GENESIS OF GENIUS™

POWER ARC
YOUR POTENTIAL
FOR GREATNESS
IN YOUR LIFE,
WORK & WORLD

INTRODUCING

POWER ARC™:

YOUR CREATIVE GUIDANCE SYSTEM®

THE MASTER SUCCESS SYSTEM FOR CREATING YOUR FUTURE ON YOUR OWN TERMS

BY
JULIE ANN TURNER

Copyright © 2013 by JULIE ANN TURNER

All rights reserved. No part of this book may be used
or reproduced in any manner whatsoever without the written
permission of the author and publisher.
Published in the United States of America.
For information address CREATOR'S GUIDE PRESS,
2124 Cliffside Drive, Plano, Texas 75023.
WWW.CREATORSGUIDE.COM

Publisher's Cataloging-in-Publication
(Provided by Quality Books, Inc.)

Turner, Julie Ann.
   Genesis of genius : power arc your potential for
greatness in your life, work & world / by Julie Ann
Turner. -- First edition.
   pages cm
   Includes bibliographical references and index.
   ISBN 978-1-933628-02-8

   1. Creative ability. 2. Creation (Literary,
artistic, etc.)   I. Title.

BF408.T847 2013   153.3'5
                         QBI13-600149

First Edition

GENESIS OF GENIUS™, POWER ARC™, CREATIVE GUIDANCE SYSTEM™, CONSCIOUSSHIFT™, WHERE, NOW, HOW™, VISIONSPARC™, VISIONSPIRAL™, CREATOR'S GUIDE®, CREATORSGUIDE.COM™, CREATIVE ARC™, CREATE YOUR LIFE, WORK & WORLD®, CREATIVE RENAISSANCE™, ORBITS OF INFLUENCE®, WHERE GLOBAL THOUGHT LEADERS GATHER® are trademarks of JULIE ANN TURNER & COMPANY/CREATORSGUIDE.COM, as indicated throughout the GUIDE by SMALL CAPS. All Rights Reserved.

Cover photos by permission of photographer Laurent Laveder - www.pixheaven.net - from his MoonGames series.

Extensive efforts have been made to ensure the information in this book series and course is accurate, and extensive research has been conducted to ensure information and quotes are attributed to their original authors and sources as much as is possible and to the extent source information was available and accessible, as we highly respect the creative expressions and contributions of creators around the world. In addition, multiple editors have made every effort to ensure the book series is error-free. However, though we are all creators, and capable of magnificent contributions - we are also human. So, if you find a typographical or grammatical error, or find anything in this publication which you believe may be in error, please let us know at constructivecomments@creatorsguide.com. Perhaps your creative gift or contribution, in part, is helping find such errors, and we value and appreciate your help, as we endeavor to make GENESIS OF GENIUS™ an ever-improving, ever-expanding resource for creators worldwide.

*To
the CREATORS -
the CONSCIOUS-SHIFTERS -
who,
in seeking and shining
their singular and true light,
express and share with the world
the magnificence of Creation.*

*And to the CREATOR'S GUIDES
who,
once they discover their unique gifts and talents
and experience the joy
of realizing their full creative purpose and potential,
shine that light for others,
so that they may do the same.*

We are all CREATORS.

We are all CREATOR'S GUIDES.

GENESIS OF GENIUS™

A CREATOR'S COMMITMENT

We are all CREATORS -
CONSCIOUS-SHIFTERS -
here to seek and shine
our singular and true light,
and to express and share with the world
the magnificence of Creation.

We are all CREATOR'S GUIDES.
who, once we discover our own unique gifts and talents
and experience the joy of realizing our full creative purpose and potential,
commit to share the Creative Process
and shine the creative light for others,
so that they may reach their full creative potential, as well.

Creator's Signature: _____   Date: _____

Those for whom I may become A Creator's Guide: _____

_____

_____

_____

I commit to share POWER ARC, the Master Creative Process, with at least ___ person(s).

* eBooks Play on Your Tablet or PC

REGISTER
YOUR GENESIS OF GENIUS SOFTCOVER BOOK NOW >
TO RECEIVE THE COMPLETE GENESIS OF GENIUS
3-EBOOK SERIES FREE! (An Additional $149 Value)

*A Journey of Discovery from Da Vinci to Oprah
that Reveals the Single, Startling Principle
the Greatest Creative Minds throughout History
Used to Consciously Shift
to Success in Their Lives, Work & World . . .*

- **BOOK ONE:** The Arc of Imagination

- **BOOK TWO:** The Once & Future Age of Imagination

- **BOOK THREE:** POWER ARC™: Your Creative Guidance System®

Plus, receive **GENESIS OF GENIUS** Owner-Only bonuses, discounts, quotes and tips, exclusive community access, and much more!

REGISTER
YOUR GENESIS OF GENIUS SOFTCOVER BOOK NOW >
at http://www.GenesisofGeniusBook.com
& RECEIVE THE COMPLETE GENESIS OF GENIUS 3-EBOOK SERIES FREE!

GENESIS OF GENIUS™
POWER ARC YOUR POTENTIAL FOR GREATNESS IN YOUR LIFE, WORK & WORLD

TABLE OF CONTENTS

WELCOME
- ORIGIN STORY VIII
  - GENESIS OF GENIUS VIII
  - ON THE QUEST IX

INTRODUCTION
- **ULTIMATE DISCOVERY** X
  - NAVIGATOR XI
    - OPEN CHANNEL XII
  - CREATIVITY RISING XIII
    - CREATIVE RENAISSANCE XIV
    - GUIDE TO THE GUIDE XV
  - EXPLORESOURCES XVII
    - ABOUT THE METACOSM XVII

PROLOGUE
- **TO THE EXPLORERS** XVIII
  - GENESIS XIX
    - SPREADING LIGHT XX
    - AN UNFOLDING DREAM XXI
    - MYSTERIES OF ETERNITY XXII
    - EXPANSIVE VIEW XXIII
    - AUTHENTIC SOURCE XXIV
  - CASCADE OF CREATION XXV
    - HONORING THE QUESTIONS XXVI
    - REFLECTIONS OF THE CREATOR XXVII
    - ON PURPOSE XXVIII
    - EXPANDING UNIVERSE XXIX

MASTER GUIDEBOOK
POWER ARC: YOUR CREATIVE GUIDANCE SYSTEM

- **THE CREATIVE GUIDANCE SYSTEM®** 1
  - CREATIVE AGE 4
  - CREATIVE WORLDVIEW 7
    - TWO WORLDS 8
    - EXPANSIVE IMAGINATION 9
  - CREATIVE MIND 10
    - MINDSHIFT: KNOWLEDGE TO IMAGINATION 11
    - NEW THINKING FOR A NEW WORLD 12
  - CREATIVE GUIDANCE SYSTEM ELEMENTS: TWO WORLDS 13
    - METADIMENSIONAL FIELD 14
  - EXPLORESOURCES: 15 FUTURE-THINK MINDSHIFTERS 15

PART ONE
THE ARC & THE SPIRAL

- JOURNEY 17
  - FIELD 19
  - FORM 21
  - FORCE 22
  - TRANSLATING LIFE 23
- CREATIVE GUIDANCE SYSTEM ELEMENTS: THE ARC & THE SPIRAL 24
  - CREATING THE FUTURE 26
- CREATIVE GUIDANCE SYSTEM ELEMENTS: THE CREATIVE FILED 27
  - CREATIVE GUIDANCE SYSTEM ELEMENTS 28
- CHART: CREATIVE GUIDANCE SYSTEM MASTER VISUAL TOOLS 32

GENESIS of GENIUS

CHAPTER ONE
STARPILOT 33
    THE FORCE IS WITH YOU 34
    SKYWALKING 36
  JOURNEYARC: INITIATION 39
  WORKSHEET #1: YOUR CREATIVE ARC WORKSHEET 40

CHAPTER TWO
CREATIVE WAY
  THE ARC OF IMAGINATION 42
    ARNOLD'S STORY 43
  ARNOLD'S ARC 44
    CREATING A LIFE 45
    ARNOLD: THE NAVIGATOR 46
    SEEKING THE HIGHEST 47
    THE EVER-RISING SPIRAL 48
    ON BEGINNING 49
  JOURNEYARC: STORY ARCS 50
  WORKSHEET #2: YOUR LIFE SPIRAL 51

PART TWO
THE CREATIVE GUIDANCE SYSTEM®

CHAPTER THREE
LAUNCH SEQUENCE 53
    LIVING INTO LIFE 54
  CREATIVE GUIDANCE SYSTEM ELEMENTS: WHERE, NOW, HOW 55
    SCALABLE THINKING 57
  JOURNEYARC: LIFE ARCS 59
  EXAMPLE #3: MASTER LIFE ARC EXAMPLES WORKSHEET 60
  WORKSHEET #4: MASTER LIFE ARC WORKSHEET 61

CHAPTER FOUR
THE PROBLEM WITH PROBLEM-SOLVING 62
    DEFINING THE PROBLEM 63
    ECLIPSING THE PROBLEM 64
  CONSTELLATIONS OF CIRCUMSTANCE 65
    A LIMITED LENS 66
  PROBLEM-CENTRIC FOCUS 68
    ANALYZING ASTEROIDS & ALIENS 69
    ENTERING THE CREATIVE FIELD 70
    INFLUX 71
  AN ARC THROUGH CHAOS 72
    BREAKING OUT OF ORBIT 73
  NAVIGATIONAL THINKING 74
    THE COLLECTIVE FIELD 75
    AHEAD OF THE CURVE 76
    POWER OF CHOICE 77

CHAPTER FIVE
CONSCIOUS CREATION 79
  WHERE POWER LIES 80
    CREATIVE TENSION 81

PART THREE
WHERE, NOW, HOW®
    THREE CORE QUESTIONS 83

CHAPTER SIX
WHERE 84
  THE END IN MIND 85
    POWER OF VISION 86
    THOUGHT SEQUENCING 88

ELECTRIC FIELD OF POSSIBILITY	89
STEPPING INTO NEW SPACE	90
JOURNEYARC: LIFE VISION	91
CHECKLIST #5: POWER OF VISION CHECKLIST	92
WORKSHEET #6: MASTER LIFE WORKSHEET - WORKING DRAFT	93
WORKSHEET #7: MASTER ARC GUIDESHEET -1-PAGE SUMMARY	94
JOURNEYARC: MINDMAPPING & MORE TOOLS FOR VISION-EERS	95
EXPLORESOURCES: 16 VISION-CREATION TOOLS & RESOURCES	96

CHAPTER SEVEN
JOURNEY TO POTENTIAL 97

EXPRESSION	98
IDENTITY	99
THE WAY OF THE HERO	100
LIGHT THROUGH THE LENS	101
THE ARTFUL LIFE	102
AUTHENTICITY	103
PERSONAL PLANES OF THOUGHT	104
LIFE BRAND	105
POWER OF MISSION	106
ENERGY FLOW	107
THE SOUL OF WORK	108
REENERGIZING LIFE	109
JOURNEYARC: IDENTITY & EXPRESSION	111
EXPLORESOURCES: CORE IDEAS FOR EXPLORING LIFE MISSION	113
WORKSHEET #8: VISION & MISSION PERSONAL WORKSHEET	114
WORKSHEET #9: MASTER GOALS WORKSHEET	115

CHAPTER EIGHT
CREW CONSCIOUSNESS 116

TEAM IDENTITY	117
THE ART & SPIRIT OF BUSINESS	118
TEAM TRAJECTORY	119
ADAPTATION	121
THE CREATIVE ORGANISM	122
TEAM VISION	123
BEYOND COMPROMISE	124
ORIENTING TO PURPOSE	125
GLOBAL THOUGHT LEADERS	126
CULTURE OF INNOVATION	127
A CAUTIONARY TALE	128
COMMITMENT	129
BOLDNESS FOR THE JOURNEY	130
JOURNEYARC: TEAM IDENTITY & MISSION	131
EXPLORESOURCES: 11 TOOLS FOR EXPLORING MISSION & IDENTITY	132
SURVEY #10: CREATIVE ENDEAVOR PRE-SURVEY TEMPLATE	133
EXAMPLE #11: TEAM ARC TITLE EXAMPLES	134
WORKSHEET #12: TEAM ARC WORKSHEET WORKSHEET #13: MASTER TEAM ARC GUIDESHEET	135
WORKSHEET #13: MASTER TEAM ARC GUIDESHEET	136

CHAPTER NINE
NOW 137

SNAPSHOT IN TIME	138
SCAN STATE	139
TWO-FOLD VISION	140
SURFING THE SITUATION	141
SCAN STEP ONE: SURVEY	142
SWEEPING THE SPACE	143
SCAN STEP TWO: ANALYZE	145
DEATH BY DATA	146

CAUGHT IN THE REAR-VIEW MIRROR	147
SCAN STEP THREE: SCOPE	148
DETERMINING SCOPE	149
THE POWER OF PLANES OF THOUGHT	151
NAVIGATIONAL THINKING TECHNOLOGY	152
SCAN STEP FOUR: MONITOR	153
THE END OF PREDICTION	154
THE SCOUT MOTTO – AND OTHER INNOVATION KEYS	155
BREAKING CREATIVE GROUND	156
JOURNEYARC: NOW RESOURCES	157
EXAMPLE #14: SWOT ANALYSIS DESCRIPTIONS	158
WORKSHEET #15: SWOT ANALYSIS WORKSHEET	159

CHAPTER TEN
HOW 160

DOING THE DREAM	161
SHORTCIRCUIT TO HOW	162
PLAN	163
FILLING THE GAP	164
MASTER ARCS & MINI-VISIONS	165
NAVIGATIONAL PLANNING: WHAT WE DO WANT	166
BEST NEXT STEPS	167
PLAN STEP ONE: PLAY	168
TOOLS FOR PLAY	169
MINDPLAY: REGAINING CREATIVE SPIRIT	170
PLAN STEP TWO: PLAN	171
PLAN STEP THREE: PRIORITIZE	172
PLAN STEP FOUR: ACT	173
LIFE NAVIGATION SYSTEM	174
POWER TO POTENTIAL	175
JOURNEYARC: HOW RESOURCES	176
EXAMPLE #16: STRATEGIC ARCS - INDIVIDUAL ARCS & MINI-VISIONS	177
WORKSHEET #17: STRATEGIC ARC WORKSHEET - INDIVIDUAL & TEAM	178
WORKSHEET #18: STRATEGIC GOAL - PLAY & BEST NEXT STEPS	179
OVERVIEW #19: WHERE, NOW, HOW MASTER SUMMARY SHAPSHOT	180
EXPLORESOURCES: PLAY - TIPS & TOOLS TO SPARK IMAGINATION	181
EXPLORESOURCES: TECHNIQUES FOR THIINKING IN XD	182
EXPLORESOURCES: PUTTING IT ALL INTO ACTION	183
WORKSHEET #20: CREATIVE GUIDANCE SYSTEM PRACTICE WORKSHEET	184

CHAPTER ELEVEN
CHANGING COURSE 185

NAVIGATING THE NEW REALM	186
CHOOSING IN THE MOMENT	187
LIGHTSHIFTERS	188
PREVENTING THE STALL I	189
PREVENTING THE STALL II	190
THRIVING ON AMBIGUITY	191
ON TRUTH & JUDGMENT	192
LOOP OR LEAP	193
OPRAH'S ARC	194
OVERCOMING THE ODDS	195
NAVIGATING TOWARD DESTINY	196
AL GORE'S ARC	197
COMMITMENT TO VISION	198
OBAMA'S ARC	199
FINDING HIS WAY	200
LIVING OUT THE DREAM	201
ERIN BROCKOVICH'S ARC	202

SLOW DOWNWARD SPIRAL	203
COURAGE TO SOAR	204
SHIFTING THE ARC	**205**
DEGREES OF POSSIBILITY	206
THE CREATIVE GROUND OF INNOVATION	207
CIRCLES OF INFLUENCE	208
HOLD THE HIGH VISION	**209**
ABOUT THE AUTHOR	210
ACKNOWLEDGEMENTS	211
INDEX	213
NOTES & REFERENCES	218-244

GENESIS OF GENIUS™
POWER ARC YOUR POTENTIAL FOR GREATNESS IN YOUR LIFE, WORK & WORLD

We shall never cease from exploration.
And the end of all our exploring
Will be to arrive where we started,
And know the place for the first time.[1]

— T. S. Eliot

GENESIS OF GENIUS

You have just taken a transformational step
in the creative adventure that is your life.

At this moment – though you have yet to realize it –
you are embarking on the voyage to your true potential.

During this journey, you will learn how to create the future.

You already have everything you need to start this journey.

The truth is, you have had the power to travel this path from the very beginning.
But that is something you must discover for yourself.
This GUIDE will aid you in that discovery.

Your creative exploration –
the journey to your dreams and your full potential -
will bring you full circle,
to the pure, complete and joyful expression of who you are,
to the miraculous meaning of your life,
and to the fulfillment of your unique contribution to the Universe.

WELCOME

ORIGIN STORY

The true signposts of a sacred quest may only be connected in hindsight ...
as timeless images and stories emerge, revealing themselves, discovery by discovery,
as eternal, self-similar patterns, woven through space and time.

Perhaps that is why, on a quest, the way forward may be navigated only by faith.

So when and why does a life quest begin?

I believe each of us reaches a turning point in life - a crossroads of choice,
when the day comes, as the writer Anais Nin so beautifully describes it,
"*when the risk to remain tight in a bud is more painful than the risk it takes to blossom.*"

That moment we realize that what has come before, no matter how comfortable it may be,
can no longer serve our highest self, and that, in order to expand into our highest potential,
we must consciously choose the path of WHAT CAN BE ... the quest of discovery begins.

For me, after success as a senior executive in international advertising/PR firms,
and as a rising star in a Global 50 tech company, I had what looked like success on the
outside ...but on the inside, my authentic self – my soul - was struggling. You see, for me,
the *higher* I rose in the corporate world, the *less* my values aligned.

It seemed that everywhere around me I saw corporate turf wars, people undercutting one
another and valuing competition over co-creation - when my values and gifts were the
exact opposite – creativity, innovation and collaboration.

Though I tried to ignore it, what emerged within me was a sinking realization
this "success" was an illusion - and, for me, a trap.

I was stuck in a loop – and I didn't know how to get out. I just knew I was not living
my highest and best life ... and I was not sharing my greatest gifts.

And then ... you know how there are moments in life – where everything changes?
They wake you up, and you never see things the same again. Here I was, already questioning
my path – and my beloved Mother got cancer – and passed away at only 48 years old.

So, for me, perhaps a bit younger than most - I came face-to-face with the reality
that we only have such a brief time to make the impact we're here to make.

I remember sitting in my stark office cubicle, knowing
that I simply could no longer go on as I had been.
I had to *know* that I was
living out my highest life purpose ...
that I was making the impact I was born to make.

So I took the leap.

I left my corporate job - without a real plan
(even though my expertise was strategic planning).

That turning-point decision - and my deep desire to live out my own true purpose,
launched me on my quest to discover - not only my own life purpose -
but ultimately, something much more eternal, universal and transcendent.

GENESIS OF GENIUS

I started a deep questioning process. And the first thing I discovered is that I wasn't alone.

Whenever I talked to my friends or my family about what I was going through, they were all saying, "Yeah, you know, I feel like that, too ... but there's nothing I can do about it ... that's just the way life is - you've got to make a living and have a job."

Everyone around me was in the same spot - they were all struggling, saying, "This is WHAT IS" - but somehow not yet consciously able to create WHAT CAN BE. They either believed it was not possible - or they didn't know how to do it for themselves. I was afraid, too.

But I believed there had to be a way.

My belief was that there was something beautiful and divine about life - and I deeply desired to discover and be in tune with that truth, more than anything else.
I set out to find that truth.

I began my quest, digging through hundreds of books across all realms of thought, and over all of human time.

With each page I turned, and with each piece of truth I gathered, I started to see the patterns emerge.

In my quest to figure out what I was here to do, I tuned in deeply to my own Highest Source, and was guided on, what was for me, a sacred journey - one that led me back to the origins of all creation, all the way back to the earliest known sacred writings of humankind, back to the *Genesis of Genius* itself.

And again, I realized I was not alone. I realized I, too, was seeking the answer to the fundamental question that humans have been grappling with since the dawn of time, and I realized there was **a pattern to the solutions**.

It became clear that the greatest human desire is for meaning, to understand our place in the world ... to make our mark - and to leave a legacy.

When you page through history, though we humans are born with nothing, you can't help but marvel at all we've created, from the cave paintings of Chauvet to the Hubble telescope.

At our core, there is a desire to create. And that desire for expression has sparked all of the creation that has ever emerged, whether in the form of a scientific breakthrough or discovery, or of dimensional perspective in drawing or painting, or of a meal crafted by Julia Child or Rachel Ray.

As a seeker, I was both humbled and in awe, as I was guided all the way back to the earliest known sacred writings of humankind - the Vedas - ancient poetry in Sanskrit, the language from which all our languages come. As you'll discover in GENESIS OF GENIUS, the Vedas are all about the master creative process ... the sacredness of it, the power of it, and the truth that we are all born creators.

ON THE QUEST

Starting with those earliest sacred writings, I began tracing the universal principles, patterns and archetypes of creation, through philosophy, theology (all major faiths and belief systems), art, myth and literature - and forward from traditional science to quantum physics and systems theory.

What I discovered on this journey astonished me.

The truth is, throughout time, all visionaries, sages and thought leaders have used a pattern of thought - an archetype of creation - to think dramatically differently from everyone else.

In fact, these visionaries begin with an entirely different WorldView that enables them to see beyond WHAT IS ... to WHAT CAN BE.

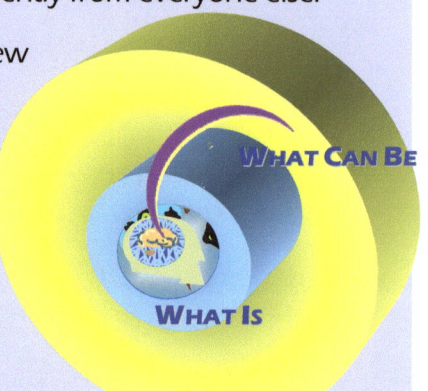

The good news is that we can adopt the same WorldView - literally a different thinking system that all world-changers throughout time have used - a profound and practical - and profoundly different - sequence of thought for the 21st Century.

Not only can we adopt this creative sequence of thought - it is now required for those who will succeed going forward in this globally connected world.

The patterns I'll share with you here have been the key for everyone who has ever broken out of the reality of WHAT IS into the fullness of WHAT CAN BE - what they were born to do.

From ancient creators from Plato to Leonardo Da Vinci, on to modern-day models like Oprah and Steve Jobs - they were all operating from one universal principle, one Conscious Shift in Worldview, that enabled them to not only imagine the next level of success, but to walk step by step into it.

It is this trail of clues you, too, will discover in this book, GENESIS OF GENIUS.

Not only the origin of genius itself, but the fact that, within you, is the origin of a unique, Signature Genius, as well.

This, it turns out, was what I was born to share.

In these pages - drawn from my 18+ years of researching and tracing the universal patterns and principles of the master creative process - you will discover how to activate and experience this for yourself, as I share with you the master sequence that all thought leaders and visionaries throughout time have used to consciously create success after success ... so that you, too, may share your genius and more consciously create the life, work and world you most desire.

Here's what I want you to understand ... this is your moment.

Let this be your turning point - and your guide on your quest.

Now is the time to come awake – and get out of the loop, and into your leap.

The world is awaiting your brilliance.

GENESIS of GENIUS

INTRODUCTION
ULTIMATE DISCOVERY

The Creative Process powers the Universe.

At its core,

GENESIS OF GENIUS

reveals the form and force
of the Creative Process -
the master process through which
all that exists in the Universe is created,
and upon which all power is based.

Through this process,
we all have the power
to create the future –
our individual, as well as our collective, future.

POWER ARC™: YOUR CREATIVE GUIDANCE SYSTEM®
captures the form and force of the Creative Process
within one elegantly simple,
yet profoundly powerful,
navigational system
that we all may use
to create
the lives, relationships, work and world
we envision.

NAVIGATOR

*You are the StarPilot,
the Navigator, the Hero -
the One with the Power
to Choose your Direction.*

Long before we were transfixed by *Star Trek* or *Star Wars*...
we have been intrigued with exploration.

"To seek out new worlds... To boldly go where no one has gone before."

Yet so few of us actually embark on the journey of exploration for ourselves.

Why?

What holds us back?

*Perhaps it has always been fear of the unknown, the uncertain.
No maps. Uncharted territory.*

For in order to discover, we must embark -
and the first step always seems the most daunting.
Yet, we know it is in this initial step that we break through familiar boundaries,
and free ourselves to move on to undiscovered realms of possibility.

By definition, no one has traveled exactly this course before.
There are no maps, no defined paths,
no one to show us *the way*...

... and yet, we don't really need or even desire
someone to tell us which way we should go
or what we should do.
We want to make those choices for ourselves.

In fact, that is the only way
we will really have what it takes -
the passion, the energy, the determination, the vision -
to see the journey through to its end.

Perhaps all we need is a guide, and a good navigational system.

Then we may find our own way.

*It is with this belief, and in this spirit of exploration,
that GENESIS OF GENIUS is offered.*

OPEN CHANNEL

As you embark on your own creative exploration, your potential for discovery will expand exponentially as you consciously remain open to the free flow of ideas, imagination and possibility.

In Japanese, this concept of remaining open to potential is often expressed as *shoshin*, the "beginner's mind," or "empty and ready mind":

> *If your mind is empty, it is always ready*
> *for anything; it is open to everything.*
> *In the beginner's mind there are many possibilities;*
> *in the expert's mind there are few ... .*
> *This is also the secret of the arts:*
> *always be a beginner.* [2]
>
> Shunryu Suzuki
> *Zen Mind, Beginner's Mind*

In his introduction to this book, Richard Baker describes this approach as "the innocence of the first inquiry": "The mind of the beginner is empty, free of the habits of the expert, ready to accept, to doubt, and open to all the possibilities."[3]

This GUIDE is all about possibilities.

So, as you begin your creative journey, consciously and intentionally open your eyes and your mind . . . to enter uncharted territory . . . to explore remarkable ways to access your creative potential . . . to discover a more creative way of thinking and traveling through the world. Look at it this way . . . the only way to tap into new realms of potential is to first open your mind to *consider the possibilities.*

Curiously, we may limit our own vision, and consequently our potential, often without even realizing we are doing so. We each carry our own set of personal filters through which we view the world. Our mental models, frames of mind, predetermined beliefs, comfort zones, voices of judgment (our own, as well as those of others), past experiences, and even "things we think we know already" - all may act to limit or distort our view, preventing us from seizing, or even from *seeing*, creative possibilities that exist within our grasp.

However, if we consciously keep an open channel, we will be able to see even familiar concepts anew - authentic, powerful creative keys such as *vision, purpose, power, choice* - as well as to perceive a creative spectrum of possibilities we may never even have imagined before.

The ability to suspend judgment, to remain receptive, to keep an open channel, unlocks the gateway to the flow of creative thought.

So look with fresh eyes, contemplate fully, evaluate deeply - keep what enlightens you, discard only with careful consideration - learn and grow.

You may only discover new worlds if you embark with a true explorer's mind.

CREATIVITY RISING

**In the midst of a Universe
many perceive as spinning faster and ever faster
into chaos and uncertainty,
there is a pattern of thought arising,
beginning to coalesce into orbit
within the realm of *creativity*.**

**GENESIS OF GENIUS
reveals that the unifying pattern –
the universal system that encompasses, aligns,
and gives structure to these swirling streams of thought -
is the *Creative Process* itself.**

Those who are watching closely have undoubtedly seen the patterns of thought forming, and have heard many more voices arising in this *creative awakening*.

There is a very strong likelihood that you, too, have seen and sensed this shift taking place in and around you.

We are crossing the threshold of a fundamental shift in our WorldView, which carries the potential to positively transform our lives beyond any shift we as humans have ever before experienced.

Much more than a fad or a trend, this creative shift of thought is massive in scope and unlimited in potential. It will alter all we know or believe we have known. It has the power to change forever the way we perceive the world and conceive of our future.

- **On a personal level,** those who make this shift to a greater creative awareness will break through to higher levels of creative expression and contribution. We each will discover our unique genius, a wholeness of being - integrating the physical, mental, psychological, and spiritual - that is accessible to each of us through the power of the Creative Process.

- **On a global level,** we have the potential to come together as never before to collectively envision, and consciously *co-create*, the higher future we imagine for our selves and our world. For many reasons to be shared in this *GUIDE*, this shift to *creative consciousness* is mission-critical for our society, our planet, our Universe. Our continued growth as a people and a planet rests on our making this creative shift successfully.

All of us. Together.

We have the opportunity not only to awaken to, but to consciously and actively help usher in, this *CREATIVE MINDSHIFT*. As we do so, we will fulfill our potential to advance into an era of INFINITE imagination, marked by unlimited achievement and growth.

CREATIVE RENAISSANCE

It is ceaseless creativity that marks the new age.[4]
Fritz Dressler, *The Wall Street Journal*

We stand at the portal to a new CREATIVE RENAISSANCE, one that carries the potential to far eclipse the first Renaissance in scope and scale - as we collectively rise to this new plane of creative thought.

This CREATIVE MINDSHIFT is not merely a beautiful dream, a desired and compelling vision - although it is both of these, and although it does carry with it the potential to transform our very existence. Ultimately, however, the CREATIVE MINDSHIFT is about *a higher choice* - a fundamental, world-altering choice.

It involves much more than a response to threat or crisis, although, admittedly, for many it is the astounding, and apparently escalating, speed of change that has arrested our attention, forcing us to acknowledge that it will take a dramatic shift in creative capacity for us to continue to cope in this chaotic, fast-fast world.

As humans, however, endowed with the power of choice, we can do more than simply react to threat. In this CREATIVE MINDSHIFT, we may proactively and *consciously choose* to move - to evolve - to a higher plane of being, where we may each begin at last to live into our full creative potential. It is, then, in using our creative power to envision and co-create across shared spheres of our existence, that we may unleash this new CREATIVE RENAISSANCE.

The perspective presented here is that this CREATIVE MINDSHIFT has actually been emerging for some time; it is now accelerating and expanding. The nucleus of creative thought is forming and gaining mass, and, as from a natural gravitational and magnetic force, it is attracting more creative minds.

As with the emergence of all our creations, this mindshift began behind the scenes, slowly and seemingly invisibly building momentum, initially veiled from our view. However, as this creative awakening breaks fully into our collective consciousness, the change will be pervasive and all-encompassing. It will alter every dimension of our lives - individual, organizational, societal, cultural, mental, physical and spiritual.

GENESIS OF GENIUS is meant to serve as a lens to enable you to:
- *first, see* this CREATIVE MINDSHIFT occurring, to provide perspective on critical factors converging to drive it, and to reveal to you the Creative Process that powers it;
- *second, perceive* the universal structure and operational principles of the Creative Process - and present POWER ARC: YOUR CREATIVE GUIDANCE SYSTEM®, the navigational model based on it - so you may consciously apply it and access its power; and,
- *third, survey* the many viewpoints that span the full spectrum of creative thought, and provide a rich collection of practical creative tools and resources you will be able to reference and revisit throughout your lifelong Creative Journey.

GENESIS of GENIUS

GUIDE TO THE GUIDE

As you explore this *GENESIS OF GENIUS GUIDE,* you will enter into an unlimited Creative Realm and discover how to tap into the creative power available to you, in every moment, through Creative Process revealed in this GUIDE.

BONUS
ALL 3 eBOOKS AVAILABLE FREE WHEN YOU REGISTER @ GENESISOFGENIUSBOOK.COM
CLAIM YOUR EBOOKS!

BONUS: BOOK ONE
THE ARC OF IMAGINATION

PART ONE – METAPHOR: CREATIVE JOURNEY

Here you will begin your own creative exploration with a broad view of the *"METACOSM"* - a new term we will use as we describe the infinite Creative Realm – which is revealed within this GENESIS OF GENIUS GUIDE. PART ONE will serve as your "flight preparation," introducing the core concepts, patterns and principles you will need for successful navigation throughout your Creative Journey.

PART TWO – METAPROCESS: CREATIVE PROCESS

You will begin to see, possibly for the first time, how the patterns and energy of the master Creative Process weave throughout the Universe, and how you can use the same principles to create miraculous change in your life, work and world.

PART THREE – METAPRINCIPLE: CREATIVE ABSOLUTE

You will discover that the universal principles and patterns of the Creative Process are - and have always been - hidden within streams of sacred and philosophical thought of both East and West. Here, we will reveal these parallel, creative streams.

PART FOUR – METAMODEL: POWER ARC: YOUR CREATIVE GUIDANCE SYSTEM®

You will get your first glimpse of the master Creative System – at first three, and, ultimately, just seven simple, but powerful, interrelated steps - that will enable you to create the future you want in your life, in your relationships, projects, work, career, community, and world.

BONUS: BOOK TWO
THE ONCE & FUTURE AGE OF IMAGINATION

PART ONE - CREATIVE METACOSM

You will learn why so many of us - though we already are travelers in an infinitely Creative Realm - have come to unnecessarily limit our own creativity to the realm of WHAT IS, when we can move into the unlimited realm of WHAT CAN BE. The universal Creative System presented here transports us far beyond these limiting views of creativity, where we may participate in new worlds of infinite possibility.

PART TWO - A NEW WORLDVIEW

You will witness the shift from Knowledge to Imagination, and realize, without a doubt, that only those who know how to consciously create will thrive in this millennium. You will take a bullet-train trip from the Flat World to the Future Age, and discover why Imagination is truly the only inexhaustible resource.

PART THREE - MINDSHIFT

Here, you will acquire the creative mindset. You will discover how to make the conscious shift in your personal awareness necessary to tap into full creative potential. Most important, you will learn that all of us can rediscover and reconnect with our creative power through a simple, but profound, shift of mind. You will learn why making this CREATIVE MINDSHIFT is an imperative for those who desire to navigate through the AGE OF IMAGINATION.

To Claim Your Bonus Books, Free Creative Resources, & Innovation Tools visit GENESISOFGENIUSBOOK.COM.

© JULIE ANN TURNER & COMPANY/CREATORSGUIDE.COM.
All Rights Reserved.

GENESIS of GENIUS

BOOK THREE - MASTER GUIDEBOOK
POWER ARC™: YOUR CREATIVE GUIDANCE SYSTEM®

PART ONE - THE ARC & THE SPIRAL

You will recognize how the timeless, transcendent forms of the ARC and the SPIRAL actually become the interrelated master tools you and your teams use to co-create and innovate.

PART TWO – POWER ARC: YOUR CREATIVE GUIDANCE SYSTEM®

You will acquire the tools to apply the master Creative Process to navigate in this new realm of unlimited potential. **POWER ARC: YOUR CREATIVE GUIDANCE SYSTEM®** *is the elegantly simple, yet profoundly powerful, navigational model of the Creative Process that enables you to create and reorient to your dreams in real time. This GUIDE will show you how to apply the POWER ARC SUCCESS SYSTEM to create the desired outcome you want - at every level of, and in every aspect of your life, your relationships, your work, your community, your world.*

CREATIVE GUIDANCE SYSTEM®

MASTER FORMS	MASTER TOOLS
THE ARC *You will quickly become familiar with the Creative Process in its simplest, three-step form*	**WHERE, NOW, HOW®**
Next, you will gain a practical, in-depth understanding of the process through its expanded pattern	**VISIONSPARC®**
THE SPIRAL *You will advance to master the transcendent seven-step pattern that weaves through all creation*	**VISIONSPIRAL®**

After introducing you to these fundamental principles and patterns of creative power, the GUIDE will reveal how this Creative Process brings dreams into reality within the lives, relationships and organizations of those who consciously apply it. Finally, you will learn how creativity tools and techniques, used at specific stages within the process, can help you generate breakthroughs in thought and perception, further increasing your personal creative power.

PART THREE - WHERE, NOW, HOW®

You acquire and put into action the CORE three-step system, which gives you the transformational tools you may use to navigate successfully in a Universe swirling with dynamic change..

PART FOUR - JOURNEY TO POTENTIAL

You will explore your own creative path, and discover the power and the process by which you may choose your own course, live as a Full Potential Person, and literally create your future.

MASTER LEVEL: PART FIVE - VISIONSPARC™ *(Available Online Only - GENESISOFGENIUS.COM)*

You gain more in-depth ADVANCED knowledge of the POWER ARC SUCCESS SYSTEM - especially critical for creative teams and organizations - plus additional practical, but transformational, master tools..

MASTER LEVEL: PART SIX - VISIONSPIRAL™ *(Available Online Only - GENESISOFGENIUS.COM)*

You will attain the highest level of understanding of the Creative Process as the very system that generates all leadership and learning, when used consciously by you and your teams..

SYSTEM KEY: CORE LEVEL - BLACK ♦ ADVANCED LEVEL - PURPLE ♦ MASTER LEVEL - ONLINE TRAINING

EXPLORESOURCES - *Throughout this GUIDE, you will be introduced to the rich and diverse perspectives of creative thought leaders, and to a world of CREATIVE RESOURCES - a wealth of quotes, articles, books, web sites, software, and even toys and games - that you may use to expand your creative exploration in the areas of most interest and importance to you.*

ABOUT THE METACOSM

META means "beyond" in the original Greek,
and signifies "transcendence";
while –COSM means "world" or "universe."

In GENESIS OF GENIUS,
we introduce the term METACOSM
because the
master Creative System presented here
transports us far beyond
the seemingly separate, fragmented worlds
that appear to divide us,
and transcends
our current, limited views
that have led us to limit our own creative power,
to reveal the true nature, not only of creativity,
but of Creation itself.

The METACOSM
reveals the Creative Realm
as a universal, infinitely dynamic System -
within which the master Creative Process –
the METAPROCESS of Creation –
constantly transforms chaos into astounding order,
and energy into magnificent form.

GENESIS of GENIUS

PROLOGUE
TO THE EXPLORERS

It is clear that you are an explorer, a seeker.

Undoubtedly, you have within you an *inner desire* that has led you to look beyond what now exists, an inexplicable "knowing" deep inside you that echoes: "*There is something more.*"
There is more to discover, more you can accomplish, more you can contribute.
You know that *there is more that you are, and still more you are meant to be.*

How is this inner desire made evident? *Though you may not yet realize it, you already have expressed this desire, and that expression is being reflected in the world.*

First, you have made a choice - an internal, fundamental choice. As you will soon see, *choice is the mechanism of creation.* You already are expressing your internal choice externally - by your very arrival here, by your *action* in reading these words. Such simple, subtle acts signal that you have already begun your quest, as does your action in choosing this *GENESIS OF GENIUS GUIDE* to accompany you.

You have chosen, and you have taken the first step. In doing so, you have set creative energy into motion. With elegant simplicity, you have activated the process of creation, the process through which inner desire is made visible. By choosing consciously to travel your own creative course, you have taken a pivotal step in the creative adventure that is your life.

And what a remarkable, miraculous adventure it will be.

This will be no ordinary voyage. This most personal, creative exploration will bring you full circle:

*To the pure, complete and joyful expression of who you are,
to the miraculous purpose and meaning of your life,
to the fulfillment of your potential
and your unique contribution to the Universe.*

This is the journey to your dreams.
What did you come into this world to do?
What kind of hero will you be? What will you discover on your journey?

Where does the journey begin? Within you.
It begins with a single choice, and ends in the full expression of your self.

> *If you asked me
> what I came into this world to do,
> I will tell you:
> I came to live out loud.*
> — Emile Zola, French writer

Within these pages you will learn that you have the power to create your future, and you will begin to discover for yourself the answers to these questions. Like all the heroes who have gone before, you will find you hold within you the power to take the creative path.

GENESIS

"How can we deal with change at such accelerating speed and on such world-altering scale?"

This *GUIDE* owes its genesis to the many variations of this question, which those with whom I live and work, across personal, business and community realms, have asked so often.

Both as individuals and members of organizations, we now, more often than not, find ourselves seemingly submerged by the tides of constant change, overwhelmed by flow and pace of incoming information, and often all but paralyzed by uncertainty. Often desperately in need of answers, we seek new, creative ways to see more clearly and to move more confidently through change.

Often, our first inclination is to seek ways *to respond - to predict, solve, stop, avoid, manage or control - this change.* The answer this *GUIDE* presents is a powerful alternative, a different way of thinking and navigating through this new world: *We cannot, and we need not, merely respond ever faster, avoid or "fix" or eliminate all problems, continually add even more controls . . . but we can learn to CREATE.*

GENESIS OF GENIUS GUIDE arose in the hope of sharing this answer - on both a personal and a global level - within a profound and powerful, yet understandable and practical, process and framework.

Clearly, the old ways of thinking and operating are no longer adequate in this ever-evolving world. Clearly, we must find a way to navigate through the blistering change and seeming chaos.

Almost invariably these days, when I am asked to help both individuals and organizations plan, create, and innovate, they are engulfed in a new wave of change, a newly emerging crisis. It is certainly not uncommon for participants - whether in corporations, service firms, creative agencies, or non-profits - to walk into an initial session enmeshed in a new conflict or problem that has just arisen, or holding reorganization or merger notices they have just at that moment been handed.

One might think it impossible to plan or create proactively in these chaotic environments - certainly participants may initially feel this way, and many express doubt and even resistance at the undertaking: *"How can we possibly (develop our strategy, create a new program, determine a career path, encourage innovation . . . you may fill in the blank) . . . when we don't even know (who is in charge, what our direction is, which organization we are part of, how we can gain a voice in these decisions, how we can possibly meet today's urgent deadline . . . fill in the blank)? . . . we'll have to wait to plan . . . we must postpone . . . let's reschedule . . . .*

Yet, change is constant and escalating. It becomes clearly and immediately evident that the most necessary step to regain focus (and any hope of a successful planning or creative effort), although perhaps the most daunting one, is to face the uncertainty head-on. One central question generally recaptures both personal and collective attention and perspective:

"If we wait until things stop changing to determine the best course, when do you think that will be?" Silence. Silence. Slow recognition. *"Never,"* is the invariable answer.

Still, we need more than traditional, static plans, as these are no longer adequate to enable us to respond, given the speed and scope of change we are facing. *We need a navigational system - a guidance system - that will allow us to create and adapt in real time.*

So, together, we draw a big circle on the white board, write "*UNCERTAINTY*" in the center, and we embark, in the midst of chaos, on a co-creative journey. And I am given the opportunity to share with these individuals, teams and organizations how they can regain their power in that moment, by learning how to navigate change through conscious use of *the Creative Process,* within the framework of the simple but powerful *POWER ARC: YOUR CREATIVE GUIDANCE SYSTEM*®.

GENESIS of GENIUS

SPREADING LIGHT

There are only two ways of spreading light —
to be the candle or the mirror that reflects it.
Edith Wharton, American novelist

I am a messenger, *a creator's guide*, if you will, whose purpose and passion is to help others discover how to use the Creative Process for themselves, to create the outcomes they desire in their lives, their relationships and their organizations.

It is my purpose, then, to serve as both a candle, and a mirror, in revealing to you to your own creative power. For, as we have said, creation begins within each one of us.

All creations begin internally - as the tiny seed of a thought, a concept, a process, an object - the initial, inner vision growing at first almost imperceptibly, invisible to the external world.

It is only through our expression that these creations are released into the world, and ultimately, are manifested in, and reflected by, the world.

This creation of this *GUIDE* followed this "inside-out" process.
First, a change began in me. This creation formed, was nurtured and grew, and is now expressed, not only through this book, but throughout my life.

In the same way, a change has begun in you.
We have yet to see what your new creations will be,
but they, too, will begin from within.

They will change you,
and they will ultimately change our world.

Each one of us has an important role to play.

One of the foundational concepts presented in this *GUIDE* is this:

We each have been given certain gifts and talents
that only we can express and share with the world.
We are each called to create,
and to share that entirely unique creative expression
that is alive within each one of us.

Yet, for many reasons we often do not fully express our creativity, and, for many reasons, it is perhaps even more important now than ever before that we rediscover how to consciously use the Creative Process, as this *GUIDE* will share with you.

AN UNFOLDING DREAM

Everywhere, individuals and organizations alike sense there is something greater, something more they can be, do, accomplish. Far too many are not creating and living their dreams. Deep down they know they are not fulfilling their potential. Their personal and collective frustration, their pain, is visible. They have lost touch with who they really are, with the full meaning of their lives, with their purpose for being.

While a few may share these thoughts and feelings directly,
it is not difficult to see their desire to find meaning - a higher purpose, a higher expression.
We can see it in their eyes and recognize it in their stories.

Like so many others, I have stood in that place, at the entryway to this journey. Undoubtedly, that makes the frustration, the hope, and the compelling desire, more apparent, more tangible to me. Not surprisingly, as a hard-headed, vastly imperfect perfectionist, I came to this place by trial, and much error, banging into walls the wrong way, until, at long last, I gave up, acknowledged my way was not working, and opened myself to listen and to be led.
Hopefully, the fact that even I have come
to this place will encourage you.

The Creative Process can transform us all.

*If we only allow it to do so,
the Universe will unfold before us.*

We will see that everything is a miracle.

I believe this is as it should be; we are always called to share what we first have had cause to learn and live ourselves. As Mahatma Gandhi said:

> *You must be the change
> you wish to see in the world.*

Then, we are able to speak out of our experience and our spirit, because we *embody* the lessons. Certainly, though, I do not claim to have all the answers; I, too, am a seeker, a fellow traveler on this creative journey.

I do know this: *All of us can use the Creative Process and its principles intentionally to reach our potential in our lives, relationships, and organizations.* I have witnessed the power of this process. I have experienced it in my own life, and watched others around me change their lives, once they are able to see and use the power of these principles.

> *This process completely alters the way I view the world.
> I want to tell you that it changes everything.
> I will never look at the world the same way again.*
> 63-year-old Executive Director
> on *Power Arc: Your Creative Guidance System*®

MYSTERIES OF ETERNITY

*The important thing
is not to stop questioning . . . .*

*One cannot help
but be in awe
when he contemplates
the mysteries
of eternity,
of life,
of the marvelous structure
of reality.*

*It is enough
if one tries merely
to comprehend
a little of this mystery
every day.*

*Never lose
a holy curiosity.[5]*

Albert Einstein, theoretical physicist

*The creative journey teaches us that the only true creative answers
come from within - we discover and create them for ourselves.*

We all have the power to live into our full potential, express our unique creations, and share with others our creative contributions.

*The Creative Process works wherever you are,
with what you have within you right now.*

The high vision I have been given to share with you is that we will each rediscover our creative natures and begin to use our personal and collective creative power consciously to bring about positive change in our lives, our work and our world.

You cannot teach people anything.

You can only help them discover it

within themselves.

Galileo, Italian astronomer

EXPANSIVE VIEW

The creative spectrum presented here is intended to be holistic and unifying. Our approach will be to allow Creative Process to work for you, in the belief that, by exposing you to many voices, viewpoints and perspectives on creativity, within the overall context of the Creative Process, the most meaningful conception of creativity will emerge for you.

By presenting an expansive and inclusive view of the *creative spectrum*, GENESIS OF GENIUS will enable you to see for yourself how widely and deeply the streams of creative thought run, through the words and works of creators from the beginning of time.

You will be exposed to philosophers, artists, mystics, clerics, psychologists, business gurus and everyday thought leaders, and to a myriad of creative sources and perspectives - ancient and recent, Eastern and Western, secular and spiritual - for the full creative spectrum encompasses all of these.

As you will soon see, true and transcendent ideas and universal themes emerge as recognizable, consistent patterns, just as spirals form within newborn galaxies.

Once you acquire the tools to discern them, you may come to view these remarkable, recurring patterns of thought as essential signs of authenticity, arising within an infinitely creative Universe. These patterns become signposts to the discovery of universal laws and truths.

So many leaders across all ages of time and all realms of thought have expressed these creative truths in a myriad of words and ways. Therefore, throughout this GUIDE, we will endeavor to share a diversity of creative views expressed by others, to provide connection points with concepts and models that may expand your understanding of the broad spectrum of creativity, and, of course, to acknowledge that we all stand on the shoulders of those who have gone before us on this path of discovery.

As you explore this flow of ideas, listen for the consistent streams of transcendent thought as they emerge and resonate across the words and works of these great thinkers, philosophers and creators. Allow the thinker and philosopher within you to emerge, as well. As you become more aware - more *creatively conscious* - you may see more clearly how these streams and patterns of thought parallel, and are contained within, the universal Creative Process.

Like the Creative Process itself, these creative constructs -
these *principles* and patterns *of thought* - are universal.

The same, universal Creative Process operates across all *domains*, from business to science to religion, from personal growth to organizational leadership, and encompasses every *dimension* - physiological, mental, psychological, intellectual, social, behavioral, philosophical, spiritual.

AUTHENTIC SOURCE

One of the greatest gifts you may gain through this book is the ability to see, quite possibly for the first time, how the Creative Process revealed here provides the unifying framework that contains and aligns these timeless, universal principles and concepts. You will discover that many familiar phrases and concepts - such as "optimism," "attitude," "positive thinking," "goal-setting" - and even processes, such as "strategic planning," "branding," and "team-building" are grounded in the Creative Process.

In fact, many of these concepts endure *precisely because their core aspects are based on universal creative principles.* The Creative Process not only encompasses the authentic aspects of these recurring concepts, but is the authentic and original source that generates them, and is actually the reason these concepts hold such potential and enduring power. These concepts, in turn, naturally align with the Creative Process.

And although some elements of Creative Process and the fundamental creative concepts within it are sometimes taken out of context, misapplied or used simply as "buzz words" or phrases - this does not diminish their validity or value. Here, we will rediscover these authentic creative concepts in their purest sense, and thus reclaim their fundamental truth and transformational power.

The Creative Process is much more than just another traditional, static plan, a repackaged program or a superficial formula. It is not simply a "rebranding" of popular concepts, nor is it merely a set of motivational maxims, although the process and its principles may indeed serve as powerful guidelines for our lives and relationships.

Many valid and varied perspectives on "the Creative Process" itself have been proposed. Therefore, we will share and contrast conceptions of the Creative Process as presented by others, while also taking care to clearly define and differentiate the Creative Process as presented in this *Guide*, including the specific stages and steps of that process as expressed here, within the unique and recognizable *Power Arc: Your Creative Guidance System*®.

As always, it is the authentic and universal creative process that is the source, and it is the process *itself that carries inherent transformational power.*

As you will discover, *Power Arc* is an authentic, dynamic system - simple to learn, remember and use - that mirrors the Creative Process and its patterns, enabling us to think, navigate and proactively create in this Universe of change.

This, then, is the ultimate flight test that distinguishes the authentic Creative Process: true creation is both transformational and universal.

The authentic creative process and its principles are *life-changing* - they have the power to transform, alter and expand not only our current frame of reference, but our lives and our world. The true creative process is *universal - it operates at every level - individual, relationship, organization, community, society, cosmos.*

CASCADE OF CREATION

Like a single candle whose light may be passed on, undiminished, to multitudes, so *the creative power that flows within each of us is the force that changes the world* . . . first, as it is shared through expression, and then, as these creations are reflected in the world.

In this way, we actually become co-creators with God, and participate in the creation of the Universe. In this way, the Universe unfolds in a miraculous *cascade of creation*.

The thought that we would be called to co-create with the Creator of the Universe always remains a miracle beyond our full comprehension. Yet, we are all invited to participate in this wondrous, creative dance.

To fully participate, we must first rediscover the creative, infinite Universe. Through a shift in our perspective, we acquire an entirely new way of looking at the world. We recognize anew the creative energy that indwells all things.

In this *GUIDE*, you will become familiar with this universal creative energy, its process and its patterns. You will come to recognize the Creative Process as it operates across the realms of science, art, thought, and spirit, and at all levels of creation - from particle to organism to person to planet to cosmos. It is the single, universal and unifying system that transforms the Universe, as both powerful *force* and elegant *form*.

This universal, creative energy and wholeness touches and transcends all time, thought and space.

> *You are so young, so before all beginning, and I want to beg you,*
> *as much as I can, dear sir, to be patient*
> *toward all that is unsolved in your heart*
> *and to try to love the questions themselves*
> *like locked rooms and like books that are written in a very foreign tongue.*
>
> *Do not now seek the answers, which cannot be given you*
> *because you would not be able to live them.*
> *And the point is, to live everything.*
> *Live the questions now.*
> *Perhaps you will then gradually, without noticing it,*
> *live along some distant day into the answer.*[6]
>
> Rainer Maria Rilke, in *Letters to a Young Poet*

Ultimately, the creative journey inevitably leads us into the realm of the divine, as it approaches the complete expression of *I am*. Here, we will walk quietly, reverently, for we acknowledge this is sacred ground. It touches the core of our identity, of who we are. We each have our own questions; we each will come to our own truth. It is something no one can tell us; we must come to know it for ourselves.

HONORING THE QUESTIONS

*All men, Socrates, who have any degree of right feeling,
at the beginning of every enterprise, whether small or great,
always call upon God.*

*And we, too, who are going to discourse on the nature of the universe,
how created or how existing without creation, if we be not altogether
out of our wits, must invoke the aid of Gods and Goddesses
and pray that our words may be acceptable...*

*First then, in my judgment, we must make a distinction and ask,
What is that which always is and has no becoming;
and what is that which is always becoming and never is?[7]*

Plato, Greek philosopher, in *Timaeus*

Perhaps the starting point of our exploration lies in acknowledging the questions themselves.

Is the Universe a Master Creative Force in which we all participate? Is there a Higher Power, or is everything just a result of the Creative Force of the Universe itself? Is this purely a matter of science - biology, chemistry, physics, psychology? Is this Creative Force a process, a presence, an energy, a collective conscience, consciousness itself, or God? Are we physical creatures, formed by nature, or are we sculpted by our environment, our experience? Or are we spiritual beings, part of a universal and divine whole? Could it be that we are within God - the Master Creator, the Creative Universe, and we are God's creations, as well as co-creators with God? Is it possible that God the Creator has given us the power of choice within all of creation?

Could it be that all of these positions are false? Or that all of them could be true?

Perhaps God and the Universe and Creative Force and Spirit and Science and Physical and Quantum and Mind and Potential all are *One*. Perhaps God is Omnipresent, Omnipotent, Omniscient - is All, In All, and Through All. Perhaps God is *All That Is*, and thus encompasses all these truths and paradoxes and concepts that so often seem contradictory to us in our own limited planes of thought.

The questions and possibilities are myriad and endless. They arise out of our universal wonder at creation, its miracles and its mysteries. Here, in GENESIS OF GENIUS, *we honor the questions themselves, and offer a spectrum of perspectives. Our hope is that you will add to them your own, and reflect on the whole.*

Bidden or not bidden, God is present.[8]

Carl Jung, Swiss psychiatrist

Ultimately, creation is more profound than any one of us can fully imagine or comprehend.

There is always infinitely more.

REFLECTIONS OF THE CREATOR

We all speak from our own experience, our own learning, our own life journey.
We all experience, and express, life differently, uniquely.
We use different words to describe Creation and the Creator.

For my part,[1] I believe that our ability to choose *WHAT CAN BE*, rather than *WHAT IS*, and to create *that which as yet does not exist*, miraculously empowers us to co-create with *God, the Master Creator*, the *Creative Absolute*.[2] Our co-created potential and our co-created works are infinitely higher than anything we might do on our own. We are born creators.

My belief is that, contained within the Creator's cosmic wisdom, lies this truth: as long as we try to pin the majesty of creation down within our limited, either-or mindset, the miracle of the unified Whole eludes us. Often, I imagine the Creator smiling patiently at our insistence on *right* or *wrong*, *either -or* answers and positions - when all along it has always been "*and*."

God, the Creator and the Creation is All That is - Wholeness and Unity, is able to encompass and reconcile all seeming paradox. We are part of this *Divine Gestalt*, and this spark of divinity dwells within all of us. We are creatures of God *and* we have the power to create. We have physical bodies *and* we are spiritual beings. In the creative realm, we see there is *infinitely more, not less*.

*In the creative realm, the answers are not **either-or**, or **but**;*
*the answers are **and**, **both**, and **YES**.*

This is indeed sacred and hallowed ground - to endeavor to illuminate the magnitude and magnificence of the Creative Process and principles that existed even before the beginning of time. I am humbled and full of awe at any insights, experiences, and understanding I have been given to share. Most assuredly, the transformational power of these principles comes from a Creator who is infinitely greater and higher.

And yet, I am most certain that this insight and this work represent a unique expression of the very creative power that is discussed in this book, the creative energy that flows through every one of us. It is therefore altogether perfect and fitting that this unique creative expression unfolds here in the form of this book, and I am blessed to lend it voice.

---

[1] *Author's Note:* I share my personal belief here for two reasons: first, because I believe all creations are blessings from a Higher Source, I believe it is only right to acknowledge this, and to give honor to the Creator, the Light that shines through each of us and illuminates our singular gifts and talents, so that we may share them with the world. As noted, beliefs about these higher concepts are inherent and integral to any book on creativity. Second, this decision is in keeping with the spirit of full truth, as well as with the philosophy of exposing you to a broad spectrum of viewpoints on creativity. In understanding the perspective of the presenter of these concepts, you will be better able to determine for yourself, and to place in appropriate context, the concepts presented.

[2] For purposes of simplicity, and only as necessary, we may use the pronoun *His* to refer to God or a Supreme Being, as this is the most familiar reference to most readers, and, for this reason, we believe this form currently carries the most general connotation (clearly, any personal pronoun used to refer to a Supreme Being is always infinitely inadequate).

ON PURPOSE

In humility and awe, we echo the perspective expressed so eloquently by a great creator:

> *Strange is our situation here on earth.*
> *Each of us comes for a short visit, not knowing why,*
> *yet seeming to divine purpose.*
> *From the standpoint of daily life, however, there is one thing we do know:*
> *That we are here for the sake of humanity...*
> *for the countless unknown souls*
> *with whose fate we are connected by a bond of sympathy.*
>
> *Many times a day I realize how my own outer and inner life*
> *is built upon the labors of my fellow human beings, both living and dead,*
> *and how earnestly I must exert myself in order to give in return*
> *as much as I have received and am still receiving.* [9]
>
> — Albert Einstein, theoretical physicist

Once again these insights and this GUIDE are offered as both a candle and a mirror.

- If the ideas and images contained in these pages help you, even for a brief time, to **think differently** about the way you conceive of and perceive the Universe, about the way you relate with other beings within it, and about your own creative way of being in and traveling through it, then this GUIDE will have fulfilled its core purpose.

- If, on a higher level, the process and tools revealed here help you move into the abundance of the creative realm and reconnect you with your own ability to access creative power, then this book will have bestowed on you the true blessing it was intended to give you.

- If, at the highest level, the creative vision presented here in even some small way plays a part in energizing and expanding a universal rediscovery of creative power, a world-altering cascade of creativity, in which we will all be participants, then the highest purposes of this book will be fulfilled, as well.

In every moment, we live in the presence of the Creator's power, and stand in awe of the infinite beauty of Creation.

May you soon discover - if you do not know it already - that *we are all creators*.

EXPANDING UNIVERSE

Although this book has been emerging as a tangible, physical creation for a number of years, in truth, it has been *in creation* an entire lifetime. It is an expression of calling, born of the heart and the spirit, a co-creation, nurtured and expressed in love and joy. GENESIS OF GENIUS will continue to be an ongoing, organic work. Like all Creation, this GUIDE is *a process*, and thus a work in progress. GENESIS OF GENIUS will always be evolving. It is my hope and intention that you will join with me in expanding this creative work, as fellow seekers and travelers on the Creative Journey.

As we cross the threshold of this Creative Age, we share the *good news* of creation:

- *That you are meant to fulfill your purpose in life, by sharing your unique gifts and talents (yes, you do have them)*
- *That doing so will bring you joy - because you will be expressing what you most love (the positive energy will be uncontainable)*
- *That doing so will bring you abundance - because you will be sharing what you alone were uniquely created to do (so you'll be the absolute best at it)*
- *That, as you express your purpose and share your creative gifts with others, they too will be blessed (in a cascade of creative power and energy)*
- *That your ultimate destination isn't so much a place, as a process of becoming - it is the full expression of your potential.*

Thus we each reclaim our power in the Universe, to create what we truly desire. This is your guidebook to discovering and directing that creative power. As we embark on the creative way, I echo a blessing a friend once shared, *"Life is choice. Enjoy your creation."*

Along our journey we learn and grow, and help others do the same.

In that way, *we are all Creator's Guides.*

GENESISOFGENIUS.COM

- GENESISOFGENIUS.COM is an inclusive, online convergence point for creative thought leaders and writers; and diverse creative viewpoints from creators of all types and walks of life; as well as a dynamic center for dialogue (through ORBITS OF INFLUENCE), creative exchanges and expert forums; creativity resources and tools.

  We hope you'll not only visit often - http://WWW.GENESISOFGENIUS.COM - but also participate in co-creating this resource-rich gathering place for creators and conscious shifters worldwide.

GENESIS *of* GENIUS

Power Arc Your Potential for Greatness in Your LIfe, Work & World

INTRODUCING

POWER ARC™: YOUR CREATIVE GUIDANCE SYSTEM®

The Master Success System for Creating Your Future on Your Own Terms

MASTER GUIDEBOOK

POWER ARC™: Your Creative Guidance System®

Julie Ann Turner

Host, Global ConsciousSHIFT Show & Founder, ConsciousSHIFT.Me

Copyright © 2013 by Julie Ann Turner

All rights reserved. No part of this book may be used
or reproduced in any manner whatsoever without the written
permission of the author and publisher.
Published in the United States of America.
For information address Creator's Guide Press,
2124 Cliffside Drive, Plano, Texas 75023.
www.CreatorsGuide.com

MASTER GUIDEBOOK
Power Arc:
your Creative Guidance System®

ISBN 978-1-933628-07-3

First Edition

Genesis of Genius™, Power Arc™, Creative Guidance System™, ConsciousSHIFT™, Where, Now, How™, VisionSPARC™, VisionSPIRAL™, Creator's Guide®, CreatorsGuide.com™, Creative Arc™, Create Your Life, Work & World®, Creative Renaissance™, Orbits of Influence®, Where Global Thought Leaders Gather® are trademarks of Julie Ann Turner & Company/CreatorsGuide.com, as indicated throughout the Guide by Small Caps. All Rights Reserved.

Cover photos by permission of photographer Laurent Laveder - www.pixheaven.net - from his MoonGames series.

Extensive efforts have been made to ensure the information in this book series and course is accurate, and extensive research has been conducted to ensure information and quotes are attributed to their original authors and sources as much as is possible and to the extent source information was available and accessible, as we highly respect the creative expressions and contributions of creators around the world. In addition, multiple editors have made every effort to ensure the book series is error-free. However, though we are all creators, and capable of magnificent contributions - we are also human. So, if you find a typographical or grammatical error, or find anything in this publication which you believe may be in error, please let us know at constructivecomments@creatorsguide.com. Perhaps your creative gift or contribution, in part, is helping find such errors, and we value and appreciate your help, as we endeavor to make Genesis of Genius™ an ever-improving, ever-expanding resource for creators worldwide.

MASTER GUIDEBOOK
POWER ARC: YOUR CREATIVE GUIDANCE SYSTEM®

The POWER ARC™/CREATIVE GUIDANCE SYSTEM captures the master Creative Process –
in at first three, and, ultimately, just seven simple, but powerful, interrelated steps -
to enable you to create the future you want in your life . . .
in your relationships, projects, work, career, community, society, world . . .

It is the One System that gives you the tools
to navigate successfully in a Universe swirling with dynamic change . . .

GENESIS of GENIUS
CREATIVE PROCESS MANIFESTO

The Creative Process powers the Universe.

The Creative Process is not *a* process. It is *THE* process.

The Creative Process underlies, informs, and transcends everything that exists, ever has existed or ever will exist.

It is the process that underlies all learning, growth and evolution.
It encompasses all natural and spiritual laws.
It aligns with both physical and quantum-level science.
Indeed, all energy in the Universe flows through the Creative Process.
Its patterns - the web, the circle, the arc, the spiral - are woven throughout creation.

The Creative Process is the source of all personal growth and achievement.
It weaves the structure for all organizational learning and development,
 from innovation and strategy to planning and implementation.
It is the foundation process of authentic leadership.
It is the generative force behind all individual and collective power.

It operates on every level,
from particle
to individual
to organization
to society
to culture
to cosmos.

The Creative Process is *archetypos* - in the Greek, "*original pattern.*"
Throughout time, all myth, all parable, all story - indeed, all art – has revealed this universal Creative Process.

It is *alpha* and *omega* – "*beginning*" and *"end,"* and it is *"meta"* – "*beyond."*
The Creative Process moves us *beyond* the realm of WHAT IS,
into the transcendent, Creative Realm of WHAT CAN BE.

The Creative Process is the master process.
It is the most fundamental and powerful process in the Universe.
And it is available to each of us.
This master process is captured, and accessible to us,
through POWER ARC: YOUR CREATIVE GUIDANCE SYSTEM.

*It is ceaseless creativity
that marks the new age.*
Fritz Dressler, *The Wall Street Journal*

We have crossed the threshold to a new CREATIVE RENAISSANCE, one that carries the potential to far eclipse the first Renaissance in scope and scale - as we collectively rise
to this new **plane of creative thought**.

*Creation is a Process of Mind,
a Process of Imagination.*

It is through the Creative Process that we MINDSHIFT
from the Limited to the Unlimited,
from the realm of what already exists, or WHAT IS –
into the infinite, Creative Realm of WHAT CAN BE.

This CREATIVE MINDSHIFT is not merely a beautiful dream, a desired and compelling Vision - although it is both of these, and although it does carry with it the potential to transform our very existence. Ultimately, however, the CREATIVE MINDSHIFT is about *a higher choice* - a fundamental, world-altering choice.

It involves much more than a response to threat or crisis, although, admittedly, for many it is the astounding, and apparently escalating, speed of change
that has arrested our attention,
forcing us to acknowledge that it will take a **dramatic shift**
in creative capacity
not only for us to survive – but thrive - in this chaotic, fast-fast world.

As humans, however, endowed with the **power of choice**,
we can do more than simply react to threat.

In this CREATIVE MINDSHIFT, we may proactively
and *consciously choose*
to move - to evolve - to a higher plane of being,
where we may each begin at last
to live into our full creative potential.

CREATIVE AGE

*Today
we are on the brink
of another
extraordinary
revolution.*

*The Information Age is already over
and an exciting new epoch
is taking its place. . . .*

*Creativity and Innovation
are the name of the game . . .*

*. . . the only answer,
is through
the genius
inherent
in human
consciousness.*[10]

— Patricia Aburdene, *Megatrends*

More than 400 years ago, Galileo raised a telescope and enlarged his view to encompass a vast Universe. Through this new lens, Galileo confirmed Copernicus' revolutionary view that the Universe did not revolve around the Earth; indeed, the Earth was actually part of a vastly larger solar system that revolved around the Sun. With that one view, t*he Earth shifted from the center of the Universe – but only within the WorldView of humankind.*

The Universe had not changed, but – through the lens of new technology – Galileo was able to see it differently, to see the greater Wholeness. The potential to see *more* existed all along; only our *perspective* had been limited.

Throughout history, humanity has faced pivotal moments like this. We are now in the midst of a MINDSHIFT of this magnitude.

Significantly, until these mindshifting moments arise, we do not even recognize our sight is limited. We accept widely held beliefs, and often never even look beyond our current view.

Today, we gaze through the lens of our technologies – which open to us infinite, ever-networked, virtual worlds – and we catch a first glimpse of the depth of our connectedness. Yet a vastly greater Wholeness – and greater creative potential – has always existed.

Our potential as Creators has existed all along. Only our WorldView has been limited.

The Field of Creation has always existed – an infinite Wholeness, within which worlds upon worlds of potential await ... for us to become aware, to accept this realm of possibility – this vast new creative space - into our consciousness. For us to step into the role of creator.

FIELD OF CREATION

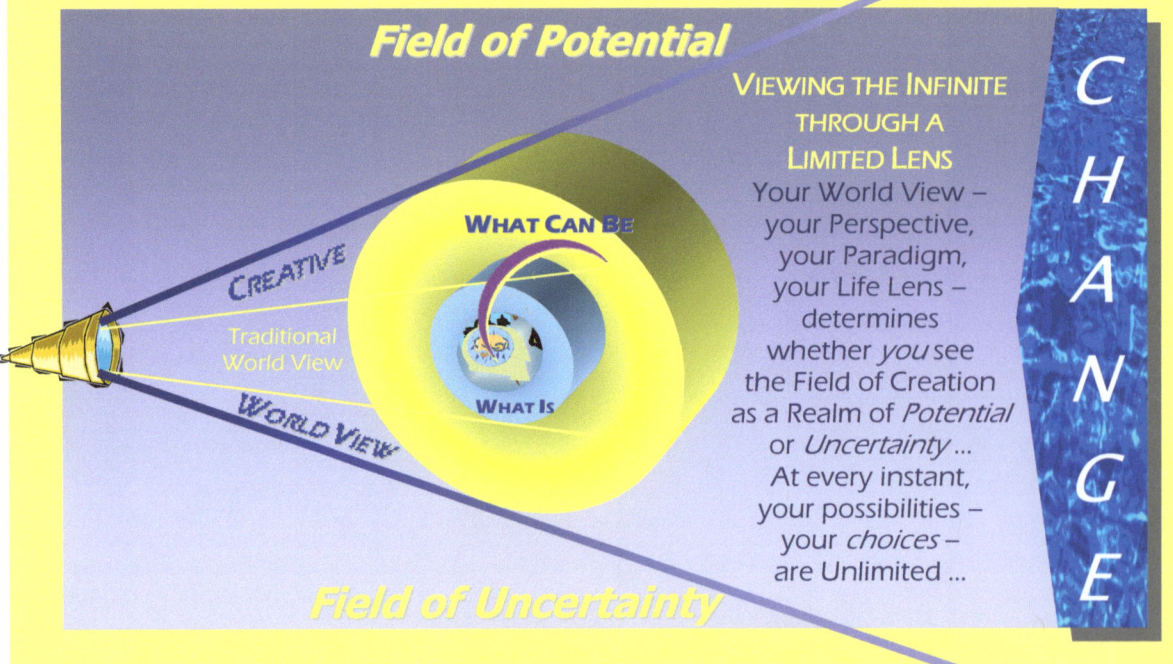

CRYSTALLIZING POSSIBILITY

> *The future is simply infinite possibility*
> *waiting to happen.*
>
> *What it waits on is human imagination*
> *to crystallize its possibility.*[11]
>
> — Leland Kaiser, healthcare expert and futurist

Like Galileo, we discover
we have been viewing the World
through a limited lens.

In that instant of discovery,
we find ourselves
in an inherently creative Field of Pure Potential
where we are vital participants,
and where choice
is the mechanism of creation.[12]

Here, imagination crystallizes possibility.

Imagination is the mode of thought
through which we access and transform
the Potential of the Field ...

For, at least initially,
we cannot see this new Realm with our eyes,
We must first navigate it with our Minds
through our Imagination.

In fact, our senses may initially discern only the turbulence of Change,
alerting us that we are crossing into the Unknown.

Nevertheless, the Arc of your Journey – your Creative Story – unfolds in this Space.

We may always choose to venture to a higher level of thought,
where new worlds of possibility emerge.

These worlds have always been within our reach –
all it takes is a *CREATIVE MINDSHIFT* for us to traverse and tap into them.

The truth is, we have already arrived.
Moreover, we play a role in this Realm,
whether consciously or unconsciously.

Again, our true creative potential originates here:
At any moment, we may make a mental leap, and *choose consciously*
to create totally new patterns of thought, new ideas, new visions, new worlds.

Where we choose to focus our thought and attention
makes all the difference in our WorldView.[13,14]

CREATIVE WORLDVIEW

*Some see things
as they are
and ask
"Why?" ...*

*Others see things
as they never were
and ask
"Why Not?"* [15]

George Bernard Shaw
often quoted by Robert F. Kennedy

TWO WORLDS

*We need a whole new view of the world.
The Creative Realm – and our Creative Power –
have always existed …
but we must expand our WorldView
to see this truth.*

*As the often-paraphrased quote originated by George Bernard Shaw illustrates –
how we choose to view the world determines the limits of our possibility:
We may either choose to "see things as they are and ask 'Why?' " …
or we may choose to imagine things as they might become, and ask "Why not?"*

*And to borrow a parallel thought from Henry David Thoreau,
"that choice will make all the difference."*

*We begin our Creative Journey here …
our journey to rediscover the Creative Realm,
and our role as creators in it.*

*First, you must see
and believe it is so.*

*Then,
in every
moment*

*you
choose
to make it so,
through the power
of the Creative Process.*

*The Creative Process
is the navigational system
of The Journey itself.*

*As we will see,
new worlds of thought
call for new modes of thinking …*

EXPANSIVE IMAGINATION

In 1798, British Economist Thomas Malthus shocked the world with his theory, introduced in *An Essay on the Principle of Population*, that "*the power of population is so superior to the power of the earth to produce subsistence for man, that premature death must in some shape or other visit the human race.*"[16]

In other words, given the current knowledge he had about population growth and the limits of food production (at that time, a description of current circumstances or WHAT IS), Malthus predicted that population would outrun food supply by the mid-19th century, causing a worldwide crisis, for which Malthus suggested population control as a solution.[17]

Malthus based his prediction on analysis of past and present population and production (WHAT IS); however, he did not take into account the power of the human imagination (WHAT CAN BE) – and thus failed to envision the transformational agricultural inventions just over the horizon, which would exponentially expand current limits of food production.[18]

Malthus's theory was very influential at that time, but is now remembered as a classic example of how relying solely on analysis from the past and present, and then simply projecting past trends into the future, can lead to major errors in prediction[19] – as analysis of this kind completely fails to factor in the potential of the human Imagination (as does most analysis and measurement, as we learned with I.Q., for instance) ....

WHAT CAN BE ... to IMAGINATION
"WHAT WE CAN IMAGINE" & "WHAT WE CAN"

WHAT IS From KNOWLEDGE ...
"WHAT ALREADY EXISTS" & "WHAT WE ALREADY KNOW"

In 1798, British Economist Thomas Malthus predicted poverty and starvation were inevitable, stating that population would always outrun food supply

Remember, the MINDSHIFT from Knowledge to Imagination involves creating "more pie" for all ...

In 1798, Thomas Malthus failed to predict – or *imagine* – the Agricultural Revolution:
- Refrigeration • Crop Rotation • Irrigation • Mechanization • & More

... Inventions of Imagination, which would dramatically expand the world's food supply

... rather than merely further dividing an existing, but limited pie.

... and the expanded worlds of possibility the human mind may create.

CREATIVE MIND

There has never been a time in history when the character of human imagination wasn't important, but ... it has never been more important than now, because ... so many of the inputs and tools of collaboration are becoming commodities available to everyone.

They are all out there for anyone to grasp.

There is one thing, though, that has not and can never be commoditized – and that is imagination.[20]

Thomas Friedman,
The World is Flat

MINDSHIFT: KNOWLEDGE TO IMAGINATION

Knowledge is power.
   Sir Francis Bacon, scientist, circa 1620

Knowledge is potential power.
   Napoleon Hill, author, 1937

Imagination is more important than knowledge.
   Albert Einstein, physicist, 1941

*Knowledge is change -
and accelerating knowledge acquisition,
fueling the great engine of technology,
means accelerating change. . . .
And so the innovative cycle,
feeding on itself, speeds up. . . . .*
   Alvin Toffler, futurist, 1970

*Knowledge grows obsolete
every half dozen years or less . . .
Imagination is the main source of value
in the new economy. . .*
   Tom Peters, management 1994

*In this economy, our ability to create wealth
is not bound by physical limits,
but by our ability to come up with new ideas –
in other words, it's unlimited.*
   Wired Magazine, 1998

*The scale of the global community
that is soon going to be able to participate
in all sorts of discovery and innovation
is something the world has simply never seen before.*
   Thomas Friedman, global economist, 2005

*Today we are on the brink
of another extraordinary revolution.
The Information Age is already over
and an exciting new epoch is taking its place.*

*Creativity and Innovation are the name of the game. ...
the only answer, is through the genius inherent in human
consciousness. ... Consciousness, the prime ingredient
in creativity, represents a higher intelligence than the mind.*[21]
   Patricia Aburdene, author, Megatrends 2010

GENESIS of GENIUS

NEW THINKING FOR A NEW WORLD

When society requires to be rebuilt,
there is no use in attempting to rebuild it on the old plan.

No great improvements in the lot of mankind are possible,
until a great change takes place
in the fundamental constitution of their modes of thought.
John Stuart Mill, English political economist

We have watched the World change,
and we have sensed the rise of a new Realm ...
but we have not fully recognized nor responded
to the massive shift
in our modes of thought
that is required to journey in this new Realm.

This new World
requires new Thinking.
This new Space
requires a new WorldView ...

The future is here. It's just not widely distributed yet.
William Gibson, author of *Neuromancer;* coined the term "cyberspace" in 1984

In this dramatically different, dynamic, **realm of constant change,**
old maps and rules, plans and operating systems, are instantly outdated,
Our existing modes of thought are obsolete,
Even in our software of language – terms like "speed" and "distance" lose meaning.
Having flashed past the Age of Information, we discover ...

Information is no longer power.

In a Field of Information, only configuration – and continuous **re-configuration** – only Creativity, imagination, innovation – count.

Knowledge is not enough.
Knowledge is not power.
Knowledge is potential power.

Everything we know at this instant is being rendered obsolete in this Field of Change.
What we know is potential in the moment, but quickly losing relevance in the next -
no matter how much it can be measured, tested, demonstrated, analyzed, graphed,
manipulated. Only what you create with knowledge matters. Because ...

Imagination is – and has always been -
more important than knowledge.

In an Age where information and knowledge exchange are free and instantaneous
and infinitely connected - in this ONCE AND FUTURE AGE - we are only now recognizing:

Imagination is the power ... the currency .... and the only inexhaustible resource.

GENESIS of GENIUS

POWER ARC™/CREATIVE GUIDANCE SYSTEM® ELEMENTS

FOCUS: TWO WORLDS

To Shift to a Higher Realm of Thought, All it takes is a Choice ...

THE ARC OF IMAGINATION

WHAT CAN BE ... to IMAGINATION
"WHAT WE CAN IMAGINE" & "WHAT WE CAN CREATE"

WHAT IS From KNOWLEDGE ...
"WHAT ALREADY EXISTS" & "WHAT WE ALREADY KNOW"

- **THE CREATIVE ARC®** BRIDGES TWO WORLDS OF THOUGHT – from WHAT IS to WHAT CAN BE ... from Knowledge to Imagination
- **THE CREATIVE ARC REPRESENTS:**
  - The Creative Process [CREATIVE GUIDANCE SYSTEM®]
  - Your Creative Journey
  - A Process of Mind

Choice is the Mechanism of Creation.

— JULIE ANN TURNER, A CREATOR'S GUIDE

METADIMENSIONAL FIELD

Noted global economist Thomas Friedman saw it. He wasn't quite the first, mind you. As Friedman himself realized, the view already had been emerging for some time. Like Einstein and Thomas Kuhn before him, Friedman acknowledges that existing mental lenses could cloud one's view of an emerging global shift:

> The perspective and predispositions that you carry around in your head are very important in shaping what you see and what you don't see.[22]

With their vision filtered through the lens of the predominant, but increasingly outdated, WorldView, virtually no one - save for a few theoretical physicists and futurists, and even fewer visionary business leaders – saw this new worldscape rising, Friedman realized, "even though it was happening right before their eyes."[23]

Peering out across this virtual Field of Information - now accessible at anytime, from anywhere, around the globe – Friedman suddenly saw a dramatically altered "flat world" coming into focus. In Friedman's view, a host of technological drivers – "the PC, the microprocessor, the Internet, fiber optics,' as well as broadband voice, video, and wireless access - and geopolitical drivers[24] ("flatteners") – now instantly and infinitely connected, or 'flattened," the world on an unprecedented scale.

> The net result of this convergence was the creation of a global, Web-enabled playing field that allows for multiple forms of collaboration – the sharing of knowledge and work – in real time, without regard to geography, distance, or, in the near future, even language.[25]

Friedman realized that new players had access, as well: "3 billion people who had been frozen out of the field suddenly found themselves liberated to plug and play with everybody else."[26] Everyone, even former "third-world" and emerging countries – like China, India, Russia, Eastern Europe, Latin America, and Central Asia – were now players in a global Creative Field.

Moreover, this Field would unleash a wave of creativity of world-altering magnitude.

> Giving so many people access to all these tools of collaboration, along with the ability through search engines and the Web to access billions of pages of raw information, ensures that the next generation of innovations will come from all over Planet Flat.

> The scale of the global community that is soon going to be able to participate in all sorts of discovery and innovation is something the world has simply never seen before.[27]

And yet, it will take an altogether new lens and a much broader focus to see and fully apprehend the multidimensional Creative Field now emerging into view, and an entirely new Navigational System to successfully traverse this dynamic space.

For the Creative Field has always existed - our technologies are just now revealing to us the flux, complexity and speed that are constants in this ONCE & FUTURE REALM.

EXPLORESOURCES

15 FUTURE-THINK MINDSHIFTERS

To complement your creative exploration, here we recommend 13 mind-altering resources guaranteed to challenge your WorldView and expand your thinking about what is possible. Highly recommended for all GLOBAL THOUGHT LEADERS (that's you!).

"NEW CLASSICS" FOR CREATIVE THINKERS

- **Consciousness: An Introduction**
  Susan Blackmore, Oxford University Press, USA, 1st Edition - 2003

- **Contagious: Why Things Catch On**
  Jonah Berger, Simon & Schuster - 2013

- **The Cultural Creatives: How 50 Million People Are Changing the World**
  Paul H. Ray and Sherry Ruth Anderson, Three Rivers Press – 2001

- **Drive: The Surprising Truth About What Motivates Us**
  Daniel Pink, Riverhead Books - 2011

- **The Field: : The Quest for the Secret Force of the Universe**
  Lynne McTaggart, Harper Paperbacks - 2003

- **The Global Brain: Your Roadmap for Innovating Faster and Smarter in a Networked World**
  Satish Nambisan and Mohanbir Sawhney, Wharton School Publishing - 2007

- **Megatrends 2010: The Rise of Conscious Capitalism**
  Patricia Aburdene, Hampton Roads Publishing Company; New Edition - 2007

- **Spark: The Revolutionary New Science of Exercise and the Brain**
  John J. Ratey, Little, Brown and Company - 2013

- **Six Degrees: The Science of a Connected Age**
  Duncan J. Watts, Vintage; New Edition - 2004

- **The Tipping Point: How Little Things Can Make a Big Difference**
  Malcolm Gladwell, First Bay Back Edition - 2002

- **Tribes: We Need You to Lead Us**
  Seth Godin, Piatkus Books - 2008

- **To Sell Is Human: The Surprising Truth About Moving Others**
  Daniel Pink, Riverhead - 2012

- **A Whole New Mind: Why Right-Brainers Will Rule the Future**
  Daniel Pink, Riverhead Trade - 2006

- **The Wisdom of Crowds: Why the Many Are Smarter Than the Few and How Collective Wisdom Shapes Business, Economies, Societies and Nations**
  James Surowiecki, Anchor. - 2005

- **The World is Flat 3.0: A Brief History of the Twenty-first Century**
  Thomas L. Friedman, Picador Trade Paperback Edition - 2007

Again, this "short list" barely scratches the surface of what is the rich - and, thankfully, ever growing – wealth of resources on creativity and the creative process.

- **Most important, the true master resource – our much-expanded, in-depth** and evolving treasure trove of creative resources – is available to you when you register your GENESIS OF GENIUS Guide at http://WWW.GENESISOFGENIUS.COM (see web site for details and benefits of registration and available bonuses to the GUIDE for *all* registered GUIDE owners.).

Again, consider this set of rich resources as a dynamic launch point for your exploration of creativity. We hope you will be inspired to become a lifetime student of the creative process.

PART ONE
THE ARC & THE SPIRAL

We have already crossed the threshold
into the AGE OF IMAGINATION.

In fact, we have always been here –
in this ONCE AND FUTURE AGE,
yet unaware
that unlimited Creative Power
has always been
within our reach.

The Creative Process,
and our power to access
and choose to use it,
has existed always.

This is the Creative Journey –
the Timeless Story
behind all Myth and Metaphor:

We become Aware
that we have had
this Power
All Along.

JOURNEY

*There is a greatness waiting for you ...
We are busy, we are distracted, we are cynical,
but this greatness waits ...
This greatness finds you in a moment, unlikely or untimely,
and suddenly you find yourself connected to humanity
in a way that shocks you.[28]*
— Jeffrey Swartz, President & CEO, The Timberland Company

With its opening words,
GENESIS OF GENIUS reminds us
that we are all adventurers
on a *creative journey* in this Universe,
whether we consciously realize it or not.

*We are on a Journey
to discover –
and express to the World –
the Greatness
that lies within us.*

*The essence of The Journey
is the unfolding experience of who we are,
the Creative Process of becoming and expressing
the full magnificence of who we can be.*
The Journey, then, is fundamentally creative.

*We are all Creators.
We have had the power to travel this path
from the very beginning.
Just as with our own Greatness, however,
we must discover this truth for ourselves.*

This central metaphor or archetype, *this universal creative journey* -
which has spanned the ages - is *your Journey, your Story*.

The Journey is the perfect metaphor –
in concept and form -
to guide us to this Greatness,
because it contains within it
the universal archetype – the original pattern –
of the Creative Process,
through which we rediscover, and live out,
our unique creative purpose and potential.

*The Creative Process is the navigational system of this universal Journey.
Moreover, the essence – the principles, stages and steps – of that process are captured
in POWER ARC: YOUR CREATIVE GUIDANCE SYSTEM®, the master system you may use to access
and apply creative power in your own life, work and world.*

Long before we were transfixed
by *Star Trek* or *Star Wars* . . .
we have been intrigued with exploration.

"To seek out new worlds. . . To boldly go where no one has gone before."

Yet so few of us actually embark on the journey of exploration for ourselves.

Why?

What holds us back?

Perhaps it has always been fear of the unknown, the uncertain.
No maps. Uncharted territory.

In order to discover, we must embark -
and the first step always seems the most daunting.
Yet, we know it is in this initial step that we break through familiar boundaries,
and free ourselves to move on to undiscovered realms of possibility.

By definition, no one has traveled exactly this course before.
There are no maps, no defined paths,
no one to show us *the way* . . .

. . . and yet, we don't really need or even desire
someone to tell us which way we should go
or what we should do.
We want to make those choices for ourselves.

In fact, that is the only way
we will really have what it takes -
the passion, the energy, the determination, the vision -
to see the journey through to its end.

In truth, all we need is a GUIDE,
and, most of all, a good Navigational System.
Then we may find our own Way.

It is with this belief,
and in this spirit of exploration,
that **GENESIS OF GENIUS,**
And **POWER ARC: YOUR CREATIVE GUIDANCE SYSTEM**, are offered.

GENESIS of GENIUS

FIELD

At the highest level, the master or "meta," level, **creativity is unlimited.** *operating in a Field of Pure Potential and infinite possibility.*

All levels of creativity are encompassed and aligned within one universal creative system, one Unity, one Wholeness, one Creative Absolute.

The universal Creative Process that operates across all levels is the same process we may use to create – to bring what does not yet exist into the physical realm.

Creation is a Process of Mind, a Process of Imagination.

With our Minds, we create Worlds.

This GUIDE gives you the master tools to use the Creative Process more consciously, more intentionally, in your Life, Work & World..

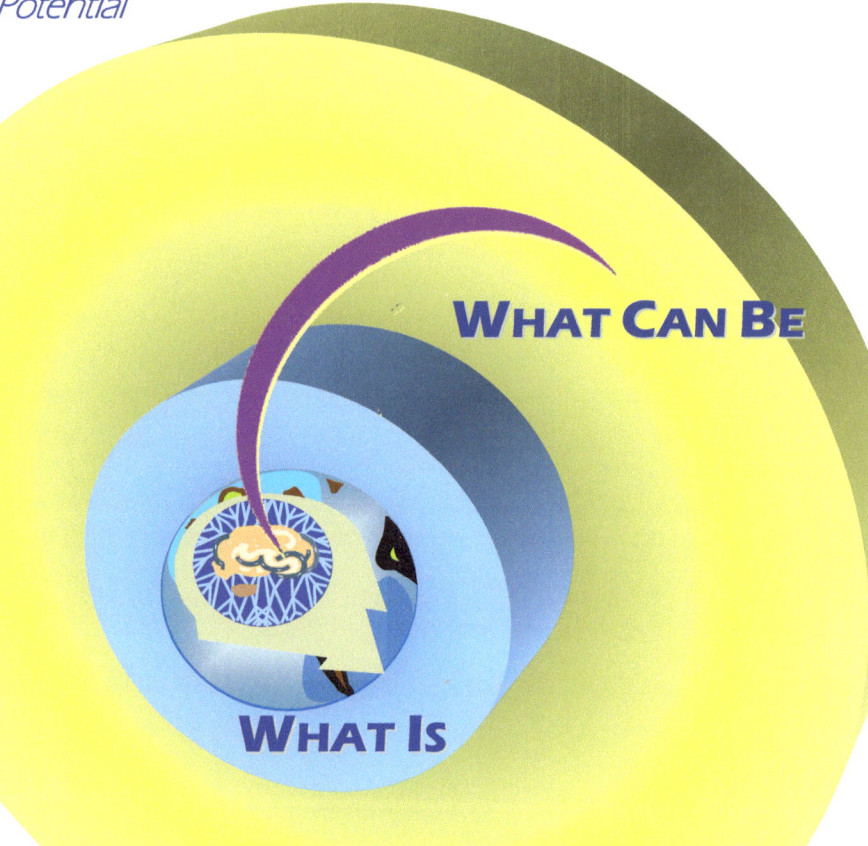

All power originates from this one truth: You may choose to create something other than WHAT IS – something other than what already exists.

This, then, is the one pivotal belief through which we can reconnect with our creative power.

Through concious use of the Creative Process, you may shift from the realm of WHAT IS, into the Creative Realm of WHAT CAN BE.

To Navigate Change at Lightspeed, You Need More Than a Plan. You Need a Guidance System.

We are explorers catapulting into uncharted territory, speeding across a vast, unfamiliar landscape shifting with continuous change.

A rush of new information, discoveries and technologies – many of which extend far beyond the limits we once considered possible – force us to revisit our current view of reality.

Stunned by this flash forward,
suddenly aware of this surrounding, unknown realm -
where massive flows of information exchange at the speed of light,
where chaos and complexity escalate at every dimension -
we desperately seek to apply our old maps,
and scramble to refresh our outdated plans.

Shocked, we find that even our traditional modes of planning themselves are woefully inadequate, given the speed and magnitude of change we are now encountering. Lag time is non-existent; reaction time zero. Simply speeding up is an inadequate answer; moreover, speed without direction is deadly.

It is precisely because we face an increasingly fast-fast world that we must shift from reaction to creation.

Few among us discern these as classic signs of a "paradigm shift" – a change of such magnitude that it requires a shift in our World View or Mindset. This uncharted territory requires us to embrace entirely new modes of thought – an altogether new, creative WorldView – and, not merely a new plan – but an entirely new navigational guidance system.

Old Mindset – Eliminate or Avoid Change.
New Mindset – Intentionally *Create* Change - for Change IS Reality.
As quantum physics and systems theory reveal, we live in *a World in Process*, where only those with a *creative guidance system* will adapt and thrive ...

In a FIELD OF INFORMATION, only configuration - and constant reconfiguration - counts. Current configuration = knowledge. Constant reconfiguration = Imagination. That means *creativity* – not only generating new connections and combinations, but new categories, and entirely new worlds of possibility.

As Einstein grasped long before the rest of the world:
"*Imagination is more important than knowledge.*"

As ever, in this ONCE & FUTURE AGE OF IMAGINATION,
Imagination is the only inexhaustible resource.

FORM

In the midst of a dynamic Universe ever enfolding and unfolding through a constant flux between chaos and order – universal patterns emerge ... traces of the Creative System at work ... revealing a master Creative Process operating at every level of creation.

The master, **Creative Process** *is fractal-like, in that the same sequence of stages and steps repeats at each level of creation, its forms unfolding in parallel, on unlimited levels.*

THE MASTER FORMS: ARC & SPIRAL

The *Arc* & the *Spiral* are the two interrelated *Master Forms* – the *Archetypes of Creation* – which mirror the Creative Process. These forms are *tools* we may use to shift from WHAT IS to WHAT CAN BE - to apply Creative Power in our Lives, Work & World.

The core Creative Process, and the **POWER ARC: YOUR CREATIVE GUIDANCE SYSTEM** that reflects it, contain self-similar, fractal-like stages that operate at all levels of creation – from particle, to individual, to organization, to society, to cosmos.

CREATIVE PROCESS OPERATES AT EVERY LEVEL
RECURRING, FRACTAL "PATTERNS WITHIN PATTERNS"
SAME SEQUENCE OF STAGES & STEPS AT EVERY LEVEL OF CREATION

In other words, once you learn the core elements and steps of the master Creative Process, you may apply them at any level of creation.

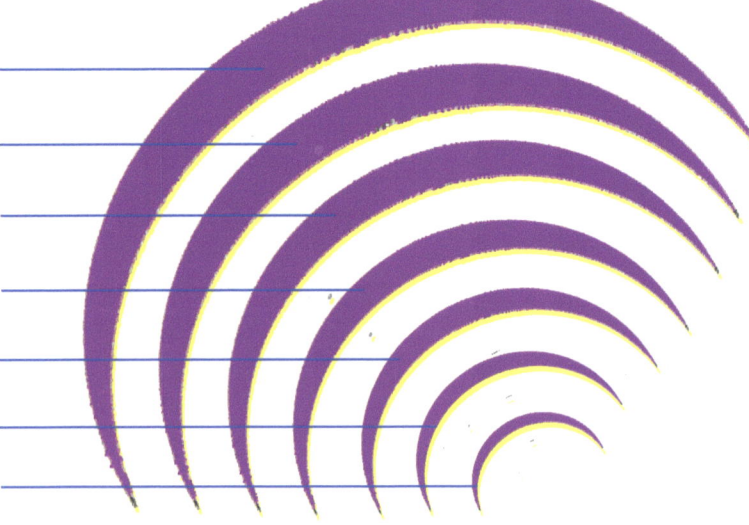

- COSMOS
- SOCIETY
- COMMUNITY
- ORGANIZATION
- RELATIONSHIP
- INIDIVIDUAL
- PROJECT

GENESIS of GENIUS

FORCE

The Tao [The Way] is ...
a Force that pervades the Universe.
It is the Source of the Universe,
but it also IS the Universe.[29]
— Anne Collins Smith, Philosophy professor, Susquehanna University

Just as Star Wars' hero Luke Skywalker was encouraged by his Guide, Obi Wan Kenobi, to

"Learn the ways of The Force,"[30]

at any moment we choose, we may tap into the Creative Force[31] that powers the Universe.

Here, in this GUIDE, POWER ARC: YOUR CREATIVE GUIDANCE SYSTEM reveals to us The Creative Way.

At any moment, you may choose The Creative Way ... The Journey to your potential.

You have had the power to travel this path from the very beginning. As always, that is something you must discover – and choose - for yourself.

THE FIRST STEP IS TO SEE IT ...

... to become Conscious of the Creative Realm, ... to realize we are One with it. Second, we choose to tap into Creative Power, consciously.

Just as the timeless hero story tells of hidden, secret powers, already existing within, we, too, discover them within ourselves.

This GUIDE reveals to you the mindset – and give you the master tools - by which you may take that Journey.

> *My ally is the Force. And a powerful ally it is.*
> *Life creates it. Makes it grow. Its energy surrounds us, and binds us.*
> *Luminous beings are we, not this crude matter.*
> *You must feel the Force around you.*
> *Here between you, me, the rock, the tree, everywhere.*[32]
> — Yoda to Luke Skywalker, *Star Wars*

TRANSLATING LIFE

Life is perpetually transforming energy into matter,
translating information into form and meaning.

In the metasystem that is life, the Creative Process is always operating, configuring information into new order. Form and pattern emerge out of possibility into creation, then dissipate and flow back into infinite possibility again, in a never-ending exchange of energy. Individuals - from bacteria to human beings - self-organize around identity - morphing into meaningful forms, expressing their diversity, expanding their capacity - either consciously or unconsciously. As if inhaling and exhaling, life takes in energy in the form of information,[33] and breathes it out into the world through expression – altering its "self" in the process.

Life is self-creative. And so are we.

With our minds we make sense out of this constant *ebb and flow* – we form patterns out of chaos. Information flows in, both randomly, and in many forms and images, some more distinct – *symbols, sounds, touch, smell, numbers, words* - and some less so – *emotions, intuitions, visions, dreams.* As part of this creative system, we *participate* in this process – and we may choose to do so consciously or unconsciously.[34,35]

With our minds, we build the networks of association and context that create meaning and identity.

In the "physical" realm, the fertile ground of creative thought rests, at base, in our brain's ability to process bits of information in new ways or discover relationships between diverse concepts, and then form different patterns and configurations among them to create something new.

We have the power to choose how we form these relationships into entirely new orders of thought and form.

However, *unlimited creativity* involves yet another step –
a step beyond mere pattern-recognition, or even associations
of that which *already* exists.

We can leap beyond the limited, "physical realm," and with our minds reach out into the creative realm - to envision and create something that does not yet exist. We make this leap to access the creative realm through the mechanism of choice.

At any moment we choose, we can tap into the creative force that powers the universe. As ancient myth, timeless metaphor and eternal image have whispered, this is the secret of the creative journey:

We discover we had the power all along.

From Dorothy clicking her ruby slippers and imagining home, to Luke Skywalker wielding his light saber energize by The Force, we have always had the power to move beyond our limited modes of thought to a higher level.

It is, as it has always been, a Process of Mind, a Process of Imagination.

GENESIS of GENIUS

POWER ARC™/CREATIVE GUIDANCE SYSTEM® ELEMENTS

MASTER CREATIVE FORM: THE ARC

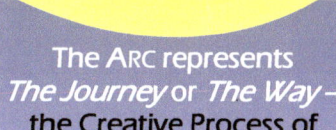

The CREATIVE ARC – the *Arc of the Journey* – is the master form or image that parallels the Creative Process itself; the ARC is the one perfect form, or archetype, that captures and reflects to us the universal stages and steps of the Creative Process.

In POWER ARC™/CREATIVE GUIDANCE SYSTEM®, the ARC symbolizes the Creative Process and its recurring sequence of steps; moreover, the ARC will serve as your master creative tool, as it represents the unfolding "Story ARCs" of your life.

The CREATIVE SPIRAL –

As your Creative Journey unfolds, the self-similar ARCS of the Creative Process generate the master form of the SPIRAL, as each fractal-like "Story ARC" of your life unfolds, shifting you to ever higher levels of experience. The POWER ARC™ SUCCESS SYSTEM® enables you to use the Creative Process more consciously – intentionally - to create the life, work & world you most desire.

The ARC represents *The Journey* or *The Way* – the Creative Process of Mind and Imagination – by which we may shift from the limited realm of WHAT IS, of what already exists, to the unlimited Creative Realm of WHAT CAN BE. In every moment, as Creators, we may choose to traverse these two Worlds of Thought.

MASTER CREATIVE FORM: THE SPIRAL

Each ARC of your life's Creative Journey will unfold, as you consciously apply the Creative Process, using POWER ARC™/CREATIVE GUIDANCE SYSTEM® that captures and reflects it. As you do, you will successfully navigate to your desired goals and visions, across a Universe of change.

You will be the StarPilot, directing each ARC in alignment, gaining power, wisdom and influence at every level of the SPIRAL. In this way, you will become a Master Creator, living into your full creative potential ... creating the life of your dreams.

To Claim Your Bonus Books, Free Creative Resources, & Innovation Tools visit GENESISOFGENIUSBOOK.COM.

© JULIE ANN TURNER & COMPANY/CREATORSGUIDE.COM. All Rights Reserved.

A NEW THINKING TECHNOLOGY

The best way

to predict the future

is to invent it [36]

> *Alan Kay, inventor of Smalltalk,*
> *precursor of windows-based computer systems*

The best way

to predict the future

is to create it.

> *Peter Drucker, management expert and author*

CREATING THE FUTURE

As our new technologies now reveal to us, our escalating experience of constant change - our inescapable role as participants within a "World in Process" – is not an aberration, but the true state in which we live.

Forever in our rearview is the era where we saw change as "variation from the norm" – as something to be avoided or eliminated, and where artificial limits on information, distance and speed lulled us into the luxury of a reactive mode, where we would wait to see what unfolded around us before determining our response or plan. Those days - of analyzing the past in order to predict the future, of avoiding change, of hoarding information, of commanding hierarchies and controlling circumstances - are fast fading into distant memory … receding ever further into the realm of myth, as they always were.

Our new awareness of this 'process reality' presents quite a shock to the system for those of us whose WorldView long focused on how our existing knowledge and 'territory" could best be protected, and on how people and materials could best be controlled.

"Knowledge is power" only in a world where information is artificially limited. As we now see more clearly, we simply cannot react fast enough in a world where information - unleashed and ubiquitous - exchanges at the speed of light, across an infinitely connected globe.

Our very sense of time and space is shaken … for, as Einstein so aptly pointed out, space and time themselves are "*modes by which we think, not conditions in which we live.*"
Our old, "sensible," logical, linear ways of thinking – seemingly adequate enough in a mechanical, industrial era – no longer serve us well in the emerging fast-fast world of ever-increasing complexity, this unpredictable age of ideas in which dynamic processes, global communication and interactive systems continuously alter the landscape of reality.

We find ourselves at a loss as our traditional modes of thinking, our standard tools for prediction, and our static approaches to planning, seem more and more to fail us.

And so it is that we find ourselves hurtling ever deeper into the 21st century, desperately in need of a new WorldView – a new lens with which to perceive this unfolding reality, a new navigational system with which to steer successfully across this dynamic space.

In this new realm, we find we can neither predict nor control our future. The only answer is to learn to create it.

It seems entirely counterintuitive – against so much of what we know or how we have been taught to think - that the only true Way forward is to focus on *intentionally creating change* – on consciously charting a course through the Creative Realm – rather than on *avoiding change,* controlling current circumstances and protecting our existing "territory."

And yet, we already are travelers in this infinite Field of Information – with no artificial buffers to shield us from the speed, complexity and connectedness. We need an entirely different "mode of thought" – a new "thinking technology" to navigate this Field of Pure Potential. In this new World, the best – and only - way to predict the future is to create it. POWER ARC SUCCESS SYSTEM is the "new thinking technology" for this Creative Realm.

GENESIS of GENIUS

POWER ARC™/CREATIVE GUIDANCE SYSTEM® ELEMENTS

THE CREATIVE FIELD

- **Your Life Story** – the ARC of your Journey - unfolds in an infinite CREATIVE FIELD.

- **The CREATIVE FIELD** IS a Field of Information, a Field of Pure Potential – where your choices in every moment are unlimited.

All we need is a new Navigation System to tap into the Creative Force that has always been here ... the Creative Force that powers the Universe.

"The Field is the Force ... . We are attached and engaged, indivisible from our world, and our only fundamental truth is our relationship with it. 'The field,' as Einstein once succinctly put it, 'is the only reality.'"
— Lynne McTaggart,
The Field: The Quest for the Secret Power of the Universe

THE CREATIVE FIELD

YOUR JOURNEY ACROSS CREATIVE SPACE

Your Life Journey unfolds through the Creative Process. Your Journey across the CREATIVE FIELD is guided by your **choices** – whether you make them consciously or unconsciously....

- WHAT CAN BE
- WHAT IS
- CREATIVE PROCESS
  - ARC OF IMAGINATION
  - CREATIVE JOURNEY
  - PROCESS OF MIND

Field of Potential

A FIELD OF UNCERTAINTY?

- CHANGE ~
- SPEED ~
- COMPLEXITY ~
- GLOBALIZATION ~
- COMPETITION ~

CHANGE

- **Often,** however, we may view this Creative Realm not as a Field of Potential, but as a Field of Uncertainty – because it is filled with constant change, which we often perceive or experience as increasing speed, complexity, globalization and competition.

- **As we will learn,** how we experience the Creative Field depends on our World View – the "lens" through which we view the World. We may find that we have been viewing the Infinite through a limited lens.

- We traverse the CREATIVE FIELD through the use of the Creative Process (shown as the purple ARC).

It is not the strongest of the species that survive, nor the most intelligent, but the one most responsive to change.'
— Charles Darwin
The Origin of the Species

We will learn more about the CREATIVE FIELD & the Creative Process (POWER ARC™/CREATIVE GUIDANCE SYSTEM®), we may use to successfully navigate change.

CREATIVE GUIDANCE SYSTEM ELEMENTS

POWER ARC: YOUR CREATIVE GUIDANCE SYSTEM® is the master thinking technology, the universal navigational system, the new mental operating system - you may use to access and apply creative power in your own life, work and world.

CREATIVE

POWER ARC: YOUR CREATIVE GUIDANCE SYSTEM operates as a master model of the Creative Process, capturing and distilling not only the universal process, patterns and principles of creation, but also placing the essential elements – the stages, steps and sequence of the Creative Process - into a working, operational framework.

Within the overarching, universal framework of this process, we are able to create, with complete freedom to choose among limitless possibilities. Both freedom and structure are captured within this master process, a single, miraculous system with the power to create beautiful order out of disorder, perfect pattern out of infinite chaos.

❶ **W**HERE
❷ **N**ow,
❸ **H**ow

The *POWER ARC SYSTEM* is one master process - at its most basic level, just three simple, yet powerful stages - *WHERE, NOW, HOW®* - that enable us to create the future we want in our lives, from our day-to-day work projects to our careers, through our relationships and our community, and always, ultimately, to our unique individual purpose, our potential and our dreams.

As we've seen, *POWER ARC: YOUR CREATIVE GUIDANCE SYSTEM is based on* two master forms *- the creative SPIRAL - and the ARC- which is actually a fractal-like form that repeats to compose the spiral itself.*

This is how the Creative Process operates - arc within self-similar arc, process within process, forming an evolutionary, creative spiral. Recall that the arcs in POWER ARC: YOUR CREATIVE GUIDANCE SYSTEM are fractals: self-similar, proportional "sub-segments" that comprise the whole. Each fractal arc is self-contained, and each builds on the next to form the expanding, master spiral pattern.

The fractal genius of nature is reflected in the POWER ARC SYSTEM in that, at every level of the model, every ARC in the SPIRAL represents the same sequence of stages that make up the whole Creative Process. Once you know the master sequence, we may apply it at every level of creation. We will see how these universal forms are transformed into the simple yet powerful creative tools we may use to remember and apply the Creative Process in our lives and relationships.

This unique system, then, captures the fundamental patterns and self-replicating, organic fractal forms that we have seen revealed in both artistic expression and natural structures. Within the system, the associative, pattern-creating process freely operates.

The Creative Process - and the *POWER ARC SYSTEM* that parallels it – provide the overarching framework that aligns different creative methods within the appropriate stage of the process – so that we may use each of them where it best serves its specific purpose.

GUIDANCE

To navigate and succeed in this Universe of searing speed and constant change, we need more than just a traditional, static plan or formula. We need a navigational guidance system that enables us to move, maneuver, assess and reorient in real time.

POWER ARC: YOUR CREATIVE GUIDANCE SYSTEM is this interconnected, dynamic navigational system. We have entered uncharted territory – a realm of constant change. *There are no maps.*

Moreover, our existing mental operating systems and planning methods are no longer adequate. To see new worlds of possibility emerging and steer through ever-evolving space, we must have a CREATIVE GUIDANCE SYSTEM to enable us to navigate through change in real time, and, most importantly, to guide us as we consciously create our future.

As we have begun to see, this CREATIVE GUIDANCE SYSTEM operates in a Field of Potential - the CREATIVE FIELD - a navigational space where *change is built-in.* Also, as in any worthy navigational system, *POWER ARC: YOUR CREATIVE GUIDANCE SYSTEM* enables you to identify, at any time, where we are in the process, to orient to our destination, and to adjust our course. In addition, by establishing a common, shared framework, the system enables us to align and co-create with others along the way.

SYSTEM

POWER ARC: YOUR CREATIVE GUIDANCE SYSTEM is much more than a static, merely descriptive model or formula; it is a dynamic, working system of the Creative Process. It is a *system*, because, like the Creative Process upon which it is based, each element within it functions independently, yet at the same time in concert with the other elements within the overall framework, while also allowing interaction with a constantly changing external environment.

Incorporating the ARC *and* SPIRAL *in this unique way – with* the ARC representing not only the Creative Process, but also your own Creative Journey, makes *POWER ARC: YOUR CREATIVE GUIDANCE SYSTEM* the ideal framework, the "right metaphor," to enable us to see and apply the process intentionally, to every aspect of life. In each instance of creation, although the core Creative Process remains the same at every level, the exact course taken to reach the creative destination will vary - with the creator, with the destination, with the environment.

This is the essence of the freedom within the framework.

Ultimately, for those seeking advanced mastery of the process, this ARC-to-SPIRAL system expands to reveal more detail at each stage in the advanced five-step *VisionSPARC*™ model, and then spirals out to mirror the overall, evolutionary seven-step *VisionSPIRAL*™ model.

Whether we realize it consciously or not, most of us use parts of the Creative Process naturally, as we should expect, given its fundamental nature. However, few recognize it for what it is, and fewer still understand how the system as a whole works, so we too rarely use the process fully, consciously, intentionally. As a result, we don't access the full power of the Creative Process, or, more accurately, our own true creative power.

That is the purpose of this GUIDE *– to enable you to use the Creative Process intentionally, to create what you desire in your life, relationships, work and world.*

GENESIS of GENIUS

POWER ARC™/CREATIVE GUIDANCE SYSTEM® ELEMENTS

FOCUS: CREATIVE SYSTEM

> POWER ARC is a dynamic, working system of the Creative Process, which enables us to apply the process intentionally, to every aspect of life. This is the essence of the freedom within the framework.
> — JULIE ANN TURNER, GENESIS OF GENIUS

WHAT CAN BE
the Creative Realm
"What We Can Imagine" & "What We Can Create"
- Unlimited
- Imagination
- Potential

... to IMAGINATION

CREATIVE PROCESS [CREATIVE GUIDANCE SYSTEM®]
- Arc of Imagination
- Creative Journey
- Process of Mind

WHAT IS
Current "Reality"
"What Already Exists" & "What We Already Know"
- Limited
- Current Knowledge [Existing Configuration of Information]
- Current Perception

From KNOWLEDGE ...

- Two Worlds ... Two Modes of Thought – Mindshifting from Knowledge to Imagination

> Some ...see things as they are and say "Why?" ...
> I dream things that never were and say "Why Not?."
> — George Bernard Shaw, often quoted by Robert F. Kennedy

> The world we have made as a result of the level of thinking we have done thus far creates problems we cannot solve at the same level we created them.
> — Albert Einstein, theoretical physicist

DARING GREATLY

This GUIDE presents a process that can enable people of all ages to produce their own designs and creations, and to self-organize with others to build a shared future.

When we make the *CREATIVE MINDSHIFT* to a new, creative orientation, and learn to use the Creative Process in the powerful yet practical form of **POWER ARC: YOUR CREATIVE GUIDANCE SYSTEM**, we regain the power to create the future for ourselves.

This creative system is elegantly and beautifully simple. In some ways, it may even appear deceptively so, for *simple* is not always, or at least at first, the same thing as *easy*, as so many who have embarked on this journey have learned. Some, who may think the Creative Process in some ways seems easy or obvious at first glance, soon realize that actually applying the process - at least initially - often takes more adjustment and practice than it may first appear.

Many are often surprised at how their deeply ingrained patterns of linear, "logical" yet mechanical thinking often unconsciously and consistently divert them from the creative path, even though consciously they acknowledge their desire to take the creative approach. Ironically, many later shrug and say: "*If it were that easy or natural, I guess we would have been doing it by now.*" This is, however, actually an inversion of the truth.

The full truth is actually the opposite: "If we were using the natural Creative Process by now, it would have been easy."

The creative way seems to us to be a new way, only because we have forgotten it. In reality, it is the most natural, simple, effortless and easy way to live, work, tap into abundance and expand our capacity.

This fact actually leads us to a central point of this book - we all have the potential to use the Creative Process, consciously and intentionally. We could be using it to create the change we want to see, right now. In fact, the Creative Process is the most natural and pervasive operational system in the Universe. Once we learn how to use it, it becomes easy for us.

It is the premise of this GUIDE that the main reason it may seem difficult for us initially, is that we are only now beginning to rediscover and consciously apply the Creative Process. GENESIS OF GENIUS is offered in the hope and belief that we may all come to use this natural process effortlessly, as we were born to use it.

> *It is not because it is difficult that you have not dared,*
> *it is because you have not dared that it is difficult.*
> — Seneca, Roman philosopher and statesman

We will embark, for there is much for us to accomplish, be and do. We must dare, for there is a much higher purpose. The simple, powerful, and fully creative path lies ahead.

The Cascade of Creation can start within you.
In fact, it can only start within each one of us.

POWER ARC™/CREATIVE GUIDANCE SYSTEM®
NAVIGATIONAL MODEL OF THE MASTER CREATIVE PROCESS

MASTER CREATIVE FORM:
THE ARC

POWER ARC™

MASTER CREATIVE TOOL:
WHERE, NOW, HOW®

1. WHERE
2. NOW
3. HOW

PROCESS STAGES

MASTER CREATIVE TOOL:
VISIONSPARC®
- **S**CAN
- **P**LAN
- **A**CT
- **R**EORIENT
- **C**OMMUNICATE

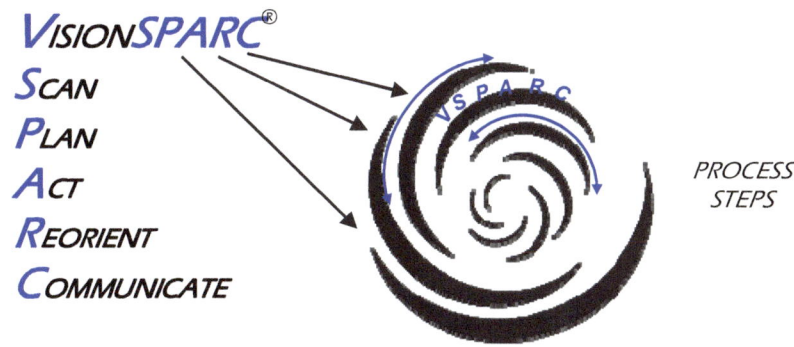

PROCESS STEPS

UNIVERSAL FORM: THE FRACTAL ARC

MASTER CREATIVE FORM:
THE SPIRAL

MASTER CREATIVE TOOL:
VISIONSPIRAL®
- **S**CAN STATE
- **P**LAN
- **I**NITIATE
- **R**EORIENT
- **A**LIGN
- **L**EARN

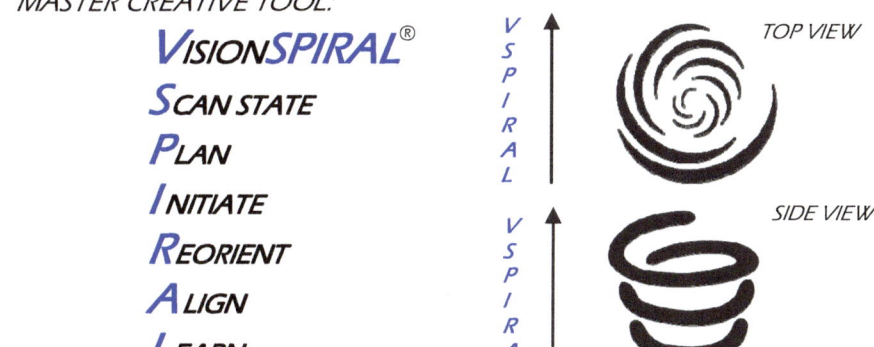

TOP VIEW

SIDE VIEW

UNIVERSAL FORM: THE EVOLUTIONARY SPIRAL

CHAPTER ONE
STARPILOT

You are the Hero,
the StarPilot,
the One
with the Power
to Choose
your own Direction –
in the Journey
that is
your Life.

First,
you must See
and Believe
it is so,
then
in every Moment
you Choose
to Make it so,
through
the Power
of the
Creative Process.

THE FORCE IS WITH YOU

Life is a journey of discovery,
of becoming what we are uniquely meant to be.
We live into that potential
through the Creative Process.

You are the StarPilot – the One with the power
to choose your own direction,
in the Journey that is your life.

Just as heroes and heroines of ancient myth
and superheroes, from Superman to Star Wars,
possess secret, hidden powers, so you, too, hold within you the potential
to wield creative power in unique and transformational ways –
expressible in different forms … expressible only by you.[37]

Why is Socrates' highest admonition "*Know Thyself*"?
Because it is only by knowing yourself
that you can discover your uniqueness, your gifts, your Greatness.

One of the hero's secrets lies in recognizing that *Greatness comes in giving* …
in sharing our gifts with the world, we find our greatest power. In this, we also find our joy.

> *We have only to follow the thread of the hero path … .*
> *Where we had thought to travel outward,*
> *we will come to the center of our own existence.*
> *And where we had thought to be alone,*
> *we will be with all the world.*[38]
> Joseph Campbell, *The Power of Myth*

There is one transformative belief
that originates all creation.
It is the secret behind all creative power in the Universe:
We have the power to choose.

The arcs within the story of our lives unfold,
unconsciously or consciously.

The true hero is a Creator.[39]

The Force already lies within. We are One with it.

All that remains is to discover it,
to choose to express it.

> *Destiny is not a matter of chance;*
> *it is a matter of choice.*
> *It is not a thing to be waited for;*
> *it is a thing to be achieved.*[40]
> William Jennings Bryan, American lawyer and speaker

It is clear you are an explorer, a seeker.

A desire deep inside calls you to look beyond what now exists ...
an inexplicable "knowing" echoes: "*There is something more.*"
There is more to discover, more you can accomplish, more you can contribute.
You know that *there is more that you are, and still more you are meant to be.*

You already have expressed this desire,
and that expression is being reflected in the world.

You have made a choice - an internal, fundamental choice.
And *choice is the mechanism of creation.*
Your very arrival here, by your *action* in reading these words,
Signal you have already begun your quest.

You have set creative energy into motion. With elegant simplicity,
you have activated the process of creation, the process
through which inner desire is made visible.
By choosing consciously to travel your own creative course,
you have taken a pivotal step in the creative adventure that is your life.

And what a remarkable, miraculous adventure it will be.

This will be no ordinary voyage.
This most personal, creative exploration will bring you full circle:
To the pure, complete and joyful expression of who you are,
to the miraculous purpose and meaning of your life,
to the fulfillment of your potential
and your unique contribution to the Universe.

This is the journey to your dreams.
What did you come into this world to do?
What kind of hero will you be? What will you discover on your journey?

Where does the journey begin? Within you.
It begins with a single choice, and ends in the full expression of your self.

> *If you asked me*
> *what I came into this world to do,*
> *I will tell you:*
> *I came to live out loud.*
> — Émile Zola, French writer

Within these pages you will learn that you have the power to create your future,
and you will discover for yourself the answers to these questions.
Like all the heroes who have gone before, you will find you hold within you
the power to take the creative path.

SKYWALKING

The Way comes about as we walk it.[41]
Zhunagzi, Taoist philosopher

Across the ancient traditions spanning East and West, a timeless truth is repeated in similar forms. In the words of Antonio Machado: *"Travelers, there is no path. Paths are made by walking."*[42]

As contemporary poet David Whyte notes, whether this truth appears in spiritual, contemplative or religious traditions, its essence is the same, and in it lies the key to living an authentic, fully creative life:

There's a way in which, if you can see your life laid out before you,
every step of the way, you know for certain that it's not your life;
it's someone else's that you mistook for your own.

Your own life you make every step of the way. In fact, your own life ...
is just the moment, when your feet are touching the ground ...
just the moment, each time, when they touch the ground ... that's your path.
And you only know it in the moment of contact ... .[43]

Today, we are experiencing more than an age of change, but, more accurately, as Eamonn Kelly says, a "*change of age*" – the phrase he uses to describe the pervasive sense of "uncertainty," a sense that the world as we knew it has shifted somehow on its axis.[44] Here, we see it literally as a shift to higher consciousness, a MINDSHIFT to a greater awareness of our creative power.

Moreover, both ancient traditions and quantum physics tell us, we are already creating our world, with every choice – conscious or unconscious. The world of our experience is constantly transforming. Ours is a "World in Process."

Choice is the mechanism of creation. Life may either be merely a series of reactions to ever-changing swirl of current circumstances, or a miraculous, remarkable creative journey – either "a great adventure," as Helen Keller said – "or nothing."[45] And yet, no matter how much we settle for the world as it exists, there is always a nagging thought tugging within the depths of our being – "*What if there's something more?*"

Nothing fails like success. The whole history of society [unfolds this way]:
Demand - response ... equals success.
New demand - old response ... equals failure.
Nothing fails like success.
The more you get centered upon principles that never change,
the more you can change your response to everything else, that can change.[46]
Stephen R. Covey, author on leadership and life management

In this FIELD OF INFORMATION, this realm of pure potential, we may choose to view any constellation of circumstance either as uncertainty and threat, or as opportunity and potential. As always, as we choose our lens – the WorldView or paradigm - through which we interpret the world. And in doing so, we determine the limits of our own possibility.

We must rediscover a more Creative Way. To create the path by walking it, we need a navigational guidance system – to create ever new, ever more creative responses in this ever-unfolding realm of change.

GENESIS of GENIUS

POWER ARC™/CREATIVE GUIDANCE SYSTEM® ELEMENTS

FOCUS: MINDSHIFT

> To Shift to a Higher Realm of Thought,
> All it takes is a Choice.
>
> Choice is the Mechanism of Creation.
>
> — Julie Ann Turner, Genesis of Genius

WHAT CAN BE

THE CREATIVE REALM
"WHAT WE CAN IMAGINE" & "WHAT WE CAN CREATE"
- UNLIMITED
- IMAGINATION
- POTENTIAL

... to IMAGINATION

WHAT IS

CURRENT "REALITY"
"WHAT ALREADY EXISTS" & "WHAT WE ALREADY KNOW"
- LIMITED
- CURRENT KNOWLEDGE
- CURRENT PERCEPTION

From KNOWLEDGE ...

CREATIVE PROCESS AS CREATIVE GUIDANCE SYSTEM®
- ARC OF IMAGINATION
- CREATIVE JOURNEY
- PROCESS OF MIND

- TWO WORLDS ... TWO MODES OF THOUGHT – MINDSHIFTING from Knowledge to Imagination

> When society requires to be rebuilt, there is no use in attempting to rebuild it on the old plan.
> No great improvements in the lot of mankind are possible, until a great change takes place in the fundamental constitution of their modes of thought.
>
> — John Stuart Mill, British economist

TRAJECTORY

> *Ideals are like stars; you will not succeed in touching them
> with your hands. But like the seafaring man on the desert of waters,
> you choose them as your guides, and following them
> you will reach your destiny.*
> — Carl Schurz, German revolutionary, American statesman and senator

*We find ourselves speeding through uncharted territory –
as our own creations and technologies reveal ever more
of the FIELD OF INFORMATION – the FIELD OF PURE POTENTIAL –
as we rediscover our place, as co-creators, in this ONCE & FUTURE AGE OF IMAGINATION.*

In truth, navigating here calls for much more than a change of plan. It calls for a "change of age" in our very modes of thought, a fundamental shift in our WorldView and our consciousness, a quantum MINDSHIFT from *reaction* and *control*, to *choice* and *creation*.

In the FIELD OF PURE POTENTIAL – the Creative Realm – in which we find ourselves, the first imperative in successful navigation through this ever-changing Universe flowing at lightspeed, is *to know our direction*.

As your LIFE ARC stretches across the realm of possibility, the FIELD OF PURE POTENTIAL you must first choose a direction and set your course toward WHAT CAN BE, into the realm of the creative, of leadership, of things dreamed of but not yet seen.

*So where did the ancients look to find universal truth
to guide them in an uncertain and changeable world?*

*To those things that do not change in the midst of change.
To "archetypos," to the original patterns of creation,
and the universal principles - that transcend time.*[47]

To navigate successfully in this Age, we need a CREATIVE GUIDANCE SYSTEM – one that encompasses the eternal, universal creative principles – one that orients not based on transient circumstances, but centered on true constants, like *Vision*, *Values* and *Purpose*.

Like constellations, *Vision*, *Values* and *Purpose* shine steadily, serving as sure guides over time, even as we traverse tumultuous stretches in crossing uncharted space. These constants carry within them deep, enduring meaning and represent that which we hold most precious. Before we embark on our journey to full potential, we must know these deep, inner constants. For when we navigate the field of uncertainty, these are our only sure, compelling guides.

> *In order to live, man must act;
> in order to act, he must make choices;
> in order to make choices, he must define a code of values.*
> — Ayn Rand, author and philosopher

Here, GENESIS OF GENIUS reconnects you with your own creative power to consciously, intentionally use the Creative Process to create the results you wish to realize in your life, work and world. In doing so, we navigate by the same universal and timeless principles of creation the ancients sought, and held most sacred and divine.

GENESIS of GENIUS

MASTERING POWER ARC™/ CREATIVE GUIDANCE SYSTEM®

INITIATION

> **JOURNEY ARC – Mastering Power Arc: Creative Guidance System®:**
> Throughout the GUIDE, these sections will pose reflective questions, based on the concepts recently presented in the book, and will introduce powerful, pivotal activities to enable you to immediately apply essential elements of the CREATIVE GUIDANCE SYSTEM to your life, work & world. We encourage you to take each step with us, completing each exercise or worksheet along the way, so that you may acquire for yourself the skills of a master creator. After all, your path is made by walking it ....

You are now taking a transformational step
in the creative adventure that is your life.
At this moment, you are embarking on the voyage to your true potential.

During this Journey, you will learn how to create the future.
You already have everything you need to start this Journey.
The truth is, you have had the power to travel this path from the very beginning.
But that is something you must discover for yourself.
This GUIDE will aid you in that discovery.

Your creative exploration – the Journey to your dreams and your full potential –
will bring you full circle, to the pure, complete and joyful expression
of who you are, to the miraculous meaning of your life,
and to the fulfillment of your unique contribution to the Universe.

To know the place of your Wholeness,
To express your singular Greatness,
To live fully your Creative Potential.

> Do not let the hero in your soul perish,
> in lonely frustration for the life you deserved,
> but have never been able to reach.
> Check your road and the nature of your battle.
> The world you desired can be won,
> it exists, it is real, it is possible, it's yours.
>
> — Ayn Rand, *Atlas Shrugged*

You will begin by revisiting the broad "Story ARC" of your life. Here, you will reflect on the dreams and accomplishments of each decade of your story. Allow yourself some creative moments now to complete YOUR CREATIVE ARC WORKSHEET. This is the first step in your Creative Journey, and will form the basis for the steps to follow.

> If you follow your bliss,
> you put yourself on a kind of track
> that has been there all the while,
> waiting for you,
> and the life that you ought to be living
> is the one you are living.[48]
>
> — Joseph Campbell, *The Power of Myth*

WORKSHEET # 1 - YOUR CREATIVE ARC WORKSHEET

YOUR CREATIVE ARC®

This simple worksheet will guide you through a brief "thought" exploration to prepare you to apply the CREATIVE GUIDANCE SYSTEM® process to your own life. The insights and perspectives revealed through this personal reflection and visioning will help guide our life exploration activities, and will help introduce some of the unique tools you will be acquiring as you learn to create your life, work and world more consciously.

So take your time, and enjoy this initial life exploration...

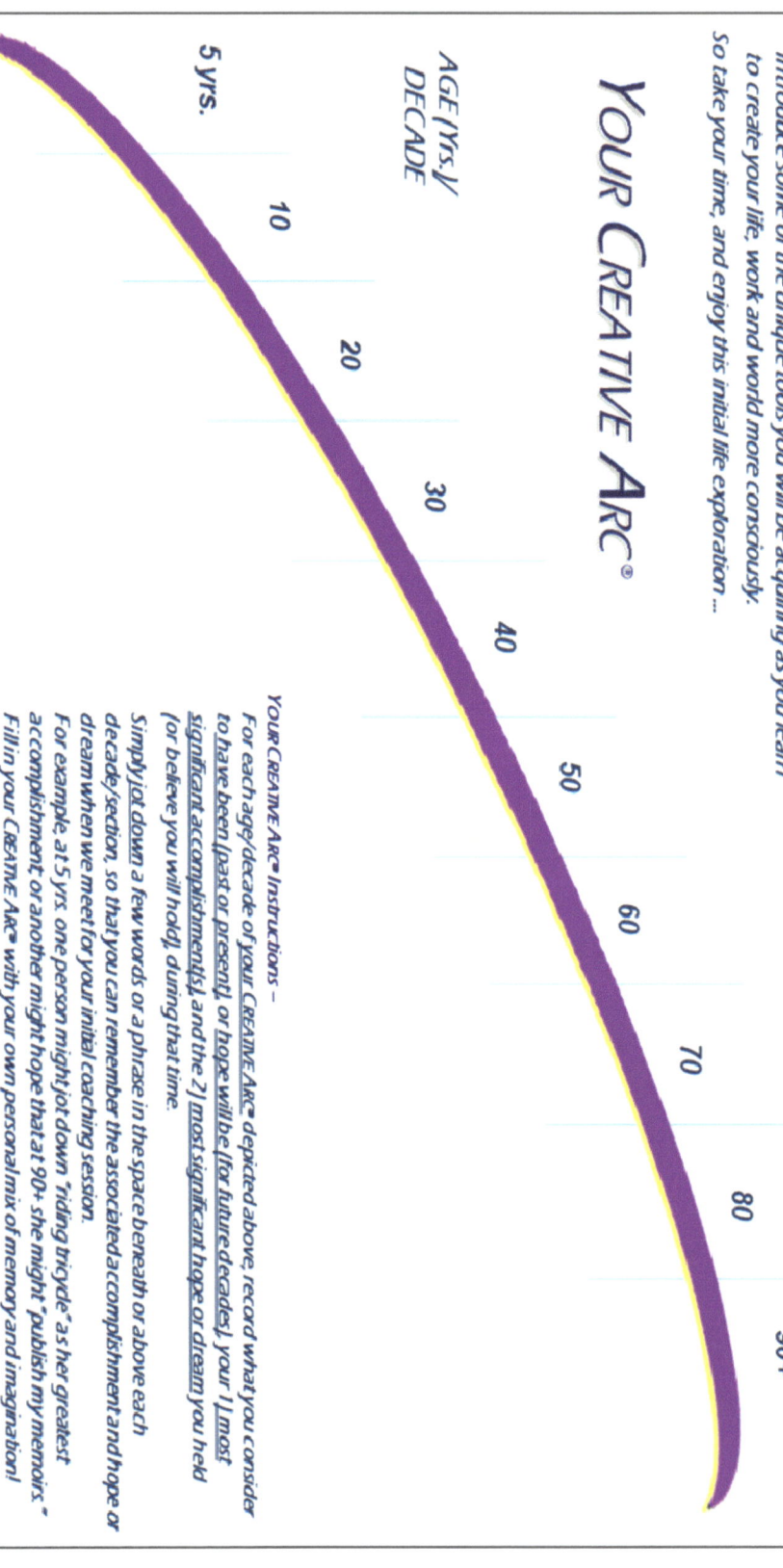

YOUR CREATIVE ARC® Instructions –

For each age/decade of your CREATIVE ARC® depicted above, record what you consider to have been [past or present], or hope will be [for future decades], your 1 [one] most significant accomplishment(s) and the 2 [two] most significant hope or dream you held (or believe you will hold), during that time.

Simply jot down a few words or a phrase in the space beneath or above each decade/section, so that you can remember the associated accomplishment and hope or dream when we meet for your initial coaching session.

For example, at 5 yrs. one person might jot down "riding tricycle" as her greatest accomplishment or another might hope that at 90+ she might "publish my memoirs."

Fill in your CREATIVE ARC® with your own personal mix of memory and imagination!

CHAPTER TWO
CREATIVE WAY

All know

The Way.

Few

actually

walk it.

Bodhidharma, Buddhist monk

THE ARC OF IMAGINATION

*What is The Way
that leads
to your full
creative potential?*

Throughout time,
this question has been framed in riddles,
with its answer revealed in story.

It makes perfect sense, then, that we would begin
with a story of a creator's journey.

As we've seen, stories make the unfamiliar familiar
and help us see new worlds of possibility - even those which previously
may have existed beyond our current WorldView.

So here, we will begin with one story –
actually, one special story within a life story –
that illustrates the answer ...
and we will use this story to introduce the tools of the Creative Process.

Starts as this creator is shifting from one story arc of life to another.
As many great stories do,
this short, simple story
actually begins in the middle
of one creator's life.

You will see,
as we trace
the full spiral path
of this creator's story,
that this vignette captures the essence
of how an ordinary life
can become quite remarkable.

It also reveals important keys to conscious creation,
accessible to all of us, through the Creative Process.

ARNOLD'S STORY

In 1976, in the city of Tucson, Arizona, a sports reporter named Steve Chandler sat down to interview a young man, a native of Austria. This young man had made quite a name for himself as a bodybuilder; in fact, this young man had recently been named both Mr. Universe and Mr. Olympia. His name was Arnold Schwarzenegger.

What attracted Steve Chandler to the interview, however, was not the young man's success at bodybuilding. It was Arnold Schwarzenegger's surprising recent announcement that he was leaving bodybuilding to pursue a career in movies.

Now, Chandler, like most who new anything of Arnold Schwarzenegger at that time, saw Arnold's publicly stated intention to shift from bodybuilder to box-office star as quite a leap, given that Arnold was then known primarily as a physical, rather than an intellectual, giant (not the first, or last, time Arnold would be underestimated), and given Arnold's his relative lack of acting experience, and his heavy Austrian accent that often overpowered his still-somewhat-stiff English.

Perhaps it was the seeming incongruity of Arnold Schwarzenegger's surprising career ambitions that drew Chandler into this interview; at the very least, this should make for a good story, even if only as a humorous anecdote. Sitting across from Arnold's massive form, one might imagine that Chandler may have held back a bit of a smile as Arnold confidently reiterated his announcement:

> "I'm going to be the number one box-office star in all of Hollywood."

And Chandler squeezed out the natural question:
"How do you intend to do that?"
Arnold Schwarzenegger answered, with a resoundingly profound, and, as it would turn out - prophetic - response:

> "It's the same process I used in bodybuilding.
> What you do is create a vision of who you want to be, and then live into that picture, as if it were already true."[49]

And Arnold proceeded to do exactly that.

ARNOLD'S ARC

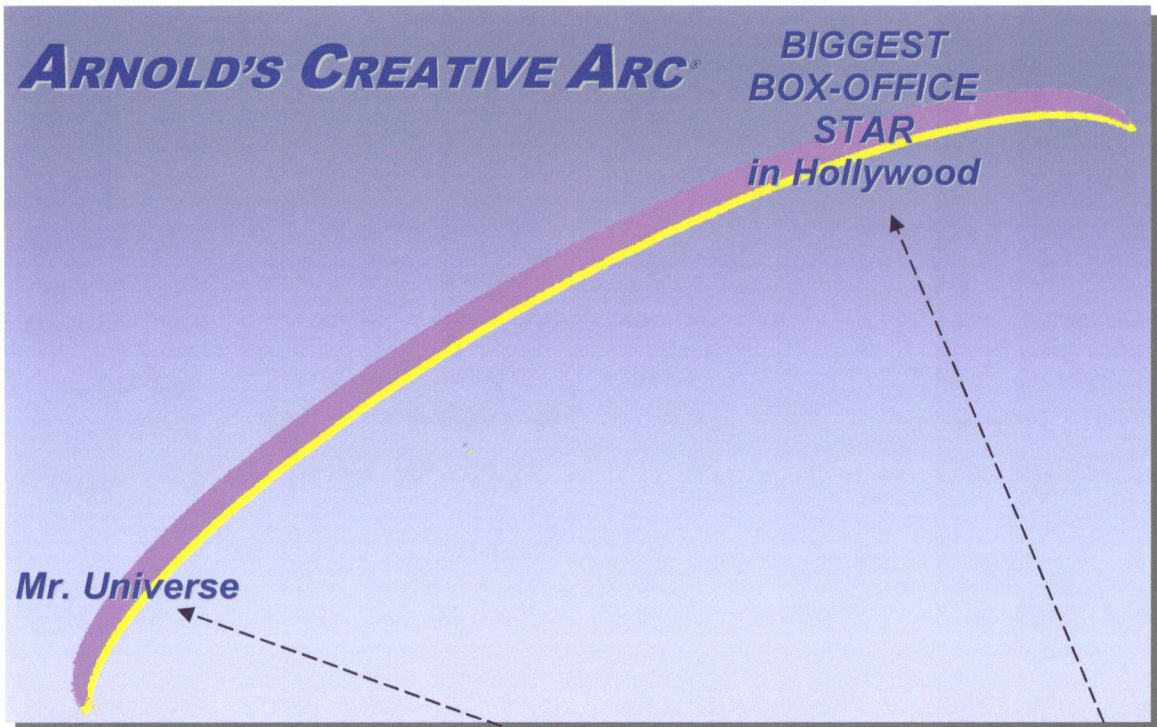

Arnold Schwarzenegger mastered the conscious, intentional use of the Creative Process to create every arc in his life's story. As revealed in this initial story, Arnold used the "same process" to create his career as a movie star that he used to create his success as a bodybuilder.

As it turns out, Arnold's story enables us to begin sharing simple secrets of the Creative Process, each hidden behind the "story arcs" that comprise his life's spiral journey to the top. Arnold's CREATIVE ARC provides a perfect model for us to demonstrate the power of the ARC and the SPIRAL as the master creative tools of the *POWER ARC SYSTEM*, which you, too, may use to create the life you desire.

Regardless of what anyone may think about Arnold Schwarzenegger – his movies, his lifestyle, his politics – the fact remains that Arnold has walked a life path largely of his own conscious creation. Along the way to many remarkable achievements, he also has made many mistakes - facing valid criticism, and overcoming challenges and failures. He is far from perfect.

Like all who follow the hero's path, he faces obstacles.[50] Though Arnold often seems larger-than-life, he is, like the rest of us, human. This is, in fact, is one of many reasons why Arnold is an excellent model for demonstrating the profound power – and the simple steps – of the Creative Process, as revealed here in *POWER ARC: YOUR CREATIVE GUIDANCE SYSTEM*.

Most of all, Arnold Schwarzenegger continues to re-create himself, and therefore shows us how the navigational nature of the master Creative Process enables anyone who uses it to move consistently and successfully, even through change and chaos, to reach their dreams.

We will use ARNOLD'S ARC as a master example as we first introduce the main stages of the CREATIVE GUIDANCE SYSTEM, and then will delve deeper into the process as we go.

CREATING A LIFE

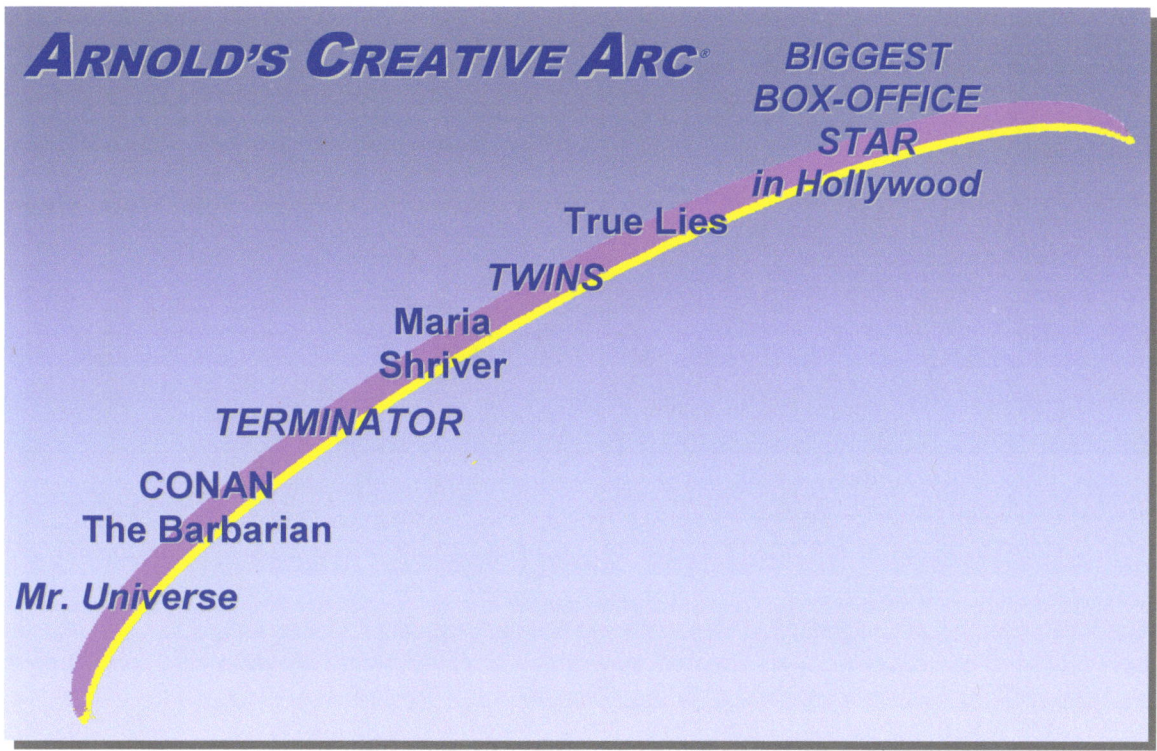

So let's follow Arnold's CREATIVE ARC a bit further, to learn how he stepped into the role of the creator of his life, how he steered his movie career, and how he achieved his dream of being the biggest box–office star in Hollywood.

In doing so, we reveal the basic steps of POWER ARC: YOUR CREATIVE GUIDANCE SYSTEM.

1) **WHERE** - First, notice that Arnold *began* by envisioning *where* he desired to be – *where* he was going (Biggest Box-Office Star in Hollywood) – rather than beginning with a focus on what his circumstances were *now*.

2) **NOW** – Arnold *built on* - but *was not limited by* - where his life was *now* (Body-builder with no acting experience, limited English speaking skills and a heavy Austrian accent).

3) **HOW** – He *then* determined *how*, step by step, to take action toward his goal - navigating his way, always in the direction of his goal - until he achieved his dream.

The order of these creative steps is crucial.

This sequence – beginning the Journey by first envisioning WHERE you wish to be – rather than by focusing on what the current (or past) circumstances or skills are NOW – or, as so many do, by immediately focusing on HOW (or whether) the goal can be reached - cannot be underestimated.

It is this powerful sequence that initiates of the Creative Process.
It requires uncommon thought, uncommon sense, and unconventional wisdom.
Yet, taking this "road less traveled" makes all the difference in your Creative Journey, as it has in Arnold's. And, it is this road that leads to uncommon success.

ARNOLD: THE NAVIGATOR

Arnold Schwarzenegger holds a much broader – and much more creative - WorldView than most. While most of those around him may initially have seen his apparent limitations, Arnold was already looking beyond what already existed – beyond WHAT IS – and beginning to "live into" the unlimited Creative Realm of WHAT CAN BE.

As it is with all great Creators, Arnold Schwarzenegger's view of the world is one of potential and possibility, rather than one of limitation. He saw before him an Unlimited Field of Creation – where he could consciously create the life and career he envisioned.

It might be easy to think that the course – and high trajectory - Arnold charted for himself unfolded smoothly and easily. In truth, it took tremendous physical and mental strength for Arnold to reach such high goals. Most of all, however, Arnold succeeded because he knew how to navigate consistently toward his Vision, in spite of every challenge, disappointment and failure - as well as the constant change - he faced along the way.

In fact, when he was being interviewed by reporter Steve Chandler, Arnold actually was promoting one of his very first movies, "*Stay Hungry*," in which he played a body-builder. The movie was not receiving positive reviews, and it ultimately made a poor showing at the box office. However, Arnold persevered – navigating and overcoming many setbacks and failures along the way, as the partial chart of his career shows below.[51] He not only went on to win a Golden Globe as Best Newcomer for "*Stay Hungry*," but moved on from starring as a body-builder (in his successful "*Pumping Iron*") to action-star roles that evolved from *Conan: The Barbarian* to *The Terminator*. At every stage, Arnold's clear Vision, his "creative guidance system," and his ability to navigate change carried him to the top.

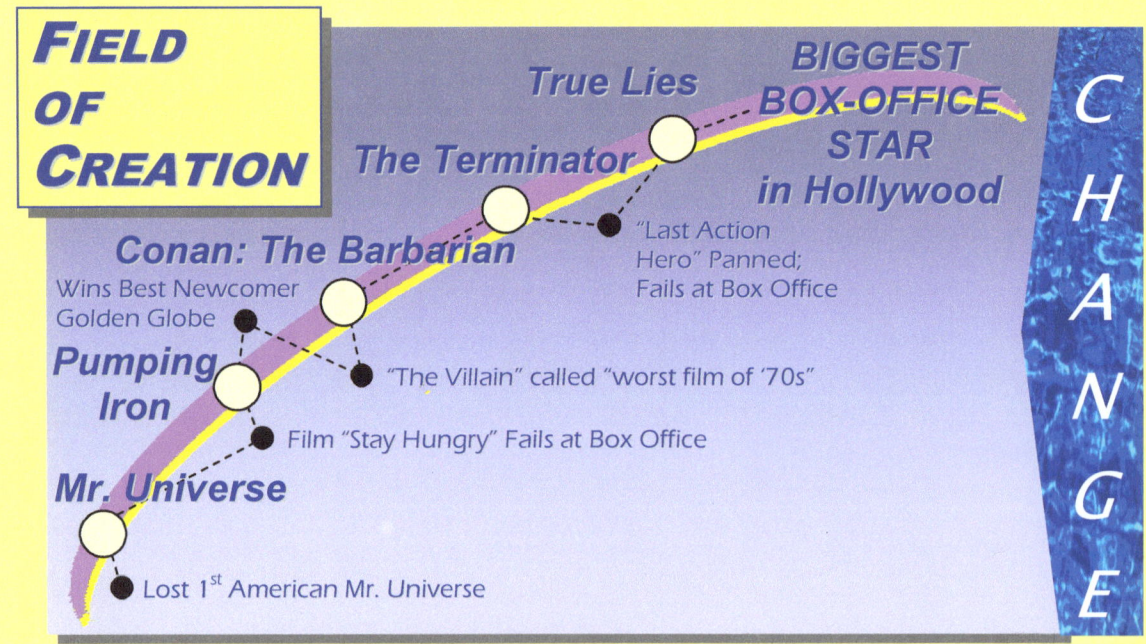

SEEKING THE HIGHEST

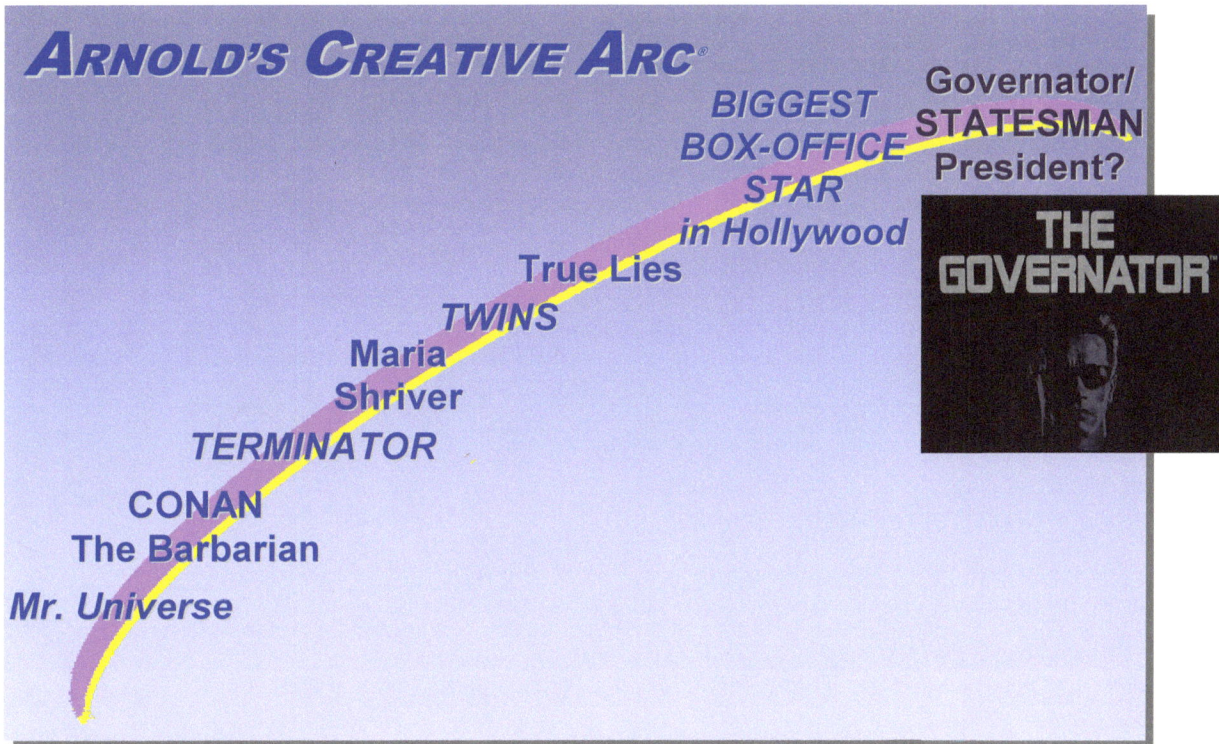

Arnold Schwarzenegger possesses a Creative WorldView.
He is a Conscious Creator.
Like all Creators, he does not see things as they are, and merely ask "Why?"
Creators see things as they never were – but "can be" – and ask "Why not?"

Where has the conscious use of the Creative Process taken Arnold?
All the way to the Governor's Mansion in California.
There is actually an Austrian postal service stamp featuring Arnold's picture.
There is talk of Arnold perhaps being president of Austria one day, and even talk of his becoming president of the United States (if U.S. law were changed to allow it).[52]

How powerful is conscious use of the Creative Process –
as revealed here in POWER ARC: YOUR CREATIVE GUIDANCE SYSTEM ?
Arnold's life trajectory and achievements prove the power of the Creative Journey.

As we shared in the preview to POWER ARC: YOUR CREATIVE GUIDANCE SYSTEM, this navigational model captures the stages and steps of master Creative Process – found throughout thought, art and nature – through which all that is created has been created.

Here, we reveal to you this POWER ARC SUCCESS SYSTEM – in simple, unfolding steps – using the master forms of the ARC and the SPIRAL to guide you. As we've seen expressed so vividly throughout Arnold's story, living a consciously creative life requires not only an understanding of what these steps are, but also how to use this creative system to navigate, in real time, through an ever-changing FIELD OF CREATION, and on to your highest dreams.

GENESIS of GENIUS

THE EVER-RISING SPIRAL

If we're built from spirals, while living in a giant spiral, then everything we put our hands to is infused with the spiral. 10:15, personal note: It's fair to say I'm stepping out on a limb, but I am on the edge, and that's where it happens.[53]
— Maximillian Cohen, in the 1998 movie "*Pi*"

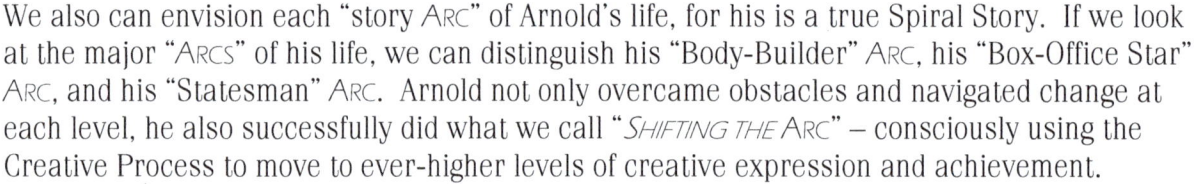

Recall that all great myth and story reveals the Hero's Journey. In this ageless archetype or "pattern of story" – represented here by the A*rc* and S*piral* – the adventurer sets out toward an envisioned destination or goal (the initial arc of the story), and is challenged to overcome obstacles and trials, which call upon creativity and test inner and outer strength (often, through several "adventure" arcs of the story).

Ultimately, the hero prevails, returning triumphant to the place where the journey began (the hero comes full circle), yet the hero is transformed, having risen to a higher place of self-knowledge, wisdom and renewed perspective. And then, the true hero sets sights on higher Vision still, and embarks on an even greater journey. *The form that emerges is an ever-rising spiral.*

We also can envision each "story A*rc*" of Arnold's life, for his is a true Spiral Story. If we look at the major "A*rcs*" of his life, we can distinguish his "Body-Builder" A*rc*, his "Box-Office Star" A*rc*, and his "Statesman" A*rc*. Arnold not only overcame obstacles and navigated change at each level, he also successfully did what we call "S*hifting the* A*rc*" – consciously using the Creative Process to move to ever-higher levels of creative expression and achievement.

Now we may begin to see more clearly why The Journey Arc is the "right" metaphor – the single perfect concept and pattern - with the power to enable us to see the master Creative Process, because revealed within this universal story A*rc* are the fundamental stages and steps of the master Creative Process itself.

Some of the elements of the Creative Process – revealed here in *Power Arc: Your Creative Guidance System* - will almost certainly be familiar to you. As we've said, "*We are All Creators.*" Deep inside our being, we sense our creative power, and, at times, we naturally use elements of the Creative Process because creating is inherent in our very nature as human beings. However, though we "know' the process instinctively, we seldom use it in full, and we even more rarely use it consciously. Moreover, we show how the conscious use of the Creative Process, amazingly, differs dramatically from the way we, especially those of us in the Western world, have been taught to think, in our fast-fast, urgency-driven environment.

Therefore, in the 21st Century, full application of the Creative Process ironically marks a radically different approach from today's "business-as'-usual" thinking. And yet, it is this refreshingly new – and yet timeless – approach that enables you to consciously create the life, work and world you most desire. For *The Journey* is your Story, too.

ON BEGINNING

Your creative journey is one of rediscovery - it is your return to your own creative power. You have always carried deep within you this creative force. By reconnecting with, and more fully expressing, the creativity that already resides within you, you return again, evolving to a higher plane of self-knowledge, purpose and contribution.

You may recall from the Introduction to this GUIDE the Japanese concept of *shoshin*, or the "beginner's mind": *If your mind is empty, it is always ready for anything; it is open to everything. In the beginner's mind there are many possibilities; in the expert's mind there are few . . . . This is also the secret of the arts: always be a beginner.* [54] As you embark on your own creative exploration, your potential for discovery will expand exponentially as you consciously remain open to the free flow of ideas, imagination and possibility.

Remember, this GUIDE is all about possibilities.

So, as you begin your creative journey, consciously and intentionally open your eyes and your mind . . . to enter uncharted territory . . . to explore remarkable ways to access your creative potential . . . to discover a more creative way of thinking and traveling through the world. Look at it this way . . . the only way to tap into new realms of potential is to first open your mind to *consider the possibilities*.

Welcome each element of the process with "*the innocence of first inquiry.*"[55] If we consciously keep an open channel, we are able to see even familiar concepts anew - authentic, powerful creative keys such as *vision, purpose, power, choice* - as well as to perceive a creative spectrum of possibilities we may never even have imagined before.

You may only discover new worlds if you embark with a true explorer's mind.

We begin by introducing POWER ARC: YOUR CREATIVE GUIDANCE SYSTEM in its simplest, three-stage form – in the ARC OF IMAGINATION expressed in the stages of WHERE, NOW, HOW, which we saw etched within Arnold Schwarzenegger's own Creative ARC. This same three-step, master Creative Process works on every level of creation. We will discover how the Arc of WHERE, NOW, HOW works first on a personal, individual level, and then on an organization level, as well as see how this same simple process can be applied to any project, challenge, change or opportunity we may face.

As is appropriate for a Creative Journey, we call the first stage of the process "WHERE" – as in "*Where are we going?*" – within the master navigational system of POWER ARC: YOUR CREATIVE GUIDANCE SYSTEM. We will explain each of the stages – WHERE, NOW, and HOW – and reveal the principles and elements within each of these stages. Later, in our Advanced and Mastery sections, we will share in more detail the stages and steps of the POWER ARC: SUCCESS SYSTEM, and reveal in more depth the power of this navigational master system, through the advanced models of VISIONSPARC – which presents WHERE, NOW, HOW in more detail - and VISIONSPIRAL – which reveals the full power of the Creative Process over time.

Throughout GENESIS OF GENIUS, the unfolding forms of the ARC and the SPIRAL are the two central visual archetypes or images we will use to represent the Creative Process. In fact, they will become primary tools to guide us through this universal, transformational process.

GENESIS of GENIUS

JOURNEY ARC

MASTERING POWER ARC™ / CREATIVE GUIDANCE SYSTEM®

STORY ARCS

LIFE SPIRAL – Mastering Power Arc: Creative Guidance System®:

Are you living your life to your full creative potential? A life expressing your Greatness? On the timeline of your life, is your path a series of ever-rising ARCS OF CREATION, or a long, flat, uneventful line, broken only by occasional unconscious reactions to whatever floats randomly into your immediate view? You may live a life of Conscious Creation, where *you* determine your own life trajectory...

Does each "STORY ARC" within your life carry you to a higher level of purpose, achievement and wisdom, with each ARC aligned with, and building on, the previous one, to form a resonant, resilient, remarkable SPIRAL of increasing imagination and realization of your dreams?

> From time to time
> it's fun
> to close our eyes,
> and in that dark
> say to ourselves,
> 'I am the sorcerer,
> and when I open my eyes
> I shall see a world
> that I have created,
> and for which I and only I
> am completely responsible.'
> Slowly then, eyelids open
> like curtains lifting stage-center.
> And sure enough,
> there's our world,
> just the way we've built it.[56]
>
> Richard Bach,
> *The Bridge Across Forever*

BODYBUILDER · BIGGEST BOX-OFFICE STAR · GOVERNATOR/STATESMAN

ARNOLD'S LIFE ARCS
Have you created your Life Journey – your Creative ARC and SPIRAL – as consciously as Arnold created his?

Now that you have seen how Arnold "shifted his ARC," reflect on the LIFE ARCS in your life thus far... (Worksheet next page).

We are all creators. We have the power in every moment to choose to create our lives (in truth, we already are creating our lives, but often, not consciously or intentionally; all the choices we have made up to this point have generated the ARCS of our lives thus far.) Through our conscious application of the Creative Process, we may choose the direction and trajectory of our next LIFE ARCS, and create a magnificent life of full creative potential.

GENESIS of GENIUS

WORKSHEET # 2 - YOUR LIFE SPIRAL WORKSHEET (SHIFTING THE ARC)

CREATIVE GUIDANCE SYSTEM®

YOUR LIFE SPIRAL™ WORKSHEET

Most people can identify several "Arcs" in their Life's Journey...

Has your Life Journey – your CREATIVE ARCS and LIFE SPIRAL – been as conscious as Arnold's?

Use this Template to sketch your initial ideas about the major "ARCS" of your life thus far...

YOUR LIFE SPIRAL® Worksheet Instructions –
Now that you have created your initial CREATIVE ARC® using Worksheet # 1 (LIFE ARC Timeline), you may review your life timeline to identify the major LIFE ARCS of your own life, thus far. Often, these may include ARCS for the earliest stages of life such as "childhood" or "school" experiences (in the medium and largest ARCS; note: if you need more ARCS to adequately capture your life's stages thus far, feel free to draw them in on the diagram, as needed). At this point, you may wish to fill in the ARCS using a pencil, so that you may revise your ARC titles as you wish, or as your reflections change. This exercise will give you a unique overall view of your life thus far, and enable you to reflect on how conscious, or perhaps how unconscious, the major ARCS of your life have unfolded thus far. Later in the GUIDE, you will discover how the CREATIVE GUIDANCE SYSTEM® will enable you to create your life more intentionally – to consciously "SHIFT THE ARC" to even higher levels of performance and potential – and we will see more examples of how other creators did this in their own lives.

PART TWO
POWER ARC:
YOUR CREATIVE GUIDANCE SYSTEM®

Power Arc: Your Creative Guidance System . . .

captures the

master Creative Process –

in at first three, and, ultimately, just seven

simple, but powerful, interrelated steps -

to enable you

to create the future you want

in your life . . .

in your relationships,

projects, work, career,

community, society, world . . .

It is the One System that gives you the tools

to navigate successfully

in a Universe

swirling with dynamic change . . .

CHAPTER THREE
LAUNCH SEQUENCE

What you do is create a vision of who you want to be, and then live into that picture, as if it were already true.[57]

Arnold Schwarzenegger
Former Body-builder and Governor of California

LIVING INTO LIFE

*As Arnold Schwarzenegger
so simply yet profoundly expressed it,
and as we paraphrase here,
living a Life of Creation
involves first creating a picture of who you want to be –
a clear image of where you want to go in life -
and then "living into that picture as if it were already true."*

*Arnold words remind us that "living into" a Creative Life is a Process –
an ever-imaginative, navigational process,
a Journey for which we need a dynamic, creative guidance system.*

*Still, though all of us are on this Creative Journey through Life,
it is amazing how few of us - whether as individuals or organizations –
embark with a crystal-clear idea of "Where" we are going – in each day, and in life.*

Too often, our only guidance systems are our To-Do Lists,
which are firmly focused solely on Now and How.
In the turbulence of a fast-fast world, our attention is arrested
by the urgent and immediate *Now*, and we're so intent
on executing How at top speed, that we too rarely pause to look up,
get our bearings, and confirm we're indeed still headed in the right direction.

That is why we smile with a deep, yet somewhat uneasy,
recognition as we read the legendary initial exchange
between Alice and the Cheshire Cat on the following page
"*If we don't know where we want to get to,
it doesn't really matter which way we go.*"[58]

One would think it would seem obvious that the first and foremost question when embarking on any new endeavor, whether on our own or with others, would be "*Where are we going?*"

Why, then, do we so rarely ask this question, and especially, ask it *first*?
Because we're so driven by what is happening Now,
and so absorbed in the details of How to do what we're already busy doing.
Not that there's anything wrong with doing what we're doing better - as long as
we know we're doing the right things in the first place - which brings us back to WHERE.

*Yet, it is precisely because of the ever-changing world in which we now find ourselves,
this question "Where are we going?" needs not only be asked first, but much more
often, to survive and thrive in this instantaneously unfolding reality.*

Moreover, as Arnold's story reminds us, and as all the ancient tales tell us,
great Journeys always start with a vivid picture of "WHERE" we are going –
a great and compelling *Vision* of where we most want to be.
If we want to accomplish great – even heroic – things, we must start
by knowing a good deal about WHERE we 'want to get to" – as the Cheshire Cat might say.

Otherwise, how can we possibly know which path to take to reach our dreams?

GENESIS of GENIUS

POWER ARC™/CREATIVE GUIDANCE SYSTEM® ELEMENTS

WHERE, NOW, HOW™

- **THREE BASIC STAGES OF POWER ARC™/YOUR CREATIVE GUIDANCE SYSTEM®** – The New Thinking Technology for the 21st Century

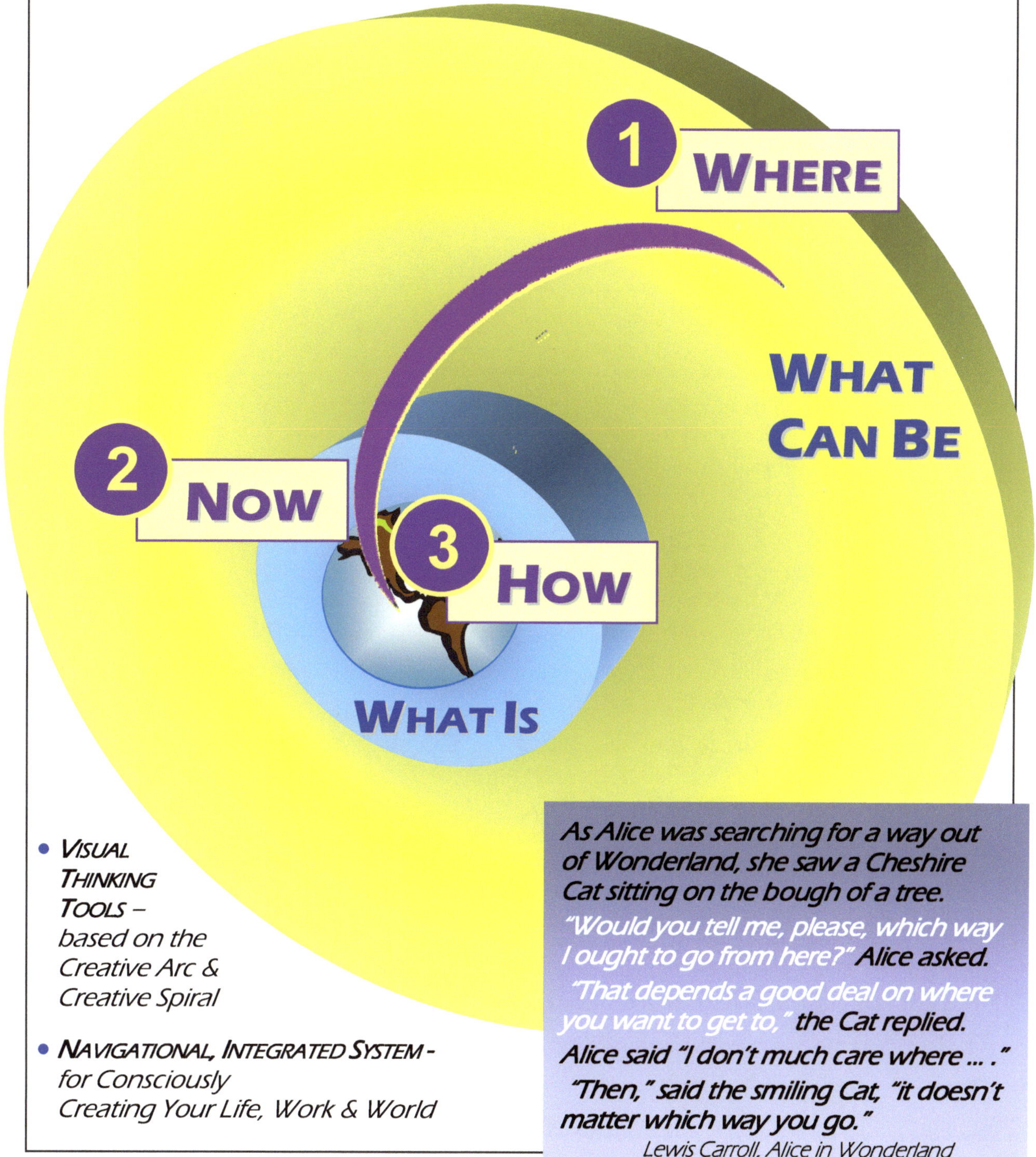

1 WHERE — **WHAT CAN BE**

2 NOW

3 HOW — **WHAT IS**

- *VISUAL THINKING TOOLS* – based on the Creative Arc & Creative Spiral

- *NAVIGATIONAL, INTEGRATED SYSTEM* - for Consciously Creating Your Life, Work & World

> As Alice was searching for a way out of Wonderland, she saw a Cheshire Cat sitting on the bough of a tree.
> "Would you tell me, please, which way I ought to go from here?" Alice asked.
> "That depends a good deal on where you want to get to," the Cat replied.
> Alice said "I don't much care where ... ."
> "Then," said the smiling Cat, "it doesn't matter which way you go."
> — Lewis Carroll, Alice in Wonderland

THE THREE BASIC STAGES

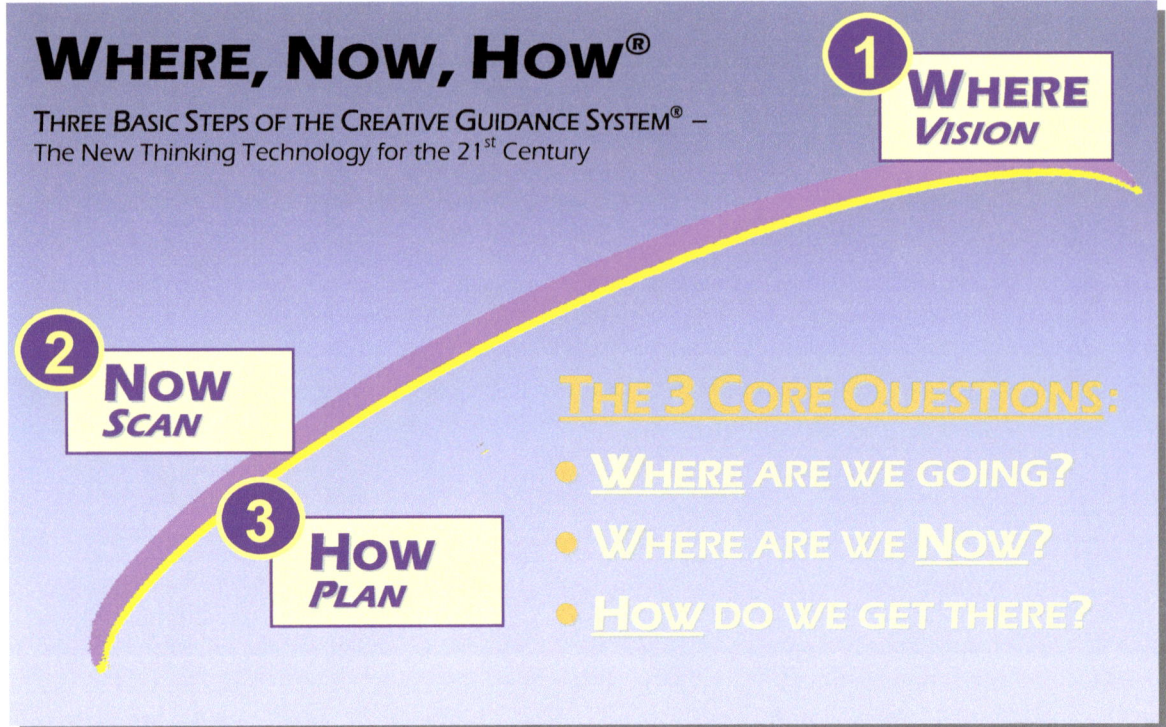

To reach your highest goals – and to live into your full creative potential - within a Field of constant change, you need more than just a traditional, static plan or formula. You need a navigational guidance system that helps you move, maneuver, assess and reorient in real time. *POWER ARC: YOUR CREATIVE GUIDANCE SYSTEM* is this interconnected, dynamic navigational system.

The *POWER ARC: SYSTEM* is not a static, merely descriptive model or formula; it is a dynamic, working system that captures the stages, steps and sequence of the master Creative Process. The *SYSTEM* is based on two master forms – the ARC and the SPIRAL – which actually become the easy-to-use tools you use to navigate your own creative journey.

The power of this POWER ARC: CREATIVE GUIDANCE SYSTEM lies in its simplicity, its sequence, and its scalability.

Simplicity - At its most basic level, the *POWER ARC SUCCESS SYSTEM* is encompassed in just three simple, yet powerful stages - *WHERE, NOW* and *HOW* - that enable you to create the future you want in your life, from your day-to-day work projects to your career, through your relationships and your community, and always, ultimately, to your purpose, your potential and your dreams.

Sequence – In many ways, it is the *sequence* of the stages that makes this *POWER ARC SYSTEM* a far superior "thinking technology," especially in dynamic times that require Imagination. And, as we'll see in more detail, this sequence is decidedly different from the way most of us have actually been taught to think. Here are the three core stages:

① *WHERE* – *WHERE* am I (are we) going?

② *NOW* – Where am I (are we) *NOW*?

③ *HOW* – How do I (we) get there?

SCALABLE THINKING

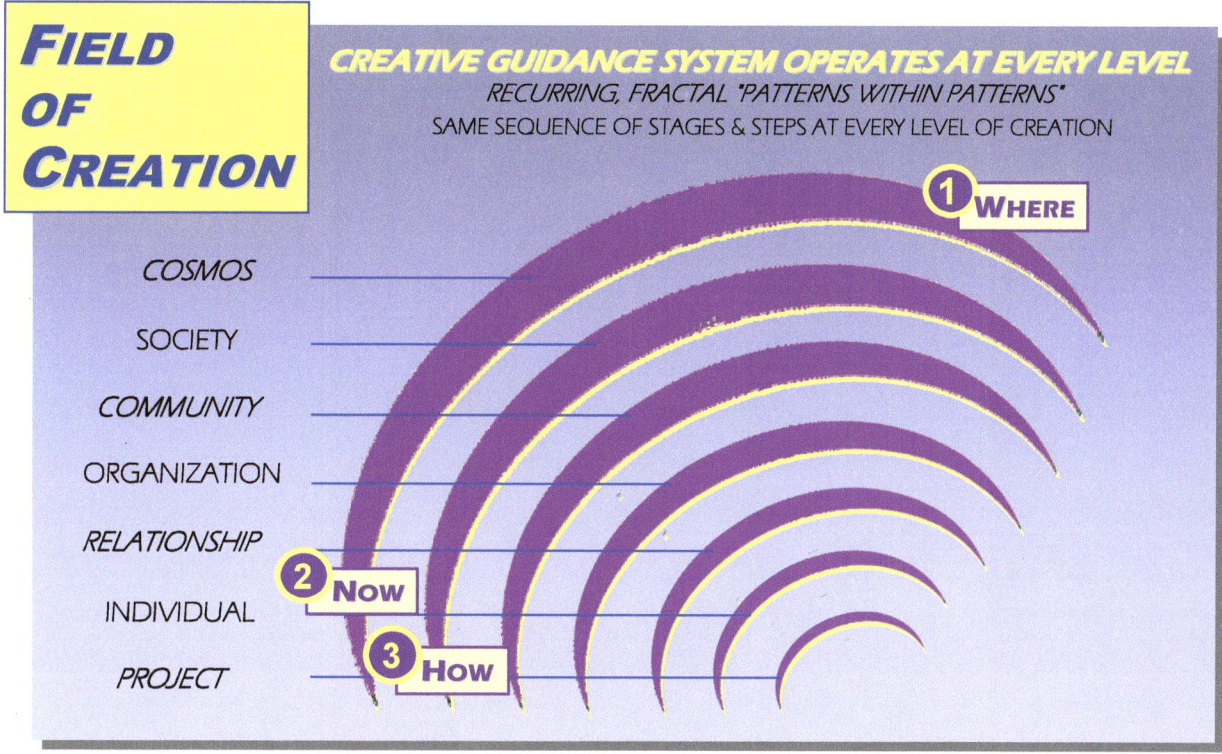

Scalability – **POWER ARC: YOUR CREATIVE GUIDANCE SYSTEM** is *scalable*. Just as the Creative Process works across every dimension of the Field of Creation, this **CREATIVE GUIDANCE SYSTEM** works across all levels of creation.

In other words, once you understand these core stages of the Creative Process, you may apply this same sequence of stages to create at any level - from project, to career, to relationship, to organization, to community, to society, to cosmos. Here, we call these levels of creation PLANES OF THOUGHT, and we discuss this concept in more detail a bit later in the GUIDE.

Remember, like the master Creative Process, the CREATIVE GUIDANCE SYSTEM is fractal-like, in that, at each level of creation, the same process repeats.

The POWER ARC of WHERE, NOW, HOW – these same core stages and steps - apply at every level of creation, from ARC TO ARC, to evolving SPIRAL.

As with the universal Creative Process it mirrors, **POWER ARC: YOUR CREATIVE GUIDANCE SYSTEM** provides *freedom within structure*, in a navigational framework within which you may freely move, reorient, and change course, with unlimited freedom to create and discover, and to access the dynamic energy that flows freely through it.

On an individual level, the Creative Process enables you to discover your true identity, your unique gifts and talents, your singular purpose and contribution to the world. It reveals to you the power you already have to chart and live into your full creative potential. In addition, by establishing a common, shared framework, the system also enables groups to collaborate and co-create, with the ARC serving as a common tool to align thought and action within and across organizations and teams.

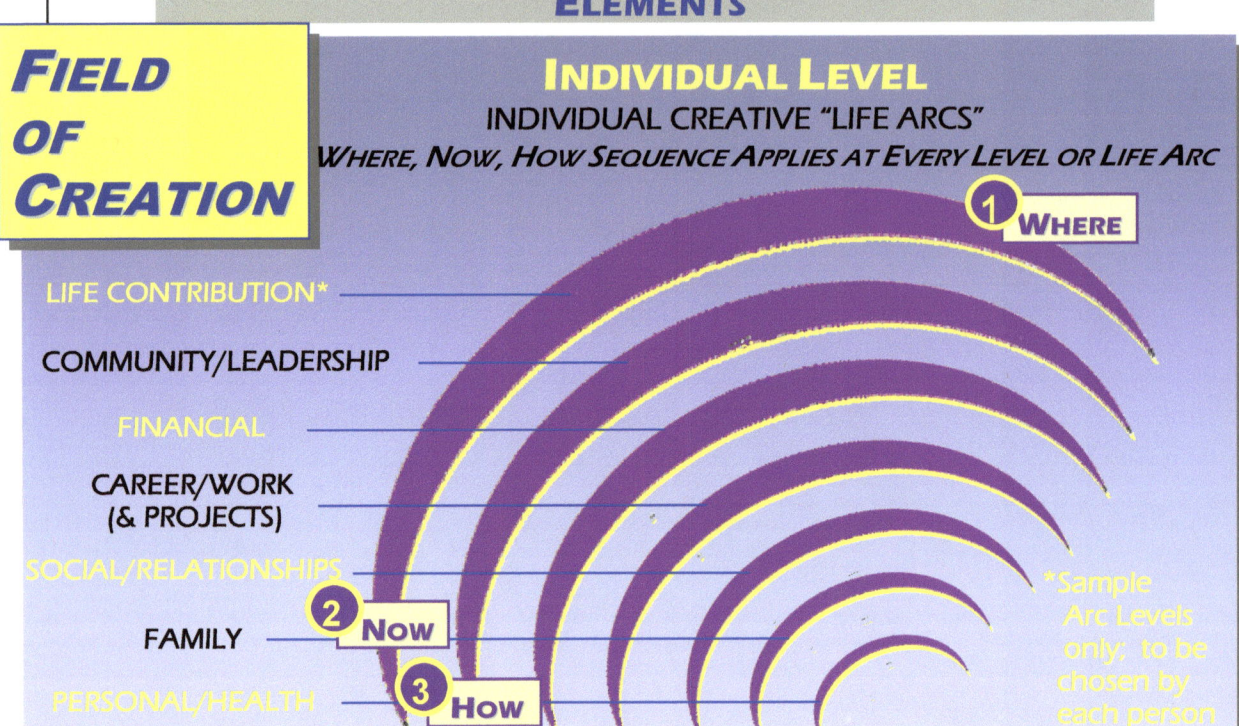

GENESIS of GENIUS

MASTERING POWER ARC™ / CREATIVE GUIDANCE SYSTEM®

LIFE ARCS

YOUR LIFE ARCS – Mastering Power Arc: Creative Guidance System®:
Each of us has his or her own unique set of Life Arcs, around which our lives are framed. Most of the time, however, we don't see our lives in such an ordered, interrelated way. Instead, all the aspects and activities of our lives often seem mixed together, making it more difficult for us to consciously focus on the most important aspects - to see What Is, and, especially, to envision and create What Can Be. Consciously identifying and choosing the Life Arcs most important to you gives you an extremely powerful way to view your life, and focus your creative efforts.

> *The mind is the limit. As long as the mind can envisage*
> *the fact that you can do something, you can do it,*
> *as long as you really believe 100 per cent.*
> — Arnold Schwarzenegger, former body-builder and former Governor of California

Some of these Life Arcs may seem obvious or automatic - perhaps Career/Work or Family - but how often do we consciously think about - and create - our Community Leadership or our overall Life Contribution? Or even allow enough focus on our own Personal/Health?

Each Arc represents a significant aspect of your life - which deserves not only your attention, but also your conscious application of the Creative Process.

> *There is a greatness waiting for you.*
> *We are busy, we are distracted, we are cynical,*
> *but this greatness waits.*
> *Through a speech by Dr. King*
> *or the story of the Grinch or even a bumper sticker,*
> *this greatness finds you in a moment, unlikely or untimely,*
> *and suddenly you find yourself connected to humanity*
> *in a way that shocks you.*
> *And this greatness will hold you up so high and strong*
> *that any previous version of yourself seems flimsy*[59]
> — Jeffrey Swartz, President & CEO, The Timberland Company

Here, you begin to fill in your own, personal Individual Life Arcs. You may use the example Arc levels and titles shown on the previous page - or you may create entirely new Arc levels and titles. You may mix and match - some example Arcs and some of your own design ... it's up to you. Whatever approach enables you to craft your Arcs to fit your own life perfectly. [See Team/Organizational Arc Worksheets on pg. 334-336.]

We've provided two Worksheets on the following pages. The first shows a set of Arcs with example titles, and space for you to begin filling in your Mini-Visions (more on this later). The second Worksheet gives you a completely open Arc template, so that you may fill in your own customized set of personal Arcs.

And remember, your life is a work in process, so feel free to play around with your Arcs and titles until you have a basic set of core Life Arc on which to focus your creative efforts starting today. You may always revise as your Journey unfolds.

GENESIS of GENIUS

EXAMPLE # 3 - MASTER LIFE ARC EXAMPLES

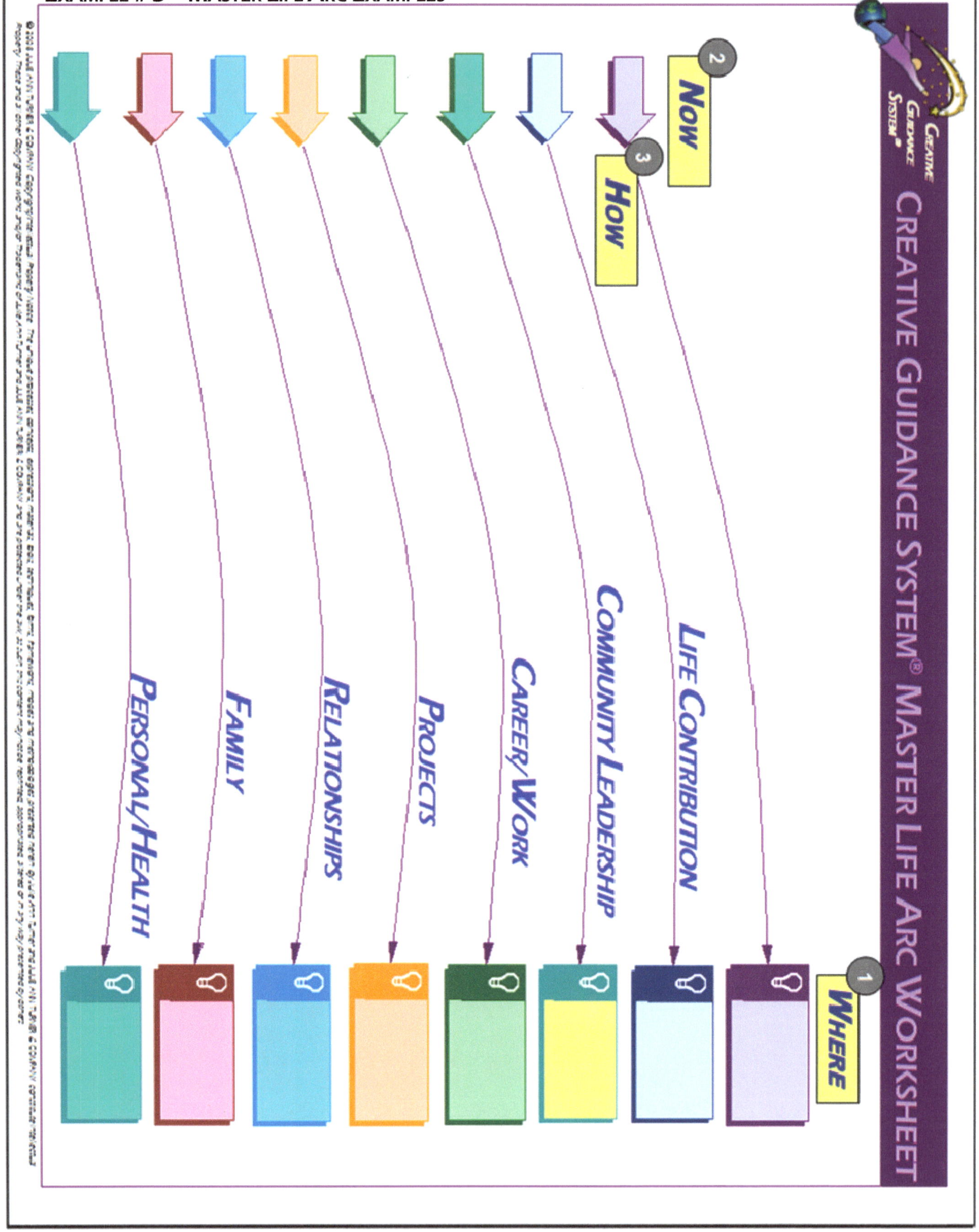

CREATIVE GUIDANCE SYSTEM® MASTER LIFE ARC WORKSHEET

1. **Where**
2. **Now**
3. **How**

- Personal/Health
- Family
- Relationships
- Projects
- Career/Work
- Community Leadership
- Life Contribution

© Julie Ann Turner & Company/CreatorsGuide.com.
All Rights Reserved.

WORKSHEET # 4 - MASTER LIFE ARC WORKSHEET

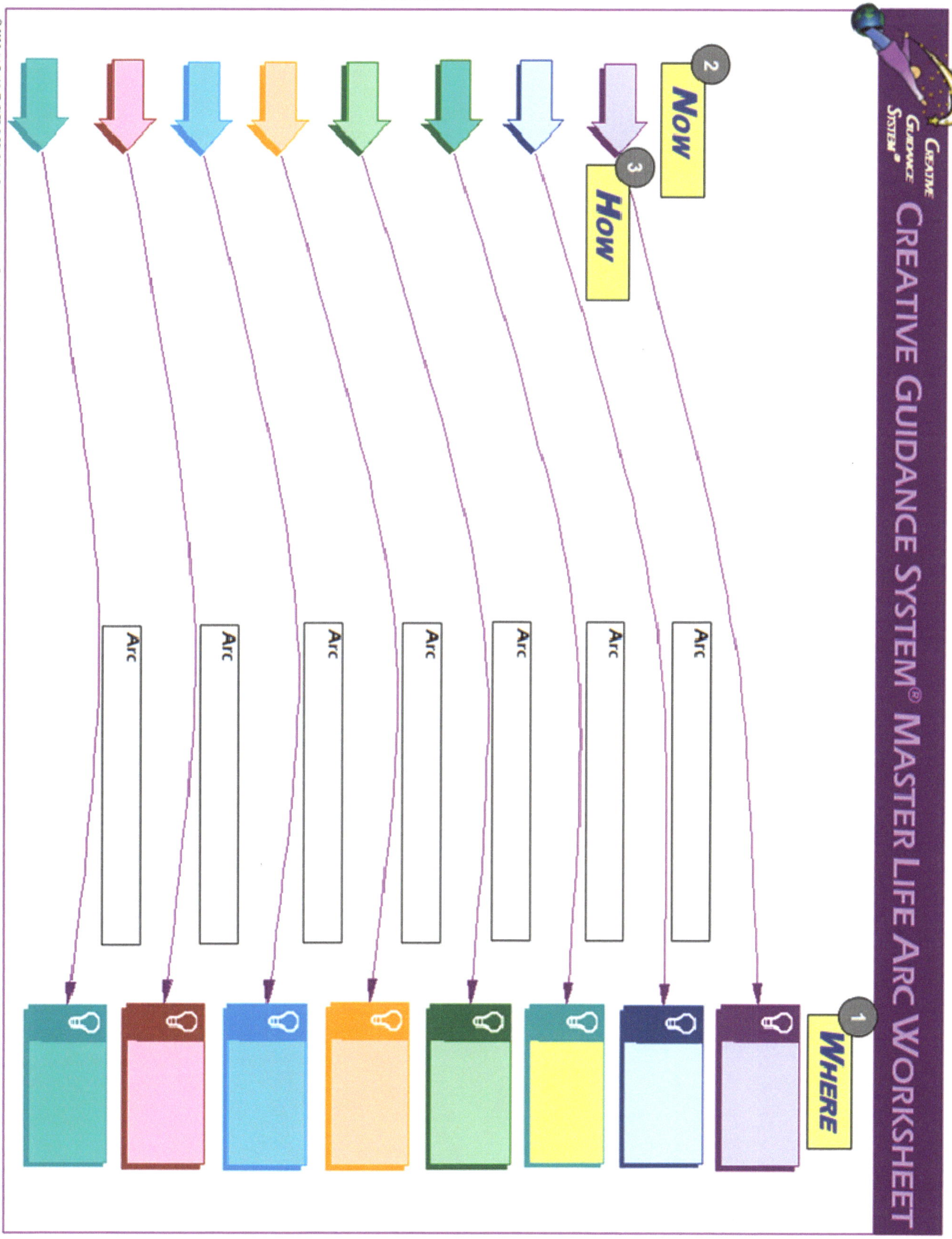
Creative Guidance System®
Creative Guidance System® Master Life Arc Worksheet
1 Where
2 Now
3 How
Arc
Arc
Arc
Arc
Arc
Arc
Arc

CHAPTER FOUR
THE PROBLEM WITH PROBLEM-SOLVING

Man is not

the creature

of circumstances.

Circumstances

are the creature

of man.[60]

Benjamin Disraeli,
Former British Prime Minister

DEFINING THE PROBLEM

I've always said that if it's conventional, it's not wisdom, and if it's wisdom, it's not conventional.[61]
Herb Kelleher, Co-Founder, Chairman and Former CEO of Southwest Airlines

If you were to read just about any general textbook on decision-making, problem-solving or even "critical thinking" – or on business management or marketing, for that matter – you would find that, traditionally, the most-recommended first step in solving any problem is:

Define the Problem.

Seems like an obvious first step, right? But, as we reveal here in this GUIDE, this approach is dead wrong. More precisely, this way of thinking – which has been ingrained in nearly all of us – is deadly to creative thinking.

How ingrained is "problem-solving" as a primary mode of thinking? If you were to search for the term "problem-solving" in *Wikipedia.org*, you would find a host of listings of problem-solving as a thinking approach in government, corporations, quality assurance processes, and scientific processes, as well as dozens of listings on related terms like "root cause analysis" (and even in the system called "*Creative Problem-Solving,* as we've seen"[62]). You would find more than 9,000 books related to problem-solving on *Amazon.com*. Many organizations post signs throughout their buildings listing "Problem-Solving Steps," listing "*Step 1: Define the Problem.*" Public school curriculum is designed to present to students problems that need to be solved, for which there is only one right answer. Even a great number of creativity trainers teach "Creative Problem-Solving" techniques as their primary model. There's only one problem with this:

Focusing on Problems rather than Possibilities.

This approach starts our thinking process with a focus on "the problem" – the WHAT IS, rather than the WHAT CAN BE.

And this immediately limits our thinking.

GENESIS of GENIUS

ECLIPSING THE PROBLEM

The future we predict today is not inevitable.
We can influence it, if we know what we want it to be.[63]
    Charles Handy, *The Age of Unreason*

Unfortunately, although it is a limited mode of thinking, "problem-solving" has been learned and practiced so much, it has become second nature to us.

And it is, indeed, second nature. Because our First Nature is as Creators.

We, as human beings, are natural creative thinkers. Think of how natural creative thinking is to children – they are always pretending, creating imaginary friends and magical places, envisioning what they might become one day. Over time, though, we have un-learned this imaginative process. Now is our chance to rediscover – and re-learn – how to think creatively, how to use the Creative Process more consciously.

Arnold Schwarzenegger never would have achieved greatness if he had focused on his "problems" – his WHAT IS, his NOW. If he had solely focused on his current limitations – his image as a body-builder (not a movie star), his strong Austrian accent, his limited English skills – Arnold might never have even attempted to move beyond where he already was in life.

The key to creating a life of greatness – and to living into our full potential – lies in focusing first on WHAT CAN BE, on WHERE we want to go and who we want to be, and on what we ultimately want to accomplish.

The greatest creators throughout the ages and across the globe, have changed the world by deliberately and wisely wielding the power of the Creative Process. It was Martin Luther King Jr.'s *Dream* and Gandhi's *Vision* – a focus on WHERE they were going, rather than a focus on problems - that captured people's hearts and imaginations, engaging them in creating a new world, in transforming society through positive change. *Yet, as we have seen, this is not how we have been taught to think.* Great leaders achieve uncommon success precisely because they use what most people today might call "uncommon thinking." The creators of the world think differently. As Charles Handy says:

> *George Bernard Shaw once observed that all progress depends on the unreasonable man. His argument was that the unreasonable man adapts himself to the world, while the unreasonable persists in trying to adapt the world to himself; therefore, for any change of consequence we must look to the unreasonable man, or, I must add, to the unreasonable woman. ... We are now entering an Age of Unreason, when the future, in so many areas, is to be shaped, by us and for us ... Change, after all, is only another word for growth, another synonym for learning.*[64]

Our new world calls for *uncommon thinking*, for more than problem-solving – for *Imagination*.

GENESIS of GENIUS

CONSTELLATIONS OF CIRCUMSTANCE

Here's some news for the new Millennium, and also a truth that transcends the ages.

A "Problem" is Simply a Set of Circumstances.

The clusters of information we often label as "problems" are merely "constellations of circumstance" – which we may use to our benefit, if only we know how.

Problems are merely specific sets of circumstances. They hold no inherent power — only the power we assign to them. When we label certain sets of circumstances as "problems," we give them power – often more power than they deserve. Give them attention? Yes. Give them power? No. Once we recognize this, we strip problems of their power to disorient and paralyze us. And we eliminate much fear and stress we often associate with problems.

We may then place problems in the right perspective, and use the information they contain to aid us in our journey toward our destination.

In fact, on a deeper level, any set of circumstances we may label as a problem is really only a configuration of information. In this light, these constellations of circumstance may alert us to potential threats we had not previously recognized. They may reveal valuable insights about the current situation or about where we are in relation to our goals. They may provide critical feedback as to how well we are fulfilling our purpose. They may reveal opportunities we may never have expected or imagined. Or, they may hold absolutely no relevance to our journey at all.

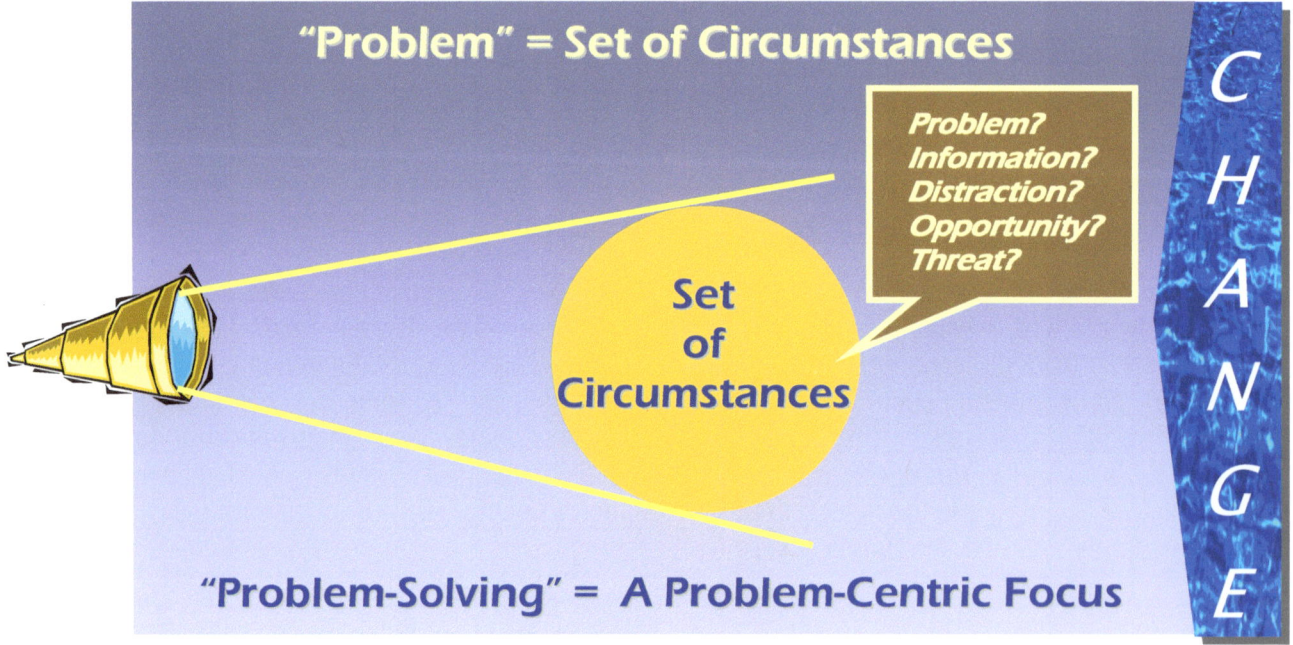

Once we shift our view to view problems merely as sets of circumstance (and this is a massive Mindshift for most of us), we free up enormous amounts of energy and resources – time, money and attention.

It is critical for us to realize here that problem-solving – often our predominant mode of thought, as we've seen – is, by definition, a "problem-centric" focus. A creative mode of thought, instead, moves us beyond problems, into the realm of potential.

A LIMITED LENS

Whether we look out over the Field of Creation and see problems - or see potential - is a matter of focus. It is a matter of choice.

If we view life through a limited lens, seeing only what already exists (WHAT IS) or paying attention only to the whatever floats into our immediate space, we will not see the unlimited potential that lies beyond, in the creative realm of WHAT CAN BE.

Current Circumstances (WHAT IS) vs. Creation (WHAT CAN BE)

But where have we traditionally focused? In business, in life and in society? On current issues and circumstances – often labeled as problems or crises. In fact, our research and analysis is designed primarily to get a snapshot, at best, of where things are now, and often, only to track a trail of what already has happened.

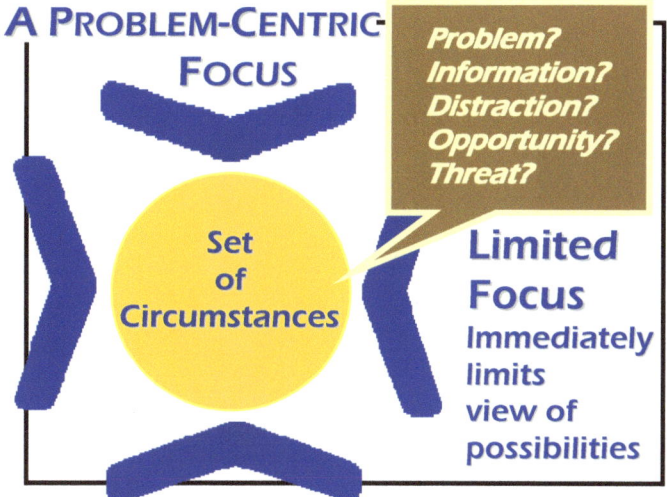

Current circumstances are only part of the picture - and not the most important part.

And so, the Creative Process begins by expanding our view of what is possible.

Arnold began each of his life arcs by imagining what was possible, rather than focusing on current circumstances. Instead of viewing each "constellation of circumstance" as a problem or limitation, and he built on the elements he could turn to his advantage (seeing his body-builder's physique not as a limitation, but an asset toward becoming a movie action-hero).

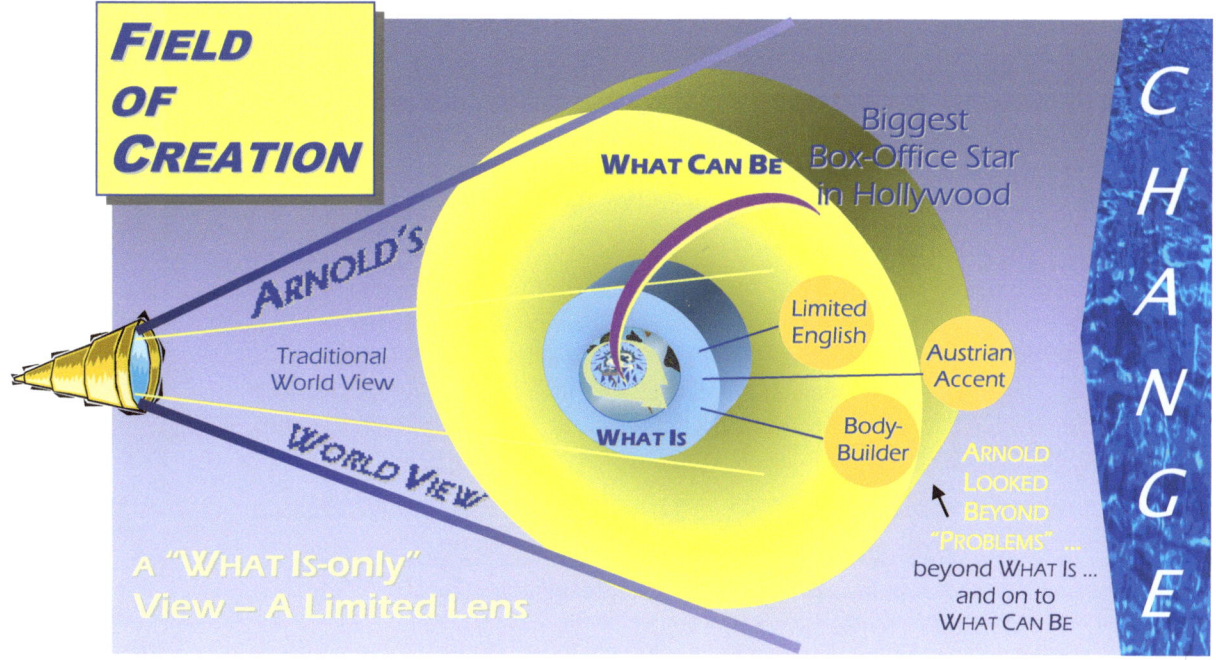

NOT IN THE STARS

Remember, the lenses through which we view the world –
our beliefs, our thought systems, our WorldViews (mindsets and paradigms), our fears,
as well as "what we already know" or "the way we've always done it" – are powerful.

These life lenses literally frame – and can limit – reality for each one of us,
determining what we see and what we don't see. Unless we are conscious
of our lenses, we may miss crucial information and opportunities.
And unless we know how to consciously create, our lenses may limit us.

We can shape the future, or simply react to the present. It is our choice, in every moment.

Moreover, as we've seen in the previous pages, problems are the *result* of our thinking.
Too often, we let circumstances dictate what we think, rather than consciously using
our thinking to determine our circumstances.

It is *our choice* how we view the world – either as a realm filled with problems
and uncertainty, or as one filled with information and potential.

It is *our choice* how we view and label circumstances – either as problems
or as valuable information, as limitations or as potential opportunities in disguise.

The fault dear Brutus, lies not in the stars, but in ourselves ... . [65]
Cassius, in William Shakespeare's play *Julius Caesar*

One of the clichés heard most often relative to creativity is "think out of the box."
Now we begin to see the origin and the outlines of this infamous yet elusive "box" –
and realize that it is one of our own creation.

As George Bernard Shaw said: "*Man is not the creature of circumstances. Circumstances are the creature of man.*" So often, however, we give our power over to circumstances – especially by labeling them as problems – and fail to remember that it is we ourselves who have labeled them. In fact, it is our own *choices* that have placed us in the exact set of circumstances we now face. We create our circumstances, and then turn around and act as if it isn't so. Too often, especially in our search to "define the problem," we look to label and blame others or external circumstances as the problem (as the cartoon on the previous pages illustrates),

Waiting for circumstances and for people to change; merely reacting to current circumstances
instead of using our own creative power to envision and choose a higher way, gives away our power.
We let circumstances guide us, instead of choosing for ourselves. We limit our own potential
with our way of thinking. We view the world through a limited lens.
All the while, creative power is always present within us, if we only choose to use it.

We have met the enemy and he is us. [66]
Pogo Possum to Porkypine, cartoon by Walt Kelly

We may just as easily choose to view these *constellations of circumstance*- and even people -
as sources valuable information, rather than labeling them as problems, if we only choose to do so.
And as we do, we discover that each contains useful elements, valuable connections
and intelligence – information about what is going right and what we need to adjust,
insights into previously unseen influences, clues to emerging opportunities, and what is possible.

And if we want to think out of the box, we must learn to think differently.

Moreover, as we've seen, the dynamic and complex issues we face today
require more than simple knowledge and traditional thinking –
they require a MINDSHIFT to Imagination.

PROBLEM-CENTRIC FOCUS

Keep in mind that problem-solving – often our predominant mode of thought – is, by definition, a problem-centric focus. When we are locked into this frame of thought, it is easy to see everything entering our space as an asteroid, a crisis, a fire-drill to which we must immediately respond.

As we'll see, the key to accurately interpreting any set of circumstances we might be tempted to call a problem or crisis, is first to know WHERE we are going.

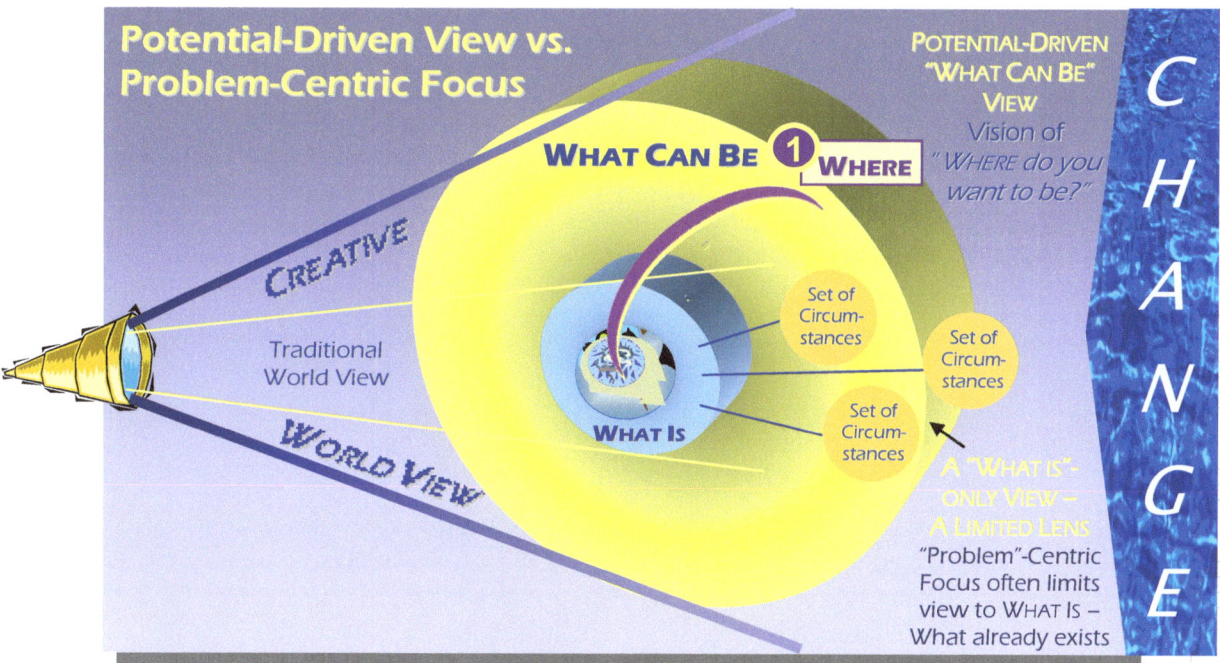

The difference between problem-solving and creating is a matter of focus.

When problem-solving is our primary mode of thought, our focus is first, by definition, on the problem(s) we perceive are currently at hand – on WHAT IS. In creative thinking, our focus is first on possibilities and potentials – on WHAT CAN BE.

This shift of focus makes a massive difference in the potential universe of ideas and possibilities we view as available to us. Focusing solely on problems – on any specific *set of circumstances* - immediately limits the scope of potential solutions. Moreover, a 'problem-centric" focus is inherently a negative one:

What You Want to Have Happen [POTENTIAL-DRIVEN/CREATIVE VIEW]
vs.
What You Don't Want to Have Happen [PROBLEM-CENTRIC/PROBLEM-SOLVING VIEW]

Once we realize this fact, we can stop giving problems the power to control us.

We can then direct all our energy toward our *Vision*, our destination — "what we want to bring into being" — instead of toward problems — "what we want to avoid or eliminate."[67]

Thus we reclaim our power to create what we truly desire.

GENESIS of GENIUS

ANALYZING ASTEROIDS & ALIENS

*The greatest danger in times of turbulence is not the turbulence;
it is to act with yesterday's logic.*

Peter Drucker, Business Management Expert

It is possible for organizations – even Fortune 500 companies – to become paralyzed by the fear of uncertainty. In the midst of a merger, a massive reorganization, or some major market upheaval, many groups freeze in their tracks, or at least hover in a holding pattern, waiting for things to become "less volatile," "more certain." More and more, these groups find themselves stalled for ever longer and more frequent periods – frozen by uncertainty (with their time, energy and creativity arrested indefinitely).

Yet it is not the unknown - or even turbulent change - that poses the real threat. It is our static, outdated modes of thought that most often hold us hostage.

As we've seen, *analysis* - our primary mental tool of choice – is deeply ingrained and nearly automatic. Analysis is attractive to us, as we like the sense of predictability and control this *sequential, linear, mechanical* approach gives us. We hold tight to the idea that anything can be understood and managed as long as we know how its parts fit together. We like being able to identify the parts – and even the people – that don't seem to fit into our model, so we can "fix" or eliminate any "problems."

However, organizations – and humans - are complex systems. As much as we may become caught up in analyzing individual pieces, fascinated by the intricacies of individual parts, our greatest errors will occur if we fail to remember that the subject we are analyzing is not a mechanical object made of separate components, but is instead a dynamic system - an irreducible, interrelated whole, within which every aspect interconnects and interoperates.

Moreover, we fail to recognize that the patterns, structures and behaviors that are so often the objects of our analysis are actually *results* of the dynamics of the system.[68] *Yet, we can never change the system by focusing on its results.* Though they are more visible, easy to analyze and tempting to focus on – we cannot "fix" the system by fiddling with its results. True change will only come from a *shift in our initial mode of thought*: We must shift our minds to a higher, more dynamic, creative mode of thought, if we are to navigate and create desired change in this new ever unfolding space. In this lies our fundamental error:

*Analysis focuses on and interprets yesterday's results.
If we depend on analysis to guide us in an ever-changing environment, we are certain to fail.*

A self-organizing system reveals itself as structure of relationships, patterns of behaviors, habits of belief, methods for accomplishing work. These patterns, structures, and methods are visible. We become entranced by their forms. ... They entice us to believe that we can change them by replacing one for another. If we dislike the structure of a system, we design a new one. If we are bothered by a colleague's behavior, we send him or her to training. Yet change efforts directed at exchanging material forms have not given us the results we hoped for. We need to look past these mesmerizing effects of organization and notice the processes that give them shape. Beneath all structures and behaviors lies the real creator – dynamic processes. Processes are not changed by focusing on their effect. Structures and behaviors are artifacts.[69]

Margaret Wheatley and Myron Kellner-Rogers, *A Simpler Way*

As long as we remain locked into a linear, logical, analytical frame of mind, we will be predisposed to resist any change– to view every unfamiliar situation as a potential "*asteroid*," and every individual who differs from us as a potential "*alien*." *Our world is driven by dynamic processes. Clearly, we need a new, more dynamic mode of thought.* Through the Creative Process, groups can rediscover their core, remember their purpose, and move forward toward their shared *Vision*, regardless of the turbulence of the space ahead. Instead of reacting to change – or being frozen by uncertainty – they embrace uncertainty as freedom to create without limits, they move boldly to create the change they wish to see.

ENTERING THE CREATIVE FIELD

How do these modes of thought - problem-solving or creativity - affect our day-to-day lives and moment-to-moment decisions? Let's consider the area of career and work.

First, imagine you are entering the Field of Creation, with a traditional, problem-centric mode of thinking. As you survey the most immediate circumstances related to your career and work, you find yourself inundated on all sides by potential decisions, and by issues you may view as problems, threats, or even crises (represented by the orange circles).

Here's the dilemma, though. How do you know, for instance, if a "Special Project" is a "problem" or an "opportunity"? What about a "Reorganization" or a "Layoff"? Perhaps these are circumstances you would be likely to label as "threats." On the other hand, what about a "Job Offer" or a "Promotion"? Your initial response may be to see these more positively, labeling them as "opportunities."

However, as so many have learned (especially in the corporate world), sometimes a "Reorganization" is actually the best thing for business, and perhaps even for your own career. Likewise, most of us know someone who, after having experienced a "Layoff," now say *"It was the best thing that ever happened to me ...,"* or, alternatively, someone who gained a "Promotion," only to land in a no-win position?

So how can you know which of these day-to-day events are a "Crisis" or just a set of circumstances? The answer? They're all just sets of circumstances – which you can only accurately interpret if you first know WHERE you are going. If you don't, you'll forever be bouncing from "Crisis" to "Crisis."

It is your view – your lens - that determines whether Life is a Field of Uncertainty or a Field of Potential.

INFLUX

*In the midst of a dynamic Field of Information – in this expanse of Open Space -
it is certainly understandable for anyone to become overwhelmed.
In fact, it is near impossible not to be overwhelmed.
We've seen the numbers, like this comparison from Fast Company:*

> *... according to some sources, the world has generated more data
> in the past 30 years than it did in the preceding 5,000 years...
> So, in this Information Age, how do you keep up with all of that, well, information?*[70]

How, indeed, can we make sense of this ever-greater influx of information? Moreover, research indicates our minds can hold only seven to nine units of information consciously at one time.[71]

Our traditional approach – attempting to move ever-faster, to *react* to every new set of circumstances that arises - is simply adequate, especially in today's world of escalating complexity. We find ourselves in "fire-drill" mode, spinning from crisis to crisis, with no sense of direction at all.

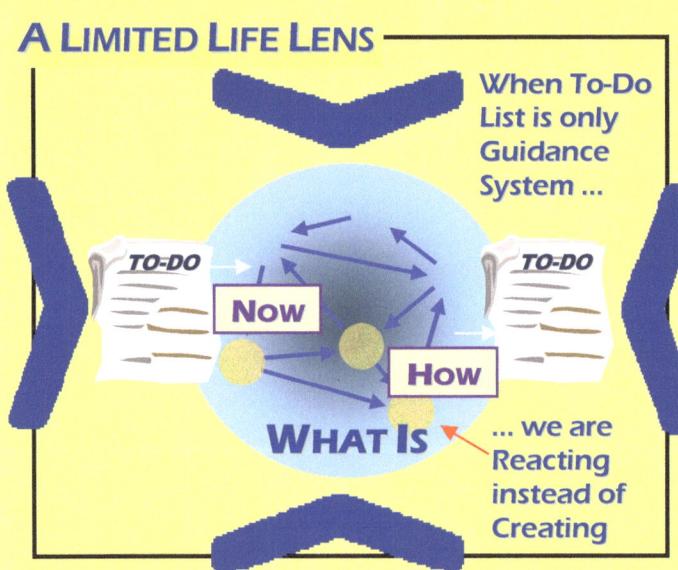

A LIMITED LIFE LENS

When To-Do List is only Guidance System ...

... we are Reacting instead of Creating

*We're "problem-solving,"
but we have no way
to determine which problems to solve.*

So we try to solve them all.

In fact, in our endless drive for increasing speed, higher productivity and instant execution, we inevitably focus even more narrowly on Now and How. Before we realize it, in the words of an unknown modern sage, "*We are too busy mopping the floor to turn off the faucet.*"

It is no wonder so many find themselves confused, stressed and exhausted.

*We often spend so much time coping with problems along our path
that we only have a dim or even inaccurate view of what's really important to us.*
Peter Senge, author, *The Fifth Discipline*

Our problem-centric mode of thinking limits both the scope of potential solutions we consider and our view of what is possible. Moreover, without first knowing WHERE we want to be – what our *Vision*, our *Purpose*, our *Values* are (elements we'll discuss further in the next section) - we cannot possibly know which options, information, or sets of circumstance are important and relevant to our journey.

It's no surprise, then, that many begin to view *all change* as threatening, as something to be avoided. Instead of a FIELD OF POTENTIAL, many only see a FIELD OF UNCERTAINTY. Often, they become paralyzed. Individuals and organizations become so entangled in the "tyranny of the urgent," they have no view of broader issues or possibilities, and are even more inclined to say they simply have no time to think about or plan WHERE they really want to go. *As we are beginning to see, however, the only way out of this criss-cross maze of "crisis management" is to consciously create the change we do wish to see.*

*We need a creative lens to accurately assess the rush of circumstances and information
we face each day. Our Life Lens determines whether we see potential and possibility,
or uncertainly and threat. If all we see and respond to are our existing circumstances
(WHAT IS), we will rarely look beyond that to explore entirely new potentials (WHAT CAN BE).*

AN ARC THROUGH CHAOS

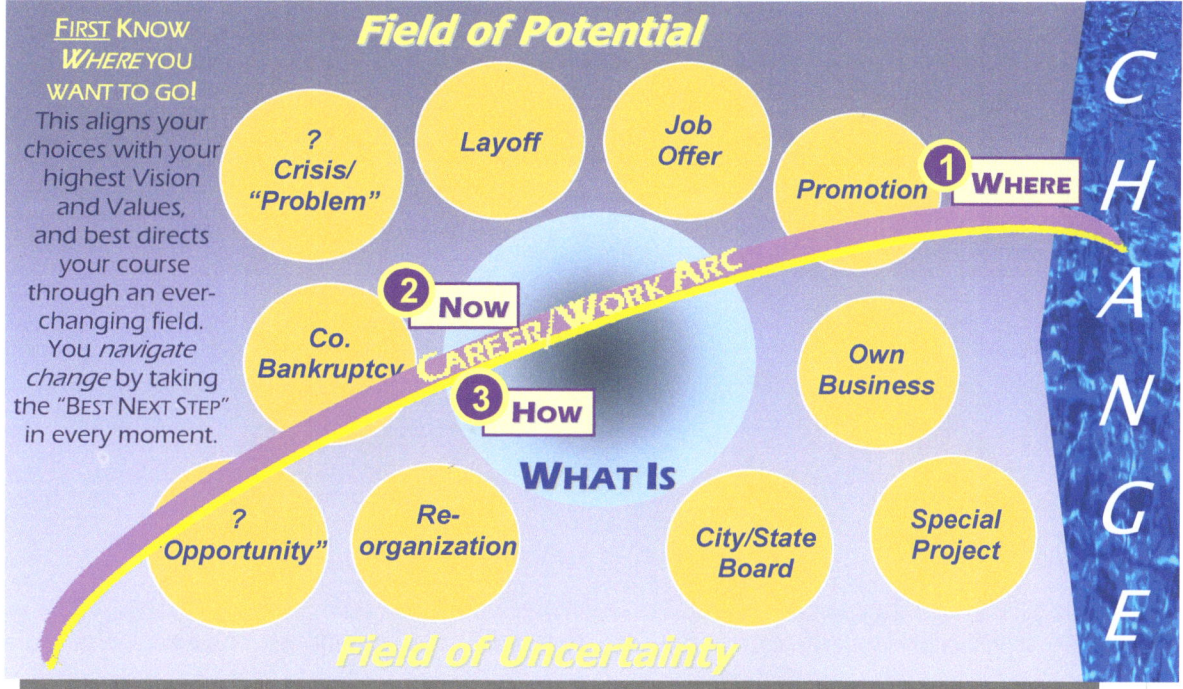

Imagine no longer feeling the need to react to every circumstance as a crisis or "fire drill," because, by knowing WHERE you are headed, you'll know what is relevant and what is not. It is the ARC of WHERE, NOW, HOW that will show us the way. On an individual level, our CREATIVE ARC will guide us in every area – career, relationships, life contribution, and more.

Once we do know WHERE we are going, we discover that, in so many cases, it may not be necessary to "solve" a perceived problem at all. In fact, many times circumstances we may have perceived as problems may not even be relevant to our Journey – for they lie far outside of our ARC. Where previously we would almost certainly have expended energy and resources on resolving them, we now realize many of these "problems" would be only a distraction. We can extract any useful information they may provide, but swiftly move right past them, and focus our attention and resources on the path to our goals.

> *Sometimes the situation is only a problem because it is looked at in a certain way. Looked at in another way, the right course of action may be so obvious that the problem no longer exists.*
> — Edward de Bono, psychologist and creativity author

For instance, is a "Promotion" in line with your conscious choices about WHERE you want to be? Is that "Job Offer" tempting, but actually just the most immediate set of circumstances that entered your mindspace? As you use the Creative Process to determine the trajectory of your LIFE ARC, you gain the *Vision* to place all information and circumstances in the right context, relative to your most important goals and values.

It is through the Creative Process of WHERE, NOW, HOW that we gain the perspective and tools to accurately interpret any set of circumstances we may encounter along our Journey.

BREAKING OUT OF ORBIT

Admittedly, it is all too tempting – and easy - to choose among those circumstances that come swirling into our immediate view, into our immediate mindspace.

If, like Alice in Wonderland, I don't know where I'm going, it is much easier simply to take the promotion that arises on my current path, or, alternatively, to take the first job offer that comes my way. After all, since I don't really know WHERE I want to be, I have no sure way or clear context to assess one opportunity over any other one that arises.

On the other hand, if I am consciously charting my own career course – knowing WHERE I want to be - I might chose to expand my experience in another area of the organization, instead of taking the immediate promotion in my current path. More than that, I might even consider a greater shift of my LIFE ARC, and decide to start my own business, in an area about which I am passionate. Of course, if I don't know where I am going, or "don't much care where," as Alice said, it may indeed be simpler to take the first path offered to me, regardless of where it might lead.

Whether in our Career Course or Life Course, we determine the trajectory of our own ARCS. We may choose a flat line, where, as they say, we may hold the same job for 10 years – with 10 years successive years of experience, or simply one year of experience, repeated over and over again. Or we may choose to set a high trajectory for ourselves, one that stretches us and leads to the expression of our full potential. And, like Arnold, we may choose intentionally to "shift" our ARC, to leap to a higher path – to change careers or start our own venture in entirely new space. In fact, in many cases, when we know WHERE we are going, we may choose to take that immediate promotion, because we know it is, indeed, part of a higher trajectory we have consciously chosen.

These considerations and choices have everything to do with creativity – at every level.

That is why it is important to we realize that, when we stay in same job, or make familiar choices about other aspects of our lives, it is not simply that these choices are easier. Choosing from what we already know – from what is familiar – is how our brains tend to function. Our brains are designed to recognize and seek out patterns, predisposed to "think" along established routes of thought, as we incorporate new thoughts into what we already know, linking them to what is already familiar to us. This pattern-seeking, associative process influences our thinking at every level, whether our choices are about what will eat next, or what our next career move will be.

Our natural tendency to categorize the familiar, and to react based on "what we already know," can actually prevent us from seeing potential alternatives and new possibilities.
There is a certain gravitational pull toward the familiar, toward our "comfort zone." Yet, a key mistake is to try to match our choices to *what already exists.* Imagination is infinitely more than pattern-recognition – in fact, it requires that we see beyond existing patterns.

The only way to break out of our current "orbit" is to consciously choose something outside it.

It is tremendously important that we recognize this fact when it comes to "creativity techniques." For many, the most familiar creativity technique is "brainstorming," a classic which is based on associative thinking.[72] As creativity author Edward de Bono notes, brainstorming typically only uses thoughts or concepts that *already exist in the minds of participants* in order to generate associated ideas, which he says, creates only "variations on a theme," rather than entirely new and innovative ideas.[73] *In fact, almost all creativity techniques are based on associative thinking and matching patterns.*[74] Yet, associative thinking is incremental thinking – it starts from what already exists. While useful at some levels, almost all of these "creativity (little "c") techniques" are inherently limiting. Matching patterns is not creating, just as knowledge is not imagination.
As Nicholas Negroponte says, "*Incrementalism is innovation's worst enemy.*"[75]

The POWER ARC SUCCESS SYSTEM offers a much broader and higher model for creative thought – one which immediately shifts us beyond brainstorming or simply associative thinking.

NAVIGATIONAL THINKING

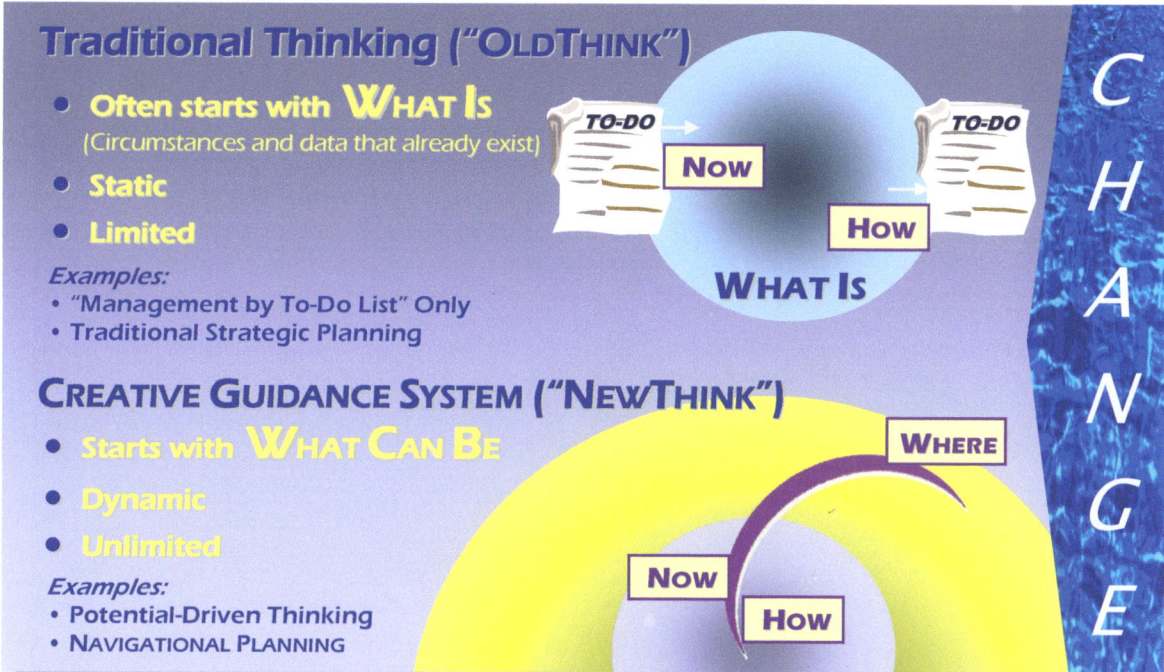

Remember, in this Field of Information, only configuration and continuous re-configuration of information – in other words, creativity, imagination, and innovation – count. Knowledge alone is not enough; knowledge is only potential power. Imagination is – and has always been - more important than knowledge.

Everything we know at this instant is being rendered obsolete in this Field of Change. What we know is potential in the moment, but quickly losing relevance in the next. Only what we create with knowledge matters. Because, in this Age where information and knowledge exchange are free and instantaneous and infinitely connected, imagination is the new currency, and it is the only inexhaustible resource.

It is precisely because we face an increasingly fast-fast world that we must shift from reaction to creation. In our rush to respond, we waste precious time and resource because we have not first envisioned WHERE we are going or determined why we are going there.

As we've seen, "Traditional Thinking" – what we might call "OLDTHINK"- often starts with and focuses primarily or entirely on WHAT IS, on circumstances and knowledge that already exist. It is problem-centric, and thus, its scope is immediately limited. This type of static, rather than dynamic, thinking – on which traditional strategic planning is based - is inadequate for our Creative Age.

We not only need a Creative WorldView – but a new type of Creative Thinking – the visionary, navigational thinking encompassed in the Creative Process, and captured in *POWER ARC: YOUR CREATIVE GUIDANCE SYSTEM.* This creative, navigational thinking – "NEWTHINK" (or "NAVTHINK," which also forms the basis for a more dynamic type of NAVIGATIONAL PLANNING we will discuss) – enables both individuals and organizations to make conscious choices and allocate resources (money, time, intelligence, creativity and energy) in real-time, to best align with the highest goals and values, as well as with emerging opportunities as they arise.

THE COLLECTIVE FIELD

Often, the greatest challenge facing an organization is recognizing and acting on opportunity rather than solving a problem.[76]
Peter Ginter, Leadership Skills Training Institute

For organizations of every kind – whether for-profit or non-profit - alignment of direction and resources is critical, because not only individuals, but teams, departments and other larger groups must work in concert to achieve goals. It is therefore even more challenging to get everyone moving together toward common goals, and much easier for the many separate groups to become paralyzed by complexity, uncertainty and lack of direction.

All the while, organizations are engaged in an instantly connected, global marketspace, where change, competition, and customer demand are only escalating. Long gone are the days when organizations could consider a five- or ten-year strategic plan – most often sitting in a binder on a shelf – sufficient. Today, successful organizations realize planning is *an ongoing process* – an always-on weekly, daily, and minute-to-minute process - not just a one-off event. A process in which all players, at all levels, must participate, contribute, proactively innovate and *create change* – new products, new opportunities, and entirely new markets. Like using an old map to traverse terrain that no longer exists, a static plan is of no use in this dynamic new space. Only a guidance system that enables diverse individuals to navigate change, make strategic choices, and allocate resources in real-time will do.

Whether to outsource, reduce or increase staff? Whether to expand into new industries, adopt new technologies, expand or consolidate product offerings? Whether to focus on driving internal innovation, spinning off an entrepreneurial division or merge with an innovative, rising competitor?

Without a shared guidance system and common navigational tools, an organization quickly finds its crew members spinning in all directions, on a ship with no set course.

AHEAD OF THE CURVE

*Leaders think and talk about the solutions.
Followers think and talk about the problems.*
Brian Tracy, leadership author and speaker

The way forward in this connected, global world will be led by potential-driven thinking, rather than problem-centric thinking. Lag time is now non-existent; reaction-time – zero. Simply speeding up is an inadequate answer, and speed without direction is deadly.

*The only way to "get ahead of the curve" is to consciously choose
our own direction and destination, create our own curve of creative change,
and then collectively focus our resources along that visionary path.*

*As we shift from reaction to creation, we craft our own course,
carve out entirely new markets, and begin to consciously direct our own destiny.*

Moreover, for organizations with limited resources – which means virtually all of them – creativity is even more crucial, because it is only with a clear view of Where we are going that we may accurately choose how best to focus those resources. Creative thought generates new connections, combinations, and categories, and innovative strategies, products and services capable of addressing more than one need or market at a time.

In the light of a clear, shared direction, many constellations of circumstance we might once have considered "problems" simply fade away in rear view, as we surge ahead knowing exactly which information and circumstances are worthy of our attention and energy.
In this *World in Process*, those with a *creative guidance system* adapt and thrive.

*To raise new questions, new possibilities, to regard old problems
from a new angle, requires creative imagination ....*[77]
Albert Einstein, theoretical physicist

POWER OF CHOICE

No static plans will do in this new space. No maps exist, for we have entered uncharted territory. Only a navigational mindset - a creative guidance system – enables us to traverse this infinitely dimensional Field of Information. We have literally entered a new realm, where our minds and thought systems must now adapt in real time.

The only way forward is the path of Imagination.

This new space requires that we be visionary at all times. We must move from response mode (problem-centric) to creative mode (potential-driven).

We do this through Choice – by choosing WHERE to direct our focus and our energy, rather than by merely reacting to circumstances.

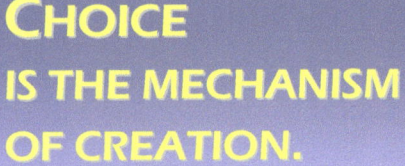

CHOICE IS THE MECHANISM OF CREATION.

Authentic power originates through choice.

At any time, we may choose to shift from WHAT IS ... to WHAT CAN BE ...

All it takes to shift our thinking from what already exists (WHAT IS) to WHAT CAN BE is a *choice* – and that choice, at all times, is ours to make. At any moment we choose, we may release the creative power that dwells within each of us – to express our unique gifts and talents, to contribute that light of genius that only we may share with the world.

All true, authentic power originates through choice. When we freely choose, all of our energy, will and passion is released, and our creative power flows fully and naturally toward whatever we endeavor. Authentic power releases our full potential and energy. Authentic power is creative and generative – it generates, and flows with, abundance.

However, far too often, we are much more familiar with another type of "power" – "coercive" power, the power of force or fear: when we are told, ordered or forced - rather than asked or allowed to choose - what we wish to do, or where we want to focus our attention or efforts. Forced or coercive power is always limited, for it carries within it an inherent inner resistance. When we are not free to choose, or feel forced to choose or do anything, our full potential and energy do not flow with our actions. Coercive power thrives on scarcity.

When we choose freely –whether individually or collectively – WHERE we want to go and who we want to be, all our creative power, energy and passion flows with us, propelling us toward our highest Vision and goals. This is the power we unleash when we consciously shift our minds into the higher creative realm of WHAT CAN BE.

GENESIS of GENIUS

MASTERING POWER ARC™/ CREATIVE GUIDANCE SYSTEM®

CONSTELLATIONS OF CIRCUMSTANCE

> *CHANGING FIELD–Mastering Power Arc: Creative Guidance System®:*
> Would you say that you "go boldly" into new space - into new situations and environments - ready to navigate and adjust to whatever you might find there, welcoming constant changes as they emerge? Well, most of us - even the most flexible among us - are often thrown off a bit by constant change. And some of us, if given the choice, would much rather have everything stay pretty much the same, thank you very much. However, as we've seen, change <u>is</u> reality - it is the norm, not the occasional aberration. We live and work n a World in Process. We can't choose a world without change, but we *can choose* to create our own change. *This, indeed, is how we regain our creative power - by choosing WHAT CAN BE, rather than WHAT IS.*

The last of the human freedoms—to choose one's attitude in any given set of circumstances, to choose one's own way.[78]
Viktor Frankl, Holocaust survivor and author, *Man's Search for Meaning*

ASK YOURSELF:

Grab a blank sheet of paper and pen, and summon up your honesty - it's time for thought! Write down the most immediate answer that comes to mind for each of these questions.

- *Top of Mind:* Think about all the circumstances in your life right now. At work, at home, with family, with friends.
    - Which circumstances are top of mind for you right now? List them for each area.
    - How do you define or perceive these circumstances? As problems? As opportunities? As information?
    - Would your attitude toward each top-of-mind issues change if you viewed it differently - rather than as a problem, as an opportunity? Or just as information?

- *Career Path:* In your career, do you typically choose to act only based on circumstances which come into your field of awareness, such as impending layoffs or news about a job opening? Or do you actively chart your career path, exploring new potentials and deliberately seeking out those opportunities that fit with your ultimate career Vision? How would you say your approach has affected your career trajectory?

- *To-Do List:* What's on your To-Do List this week (whether written or unwritten; in any area of your life - personal, work, relationship, health, etc.)?
    - Choose one item which you may have identified as a problem. Write it down.
    - What aspects of this issue cause you to perceive it as a problem?
    - What aspects of this issue could you view simply as information?
    - How might you shift your view to see this issue as an opportunity?
    - Ask "What would I really would like to have happen?" in this area. Jot down where would you most like to see this issue going
    - Does this change your view about actions you might take in this area? How might you change or adjust course toward WHAT CAN BE with regard to this?
    - Is there one change in attitude or action that would move this issue forward? If so, do it.
    - How might changing your view from WHAT IS to WHAT CAN BE change your life?

CHAPTER FIVE
CONSCIOUS CREATION

Your consciousness creates your destiny.[79]

Sandra Anne Taylor, *Quantum Success*

Everything ever made by a person started out as a thought inside someone's head.[80]

Mark Joyner, *Simple-ology*

WHERE POWER LIES

Power does not lie in technology, information, or even in knowledge, alone.[81]
Power and value are created as our minds transform Information through Imagination.

Imagination is infinitely more than pattern-recognition – in fact, it requires
that we see beyond existing patterns, and consciously choose to create
totally new patterns of thought, to explore totally new worlds of possibility.

We now realize we are participants in an infinitely dimensional Field of Information - where information is shared, not restricted – a commodity increasingly available to all, for us to shape and mold into ever-new forms and creations. And through our technologies, we are now experiencing the truth of our universal connectedness. The artificial limits of previous technology long shielded us from full realization of the complexity, speed, connectedness that is the actual state of the Universe. Now, new science and technologies have lifted the veil. And though some still apply "*The Information Age*" as the primary tagline for our time, we realize we have moved beyond that ... something more, and much greater, is emerging.

Creativity is rising across this infinitely connected Field of Information: the blogosphere, social networking, co-creation and peer production, decision and innovation markets – rising even through participation-driven, multimedia phenomena such as *American Idol*. Indeed, infinite possibility exists – and awaits - beyond WHAT IS, in the realm of WHAT CAN BE.

How crucial is this shift from Knowledge to Imagination as our primary mode of thought?
As we've seen, Imagination is the new Mindset, Power, and Currency for our time –
essential to enabling us to navigate and to succeed in this new World.
How important is our reconnection with – and our conscious use of - our Whole Minds,
our Creative Power, our Imagination? The future of our planet - and of civilization itself –
depends on this Mindshift to Conscious Creation.

This shift in WorldView affects everything – our social, economic and political systems, our organizational structures and processes, our culture, and even our spiritual perspectives.

It also reveals where true power and value lie. The power lies within us.

Creative power – the power to choose something other than what already exists – exists within each of us. At any moment we choose, we may make the mental leap, beyond current circumstance, to consciously create totally new patterns of thought, new visions, entirely new worlds of possibility. As we do, we step into the Field of Potential.

The only way to traverse this new realm is to consciously navigate and create in real time.

In the present realm of speed, connection, complexity, we can no longer react fast enough to changing circumstances. The illusion of control dissolves before us in the light of this new reality. *As we shift our focus from circumstance (external) to creativity (internal), power shifts back to us.*

We cannot control. But we can create.

As uncertain and unnerving as on this new trajectory may seem at first, it is the only path to full potential, whether on our own personal journey, or on a collective one.
This path releases us into a new plane, where we are no longer limited by circumstances, because we are consciously creating our own. Doing so moves us to a higher plane of consciousness – to the level of Conscious Creation.

CREATIVE TENSION

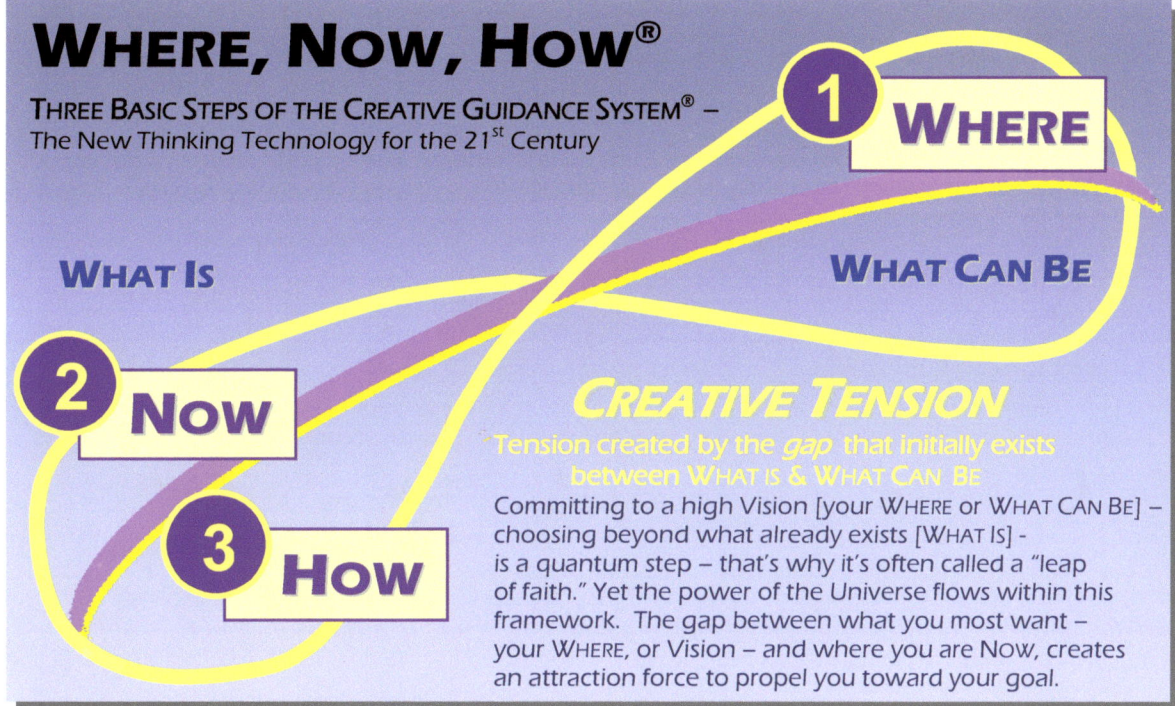

Creative tension comes from seeing clearly where we want to be, our "vision," and telling the truth about where we are, our "current reality." The gap between the two generates a natural tension.[82]

Peter Senge, author of *The Fifth Discipline*

Imagine your mind creating a connection between two worlds – WHAT CAN BE and WHAT IS ... a connection between WHERE you want to be, and where you are NOW.

We are unique beings in this world because we may conceive and create that which does not yet exist. Choosing outside what already exists is a quantum step, one that establishes a relationship between potentials, across dimensions, within a Field of Pure Potential.

When we reach out with our minds and create a vivid, compelling Vision of WHERE we most want to be, the imbalance between where we are NOW and our desired Vision establishes a positive "creative tension" in the direction of the desired Vision.

In every instant, we have the power to consciously choose among limitless possibilities. Creative energy already exists – infusing All That Is. This energy only needs a direction. Creative energy flows when choice comes from within, rather than as a response to any external force, coercion or circumstance. We create a positive flow - an *attraction force* - in the direction we choose.[83] Remember, true intelligence ("intelligentia") comes from our capacity to "*choose from within*" - based on our *Vision* and *Values* - rather than merely as a reaction to current circumstances.[84]

In the CREATIVE GUIDANCE SYSTEM, we set our sights not what is transient – not on problems and circumstances - but on principles that are universal, unchanging, transcendent. This is the true way to "go with the flow," the flow in alignment with the forces of the universe: through choice, we set up a relationship with a future reality, and energy flows toward that envisioned future.

PART THREE
WHERE, NOW, HOW®

Imagination

is the beginning

of creation.

You imagine

what you desire;

you will

what you imagine;

and at last

you create

what you will.

George Bernard Shaw, English author and playwright

GENESIS of GENIUS

THREE CORE QUESTIONS

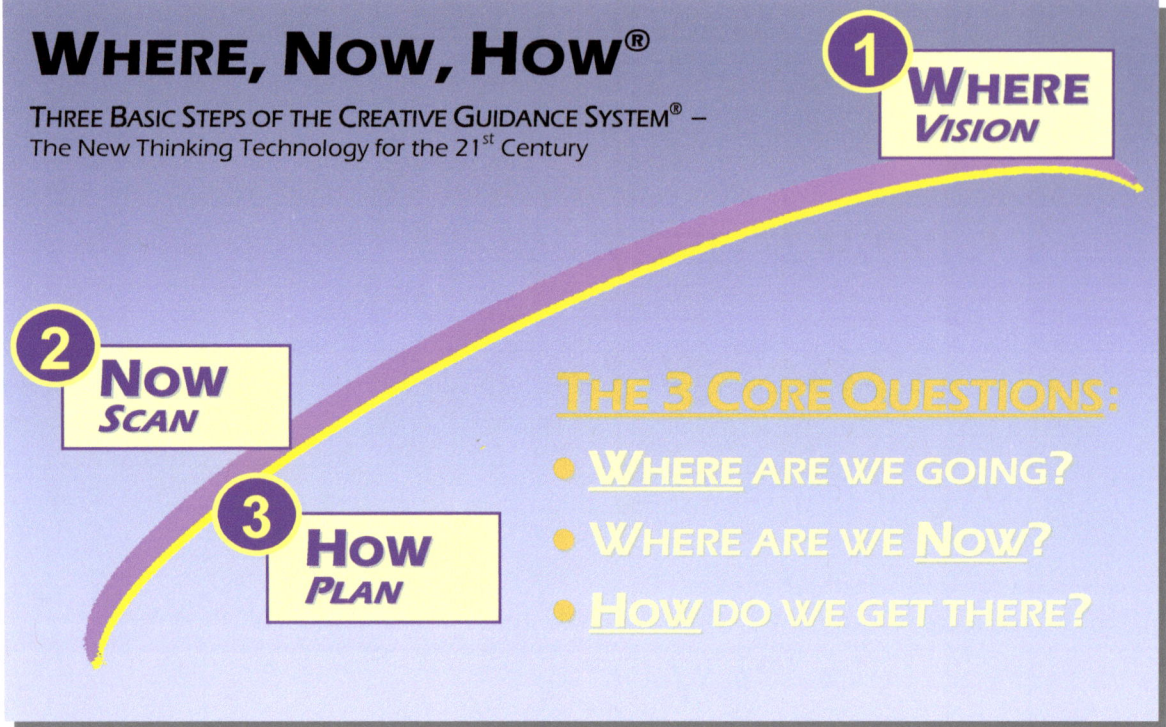

POWER ARC: YOUR CREATIVE GUIDANCE SYSTEM® is the master thinking technology, the universal navigational system, the new mental operating system - you may use to access and apply creative power in your own life, work and world.

The ARC represents the Creative Process - the translation system by which we may consciously transform energy and information into new forms and desired Vision.

As we begin, remember that this *POWER ARC SYSTEM* captures and distills the essential stages, steps and sequence of the master Creative Process, placing them into this simple but powerful framework you may use to create at every level of your life.

We now introduce the POWER ARC SYSTEM in its simplest, three-stage form – WHERE, NOW, HOW – and reveal the key elements and steps within each stage.

Recall that, at its most basic level, the Creative Process involves three questions:

1. *WHERE – WHERE am I (are we) going?* - the first stage, in which we create our "VISION"
2. *NOW – Where am I (are we) NOW?* - the second stage, in which we "SCAN" our space
3. *HOW – How do I (we) get there?* - the third stage, in which we "PLAN" our course

Finally, remember that it is the *sequence* of the stages that makes this *POWER ARC SYSTEM* a far superior "thinking technology," especially in these dynamic times requiring Imagination. This thought sequence is quite different from the way most of us have actually been taught to think, for, as Creators, our first Question is not "*What should we do now?*"- but instead, the crucial *directional* question: "*WHERE are we going?*" or "*WHERE do we want to be?*"

CHAPTER SIX
Where

Quo

Vadis?

Latin phrase
["Whither goest thou?" or "Where are you going?"]

THE END IN MIND

THE POWER OF VISION

VISION is the vivid, pleasing, sensory description of the desired experience

- **clearly describes what the successful experience looks, feels, smells, tastes, and sounds like ...**
- **is concise and compelling ... creates an attraction force**
- **reflects, embodies values and evokes emotion**
- **provides direction**
- **organizes information and prioritizes activities**
- **enables allocation of limited resources to highest impact**

The end is where we start from. [85]

T.S. Eliot, poet

Though ancient sages and poets have long proclaimed this timeless truth, it seems only recently have we rediscovered the paradoxical wisdom summarized by Stephen R. Covey: "*Begin with the end in mind.*"

As we now know, it is our initial view of the World that makes all the difference.

For even before we even start making daily decisions or taking any actions, it is this initial choice - the choice of Creation over a choice of mere Circumstance, the choice of Power over Powerlessness - that determines our Field of Potential. Our scope of possibilities is set in that instant of choice. When we choose first only from the realm of WHAT IS – from what already exists – our potential is immediately limited. However, when we choose first from the realm of WHAT CAN BE – the unlimited realm of creation, all possibilities are open to us.

All too often, in our focus on immediate results, we become so intent on "making progress" we fail to *set our course* before we embark. Yet, how useful is progress, if we are not moving in the right direction? And how may we expect to arrive where we most wish to be, if we do not first create a clear *Vision* of what that our dream destination looks like?

Here, with the initial steps of *POWER ARC: YOUR CREATIVE GUIDANCE SYSTEM* – in its simplest 3-stage form of WHERE, NOW, HOW – we first focus on the *WHERE stage* of the Creative Process, and introduce its 2 core elements of *Vision* and *Mission,* which are essential to determining WHERE we are going on our Creative Journey (first, *Vision,* then *Mission*).

After all, in a world that is constantly changing, where do we look for constants?
To Vision, Mission, Purpose, Values ... the stars of a navigational system which guide our Way, no matter how fast the territory changes or how much the space ahead shifts.

POWER OF VISION

THE POWER OF VISION

VISION is the vivid, pleasing, sensory description of the desired experience

- clearly describes what the successful experience looks, feels, smells, tastes, and sounds like ...
- is concise and compelling ... creates an attraction force
- reflects, embodies values and evokes emotion
- provides direction
- organizes information and prioritizes activities
- enables allocation of limited resources to highest impact

WHAT CAN BE — **WHERE** / **VISION** / Vision / Mission / ▶ Purpose / ▶ Work(s) / ▶ Values / **①** / **② Now** / **③ How** / **WHAT IS**

> *Nothing happens unless first a dream.*[86]
> Carl Sandburg, poet

In our "Navigational Thinking" model, we begin by determining WHERE we are going. We first set our sights on things that are universal, unchanging, transcendent – the elements of Vision, Mission, Purpose and Values, as we will discuss here – rather than on things that are transient – such as problems or sets of circumstances.

Though some of these concepts may sound familiar, it would be a mistake to dismiss them, as each one is actually an authentic, powerful key to creativity. As Jean-Marie Dru notes: "... *Despite [the term's] overuse, I believe that vision in its truest sense remains pertinent*":

> *A vision is a shaping force. ... The future can be imagined, not predicted. The same goes for vision. ... It can lead to a disruption, which in turn gives it its power. ... That is disruption's principle advantage. It accelerates the journey to the vision.*
> Jean-Marie Dru, *Disruption: Overturning Conventions and Shaking Up the Marketplace*

To grasp the emotional and motivational power of *Vision*, we need only think of what is arguably one of the most inspiring *Visions* ever written, as expressed by Martin Luther King, Jr., in his timeless "*I Have a Dream*" speech. His words paint a vivid and compelling picture of a high *Vision* – a guiding, emotion-evoking image of what success looks like in an ideal future or "dream", as areas "*sweltering with the heat of oppression ... will be transformed into an oasis of freedom and justice,*" and that "*... children will one day live in a nation where they will not be judged by the color of their skin but by the content of their character.*" We suggest you read the full speech online to experience the powerful attraction force of *Vision*.

The elements of a powerful Vision, summarized in the graphic above, will serve as a checklist as we develop vivid, sensory descriptions of the desired experiences that will guide us at each level of our individual and collective Creative Journeys.

GUIDING VISION QUESTIONS

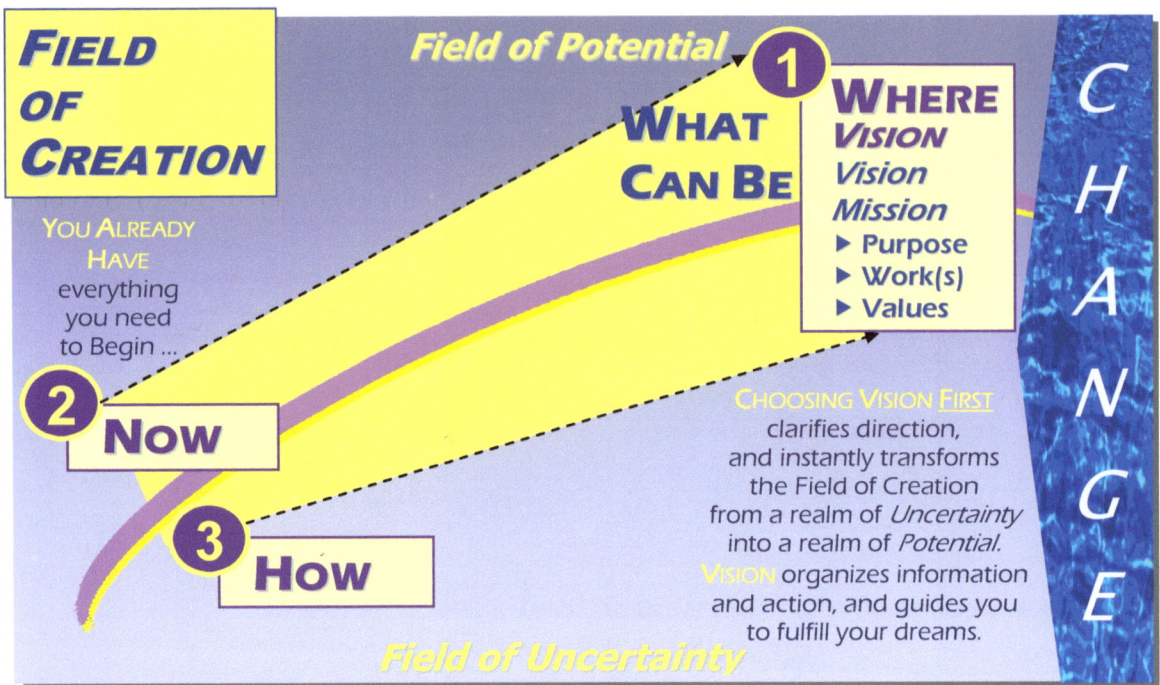

Vision is the first "creation" in the Creative Process. A Vision is a creation of mind – it is a vivid, compelling, multi-sensory description that answers one or more of the key WHERE – or Vision - questions:

1) **WHERE** am I (are we) going?

2) **WHERE** do I (we) most want to be?

3) **WHAT** do I (we) most want to create?

4) **WHAT** does success look like (sound like, feel like, etc.) for me (us)?

As Conscious Creators, the first – and most critical - step of our Creative Journey begins as we envision a highly compelling image of what we most want, at every level of our desired life, work and world. We will use the four key questions above, the elements of Vision on the previous page, and the simple, step-by-step Worksheets to follow, to guide us through this powerful, life-transforming process.

Every compelling *Vision* reflects the essence of dream, of want, of wish. *Vision* must hold personal, emotional meaning – for you as an individual, or for each person in a group or team. In order to inspire and motivate, it must capture your own highest hopes; to hold inherent power, it cannot be someone else's *Vision* for you. A high *Vision* is the outer expression of your deepest inner desire, a statement that draws out the highest and best within you, sparks your drive to excel and achieve, and holds a magnetic pull for you.

Vision is an idealized statement that carries inherent motivation; therefore, Vision is always intertwined with Purpose, an expression of our Passion. We always state Visions in the present tense, as, for each, we "live into it, as if it were already true."

THOUGHT SEQUENCING

You must first be who you really are, then do what you need to do, in order to have what you want.[87]

Shakti Gawain, Creative Visualization

All of us are already participants in the inherently creative Field of Pure Potential where choice is the mechanism of creation. We are always creating - either consciously or unconsciously – our lives, work and world. As our new technologies now reveal to us, our escalating experience of constant change – our inescapable role as participants within a "World in Process" – is not an aberration, but the true state in which we live.

We must first navigate New Space with our Minds - through our Imagination, for Imagination is the mode of thought through which we transform the Potential of the Field.

The most crucial shift to grasp is in our "Thought Sequencing": Imagination must become our initial, and preeminent, mode of thought. This truth is so deceptively simple – and so essential to Navigational Thinking in this AGE OF IMAGINATION – and yet, it is this sequence, this "order of thought" – we so often fail to absorb fully into our consciousness:

We must <u>first</u> decide WHERE we are going
before we decide HOW to get there.

In our rush to find fast fixes, it is the immediate question "HOW?" that arrests our creative thinking, collapsing the wave of Possibility before Imagination is ever even allowed generate Potentials. Choosing at the level of NOW or HOW first – WHAT IS – instantly confines us to a limited realm, In new, uncharted space, the First Question is most decidedly *not* "What should we *do*? (NOW-HOW)" - or the all-too-common, fear-based exclamation: "*But, I don't know what to do!*"

So, what is your Navigational System - your "Thought Sequence" for Life? What "stars" are you navigating by? By current circumstances? By what you already know?

People are always blaming their circumstances for what they are. I don't believe in circumstances. The people who get on in this world are the people who get up and look for the circumstances that they want, and if they can't find them, make them.

George Bernard Shaw, English author and playwright

Your First Question – your initial, instinctual thought - must become "WHERE am I going?" First, determine where you want to go. As Gay Hendricks writes: "*By making this agreement you have joined forces with the creative power in the universe, the same power that makes oak trees where no trees were there before.*" With this first step, you embark on the voyage to your true potential. Indeed, your "WHERE" represents your potential at every level.

You already have everything you need to start this Journey. This is the message of Dorothy's Ruby Slippers in the *Land of Oz*: *You have had the creative power to travel this path from the very beginning.* You now know you are free to start from wherever you are. Circumstances (even those previously known as "problems") are merely sets of Information. They cannot hurt you; indeed, you will use them to guide you. You don't have to know it all to begin. In fact, it is in the realm of Uncertainty that you possess the greatest creative power, as all possibilities are open to you. *This navigational sequence will guide you to whatever you need to know, obtain, or do to traverse the path to your destination.*

You are rediscovering your Creative Freedom: you are not dependent on current abilities, current resources, or even what you may currently believe is possible at the current moment. Released from perceived limits, you need not match your choices to what you already know exists. You are free in every instant to make what we call the "BEST NEXT STEP." No "next best" steps for you – no watered-down compromises for your life – but each step a conscious choice you know will move you toward your dream.

ELECTRIC FIELD OF POSSIBILITY

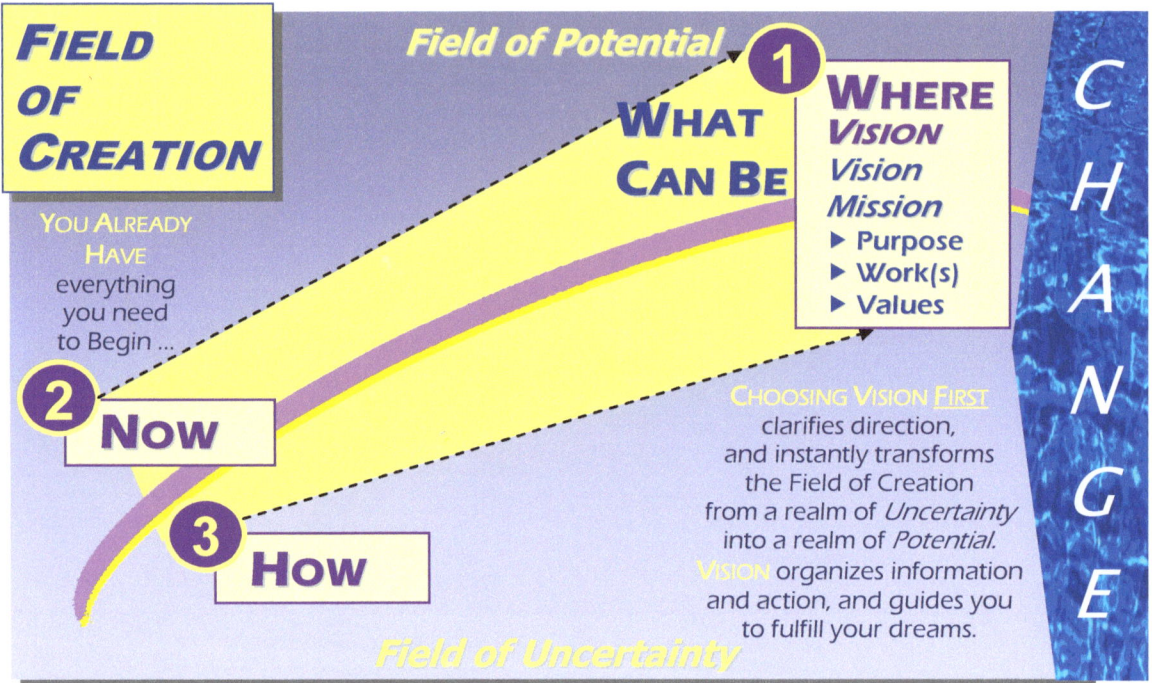

If your intention is clear, you create an electric field of possibility that actually pulls creativity out of yourself and those around you. This is the real power of intention. It inspires you in ways you could not predict.[88]

Gay Hendricks and Kate Ludeman, *The Corporate Mystic*

It is this first Vision step of your Creative Journey that sets the scope of possibility, sets the direction to your chosen dream, and sets in place the power of the Creative Field.

Creating and committing to a *Vision* is no less than a quantum choice, as author Gay Hendricks might say, you establish "*a sacred covenant with the universe*": "*You designate a future that does not yet exist and create an image of yourself there.*"[89] Imagine you are establishing a relationship between your present reality and your future *Vision*, just as quantum physics tells us that, once established in a relationship, particle pairs spin in equal and opposite directions across dimensions, no matter how distant they may be separated in space.[90] Like a magnetic field between two poles, the creative field you establish by committing to a highly compelling *Vision* encourages movement in the direction of your goal, and generates an attraction force to draw resources to aid your journey.

Once you set your direction in this is navigational system, each step moves you toward your goal. You clearly see before you the field that leads to your *Vision*. You need not be distracted by irrelevant circumstances that lie outside your path, needless "fire drills" that once caused stress and drained energy. Now, all your energy and imagination is easily focused on information and ideas that propel you forward on your chosen trajectory. Because you have first chosen to begin from the higher realm of *WHAT CAN BE*, a multitude of issues that once might have confused or confounded you simply fall by the wayside. As you set *Vision* at every level of your life, your destination is always your highest potential, with each step energized by your passion.

Follow your bliss, and what look like walls will turn into doors.[91]

Joseph Campbell, *The Power of Myth*

STEPPING INTO NEW SPACE

StarPilots step out into uncharted space.
Remember, it's not leadership if everybody's been there already.
The Creative Process is the Leadership Process. The Creative Realm is the Leadership Realm. [92]

Remember, the most visionary and profound leaders of all time – from Jesus of Nazareth to Mahatma Gandhi to Martin Luther King Jr. – *assumed* their leadership power to make a difference (their creative power *to choose to create something other than what already existed*), not by virtue of public office or a job title bestowed on them by others, but by stepping into their inherent creative power, venturing into new creative space, moving into alignment with high *Purpose*.

As each of us, as Creators, actively begin to envision and move into a higher future we have imagined, we also may transform our selves and our world. The key is to *assume* our inherent creative power –

not to expect or wait for someone else to give us permission or give us a title – but to step out into new leadership space – to *be* the leaders of our lives, our work and our world – through conscious use of the Creative Process.

Nobody told Arnold Schwarzenegger that he could become the biggest box-office star in Hollywood; he did not ask nor expect permission. He chose to envision and create his life first; titles came later.

Orville Wright did not have a pilot's license. [93]
Motto of Richard Tait, CEO, Cranium

As many historians have pointed out, had the Wright Brothers imagination stopped at what was believed to be possible in their time, their "flying machine" never would have - either literally and figuratively - gotten off the ground. Managers of a bicycle shop, these visionary brothers ventured into the leadership realm – and into higher spade - with an astonishing *Vision* of the impossible: "heavier-than-air" flight. [94]

No one initially engaged – or encouraged - struggling single mother Erin Brockovich to take on powerful Pacific Gas & Electric Company in 1993 over dangerous groundwater contamination of the small town of Hinkley, Calif. Still, though she had no formal law school training, Brockovich helped settle the case in 1996 for $333 million, the largest settlement ever paid in a direct action lawsuit in U.S. history. [95]

Sparked not by outside authority, but by inner conviction, 17-year-old Gustavo Jimenez Jr. sat down one Sunday night in March 2006 to post a *My Space* message, encouraging more than 100 friends to join an immigration walkout the following day in Dallas. Not only did this one teen rally more than 4,000 students to walk out that Monday, but his efforts helped propel a half a million to march on City Hall. [96]

Leaders do not wait for official appointments or formal titles (although many often gain these along the way) to begin changing the world. They start where they are, with what they have now. Like all creators, Orville Wright was charting new space – no formal authority, licensing agency or set of qualifications even existed for this new realm, except his and his brother's belief in their own creative power.

It is the stories of these creators, explorers, overcomers – leaders – the amazing achievements of those who, without money, education, social class or physical ability – that inspire us. Those like Helen Keller, Christopher Reeve, and Stephen Hawking – or cancer-surviving bicyclists, wheelchair basketball stars, quadriplegic painters, and so many more[97] – teach us that our true limitations lie not in our circumstances, or even in our physical bodies – but only in our minds.

The difference between power and powerlessness lies not in any physical construct – not in a strong arm, a gun, a bomb or even in money – it lies in our creative ability. True power lies in our capacity to create something different from that which already exists. Leaders are creators who assume that power - to choose among infinite possibilities, to step into uncharted space, to shape the future.

History will be kind to me, for I intend to write it.
Sir Winston Churchill, British statesman and former Prime Minister

GENESIS of GENIUS

MASTERING POWER ARC™/ CREATIVE GUIDANCE SYSTEM®

LIFE VISION

YOUR CREATIVE VISION – Mastering POWER ARC™:
Where are you going? What does a life of success look, feel and sound like for you? Do you have a clear and compelling answer to these questions? If so, you have a Life Vision - a clear, compelling, multidimensional image of the experience you most desire to live. In the previous section of the GUIDE - and in the following WORKSHEET pages - we provide tools and additional resources - to guide you in developing a compelling Vision for every ARC of your life. This is the first step in creating the life of your dreams.

Vision initiates the Creative Process. It is always the first, essential step - the MINDSHIFT - that moves you from the limited realm of WHAT IS into the unlimited, creative realm of WHAT CAN BE. From Knowledge to Imagination.

Initially, we will focus on guiding you in developing your overall LIFE VISION.

In the process, core aspects or elements of your life will naturally emerge, and you may use these to fine-tune your LIFE ARCS, which you began crafting in the preceding JOURNEYARC section (Worksheets #1-4.).

Note: In many cases, our work will feed into or build on previous WORKSHEETS, so that, at the end of the process, you will have - summarized on one or two POWER ARC: CREATIVE GUIDANCE SYSTEM WORKSHEETS - concise results of your creative work to guide your efforts.

TOOLS FOR VISION-EERS:

- **Vision Checklist:** On the next page, we provide a one-page checklist of the master characteristics of a vivid, compelling Vision. Use this sheet as a guide to ensure your Vision taps into multiple senses, and captures a multidimensional image of your ultimate life experience.

  Vision need not be expressed in words only - but as a multidimensional image or experience.

- **Sculpt or Draw:** It is often extremely valuable and insightful to begin the Visioning process - not by writing (or writing only, although words are certainly important, too), but by visual and kinesthetic (action-based or touch-based) methods.

  Sculpt Exercise 1: We suggest you grab some Play-doh® or modeling clay (available at most toy, art supply or department stores), or some colorful, flexible toys (anything from simple pipe cleaners toy sets like ⟲Zoob®, ⟲Zolo®, or ⟲Toobers and Zots®, three of the favorites GENESISOFGENIUS.COM uses for our creative sessions with clients and collaborative teams). Then set aside some time to sculpt your Vision, using only these 3D, tactile materials, as an answer to the main Vision questions, such as "What do I most want to be?" You will very likely be surprised at what emerges, as your creation will give you deep insight into your true desires.

  Draw Exercise 2: Follow the same instructions as *Sculpt Exercise 1*, above, but instead of sculpting your Vision, use paper and colored pencils or even crayons to draw your Vision and its various elements. Colored pencils, crayons may also be used in MindMapping (see below).

  The ⟲SPIRAL symbol signifies **GENESISOFGENIUS.COM RESOURCES** - tried-and-true, tested resources and tools, which we recommend through the GENESISOFGENIUS.COM web site.

  MORE TOOLS FOR VISION-EERS on following pages ▶

  Starting on the next page, you will find additional Vision WORKSHEETS, resources and tools to guide you in creating your own LIFE VISION and CREATIVE ARCS. Enjoy your creation!

GENESIS of GENIUS

CHECKLIST #5 - POWER OF VISION CHECKLIST

THE POWER OF VISION CHECKLIST

A One-page Checklist of the master characteristics of a vivid, compelling Vision. Use this sheet as a guide to ensure each Vision you create taps into multiple senses, and captures a multidimensional image of your ultimate experience.

THE POWER OF VISION

Vision is the vivid, pleasing, sensory description of the desired experience

- ☐ clearly describes what the successful experience looks, feels, smells, tastes, and sounds like ...
- ☐ is concise and compelling ... creates an attraction force
- ☐ reflects, embodies values and evokes emotion
- ☐ provides direction
- ☐ organizes information and prioritizes activities
- ☐ enables allocation of limited resources to highest impact

WHAT CAN BE

WHAT IS

2 NOW
3 HOW

1 WHERE
▼ Vision
▼ Mission
▼ Purpose
▼ Work(s)
▼ Values

© Julie Ann Turner & Company/CreatorsGuide.com.
All Rights Reserved.

To Claim Your Bonus Books, Free Creative Resources, & Innovation Tools visit GENESISOFGENIUSBOOK.COM.

WORKSHEET # 6 - MASTER LIFE ARC WORKSHEET - WORKING DRAFT PAGE

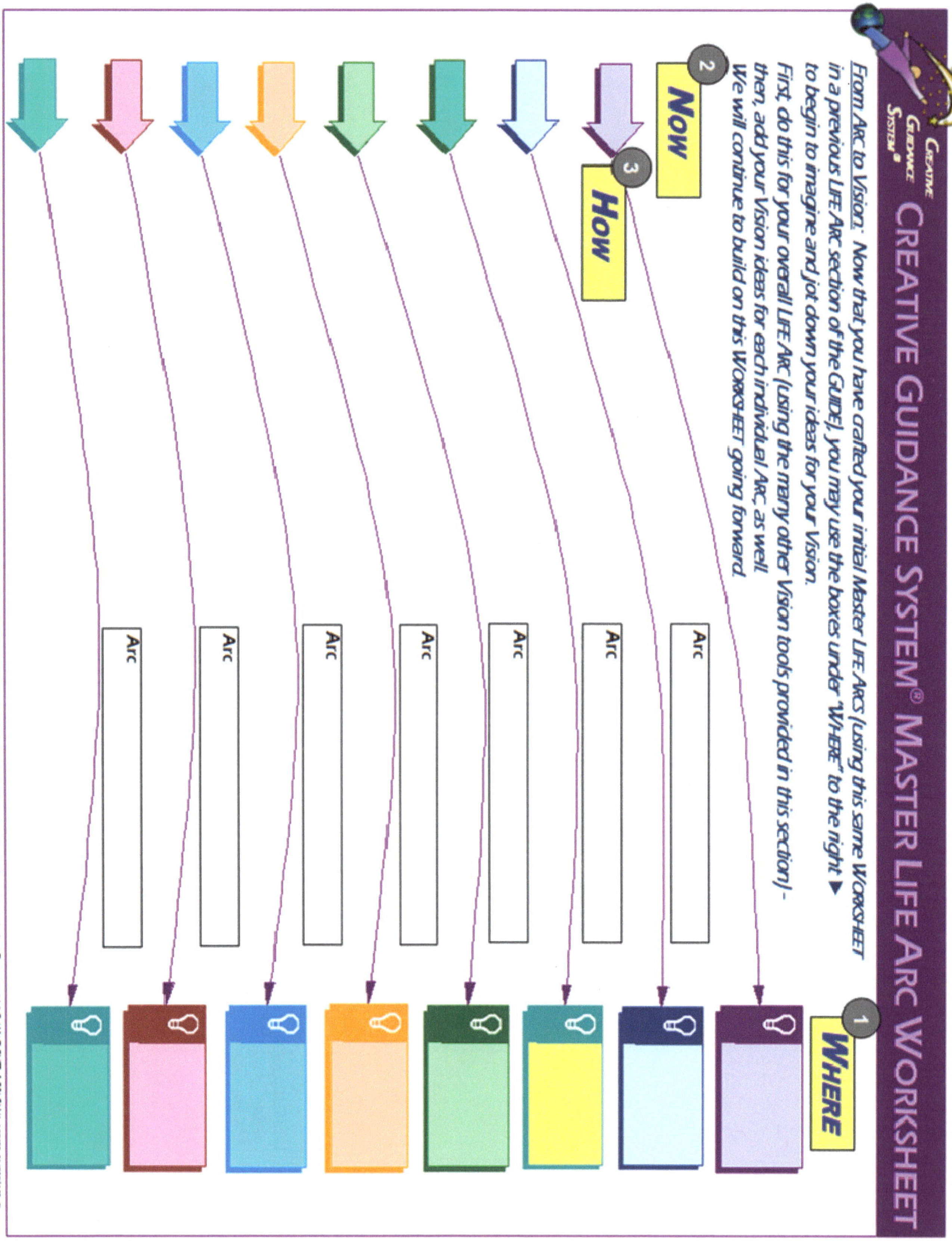
Creative Guidance System®
Creative Guidance System® Master Life Arc Worksheet
From Arc to Vision: Now that you have crafted your initial Master Life Arcs (using this same Worksheet in a previous Life Arc section of the Guide), you may use the boxes under "Where" to the right ▶ to begin to imagine and jot down your ideas for your Vision.
First, do this for your overall Life Arc (using the many other Vision tools provided in this section) - then, add your Vision ideas for each individual Arc, as well.
We will continue to build on this Worksheet going forward.
1 Where
2 Now
3 How
Arc
Arc
Arc
Arc
Arc
Arc
Arc

Worksheet # 7 - Master Life Arc Guidesheet - One-Page Master Summary (Daily Reference)

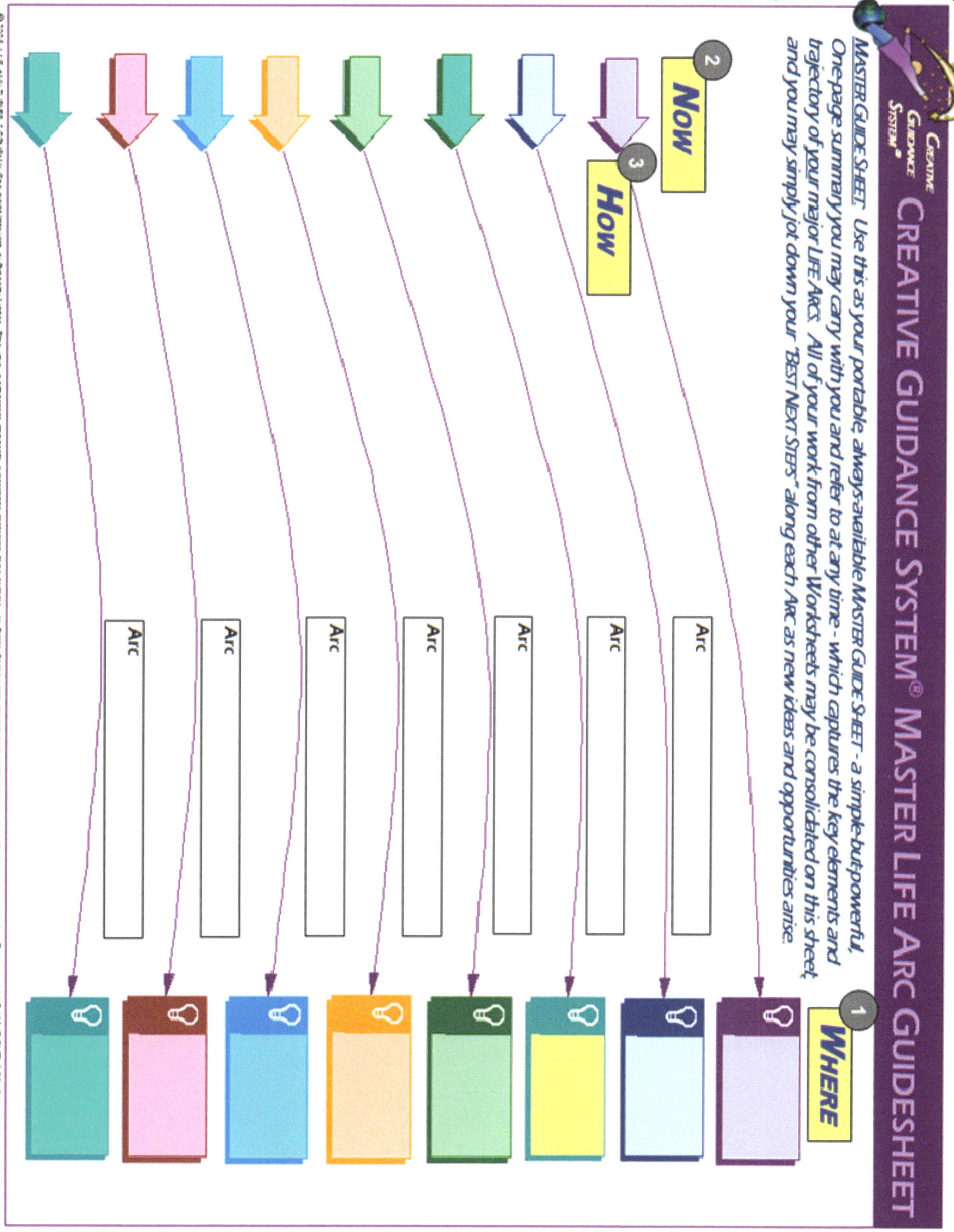
Creative Guidance System®
Creative Guidance System® Master Life Arc Guidesheet
Master Guide Sheet: Use this as your portable, always-available Master Guide Sheet - a simple-but-powerful, One-page summary you may carry with you and refer to at any time - which captures the key elements and trajectory of your major Life Arcs. All of your work from other Worksheets may be consolidated on this sheet, and you may simply jot down your "Best Next Steps" along each Arc as new ideas and opportunities arise.
1
Where
2
Now
3
How
Arc
Arc
Arc
Arc
Arc
Arc
Arc
Arc

MINDMAPPING & MORE TOOLS FOR VISION-EERS:

Nothing much happens without a dream.
For something really great to happen, it takes a great dream.
— Robert K. Greenleaf, author of *Servant Leadership*

A Vision possesses immense power, when created by the full force of the human imagination.
Not only does initiate the Creative Process and compel us forward, but, as writer Ann McGee-Cooper notes, a great Vision is life-giving: "In a new field of study called psychoneuroimmunology, we are learning that just thinking vividly about an exciting dream or goal, and imaging it as complete with all its benefits, can cause our body to create chemicals and hormones (such as endorphins) that balance our immune system, counter stress, and seem to create new energy."[98]

The opposite is also true. Worrying - essentially, imagining a "negative" Vision - works against us, sapping our energy and even damaging our bodies through the stress it generates (some even call worrying "negative prayer"). Based on our body's reactions, some even posit that our bodies do not recognize the difference between real and imagined stress, as they respond with the same chemical reactions either way.[99]

So how do we use the full force of our imagination in creating our Visions?
As we noted above, a central way to do so is to use all our senses and emotions to imagine the full, vivid experience - the "fantasy" - we wish to make real. Here are some additional creative tools for doing so.

- **MindMapping:** Mindmapping is an ideal tool for Visioning (and for creative thinking in general), in that it fuses both words and images together into a visual, relational "map" (see below). Mindmapping therefore taps into the multidimensional way our minds actually work (rather than restricting our expression only to the linear nature of written words). Mindmapping is a valuable creative tool for all levels of creation.

  Mindmaps are incredibly flexible, and can be constructed simply and quickly by hand, or be made more elaborate by adding magazine or other vivid images, or by using specialized MindMapping software, which generally includes images (as shown below). Mindmaps begin with a "central idea" or concept (here, "My Life Vision"), around which related ideas are added and arranged as the individual - or group (Mindmapping is a very effective creative tool for groups, as well) thinks of them.

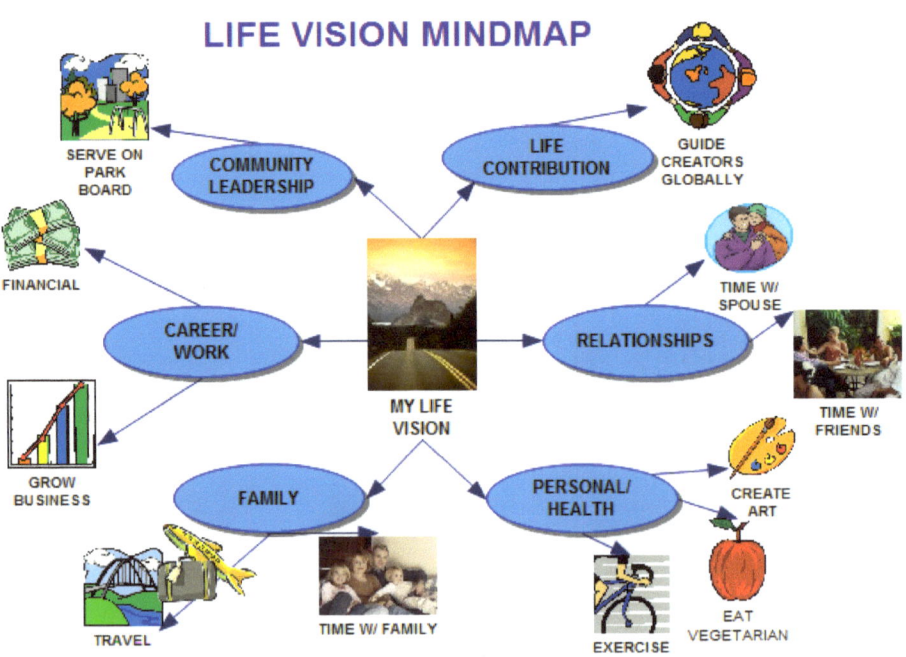

The relational "map" emerges, enabling more ideas to be added to each additional topic or subtopic.

In addition, Internet can turbocharge your creation of Mindmaps, by providing access to a world of images and ideas to spark and expand your thinking, about virtually any topic imaginable.

<u>Mindmap Exercise 3</u>:
Create a Mindmap of your LIFE VISION, using your own topics, ideas and images.

EXPLO RESOURCES

16 VISION-CREATION TOOLS & RESOURCES

The ⊙ SPIRAL symbol signifies **GENESISofGENIUS RESOURCES** - *tried-and-true, tested resources, which you will find available through the GENESISOFGENIUSE.COM web site.*

⊙ VISION CREATION CLASSICS

- **The Personal Vision Workbook**
  Tobin Burgess, Kevin Pugh and Leo Sevigny, Thomson Delmar Learning - 2007

- **Do It! Let's Get Off Our Buts: A Guide to Living Your Dreams**
  Peter McWilliams, Prelude Press - 1997

- **I Could Do Anything If Only I Knew What It Was**
  Barbara Sher, Dell Trade Paperback, Dell Publishing - 1995

- **2013 What Color Is Your Parachute: A Practical Manual for Job-Hunters and Career-Changers**
  Richard Nelson Bolles, Ten Speed Press - 2012; Excellent Sections on Vision & Mission

- **Zen and the Art of Making a Living**
  Laurence G. Boldt, Penguin, Revised Expanded Edition - 2009

⊙ MINDMAPPING & VISUAL THINKING CLASSICS

- **Mind Map**
  http://www.Wikipedia.org - Definition and pictures

- **The Mind Map Book: How to Use Radiant Thinking to Maximize Your Brain's Untapped Potential**
  Tony Buzan and Barry Buzan, Plume; Reprint Edition - 1996

- **Mapping Inner Space: Learning and Teaching Visual Mapping**
  Nancy Margulies and Nusa Maal, Zephyr Press, Second Edition - 2001

- **Mindmapping: Your Personal Guide to Exploring Creativity and Problem-Solving**
  Joyce Wycoff, Berkley Books, The Berkley Publishing Group - 1991

- **Use Both Sides of Your Brain: New Mind-Mapping Techniques**
  Tony Buzan, Plume, Third Edition - 1991

- **Beyond Words: A Guide to Drawing Out Ideas**
  Milly R. Sonneman, Ten Speed Press - 1997

- **Reinventing Communication: A Guide for Using Visual Language for Planning, Problem Solving, and Reengineering**
  Larry Raymond, ASQ Quality Press - 1994

⊙ MINDMAPPING SOFTWARE

- **Bubblle.us, Freemind and xMind**
  Bubble.us, Freemind.Sourceforge.net, xMind.com - Free, online Mindmapping applications

- **Glliffy, Mindmeister, TheBrain and Edraw Mindmap,**
  Gliffy.com, Mindmeister.com, TheBrain.com and Edrawsoft.com - Free and paid online Mindmapping applications

- **Inspiration®**
  Inspiration Software, Inc.

- **MindManager®**
  MindJet Corporation

- **Most important, the true master resource** – our much-expanded, in-depth and evolving treasure trove of creative resources – is available to you when you register your **GENESIS OF GENIUS** Guide at http://WWW.GENESISOFGENIUS.COM (see web site for details and benefits of registration and available bonuses to the GUIDE for *all* registered GUIDE owners.).

Again, consider this set of rich resources as a dynamic launch point for your exploration of creativity. We hope you will be inspired to become a lifetime student of the creative process.

CHAPTER SEVEN
JOURNEY TO POTENTIAL

Life

is either

a daring adventure

or nothing.

Security does not exist

in nature, nor do

the children of men

as a whole experience it.

Avoiding danger

is no safer

in the long run

than exposure.[100]

Helen Keller, American author, activist and visionary

EXPRESSION

There is an explanation

the ultimate end of which

is to find what is uniquely yours

in an expression that is uniquely yours

and in sharing it with others

we finally find ourselves.

T.S. Eliot, poet

IDENTITY

Our creative expressions tell us – and others – who we are. They tell us how we are each distinct and unique, as well as how we are part of a unified Whole.

We all embody this paradox - on the one hand we desire to express and be recognized for our unique identities and contributions, and on the other, we desire to be accepted, to belong, to be included as part of the Whole.

We all seek a balance between uniqueness and unity, distinctness and harmony

Every creative expression - the words we say, and how we say them; the actions we take; the gestures we make toward others; the works we create; our physical appearance; what we wear; what, and who, we surround ourselves with - *communicates who we are.*

Your unique self - your essence, your state of being, your identity - is revealed through the Creative Process.

Your expressions are inherently valuable, at the most fundamental level, because you are a unique creative being.

You have the capacity to express and share with others an essence that is wholly unique. You are the only one who can share the singular mixture of gifts, talent, intelligence, emotion, perspective – your unique light, your contribution to the Whole.

This full expression of your unique light is also the source of true joy.

No one else can make the contribution you are perfectly designed to make.

Your unique expression perfectly aligns with and complements that of others doing the same. Your projection of identity – whether shared in part, or in full - communicates information about the Whole.

> *Identity is the filter that every organism or system uses to make sense of the world.* [101]
> Margaret Wheatley and Myron Kellner-Rogers, *A Simpler Way*

The act of creation moves from the inside out.. Any creation, any change, whether it be changing a life or changing the world - starts from within, and emerges into the world through expression. So it is that the creative energy that moves through us - within you, within each of us - is the force with the power to change the world.

If we do not share our expressions, as Martha Graham says, "the world will not have them."

Unless we all are fully and authentically expressing ourselves, we all are less than complete. We all experience less than the Whole. Moreover, we cannot experience the full glory and magnificence of the Creative Absolute, without full creative expression. In this way, our unique expressions not only complete and fulfill our own potential, but also contribute essentially to the potential and fulfillment of the Whole.

Perhaps this is the true essence of Purpose – our unique creative expressions aligning in contribution to the greater Whole.
We come to know who we are, in the light of creation.

THE WAY OF THE HERO

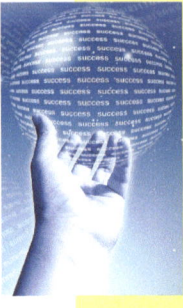

*The Way is not far from man; if we take the Way
as something superhuman beyond man, this is not the real Way.* [102]
Confucius, Chinese philosopher

This is the courageous path of creative rediscovery, the essence of the hero's quest.

As Joseph Campbell reminds us, our creative potential has been within us all along. *"The godly powers sought and dangerously won have been within the heart of the hero all the time."* The hero *"has come to know who he [or she] is,"* having discovered his or her unique spark of divinity, *"which is hidden within us all, only waiting to be known and rendered into life."*[103]

The only journey is within yourself. [104]
Rainer Marie Rilke, German poet

The Arc and the Spiral of the hero's journey – your journey, your life story, your unique expression – reveal your creative power. It is within you now, and always has been.

*Our deepest fear is not that we are inadequate.
Our deepest fear is that we are powerful beyond measure.
It is our light, not our darkness, that frightens us.
We ask ourselves 'who am I to be brilliant, gorgeous, talented and fabulous?'
Actually, who are you not to be?* [105]
Marianne Williamson, from her book "Return to Love"

*Moreover, we can start instantly, the moment we have this realization.
We already have everything we need to start.*

*The greatest obstacle to being heroic is the doubt. Whether one may not
be going to prove one's self a fool; the truest heroism is, to resist the doubt ....* [106]
Nathaniel Hawthorne, American novelist

The world will never be whole until we do. Like light shining through a single fragment of a hologram, as we each express our *self* – as we share our light - we contribute to the wholeness of the world.

*The hero's will is not that of his ancestors, nor of his society, but his own.
This will to be oneself is heroism.* [107]
Jose Ortega y Gassett, Spanish philosopher

The important thing is to be willing to start. To discover our gifts and have the courage share them – no matter how small or how grand they may seem to us.

Not I – not anyone else, can travel that road for you. You must travel it for yourself. [108]
Walt Whitman, American poet

*In fact, the secret of the Way is to learn to express creativity in everything we do.
To see and cherish the sacred in all things – from the most minor to the most magnificent.
For, as the universal patterns woven throughout creation tell us, there is divinity in all things.*

*... when you discover what you will be in your life, set out to do it as if God Almighty
called you at this particular moment in history to do it. don't just set out to do a good job.
Set out to do such a good job that the living, the dead or the unborn couldn't do it any better.
If it falls your lot to be a street sweeper, sweep streets like Michelangelo painted pictures,
sweep streets like Beethoven composed ... Sweep streets like Shakespeare wrote poetry.
Sweep streets so well that all the hosts of heaven and earth will have to pause and say:
Here lived a great street sweeper who swept his job well. ... Be a bush if you can't
be a tree. If you can't be a highway, just be a trail. If you can't be a sun,
be a star. For it isn't by size that you win or fail. Be the best of whatever you are.* [109]
Martin Luther King, Jr., American civil rights leader

LIGHT THROUGH THE LENS

*Ask yourself,
"What are the qualities
that I'm representing
by being myself?"*

*What makes you different
from another individual
and at the same time very similar?
We're all expressing the same qualities,
but each in a unique way.*

*It's kind of like having a lens
against a beam of light
and each one of us has a different way
of taking that energy and expressing it.*

*And maybe that's what purpose is . . .
Each one of us contributes something very special
and very unique to the greater whole.*[110]

Psychologist Caroline Hwoschinsky,
Quoted in *Creativity in Business*, Michael Ray and Rochelle Myers

THE ARTFUL LIFE

> *Your work is to discover your work*
> *and then with all your heart to give yourself to it.*[111]
> — Buddha, Indian spiritual leader and founder of Buddhism

The importance of our conscious reconnection with our creative power,
and of sharing our unique creative expressions - on both a personal
and collective level - becomes clearly evident, for in this way,
we create our lives, we create our work, and together, we create our world.

In A CREATORS' GUIDE, we view work not in the traditional, often tedious sense of a burden to be carried or of a duty to be fulfilled. Certainly, we first acknowledge that "work," as a concept, tends to have a negative meaning.[112] Indeed, it is often considered the opposite of fun. We have work – and fun; work – and play. In fact, the American Heritage Dictionary provides this definition of "work": *"To exert one's mental or physical powers, usually under difficulty and to the point of exhaustion."*[113] This conception not only makes it difficult to see work as a creative expression, but challenging when we see it as something we have to do every day.

Instead, here we view the concept of work with a broader, and yet more central,
meaning – as a creative expression of identity, as a way of being in the world.

People are rewarded by creative process itself . . .
Everyone wants to do meaningful work.[114]
— Warren Bennis, *Organizing Genius*

Moreover, we often refer not merely to work, but to "works" -
in the same sense as one refers to a "work of art."

Work is love made visible.[115]
— Kahlil Gibran, *The Prophet*

This view of work as creative expression - of our "works" as art – is not new, but ancient - and it is an idea that has been explored by psychologist Carl Jung and Eastern philosopher Kahlil Gibran to current-day philosophers Thomas Moore and business leadership gurus Warren Bennis and Peter Senge.

Learning organizations are organizations
where people continually expand their capacity
to create the results they truly desire.[116]
— Peter Senge, *The Fifth Discipline*

In fact, Thomas Moore, author of Care of the Soul,
notes that the Latin word for "work" was actually "opus" -
a term also used to refer to works of art, particularly musical compositions.[117]
Moore also remarks on the idea that our work as creative expression
often reveals to us our own identity, or self -
as he says, we often "find ourselves in our work" -
and that "culture is the totality of all of us doing our work."[118]

Art is the proper task of life.[119]
— Friedrich Nietzsche, German philosopher

AUTHENTICITY

An artist is not a special kind of person. Every person is a special kind of artist.[120]
Catherine Kapikian, *Creativity: Touching the Divine*

Joseph Campbell tells us this is the core theme of the Grail legend, the eternal tale of the hero – that "the world of people living inauthentic lives" ultimately returns, to live out their purpose and potential.[121]

Follow your heart. Any other path leads to someone else's dream.
Lyn Christian, CEO, Soul Salt Inc.

Are you living an authentic life? One which fully expresses your unique gifts and potential? So many today are living what Henry David Thoreau described as "lives of quiet desperation." As we've seen, an authentic life may only be lived through conscious, creative choice.

Life isn't about finding yourself. Life is about creating yourself.
George Bernard Shaw, English playwright

At every moment, you are determining your life's trajectory, whether you are choosing Purpose, or simply floating through time, merely reacting to random circumstances that drift into your space.

Everyone has been made for some particular work, and the desire for that work has been put in every heart.[122]
Rumi, Persian poet and theologian

"Realizing" your dream is an active process – making your dreams real, bringing them into the physical world involves the conscious act of creation. Whatever your life Purpose or "Calling" may be, you must consciously choose it – at the highest level, for the whole of your life's contribution, and in every instant, no matter how seemingly insignificant any moment may be.

A little bit of confidence in yourself and work. Don't ever forget your art, sic itur ad astra. [trans: "thus one reaches the stars"][123]
Paul Cezanne, French Post-impressionist painter

As Thomas Moore says, "*Creativity is, foremost, being in the world soulfully.*"[124] And, no matter how ordinary the task, when working with creativity, the results are affected by our creative power. Ultimately, our work and works have greater impact and authentic influence. This is true even though we may not always feel "inspired" in the romantic sense. As Edison said: "*Genius is 1 percent inspiration and 99 percent perspiration.*"[125] Even the composer Igor Stravinsky described his work as the "*day-to-day craft of making music,*" which he viewed "*much like a person who makes shoes.*"[126]

Everybody can be great. Because anybody can serve. You don't have to have a college degree to serve. You don't have to make your subject and verb agree to serve. You don't have to know about Plato and Aristotle . . . (or) Einstein's Theory of Relativity . . (or) the Second Theory of Thermodynamics in physics to serve. You only need a heart full of grace. A soul generated by love.[127]
Martin Luther King Jr., American civil rights leader

Dr. King is describing authentic, creative leadership – what many today call "*servant leadership.*"[128] Remember, true power and energy flow only through *choice*. As Stephen R. Covey said, "*leadership is a choice, not a position,*" and Bruce Avolio emphasizes, "*leadership is not a role, it's a process.*"[129]

The Creative Process, ARC diagrams, workbook pages and tools in this section will guide you not only in discovering your life's ultimate contribution, but also in revealing how you may integrate all levels – or ARCS - of your life, in alignment with your unique Purpose.

You love something ...there's something each one of us loves – that's [our] passion. Passion infuses every bit of our lives.[130]
Marianne Williamson, author and visionary

GENESIS of GENIUS

PERSONAL PLANES OF THOUGHT

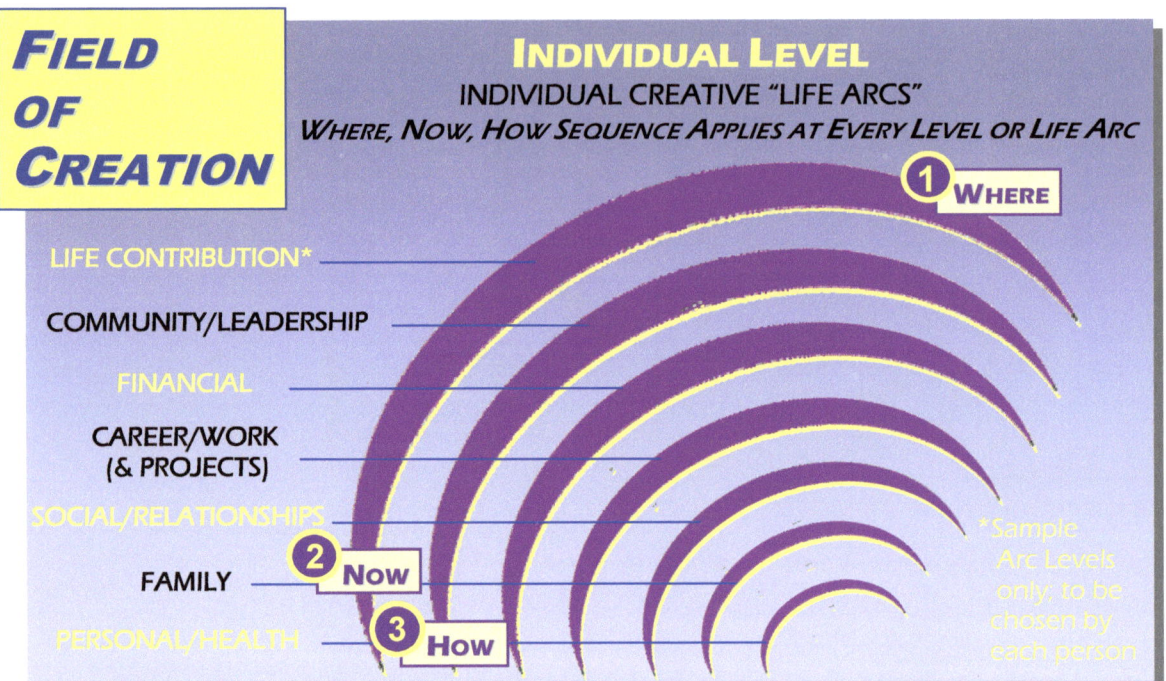

One of the most beautiful - and powerful - benefits POWER ARC: YOUR CREATIVE GUIDANCE SYSTEM provides is that it enables you to integrate and align all aspects your life around your core Mission and Purpose.

All ARCS are in alignment (above), each representing an important aspect of your life – from personal and health levels, to social and financial levels, to community and life contributions (and these are only examples; you may choose other aspects most important in your own life).

You already have begun filling in your own Visions for each ARC in the previous "MASTERING THE CREATIVE GUIDANCE SYSTEM" VISION WORKSHEET. In this section, you will begin developing your life Mission or Purpose – which will form the core of your own ultimate contribution, and will serve as the central navigational frame for your creative life journey. Your life Mission will emerge as you as you explore and evaluate your unique strengths and passions.

As you craft your own unique ARC for each aspect of your life, you are building a powerful navigational framework that will ensure your direction is aligned with what you most desire, leveraging your greatest strengths and the energy of your passions. Moreover, your personal guidance system will guide each step as you move confidently forward, knowing you have chosen consciously, at every level, what you wish to create in your life, work and world. In addition, *POWER ARC: YOUR CREATIVE GUIDANCE SYSTEM* framework will give you the power to identify and intentionally create strategies that move you toward your goals on *more than one level at the same time* – enabling you to discover unique synergies that were previously inaccessible to you.

> *The master in the art of living makes little distinction between his work and his play, his labor and his leisure, his mind and his body, his information and his recreation, his love and his religion. He hardly knows which is which. He simply pursues his vision of excellence at whatever he does, leaving others to decide whether he is working or playing. To him, he's always doing both.*
>
> James A. Michener, American author

LIFE BRAND

Everything we do communicates.
As we walk through the world, we are telling our own story – with much more than words.

Today, our creative expressions extend far beyond the words we say, and how we say them; beyond our physical appearance what we wear, beyond what, and who, we surround ourselves with. Today, we not only have a physical expression – often limited by time and space (but not always), and a virtual expression – a potentially limitless presence projected through cyberspace.

Every expression communicates who we are. We are constantly projecting our identity into the world. And now, more than ever before in all of human time, our expressions are more visibly creating and shaping the world in which we live.

There's this large trend – I think the next trend in the Web .... which is to have users really express, offer, and market their own content, their own persona, their identity. I don't mean identity as in credit cards. I mean like apparel is a way we express our identity, how we dress, the music we listen to.[131]
  — John Doerr, general partner/Kleiner Perkins Caufield & Byers

In BOOK TWO of the GUIDE, we've traced in detail the global MINDSHIFT to Imagination, and the surge of creativity our networked world is unleashing, as instantaneous information and collaboration become the norm. Trendwatching.com calls this massive creative movement "GENERATION C" – "C" for "*Content*" – which reveals itself in related trends generating creative content worldwide, such as "CUSTOMER-MADE" and "CROWD CLOUT."[132] This is all part of "THE GLOBAL BRAIN," identified as a transcendent global trend, in which "*all of the world's intelligence and experience, [is] fully networked, incorporating not only the usual suspects like gurus, professors and scientists, but the experiences and skills of hundreds of millions*" of individuals across the planet, as well. Here's the point:

Today, we each have much more power to project our identity, and express our unique voice.

Yet the desire to express ourselves is timeless. The tools of expression change over the ages, and recognizable forms cycle over the decades: from the Beatle haircuts, love beads, peace signs and psychedelic clothes (and drugs) of the 60s, to the sideburns and bell-bottoms of the 70s, to the spike-n-shock colored punk hair and piercings of the 80s, to the loose, low-slung pants and tattoos of the 90s. Pop culture captures our imaginations, as we are intrigued along the way by self-expressive "theme songs" from TV shows, by "superpowers" of graphic heroes, as by ringtones and avatars today.[133] Business gurus alert us to the need for "personal branding" in a growing "Free Agent Nation," and a few voices break through to warn of an impending creative crisis, a global fight or "flight" for "talent."[134] The truly savvy have picked up on the significance of this shift, acknowledging the emergence of "*participation*" as the new "fifth P of marketing" – co-equal with product, package, promotion, place.[135] Parents are befuddled by the attraction of *Instagram* – few perceiving what their kids so easily see – that these virtual spaces are labs for limitless creativity, broadcast nodes for near-ultimate expressions of personal identity, projected for the world to behold.[136] But here's the essential, eternal bottom line:

We all want to be known, understood, valued, loved. What do you want to be known for?

Others "know you" by your creative expressions, by your "works," in all forms.[137] Ultimately, our "*works*" are a reflection of our selves - something that emerges from within, and manifests outside ourselves – a mirror of identity. All the more reason why, here, we encourage you to take a more conscious, artful approach to life, *choosing* your life expression. As Peter Senge says: "*People with a high level of personal mastery… approach life as an artist would approach a great work of art,*" reflecting a more "*sacred view*" of work, where we reap intrinsic benefits from creative expression. This is, in part, what led *Yahoo!*'s Tim Sanders to proclaim that "*love is the killer app.*"[138] It is in expressing what is uniquely yours to share, by directing your passion, energy – and love - toward "*a cause greater than oneself,*" as Viktor Frankl said – that you reach your full creative potential.[139]

POWER OF MISSION

We have talked about the power of Vision – the primary element of "WHERE we are going," and the magnetic center of attraction in your Creative Journey. Remember, Vision is always intertwined with Mission or Purpose, an expression of our passion.

Like *Vision*, your life's *Mission* or *Purpose* holds powerful personal meaning and motivation, and a personal "*Mission Statement*" will draw out the highest and best within you, spark your drive to achieve, and hold a natural magnetic pull for you – what we call "*the pull of passion*."

A Mission Statement, whether for an individual or an organization, expresses our core Purpose – our reason for being, why we exist, and what we seek to accomplish.

① WHERE
VISION
Vision
Mission
▶ Purpose
▶ Work(s)
▶ Values

Mission also includes the element of *Work* (or "*Works*," used here to reflect *creative contribution;* others say "Business") – or *what we do* – the main activities or methods we use to fulfill our *Purpose*. Finally, *Mission* includes *Values* – *what we care most about* – the principles or beliefs that guide us as we pursue our Purpose. *Vision* and *Mission* together form our "guiding image of success," express the principles we live by, and frame our character.[140] We may also think of *Mission* as our life's Master Goal.[141]

How important is Mission?

To answer this question, consultants from Zig Ziglar to Tony Robbins have long cited a Yale Study of the Class of 1953 – since debunked by *Fast Company* - which supposedly showed that the 3 percent of seniors who, in 1953, said they had written, specific life goals, were found 20 years later to possess more financial wealth than the rest of their class combined.[142] The real point, however, is this: this example was the one used by major consultants to illustrate the importance of *Mission* and *Life Goals*, but the story focuses only on financial wealth as the measure of success.

However, life goals and life success are not solely about money and tangible gain. They are about fulfilling potential, which encompasses much more than financial wealth.

There is a school in South Dallas, located in the middle of a low-income, crime-plagued sector of the city, where every morning, students starting at 3 years of age recite from memory the St. Philip's Creed, a *Mission Statement* around which the school and its curriculum is organized. Notice in this excerpt how this *Mission* captures the essence of creative vision, power and choice:

> *Look at me. I am more than what you see. Destiny is mine! If it is to be, it's up to me. …*
> *I will use my education to explore new heights. The sky is the limit, if I just put my mind in it. …*
> *Success is my right…. I have the voice. The consequences I will accept, for I made the choice.*[143]

On national tests, students in surrounding schools score at the 45th percentile, while students from St. Philip's consistently score at the 87th percentile. Remarkably, 97 percent of St. Philip's students graduate, and a full 88 percent go on to college. While the Creed is not alone responsible for this success, Headmaster Terry Flowers credits its power as the core statement of belief and organizing *Mission* of the school.[144] Similarly, a young man named Denzel Washington was once a 20-year-old college dropout. But a woman at his mother's beauty shop wrote a note about him, which said: "*This boy is going to speak to millions of people.*" Denzel adopted this "*Mission*" as his own, and it inspired him to return to college, where he discovered his acting talent, and went on to win an Academy Award. Denzel says of the original note: "*I still keep it with me all the time.*"[145]

It is never too early - or too late - to create your life's Mission. Hopefully, you have begun your Vision Worksheet (p. 314). At the end of this section, you'll find resources to create your Mission.

ENERGY FLOW

Not surprisingly, finding your life's Mission or Purpose has an amazing way of plugging you into a natural flow of creative energy.

In On Meaningful Work, *Thomas Moore sheds light on this aspect of work, noting that the Greek word for "work" is "ergon" – which also gives us rise to the word "energy."[146] This work as "energy" concept can actually help guide us, as we seek to discover meaning and Purpose in our lives, both individually and collectively.*

As we noted on the very first page of this GUIDE, the essence of *The Journey* itself – this universal, transcendent concept shared in some form by virtually all belief systems - is the human quest to discover meaning, purpose and potential. We are all adventurers on this Journey, whether we realize it consciously or not.

One powerful secret to discovering purpose and potential is to ask the question: "Does this give me energy? Or does it take energy away?"

This question is a key to our discovering our passion, as it guides us toward the source or "flow" of our natural creative energy. We may ask "*what part of your work are you most passionate about?*" or "*What do you most love to do?*" This simple question – and other questions like it, which we share in this GUIDE – will become powerful "life navigation" tools in your *POWER ARC SUCCESS SYSTEM*. Questions open space, instead of closing it, and thus open our minds and lives to new possibilities. As we search for *Purpose* and *Mission*, we may use this energy – as it arises in various forms such as excitement, commitment, passion, joy and love – to guide us, to help us discover what our unique talents are, what types of activities we are most attracted to, where our creative energy flows most powerfully and freely.

If you don't have passion, change.[147]
Lauren Hutton, Actress

Each of us is a unique bundle of potential energy and potential power – an "*Identity in Motion*," to use Margaret Wheatley's phrase.[148] We are always revealing our identity – in everything we do. Our lives – our work and our "works' - are always in process, revealing who we are, and who we are becoming. In essence, it is through our actions - initiated by our choices – that our identity is revealed, and "set into motion" (from "potential" energy to "kinetic" energy, the "energy of motion"). We may think of ourselves as releasing our potential energy and power through our creative expressions, through our "works." Dr. Larry Dossey says the "*two most important sources of energy*" in life, are, first "*a sense of purpose that goes beyond the details of the job – that what I do is somehow congruent with the overall purpose, design and flow of the universe as I experience it,*" and second, "*a sense of the top line, as opposed to the bottom line, a concern for people and quality of life.*"[149] Creative expression energizes us.

Interestingly, Thomas Moore observes that our creative expressions "*reveal the person we are,*" that person "*we don't even recognize until it is revealed in our work ... we are seeing our selves mirrored in the world outside of us.*" This, he says, is how "*we find ourselves in our work.*"[150] Sometimes, too, once we've found our true *Purpose*, our *Mission* or *Calling*, we enter such a state of *flow* – a term Mihaly Csikszentmihalyi popularized[151] - that we may, in the process, then "*lose ourselves in our work.*" As T.S. Eliot said:

Time past and time future Allow but a little consciousness.
To be conscious is not to be in time ... .[152]

THE SOUL OF WORK

There will be hundreds of people out there with your same degree; there will be thousands of people doing what you want to do for a living. But you will be the only person alive who has sole custody of your life. Your particular life. Your entire life. Not just your life at a desk, or your life on a bus, or in a car, or at the computer. Not just the life of your mind, but the life of your heart. Not just your bank account, but your soul. People don't talk about the soul very much anymore. . . . It's so much easier to write a resume than to craft a spirit.[153]

Anna Quindlen, author, written for 1999 Villanova Graduation Speech

Indeed, how do others come to know us? By our "works" - our creations and creative expressions. They come to know who we are, and we come to know ourselves more fully, as we express our uniqueness, our true essence, our higher selves.

In *On Meaningful Work*, Thomas Moore notes that the idea of a "*profession*" also reflects this sense of our work or works as a "*profession*" or expression of identity, of self, or soul. The psychologist Carl Jung spoke of work with a sense of "*becoming*," as in "*the work of making meaningful life*," one which satisfies our soul (the "*Birth of the Soul*"). Aristotle expressed this concept of becoming as "*potentia*," while psychologist Abraham Maslow used the term "self-*actualization*." Moore echoes this idea: "*Creativity is the soul being expressed.*"[154] Moore emphasizes the importance of this *creative process*:

The very process of our work is extremely important. ... not just the product, but the process, so that doing of what we are engaged in may be as important, if not more important, than whatever it is that we have produced.[155]

The essential point: It is just as important for us to express it as it is for others to perceive it. There is value in the creative expression itself. From this expression of what you love to do, what fulfills you, what integrates all your gifts – comes true joy.

No one need feel guilty for being happy in work. Only two things are required:
1) that you not be afraid to be free, not be afraid to love work and enjoy it as creative play; and
2) that you display the will and courage to make personal choices - not because others esteem them, but because they fit who you are (your character) and what you are (your talent). Before you can please a single other human being, you must first please yourself.
It works in no other way. ... it is much easier to be miserable in work than to have a love affair with what we are and do.[156]

James R. Fisher, Jr., Author, Personal Excellence Newsletter

Moore sees this as a spiritual aspect of life - a "*natural spirituality*," a "*spirituality of everyday life*" – that is part of "*giving yourself to something that is bigger than yourself.*"[157] As we search for our *Purpose* in life, we often use words like "*mission*," "*calling*," "*profession*," or "*dharma*," which carry a sense of this more personal, even sacred, view of work, one that pollster Daniel Yankelovich says is on the rise.[158] Deepak Chopra explains that "*dharma*," or *Life Purpose*, means to "*discover your divinity - your special gift or talent*," and to share "*the creative expression of this gift or talent ... what you love to do, that also serves others.*[159]" It is this higher sense of self and *Life Purpose* that moves us past fear. As Ambrose Redmoon says: "*Courage is not the absence of fear, but rather the judgment that something else is more important than fear.*"[160] In our creative journey toward higher *Purpose*, we find our power.

When I dare to be powerful – to use my strength in the service of my vision – then it becomes less and less important whether I am afraid.[161]

Audre Lorde, writer and poet

When one is engaged in a favorite pursuit or a subject absorbingly interesting, the normal conceptions of labor or time disappear from the mind. In fact, life itself is absorbed in the engagement, or it may be said that one's life is tuned in harmony with eternal life.[162]

Gunji Koizumi, Judo Master

REENERGIZING LIFE

> *Wishing is good for us. Daydreams, fantasies, castles in the air, and aspirations all drive us forward, impel us to make things happen. They also tell us a lot about ourselves. Our wishes come straight from our core, and they are loaded with vital information about who we are and who we can become. Keeping track of our wishes helps us tap into the energy that propels us to go after our happiness.*[163]
> — Barbara Ann Kipfer, *The Wish List*

This creative view of work is, in itself, reenergizing – to our lives as a whole. By approaching our work as "works" - by aligning "what we do" with "who we are" - we also move into the flow of our natural creative energy. Creativity becomes "a way of being in the world," rather than an isolated, occasional activity.

> *Life is in motion, 'becoming becoming.' The motions of life swirl inward to the creating of self and outward to the creating of the world. ... The motions of life have direction. Life moves toward life. We seek for connections and restore the world to wholeness. ... Meaning deepens as we move into the dance ...*[164]
> — Margaret Wheatley and Myron Kellner-Rogers, *A Simpler Way*

Through conscious use of the Creative Process, we *integrate* aspects – the "ARCS" – of our lives, which we often have previously kept separate. We create life synergies. *Our work need no longer be compartmentalized, separated from life and living.*

> *Work can provide the opportunity for spiritual and personal, as well as financial growth. If it doesn't, we're wasting far too much of our lives on it.*[165]
> — James Autry, from *The Corporate Mystic*

Through POWER ARC: YOUR CREATIVE GUIDANCE SYSTEM, our Life ARCs all become aligned and oriented toward our highest Vision and our life's Mission and Purpose. We discover and express our unique self in contribution to the world.

> *The [new] mind-set says work is personal. That what I'm doing is not just making a living - I'm making a difference. The mind-set says I'm having more fun at work than I ever imagined would be possible... The mind-set says there are values in work that are really quite important. That what I do, how I do it and the people with whom I do it stand for something.*
>
> *The old model was leave yourself at home. If you have any emotions, any creativity, if you have any personal investment, check that at the door. Just give us your hands. We're not hiring you for your brain and your spirit, or your heart. ... For us that is really old news, and it no longer works.*[166]
> — *Fast Company* Editor and Co-founder Alan Webber

As we allow life's energy to flow through the Creative Process, across all ARCS of our life – personal, social, work, community – "*swirling inward to the creating of self and outward to the creating of the world,*" we rediscover life's fullness and wholeness. We heal the brokenness and fragmentation of life. We "re-member" who we are as individuals, we express our creations as part a whole, we engage in the process of *creating life*. Wheatley and Rogers say:

> *... Most people have a desire to love their organizations. They love the purpose of their school, their community agency, their business. They fall in love with the identity that is trying to be expressed. They connect to the founding vision. They organize to create a different world.*[167]

REDISCOVERING LIFE'S TOP LINE

*I went to the woods because I wished to live deliberately ...
and not, when I came to die, discover that I had not lived.*[168]
  Henry David Thoreau, American author, *Walden*

What will you do with your creative energy, your creative power?

Everything we do involves some exchange of power.[169]
  Lili Fornier, producer and director

All tangible products and services, and money itself, are merely representations of energy.

I love myself enough ... I respect my life force enough to no longer waste it.[170]
  Carolyn Myss, author

LIFE'S TOP LINE — LIFE LIVED TO FULL POTENTIAL — JOY, LOVE, FULFILLMENT, CONTRIBUTION

LIFE'S BOTTOM LINE — LIFE LIVED FOR TANGIBLE "THINGS" — MONEY $, TANGIBLE PRODUCTS/SERVICES

What do we receive in exchange for our energy? WHAT CAN BE / WHAT IS / 1 Where / 2 Now / 3 How

On a higher level (a higher energy "vibration," if you will), love, joy, fulfillment, respect, contribution or service – all are also exchanges of energy or power. Will we exchange our energy only for tangible "things" (though these are certainly valid, worthy, and enjoyable rewards), only concerned with the "bottom line" - or will we also choose to exchange our energy and power for a higher Purpose - what we call here "Life's Top Line" – to reach our full potential and leave a lasting legacy?

The greatest darkness of our time is the legitimization of selfishness. When everybody is selfish, that's a very low-level [energy] vibration. The universe doesn't support it.. ...When the only point of a project is to make money, regardless of the effect it has on children's minds, regardless of the effect it has on the environment – yes, it might make money - but it has no cosmic impetus [force].[171]
  Marianne Williamson, activist and author

Williamson adds: "*We have a desire, a natural desire – all people, in any age - to create, to express, and to experience a sacred dimension.*"[172] And, as we've said from the outset of the GUIDE, creativity always touches the divine.[173] Many have expressed this deep desire to live to their deepest and fullest potential.

I would rather be ashes than dust! I would rather my spark should burn out in a brilliant blaze than it should be stilled by dry rot. I would rather be a superb meteor, every atom of me in magnificent glow, than a sleepy and permanent planet. The proper function of man is to live, not to exist. I shall not waste my days in trying to prolong them. I shall use my time.
  Jack London, author

So many today feel a call to live for more than the bottom line – to rediscover, and "live into" Life's Top Line, which encompasses higher Values and Purpose, and expresses life's true and full creative potential.

The worst thing we can ever do, the greatest risk we that we can ever take, is playing it safe, because we risk not living the life we were meant to live. We risk losing the very thing we want to have.[174]
  Marianne Williamson, activist and author

The more we express who we really are and share our creative expressions, the more we are reflected in our life's "works." In this, we experience true joy, and rediscover the love we have been seeking all along.[175]

Twenty years from now you will be more disappointed by the things that you didn't do than by the ones you did do. So throw off the bowlines. Sail away from the safe harbor. Catch the trade winds in your sails. Explore. Dream. Discover.
  Mark Twain, humorist

It is never too late to be what you might have been.
  George Eliot, novelist

GENESIS of GENIUS

MASTERING POWER ARC™/ CREATIVE GUIDANCE SYSTEM®

IDENTITY & EXPRESSION

CREATIVE SELF – *Mastering Power Arc: Creative Guidance System®*:
Just like a fragment of a hologram, you possess a uniqueness that only exists within you ... you may allow light to shine fully through you, and express your magnificent, singular uniqueness in the World ... or you may choose to keep it to yourself - to "keep your light under a bushel," hidden from others, and, perhaps, even from yourself. Yet, if you seek to discover, and fully express, your creative gifts and talents, it will bring you joy ... and you will serve the World - because you are the only one who can shine your singular light.

The simple truth is, every person is unique, and success doesn't always mean uniformity, or conformity. Everyone's learning curve is different. The common factor among those who succeed is consistency, or the ability to utilize stick-to-itiveness.

What is equally as common is the fear factor among those who fail, who are afraid to see themselves for who and what they really are an accept it. ... they therefore fail to develop their individuality, their talent, to celebrate what is unique about them. I call this the "ear of individualism" that is so pervasive in our society. ... This need to confirm is killing our most creative minds.[176]

Erin Brockovich, *Take It From Me*

One of the most common tendencies - a result of our focus on WHAT IS, rather than on WHAT CAN BE - is to seek "outside" ourselves to match who we are (our identity) and what we can do (our gifts and talents) to what already exists (perhaps to try to be like another person, or to fit into some already existing category, job title or line of work) ... rather than to seek "within" ourselves, explore and honor our unique gifts and talents, and allow our life purpose and our "works" to arise out of who we truly are.

Even after we have embarked on our own Creative Journey, we want to remain aware of this tendency to take a new discovery about ourselves or our work and try to force-fit it into an already existing container or category ... and instead remember to allow whatever we discover to keep its uniqueness, its singularity.

This often tends to occur when we first begin to discover our creative gifts and talents, but then take these new and fragile potentials and try to wedge them into an existing job description or title. Instead, if we allow these newfound gems of self to breathe, to nurture them so that they may grow and begin to shine, we will recognize that we have truly found our own Way - that we have arrived on that path of Life Purpose that we have been searching for all along.

*Everything - a horse, a vine - is created for some duty ...
For what task, then, were you yourself created? ...
A man's true delight is to do the things he was made for.*[177]

Marcus Aurelius, Roman Emperor-Philosopher, from *Meditations*

In this section, *you will find some special tools, recommended resources, and personal Worksheets, to guide you in your own exploration of Vision and Mission. The exercises and the results you generate, as you use these tools to delve deeper into your own special uniqueness, may then be consolidated into Worksheet #7's "Top-Level," One-Page Summary.*

EXPLO RESOURCES

5 COOL TOOLS FOR EXPLORING LIFE MISSION

In addition to the wealth of Vision-exploration resources in the previous section, here we offer a compact guide to tools you may use to explore your Life Purpose and Mission.

The key to the ability to change is a changeless sense of who you are, what you are about and what you value.
Stephen R. Covey, author of *The Seven Habits of Highly Effective People*

That we find the ability to change only in light of changeless knowledge about who we are highlights the paradox we find underlying almost all profound statements of truth. We must first know who we are, so we may do what we are meant to do. It is no accident that the late Stephen Covey, who reintroduced the world to the importance of personal Mission and Purpose with his best-selling book *The Seven Habits of Highly Effective People*, should be the source of such a profound statement.

Covey's quote expresses the essence of what this GUIDE has emphasized: In the midst of an ever-changing Field of Potential, the stars we must navigate by are *Vision, Mission* and *Values.*

That is why the ancient Oracle said that all truth was captured by these words: "*Know Thyself.*" If we do not *invest* the time - and this is a true and valuable *investment* in our own potential - to explore who we are, to discover our unique Life Purpose, and to express our full creative nature, then all our actions, no matter how precisely and efficiently performed, may not possess the meaning nor carry the impact for the world, or joy for ourselves, than might one moment of living out our true Life Purpose. For, as business management expert Peter Drucker said:

There is nothing so useless as doing efficiently that which should not be done at all.

Especially in a fast-fast, imagination-driven world, we must have sure and true stars by which we navigate the new and uncharted space ever-unfolding before us. If we try to navigate by changeable circumstances, we will find ourselves spinning aimlessly, disoriented and confused. Yet if we know Where we are going - our Vision - and our Purpose, or Mission, these contain the steady light to guide us surely, even through turbulent times.

"*A Mission,*" as defined by Stephen Covey, means "*An inner urge to pursue an activity or perform a service. A calling. What one intends to do or achieve. ...*" And one of the best, yet freely available tools for crafting an initial Mission or Life Purpose is Dr. Covey's *Mission Statement Builder*.

MISSION CREATION RESOURCES

- **Mission Statement Builder - FranklinCovey**
  Online Mission Statement Wizard, www.franklincovey.com/msb/, Library & Resources - 2013

- **The Path: Creating Your Mission Statement for Work and for Life**
  Laurie Beth Jones, Hyperion - 1998

- **2013 What Color Is Your Parachute: A Practical Manual for Job-Hunters and Career-Changers**
  Richard Nelson Bolles, Ten Speed Press - 2012; "Chapter 12: How to Find Your Mission in Life"

- **The Pathfinder: How to Choose or Change Your Career for a Lifetime of Satisfaction and Success**
  Nicholas Lore, Touchstone Books, Revised Updated Edition - 2012

- **The Brand You 50: 50 Ways to Transform Yourself from and "Employee" into a Brand**
  Tom Peters, Alfred A. Knopf - 1999

The SPIRAL symbol signifies **GENESISOFGENIUS.COM RESOURCES** *- tried-and-true, tested resources and tools, which we recommend through the* GENESISOFGENIUS.COM *web site.*

CORE IDEAS FOR EXPLORING LIFE MISSION

Stephen Covey believed that *who you are* and *how you express that essence* - which he calls "*character*" – is *more important than anything that you do or can do.* As he says:

I believe that character (what a person is) is ultimately more important than competence (what a person can do). Obviously both are important, but character is foundational. All else builds on this cornerstone. ... Even the very best structure, system, style, and skills can't compensate completely for deficiencies in character.[178]

Character - who a person is - is more important that competence. That's how important it is for you to know your essence, to discover and share your uniqueness. More important than *anything you can do.* In a world where we tend to value *doing - tangible activity -* more than anything, even more than we value *thinking -* the truth is, to echo Peter Drucker, *what we do doesn't matter* if the activity is not in service of Purpose or Mission. We may look busy, but, without Purpose, in reality, we are often just wasting our time. *And, often, missing out on our authentic lives.*

What is your mission? aim? ambition? dream? goal? intent? objective? target?
It's up to you to determine what guides you ... what inspires you ...
what gets you out of bed in the morning?
But does your mission have to be HUGE to be worthy?
Must it be big enough to change the world ? No!
Just big enough to change your world, your life, your future
You can choose what you value, dream, hope for, become.[179]

— Quote from *FranklinCovey Mission Statement Builder*

As Covey said, Mission Statements are 'written to inspire you, not to impress anyone else. Here, we present key elements of *Mission*:

▶ *Purpose -* "why we are here," why a person, team or organization exists, what it seeks to accomplish and contribute (statement begins with word "To ...").

▶ *Work(s)* – "how we do it," the main method, activities or "*business*" through which a person, team or organization achieves this *Purpose.*

▶ *Values. -* "what we care about and share," principles or beliefs that guide a person or team participants as they pursue *Purpose.*

If we don't have *Purpose* or *Mission*, we also miss out on our life's true *works -* and the energy and flow that comes from expressing our creative passion, which is unique to each of us. It's not necessarily the act or the nature of work itself that gives it purpose for you; it's how you *feel* about the work and how fully your talents are expressed in doing it. A simple example,? You may absolutely dislike auto maintenance, while someone else's true talents and passion emerge when he or she is working on cars ... others when working in a garden, cleaning a house, or cooking. For each person, fulfilling *Purpose* makes the difference between waking up every morning looking forward to doing what you love, or dreading each morning you must get up and go to "work." Without *Purpose,* as Suzanne Falter Barns suggests, ultimately we miss out on our life's joy:

You may be thinking that living life without a sense of purpose is fine ... and it is!
I just want you to know, however, that if that's you, you're missing out on some serious goodies. Here's what knowing your Soul Purpose can do for you:
Give you a sense of passion and direction when you wake up in the morning ...
Make it hard to go to sleep because you're so darn fired up about what you're doing ... Make decisions about how to spend your time more easily ... Find it easier to protect your time by saying 'no' ... Live more authentically ... Go to sleep at night knowing you made your contribution today.[180]

WORKSHEET # 8 – VISION & MISSION PERSONAL WORKSHEET

Creating Space - Set aside some private time to explore the *Vision* and *Mission* tools in the GUIDE, and then use the space on this Worksheet to jot or draw your initial ideas and imaginings about your *Vision* and *Mission* - including the three elements of *Mission*: *Purpose*, *Work(s)*, and *Values*. You may transfer your final ideas to your MASTER GUIDESHEET (WORKSHEET # 7). You may make copies for each Arc.

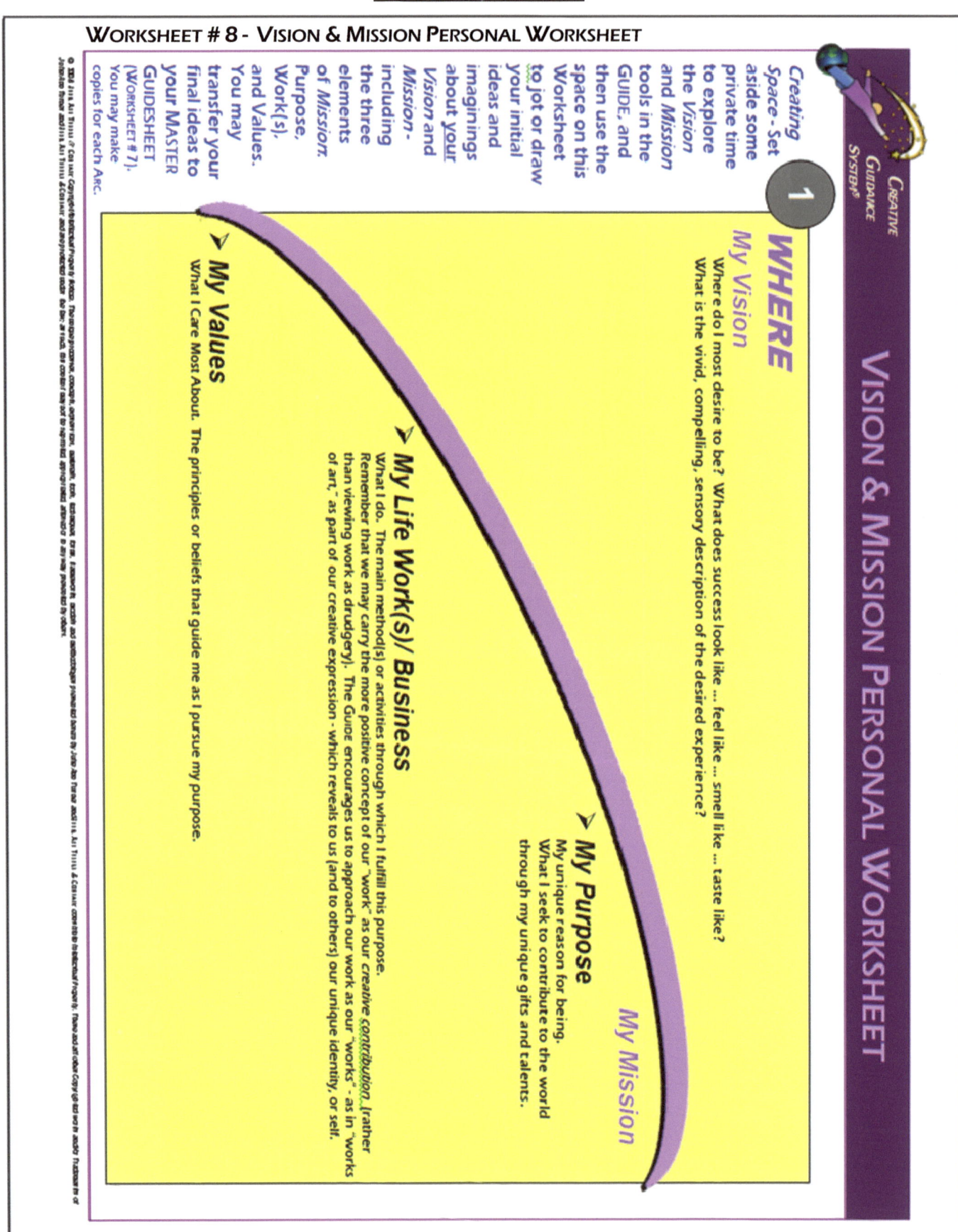

1 WHERE

My Vision
Where do I most desire to be? What does success look like ... feel like ... smell like ... taste like? What is the vivid, compelling, sensory description of the desired experience?

My Life Work(s)/ Business
What I do. The main method(s) or activities through which I fulfill this purpose. Remember that we may carry the more positive concept of our "work" as our creative *contribution*, (rather than viewing work as drudgery). The GUIDE encourages us to approach our work as our "works" - as in "works of art," as part of our creative expression - which reveals to us (and to others) our unique identity, or self.

My Purpose
My unique reason for being. What I seek to contribute to the world through my unique gifts and talents.

My Values
What I Care Most About. The principles or beliefs that guide me as I pursue my purpose.

My Mission

VISION & MISSION PERSONAL WORKSHEET

CREATIVE GUIDANCE SYSTEM

GENESIS of GENIUS

WORKSHEET # 9 - MASTER GOALS WORKSHEET

CREATIVE GUIDANCE SYSTEM® MASTER GOALS WORKSHEET

TOP 3 PERSONAL PASSIONS/INTERESTS (Things I absolutely love to do)

1.
2.
3.

TOP 3 PERSONAL STRENGTHS (Things I do extraordinarily well)

1.
2.
3.

Considerations: May or may not be what you currently do at work... And remember, "do well and love to do" are not necessarily the same... — Interests - arts/culture, technology, sports, entrepreneurship, gardening...

Bonus — MY TOP COMMUNITY PASSION: Issue I Care Most About

1.

Issues - education, healthcare, housing, kids, the elderly, homeless, crime?...

TOP 3-5 PERSONAL "ICEBERGS"/OBSTACLES to achieving goals/dreams

1.
2.
3.

Can be character traits, skills/abilities, talents... Real or perceived...

TOP 3-5 PERSONAL OPPORTUNITIES I could foresee arising in the next 5 years

1.
2.
3.

May (should) include dreams/wishes.

This Worksheet will help you think more creatively about your Where Vision & Mission, as well as provide input for your Now Goals & Obstacles in the next section.

To Claim Your Bonus Books, Free Creative Resources, & Innovation Tools visit GENESISofGENIUSBOOK.COM.

© Julie Ann Turner & Company/CreatorsGuide.com. All Rights Reserved.

CHAPTER EIGHT
CREW CONSCIOUSNESS

*If any one idea about leadership
has inspired organizations for thousands of years,
it's the capacity to hold a shared picture
of the future we seek to create . . .*

*When there is a genuine vision . . .
people excel and learn,
not because they are told to,
but because they want to.*[181]

                    Peter Senge, *The Fifth Discipline*

*The leader is the drum major,
the person who keeps a vision in front of people
and reminds them of what it is that they're about.*

*People are hungry for leadership.
They'll gravitate toward leaders who have a vision . . .
People want to be about good things.*[182]

         Lorraine Monroe, principal of Harlem's Frederick Douglass School

*The most important factor is individual recognition –
more important than salaries, bonuses, or promotions.*

*Most people, whether they're engineers,
business managers, or machine operators, want to be creative.*

*They want to contribute to giving society more comfort, better health,
more excitement. And their greatest reward is receiving acknowledgment
that they did contribute to making something meaningful happen.*[183]

                Paul Cook, CEO, Raychem Corporation

**Reenergizing is more important than restructuring.
People are hungry for meaning, for a chance to create.**[184]

                Gary Hamel, business restructuring author

*People don't do the wrong thing
because they want to do the wrong thing.
They do the wrong thing,
because they're not clear on what the right thing is.*[185]

             Debra Dunn, General Manager, Hewlett-Packard

*Leadership is about change.
It's about taking people from where they are now
to where they need to be.*

*The best way to get people to venture into unknown terrain
is to make it desirable by taking them there in their imaginations.*[186]

                Noel M. Tichy, *The Leadership Engine*

TEAM IDENTITY

We have a mission to create ... .[187]
Howard Bloom, *The Global Brain*

*Collectively, as well as individually, our master mission is to create.
And in the fast-fast, self-organizing, global space in which we now find ourselves, how do we collectively agree on, much less reach, a common destination?
As humans have done throughout time, and as we continue to do at every level, we organize and orient around Identity – around a shared Vision and Mission.*

As *Wikipedia* founder Jimmy Wales says, even in the vastness cyberspace, only one thing is essential for co-creation and collaboration, even on a global or virtual level:

A successful collaboration requires a shared vision. A good example of this is a successful wiki called wowwwiki.com, a wiki about the online computer game "World of Warcraft." There, participants work together successfully because they have a shared vision of the kind of work they are trying to complete: a comprehensive guide to all things World of Warcraft. We see the same pattern over and over: A charitable goal like that of Wikipedia is not necessary. Neutrality is not necessary. But a shared vision is.[188]

Whether we witness the Creative Process at work in the "creative space" of the blogosphere, in collaborations spawning open source software, grassroots campaigns swarming around a political candidate or environmental issue, or crowds co-creating virtual online worlds or products or advertising – always, as Wheatley and Rogers say: "*Identity is the source of organization. Every organization is an identity in motion, moving through the world, trying to make a difference. ... Therefore, the most important work we can do at the beginning of an organizing effort is to engage one another in exploring our Purpose.*" However, as they immediately add: "*Most of our organizing efforts do not begin with such a focus ... Whether we are beginning a relationship, a team a community organizing effort, or a global corporation, we need together to be asking: What are we trying to be? What's possible now? How can the world be different because of us?*"[189]

*Why do we organize – into teams, organizations, communities, societies? To create.
To express identity, to generate abundance, to expand capacity, to create worlds.*

People don't connect with other people to accomplish less. Behind all our organizing is the desire to accomplish, to create something more. In this desire, we mimic the world. Life organizes to discover new varieties, different capacities ... .[190]
Margaret Wheatley and Myron Kellner-Rogers, *A Simpler Way*

Across time and space, we come together - as fragments of a hologram, sharing our diversity, light shining through our unique facets - to tell a new story, to create something greater, to evolve to a higher plane of potential. This CREATIVE GUIDANCE SYSTEM gives us a new, shared framework for "choosing together" – across boundaries – in real time, so that we may co-create more consciously. Collectively, just as individually, we begin with *Vision* and *Mission*.

*In organizations, as in people, identity has many dimensions.
Each illuminates some aspect of who the organization is. Identity includes such dimension as history, values, actions, core beliefs, competencies, principles, purpose, mission. None of these alone tells us who the organization is. Some are statements about who it would like to be. Some are revealing of who it really is.
But together they tell the story of a self and its sojourn in a world it has created ... .*[191]

THE ART & SPIRIT OF BUSINESS

*The highest art form is really business.
It is an extremely creative form,
and can be more creative than all the things
we classically think of as creative.*

*In business, the tools with which you're working
are dynamic: capital and people and markets and ideas.*

*These tools all have lives of their own.
So to take those things and work with them
and reorganize them in new and different ways
turns out to be a very creative process.*[192]

Wayne Van Dyck, founder of Windfarms, Ltd.

The business of business is ideas.

Jerry Hirschberg, president, Nissan Design International, author of *The Creative Priority*

Microsoft's only factory asset is the human imagination.[193]

Fred Moody, journalist for *The New York Times* Magazine

*Being good in business
is the most fascinating kind of art.*[194]

Andy Warhol, artist and businessman

*A wise man has said, "Art is basically the production of order out of chaos,"
and isn't chaos the natural environment for business?*[195]

Michael Ray, author of *Creativity in Business*

When is enough enough?

*Our world already has quite enough guns,
political platitudes, arrogance, disingenuousness,
self-interest, snobbishness, superficiality, war
and the certainty that God is on one side or the other.*

*But it never has enough conscience, tolerance, idealism,
justice, compassion, wisdom, humility, self-sacrifice
for the greater good, integrity, courtesy, poetry, laughter,
and generosity of substance and spirit."*

*I'm saying: Think about your contribution to society. ...
Broaden your idea about what's enough.*

And for God's sake, think about who you are.[196]

John Bogle, Founder of Vanguard Group, Inc. and pioneer of the index mutual fund

*The very best kind of mystics – those who practice what they preach –
can be found in the business world.*

*We are now convinced that the qualities of these remarkable people,
and the principles they live by, will be the guiding force
for the twenty-first-century enterprise. ...*

*Successful corporate leaders of the twenty-first century
will be spiritual leaders. The most successful leaders of today
have already learned this secret. ... an organization
is a collective embodiment of spirit, the sum total of the sprits
of the individuals who work there..*[197]

Gay Hendricks, *The Corporate Mystic: A Guidebook for Visionaries with Their Feet on the Ground*

GENESIS of GENIUS

TEAM TRAJECTORY

Why not spend some time determining what is right for us, and then go after that.[198]

Sir George William Ross, Canadian political leader

As obvious as this suggestion from Sir George William Ross may seem, it is the rare team or organization which actually begins – and sustains – its efforts by consciously creating, and constantly orienting toward, a shared *Vision* and *Mission*. The time spent on determining common *Purpose* is repaid many times over, however, through increased productivity, efficiency and energy – and not to mention with higher achievement levels than would ever otherwise be envisioned or attempted. At the end of this section, we will guide you through this process.

As team members ask and answer questions such as - *What do I contribute? What do we contribute as an organization?* – individuals discover how best they can express their unique talents, in alignment with the contribution of the whole. Not only do these high-level *Vision* and *Mission* questions create a compelling frame for collaborate endeavor and achievement, but, as each individual is allowed to choose and express fully his or her unique contribution, creative energy is free to flow, uncoerced and unforced. As always, it is released through *choice*.

In practice, all systems do insist on exercising their own creativity. They never accept imposed solutions, pre-determined designs, or well-articulated plans that have been generated somewhere else. Too often, we interpret their refusal as resistance. We say that people innately resist change. But the resistance we experience is not to change itself. It is to the particular process of change that believes in imposition rather than creation. It is the resistance of a living system to being treated as a non-living thing. It is an assertion of the system's right to create. It is life insisting on its primary responsibility to create itself.[199]

Margaret Wheatley and Myron Kellner-Rogers, *A Simpler Way*

In this Creative Guidance System, participants choose consciously, at every level of organization.

CREW DYNAMICS

I don't run things. I lead things[200]
Steve Case, Chairman, AOL Time-Warner Media

Grasping the difference between leadership and management is literally mission-critical. As AOL Chairman Steve Case says, it is the difference between *leading* things and *running* - or *managing* - things. As Stephen R. Covey said – referencing both Peter Drucker and Warren Bennis - it is distinquishing that "*Management is doing things right; leadership is doing the right things.*"[201] And, as we have made clear in this GUIDE, it is the difference between *managing* what already exists – WHAT IS – and *leading* beyond that into the creative realm of WHAT CAN BE. While both are important to success, the *sequence* – putting creeation, or leadership, first – is essential. As Covey said:

Leadership is the first [mental] creation. Leadership is not management. Management is the second [physical] creation ... But leadership has to come first. ... Management is a bottom line focus: How can I best accomplish certain things? Leadership deals with the top line: What are the things I want to accomplish? ... Management is efficiency in climbing the ladder of success; leadership determines whether the ladder is leaning against the right wall.[202]

Covey adds: "Efficient management without effective leadership is, as one individual has phrased it, "*like straightening deck chairs on the Titanic.*"[203] As we've seen, however, a leadership *Vision* cannot simply be imposed on the crew from above; if so, the energy to drive and sustain the *Mission* will not be sufficient. NASA researchers, who have conducted extensive studies on crew, or "human systems," dynamics,[204] have found that, for high-level thought and creativity to flow, all members of the crew must assume personal leadership, know the navigational system, and be involved in the Creative Process itself.

Crew dynamics are vital to a mission's success.[205]
Lisa Reed, training team lead at NASA's Johnson Space Center in Houston

As we now know, teams and organizations are living systems – much more like organisms than machines, operating as dynamic, organic, self-organizing systems. In order for a crew or team to generate high performance and innonvation, it must have what NASA's Owen Gadekan calls "*activation energy*" – an "infusion of energy" sufficent to drive particpants to create new products and creative solutions, to "move past restraining forces to high performance."[206] This *activation energy* is only generated through participation in an ongoing orientation toward the shared *Vision*, through consistent, open and honest communication, and through individual choice and unique contribution to the *Mission*. Remember, organization is a verb, not a noun – a process, not an object or a machine. A high-performance crew is always self-organiing around a common *Vision* and *Mission*, always recognizing that visioning and planning are ongoing, dynamic processes. As Peter Senge explains in *The Fifth Discipline*:[207]

The essence of the discipline of shared vision..., lies in bringing individual vision into harmony with a larger vision. If the organization's vision is imposed on local units, it will, at best, result in compliance .... If there is an ongoing "visioning" process, local visions and organizational visions will continually interact with and enrich one another. The combination of mission, vision and values creates the common identity that connects thousands of people within large organizations.

In order to faciliate this dynamic, navigational journey toward *Mission*, the U.S. Army invented a concept called "*Commander's Intent*" (*CI*) – "*a crisp, plain-talk statement ... specifying the plan's goal, the desired end-state of an operation.*" Steve Case uses a similar term – the "strategic endgame" - as the common target of team focus. Rather than being required to follow play-by-play instructions, team members with a *Mission* or *CI* are free to improvise: "*As soon as peope know what the intent is they begin generating their own solutions.*"[208] Creative energy is unleashed. This navigational approach recognizes that in an ever-fluctuating environment, we cannot control or predict the future – "*No plan survives contact with the enemy*" (a strict plan "*risks being rendered obsolete by unpredicatble events*") – but we can *create*. Case's counsel? "*Nobody can predict the future. Place your bets and stick to your vision. ... Hire terrific people, point them generally in the fight direction and let them go.*"

ADAPTATION

'Adaptive leadership' is required to help the organization do what it has never done before.[209]
James Barrowman, Goddard Space Flight Center

A shared image of WHAT CAN BE is the guiding force that enables teams and organizations to evolve to new and higher orders and expanded realms of possibility.

Life, and work, is *process* – "*identity in motion*,"[210] organizing *around shared meaning, higher Purpose, common Mission*. Our lives and our work arise from *autopoiesis,* or "*self-creation* – a "natural poetry" - an ongoing, systems-sustaining *process.*[211,212] All forms, structures and patterns arise from the dance of this ubiquitous *Creative Process*. As Wheatley and Kellner-Rogers point out, "*The organizing tendency of life is always a creative act,*" for, "*beneath all the structures and behaviors [of the system] lies the real creator – dynamic processes.*"

More today than ever before in human history, people across the planet are self-organizing. Tapping into the instant communication that enables them to swarm around issues and ideas, humans are drawing on globally networked intelligence – and are feeling the buzz of their co-creative power.[213]

Time writer Lev Grossman describes the globally networked "organism" now enabled by collaborative technology: "*There's no road map for how an organism that's not a bacterium lives and works together on this planet in numbers in excess of 6 billion.*"[214]

True. There is no road map. But there is a navigational, self-organizing, creative system.

It is called the Creative Process, and if we can rediscover it, if we can learn to apply it consciously, we can self-organize around a common Vision and Mission – in clusters of 3 or 4, or in swarms of thousands, or in global networks of millions or even billions.

Life leaps forward when it can share its learnings. The dense webs of systems allow information to travel in all directions, speeding discovery and adaptation.[215]

Self-organization, at all scales, requires only a shared Vision, a common Purpose - and a Navigational Process. Vision and Mission are the steady stars that the one and the many may navigate by, from across organizations, across the globe, or across virtual space. Time and distance are not barriers. Our only limits are our own imaginations.

The Internet has enabled us to recognize and tap into our collective, creative, self-organizing power as no technology has before. As Kevin Kelly says, self-organizing "hives" now "*detonate hierarchies in favor of organic organizational structures.*"[216] As NASA crew-master James Barrowman says: "*This age of paradox that requires you to do more with less demands paradoxical solutions, for example, the need to serve at the same time as the leader and the follower.*"[217] It is only through creative adaptation that we may navigate this new reality.

Indeed, for 300 years leaders have built their organizations on the seemingly unassailable principles of Newton's mechanics, as if people were the gears of a timepiece. And it worked – until the speed and complexity of modern life began to overwhelm even the grandest control structures, from the Soviet Union to the mainframe computer. The new model for organizations is the biological world, where uncontrolled actions produce stunningly efficient and robust results, all through adaptation and self-organization.[218]
Thomas Petzinger, Jr., *The Wall Street Journal* "Front Lines" column

THE CREATIVE ORGANISM

You may never know what creativity you can forge out of chaos. [219]
Charlie Stegemoeller, Johnson Space Center, *Chaos Is the Fraternal Twin of Creativity*

What happens when we step into self-leadership,
connect on multidimensional levels,
and co-create what we most want?

We discover we are the leaders we've been looking for.

When we do, what does success look like?

We've been trying to create a day-care program at Timberland.
Several years ago, I commissioned outside people to design a program.
They came back with a model that no one wanted.

But at a company rally recently, a woman asked me what I was going to do
about day care. I told her that I was not going to do anything about it.
My kids are getting older, and they don't need day care. The place went silent.
But then I said that if she needs day care and if it's relevant for the company,
then she should let me know what she wants to do about it. So what did she do?

She organized a group that polled other employees, researched the cost of a day-care program,
and identified where the funding would come from. Then she held a meeting to present the
group's case to me.

When I asked her why she had invited me to the meeting, she said, "To applaud."

That meeting was spectacular! The group still has some issues to work out before the program
is implemented, but the way the group tackled the problem was amazing.

All I did was to move out of the way. [220]
Jeffrey B. Swartz, President/CEO Timberland Company, *Fast Company*, "The Art of Smart"

No school can teach you how to do business in today's world.
Instead, companies have to rely on their own internal-learning practices to succeed.
Everyone is capable of reinventing themselves and their businesses. And the one thing that
people really want to be assured of is that it's all right to spend time thinking crazy thoughts –
and that those thoughts will be taken seriously by their companies.
Create this environment, and watch where imagination can lead you. ...
Basically, if you give people the space and the support to learn and to change, they will. [221]
Eric Hippeau, Chairman and CEO, Ziff-Davis Inc, *Fast Company*, "The Art of Smart"

Today, if you're going to have a successful company, you have to recognize
that no leader is going to have all the answers. The leader may have a vision.
But the actual solutions about how best to meet the challenges of the moment
have to be made by the people closest to the action — the people at the coal face.
The leader has to find a way to empower these frontline people, to challenge them,
to provide them with the resources they need, and then to hold them accountable. [222]
Richard Pascale, Fellow at Oxford University

Strategic planning is considered futile at Cardinal Environmental Inc. of Oklahoma City,
which instead relies on its 12 employees to act on ever-changing customer clues.

'We function like an amoeba that flows with the environment
and constantly reshapes its body,' says owner Steve Mason.
Steve Mason, quoted by Thomas Petzinger, Jr., *The Wall Street Journal*

TEAM VISION

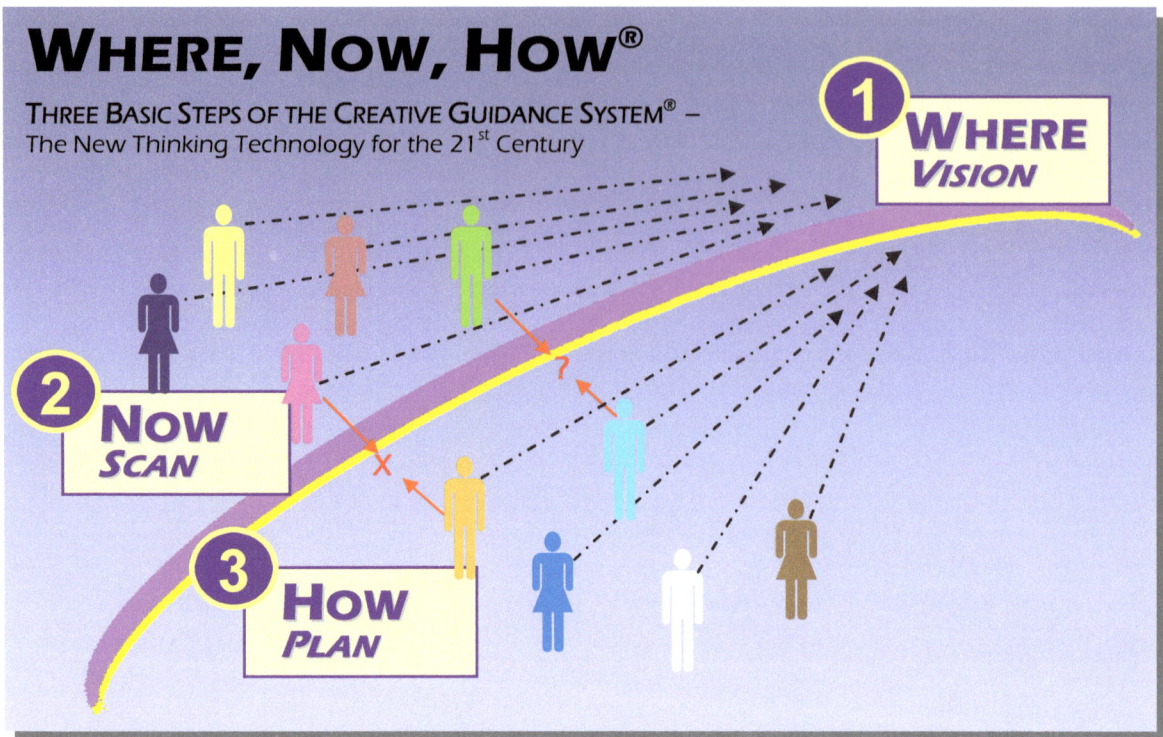

Vision and Mission are the higher guiding stars that enable diverse individuals to come together across boundaries. Vision and Mission encompass lasting, shared values - they represent the highest potential in our selves and in our organizations.

Because *Vision* and *Mission* focus our attention, imagination and energy on a higher plane – we are able to look past silos (organizational divisions, departments, and functions) and come together, bringing talent and perspective from across spheres of influence.

Remember, groups, like individuals, are multidimensional.[223] Each participant brings a wealth of experience, knowledge, imagination – a different lens through which each may view the space ahead, while together bringing broad talents and gifts to contribute to the whole.

It is in this MINDSHIFT to a higher plane of potential that true creative power is revealed. Why? When we agree on a higher shared *Vision* and *Mission* – when we agree on WHERE we're going (see above) – it is no longer necessary for every person or team to agree on How we get there. In fact, the beauty of the Creative Process – revealed in the sequence of this CREATIVE GUIDANCE SYSTEM - is that we need no longer collapse our diverse, innovative ideas about How to reach our goals into mere compromise (see following page). In fact, as long as we agree on WHERE we are going, our diverse efforts - working in parallel - will often propel us to our goals faster than any single, unified (compromised or coerced) effort would. Moreover, as a whole, our learning process is accelerated, and across the whole, individual and team energy continues to flow, in alignment with these higher goals. Creativity is not stifled, but unleashed. All are able to choose consciously at each level where they may best contribute.

As we self-organize around higher Vision, we navigate toward that common star. By adopting this new way of thinking, we shift from artificial control to authentic creation.

BEYOND COMPROMISE

*Thinking creates the structures that create an organization's behavior.
Learn how to rethink, and you start to change.*[224]
— Chris Turner, Xerox Business Services "Learning Person" and author

If we create Vision and Mission first, all potential solutions remain open to us.

Yet, as we've seen, in our typical thinking processes we each focus on sharing our own views on the "problem" or issue at hand – asking "*What's going wrong?*" - each trying to get others to see the problem our way – but rarely, if ever, stopping to ask "What do we really want to have happen?" – and other questions that would shift us to the higher, creative plane of thought.

All too often, we focus at the "problem" level, so caught up in debating how to "fix the problem" that any consideration of *what we might create together* never even enters the conversation. At this point, we have already limited any potential solution to our different views of how to solve "the problem." With our energy tied up in debating which solution to choose, we often never rise above the level of *conflict*. We remain stuck at ground level, often unable to reach any agreement at all. Unfortunately, at this "problem" level, the highest solution we may hope for is *compromise* – a forced choice which generally results in a weaker solution overall, and which almost inevitably reduces energy behind the "solution."

*The world we have made
as a result of the level of thinking
we have done thus far
creates problems we cannot solve
at the same level we created them.*
— Albert Einstein, theoretical physicist

*When society requires to be rebuilt,
there is no use in attempting to rebuild it
on the old plan.
No great improvements in the lot of mankind
are possible, until a great change takes place
in the fundamental constitution
of their modes of thought.*
— John Stuart Mill, British philosopher and economist

HIGHEST POWER: CREATION
LESSER POWER: COMPROMISE
LEAST POWER: CONFLICT

Consider instead the power of first choosing together a shared, compelling *Vision* and a *Mission* that encompasses purpose and value for all involved. This thinking process shifts potential to the highest level. We need no longer lose the power that lies in our diversity, or force a compromise in which no one is fully engaged. By choosing first at the level of WHERE – the level of *Vision* and *Mission* – this CREATIVE GUIDANCE SYSTEM enables choice within this higher framework. Energy continues to flow, creative ideas continue to be generated. Moreover, within this framework, all are able to see where others are in the process, communicate more clearly, allowing new participants to join in at any stage, where they can best contribute. In other words, we are better able to think, communicate and navigate together in real time. A critical point: It is not that synergy across different approaches to on "HOW we get there" are not important, but such strategic alignment is only enabled from a higher-level view. In fact, *Vision* and *Mission* make it much more possible for us to identify and pursue strategies and solutions that are synergistic, addressing more than one goal at the same time.

Every man takes the limits of his field of vision for the limits of the world.[225]
— Arthur Schopenhauer, German philosopher

ORIENTING TO PURPOSE

*To make a contribution to the world
by making tools for the mind that advance humankind.*[226]
Original Apple Inc. Vision Statement

While a *Vision* statement express how the world is different because of our contribution, *Mission* statements tell the world how and why we seek to fulfill this high vision. Sometimes these elements – *Vision, Mission, Purpose, Work* and *Values* – are combined in various ways, and in some cases, statements may be "hybrid" *Vision* and *Mission* statements. What is most essential is - whatever Vision and Mission statement an individual or organization creates –
   that all of these key elements are included (typically, values are the most often overlooked).

① WHERE
VISION
Vision
Mission
▶ Purpose
▶ Work(s)
▶ Values

For example, the original Apple Inc. statement above is somewhat a "hybrid" statement, in that it expresses high-level *Vision* elements such as "advancing humankind," and could be restated (in present tense) as a more "pure" *Vision* statement as follows: "*We make tools for the mind that advance humankind.*" It is the opening phrase "*To make a contribution to the world*" (or any phrase starting with "To + (verb)" that signals a *Mission* or *Purpose* statement). The *Purpose*, as stated above, is "*to make a contribution to the world*," and the "*work(s)*" are expressed "*by making tools for the mind.*" *Values* are also expressed in this statement, though somewhat indirectly, as it is clear that "advancing humankind" is valued (as well, arguably, is "*making a contribution to the world.*").[227] Weaving these elements together creates a powerful, guiding "*purpose story,*" what Peter Senge describes as a "*larger 'pattern of becoming' that gives unique meaning*" to both "*personal aspirations and highest hopes for the organization.*"[228]

Whole Foods Market states its *Vision* as "*Our children and grandchildren will be living in a world that values human creativity, diversity, and individual choice by changing the way we think about the relationships between our food supply, the environment, and our bodies.*"[229] This statement clearly expresses how the world is different (though Whole Food's states this in future tense, using "*will be*") because of the organization's contribution. Whole Foods lists Core *Values* and *Mission* elements separately, and also uses a "motto" which concisely combines all elements: "*Whole Foods, Whole People, Whole Planet.*" Note that the company specifically states that "*our vision reaches far beyond just being a food retailer.*"

It is most essential that Vision and Mission be high-level and inherently compelling.

As architect Daniel H. Burnham said, "*Make no little plans; they have no magic to stir men's blood and probably themselves will not be realized.*" He advised: "*Make big plans; aim high in hope and work, remembering that a noble, logical diagram once recorded will never die, but long after we are gone will be a living thing, asserting itself with ever-growing insistency.*"[230] This is why, as Senge says, "*the first leadership design task concerns developing vision, values, and purpose or mission.*"[231] As Jeffrey Liker relates, these elements distinguish greatness.

Throughout my visits to Toyota in Japan and the United States…. every person I have talked with has a sense of purpose greater than earning a paycheck. They feel a greater sense of mission … and can distinguish right from wrong with regard to that mission. … the message is consistent: Do the right thing for the company, its employees, the customer, and society as a whole. Toyota's strong sense of mission and commitment … is the foundation for all other principles and the missing ingredient in most companies trying to emulate Toyota.[232]

GLOBAL THOUGHT LEADERS

Change the way you think, and you are halfway to changing the world.[233]
Theodore Zeldin, Oxford historian & author

Clearly, we need new ways of talking and thinking together, in order to reach our collective potential – in order to consciously create the world we wish to see.

Our old ways of talking and thinking together are centered around **WHAT IS** – analyzing, arguing and debating different views on *what already exists*, or about *what is already past*.
Yet, as we've seen (MINDSHIFT, p. 176+ and Problem-Solving, p. 262+), our old ways of thinking are no longer sufficient to navigate and succeed in the dynamic WorldSpace in which we now find ourselves. We need a shift of mind – from knowledge to imagination, from analysis to co-creation, from WHAT IS to WHAT CAN BE – if we are to shape the future of our lives, our work and our world.

In this new WorldSpace, we must all become "global thought leaders."
We must all gain the capacity, not only to engage diverse individuals in dialogue to gain a 360-degree "global" view of WHAT IS, but to guide them – through their imaginations, through the Creative Process – to envision the highest potentials of WHAT CAN BE.

As Deborah Flick says, we live in a "debate culture," an "argument culture" – in which we seek foremost to win our points and prove others wrong.[234] This way of thinking and talking is so ingrained in us, and especially in the Western mindset, that we hardly recognize this approach immediately limits the potential and creativity that only emerges from other points of view. In our rush to force people to our own way of thinking, our debate mode of thought cuts us off from the co-creative power of the collective. We must rediscover authentic tools of talking and thinking together – shifting from *debate* to *dialogue*, and from *analysis* to *visioning*. As physicist David Bohm notes, *"Dialogue comes from the Greek word 'dialogos' ~ 'Logos' means 'the word,' or in our case, we would think of 'the meaning of the word.' And 'dia' means 'through' - it doesn't mean 'two.' A dialogue can be among any number of people, not just two ... ."* Bohm emphasizes that *dialogue creates the initial ground for co-creation*:

> *The picture or image that this suggests is a stream of meaning flowing among and through us and between us. This will make possible a flow of meaning in the whole group, out of which may emerge some new understanding. It's something new, which may not have been in the starting point at all. It's something creative. And this shared meaning is the 'glue' or 'cement' that holds people and societies together.*[235]

To co-create our future, individually and collectively – we must shift to a higher plane of thought.

Dialogue
- Inclusivity
- Equality
- Listening to Understand
- Non-judgment
- Examining Assumptions
- Reveals Potential for Shared Action

Debate
- Exclusivity
- Winners & Losers
- Seeks to Prove Point, Argument
- Criticizes Other Points of View
- Defends Assumptions as Truth
- Forces Conclusion or Decision

Strengths
Conversation and dialogue are the heart of our creative process.
Margaret Wheatley

CULTURE OF INNOVATION

Every organization – not just business – needs one core competence – innovation.[236]
Peter Drucker, *Management Challenges for the 21st Century*

Whether in the realm of community or business …. *creating change* is an imperative.
We can no longer wait – and expect to have time to respond to change.
Before us extends new space swirling with complexity, speed, competition, globalization.

Can we afford … the time … the resources … the risk … to be innovative?

Innovation will be the dominant value proposition for the next century.[237]
Trevor Davis, PricewaterhouseCoopers, 1999 PricewaterhouseCoopers Innovation Study

In truth, we can no longer afford not to be creative.
Creativity is the one capacity that holds its value, while everything information-based becomes more a commodity. The free flow of information – across global networks – has shifted the fundamental dynamics. The only competitive advantage is creativity.

Let's be clear: Creativity and innovation are not simply one more "program" added to our work.

Creativity is the process by which we do our work.

Creativity and innovation are *the way* … *the way* we become more strategic and more competitive … *the way* we do more in less time … *the way* we stretch and multiply resources.

Creativity is the ground of innovation; we must build it into the culture.
A plan is not enough; we must have a creative guidance system.

Innovation is as much a mindset as it is a set of principles, practices, skills, tools and techniques. It is a belief in the future; conviction that things can always be better; confidence in the positive force of new ideas; faith the power of people working toward a common objective; trust in the imagination, ingenuity, intuitions and instincts - as much as rational thought, evaluation and measurement.[238]
Joyce Wycoff & Ruth Hattori, *Innovation Training*

As innovation expert Joyce Wycoff appropriately emphasizes: "*Innovation is a mindset, a collective willingness and ability to deconstruct what is in order to construct what could be.*" Creativity and innovation require a culture in which to thrive – a participatory culture that emerges from the creative expressions and contributions of all involved – dynamically self-organizing around common *Vision* and *Mission*. *InformationWeek* editor Bob Evans contends that culture is a critical component in innovative organizations, those which have "*the courage to foster [a culture] that treasures risk-taking, unconventional thinking, new approaches … .*"[239]

What ties this all together is one simple, incredibly powerful idea: Innovation.
More than financial muscle, unmatched physical presence, or clever advertising and highly caffeinated salespeople, companies of all stripes are striving for and battling to master the power to innovate: to move quickly to new opportunities; to know almost innately what customers will want in six or 12 months; to feel the ground preparing to shift so they can reposition before it does; to understand and be comfortable with new forms of partnership, competition and success; to slash development cycles; to foster a culture that promotes risk-taking, customer intimacy, and operational brilliance.[240]

A CAUTIONARY TALE

We trained hard but it seemed that every time we were beginning to form up into teams we were reorganized. I was to learn later in life that we tend to meet any new situation by reorganizing, and what a wonderful method it can be for creating the illusion of progress while actually producing confusion, inefficiency, and demoralization.
  Petronius Arbiter, Roman writer, circa 27–66 A.D.

Lest we are tempted to kid ourselves that tweaking our approach here, and replacing an individual over there, will transform our teams and organizations into an "innovation machine," we should consider ourselves duly warned, as leaders throughout the ages have made this inevitably fatal mistake.

Creating a culture of innovation requires an entirely new mindset – a new way of thinking.

Organization as a process, organization as a self-organizing system, organization around shared meaning and purpose. In an innovation culture, we realize we're all part of a symbiotic, self-creative Whole.[241]

Yet, from ancient times to today, we repeat the same elemental errors: controlling the system as a "machine," treating people as "parts," and undervaluing process in favor of "products." Though ancient Romans may have called it "reorganizing," in the 1990s corporations called it "re-engineering," and though it recurs in different forms, as it did during the "dot.com crash," the timeless truth is that any "fad or fix" that disrespects people, their connectedness, and their creative potential, is doomed to fail.[242] *The fundamental error is that of* cycling back *– to analyze, categorize and control people and systems – instead of* shifting up *- to an altogether higher plane of innovative thinking.*[243] Meg Wheatley cautions us:

We can't predict the system by looking at the individuals. Yet we spend long hours analyzing ourselves as individual parts. From quick magazine quizzes to elaborate assessment procedures, we've become a culture fascinated with knowing our selves. We want to know our style: our learning styles, our leadership styles, our communication styles. Many organizations use multiple assessment tools to categorize people. From such information, managers can assemble dream teams by recipe. Two of this, three of that, perhaps one renegade or intuitive to spice things up. We reassure one another that if we combine diverse styles in just the right proportions, we can cook up high-performing teams. We don't engage in all this assessment because we are curious about the many ways people engage with life. We analyze people because we want to control them. We need to predict what will happen. ... We fill out a form, learn our scores, and pretend that we know how life will unfold. When we realize that the world creates newness in every relationship, we can only laugh at these studied attempts to control.
We can't predict at all how we or others will perform together. We can't know ourselves in isolation. Life seeks systems. Systems are full of surprises. Life is unpredictable. So are we.[244]

Some of these efforts are primarily well-intentioned – and, arguably, demonstrating to team members that each brings unique strengths and various learning and communication styles is, in itself, valuable. Too often, though, this focus on testing and analysis may ultimately reinforce fragmentation, rather than enabling dynamic flexibility, adaptation and personal growth.[245] *It fails to shift teams to full potential through a creative, system mindset.* After all, as Richard Florida notes, the value of "*creative capital*" within an organization "*isn't just embedded in individuals' heads; it also exists in the relationships between people,*"[246] which cross multidimensional boundaries of time and space, issues and interest, race and class.[247] Even more than the *connections*, it is the *potential for creation and co-creation* that is transformational.

Our connectedness matters.[248] *When we fragment the system, we lose information about the Whole; we reduce diversity and collective intelligence. We can't downsize our way to innovation.*[249]

You can't shrink your way to greatness.[250]
  Arthur Martinez, former Chairman of the Board, President and Chief Executive Officer of Sears, Roebuck and Co.

The Creative Process shifts us beyond separateness, so we may reach full potential and higher Purpose.

COMMITMENT

How do we give away the issue of leadership to everyone?
How do we celebrate the importance of every person in organizations
having a part to add to the greater whole? [251]
  Ron Patrick, Director/Mentor ESD, *Dialogue: Rediscovering the Transforming Power of Conversation*

In order for us to shift together to a higher - more imaginative - plane of thought ...
to reach our individual and collective potential within the whole ...
we first must choose to do so. As always, "Choice is the mechanism of creation."

What does it take for diverse individuals to *choose* to contribute their full energy, talent and creative genius behind a shared *Purpose*? It takes the power of the Creative Process – a new way of thinking – which begins with engaging all in generating *Vision* and *Mission*.

Even more important than what Vision is ... is what Vision does.

Only by engaging our multidimensional, multitalented teams in determining "WHERE we are going, "will we access the diverse perspectives necessary to successfully co-create our future, and form innovative, dynamic teams savvy enough to navigate change to reach our higher goals. We can no longer coerce or force individuals to commit. Each must choose to do so. Moreover, we cannot co-create together unless there is first trust and respect.

Trust breeds innovation, and communication breeds trust. [252]
  Martha Heller, CIO Director Best Practice Exchange

As Linda Ellinor and Glenna Gerard explain: "*Trust is built by taking the time to deeply listen to one another and to get to know one another. This is the secret of high-performance teams, whether they be related to sports, music, or work.*" Trust is what turns a handful of scattered individuals into a powerful, dynamic crew, capable of creative breakthroughs and innovation that literally open new realms of possibility. Ellinor and Gerard pinpoint the role of dialogue in building trust and commitment, and in unleashing creative power: "*The larger core dilemmas of our times – such as alienation in the workplace, integration of diversity, running from one crisis to another, or making sense of increasing levels of complexity – can no longer be addressed piecemeal and only at the individual level. These seemingly intractable organizational problems can only be chipped away if seen through the lens of a system as a whole entity. Dialogue is by its nature such a lens.*" [253] Only choice and commitment allow full creative power to flow.

Until one is committed, there is hesitancy, the chance to draw back,
always ineffectiveness. Concerning all acts of initiative and creation
there is one elementary truth, the ignorance of which kills countless ideas
and splendid plans: that the moment one definitely commits oneself,
Providence moves too. All sorts of things occur to help one that would never otherwise
have occurred. A whole stream of events issues from the decision, raising in one's favor
all manner of unforeseen incidents and meetings and
material assistance, which no man could have dreamed would have come his way.
I have learned a deep respect for one of [Johann Wolfgang Von] Goethe's couplets:

  'Whatever you do, or dream you can, begin it.
  Boldness has genius, power and magic in it. [254]
    W.H. Murray, Scottish Himalayan Expedition

BOLDNESS FOR THE JOURNEY

*When you are inspired by some great purpose,
some extraordinary project, all your thoughts break their bounds:
Your mind transcends limitations,
your consciousness expands in every direction
and you find yourself in a new, great and wonderful world.
Dormant forces, faculties and talents become alive,
and you discover yourself to be a greater person by far
than you ever dreamed yourself to be..*[255]

Patanjali, Yoga Master

Be bold, and mighty forces will come to your aid.[256]

Basil King, Canadian cleric and author

*I am in search of the simple elegant seductive maybe even obvious IDEA.
With this in my pocket, I cannot fail.*[257]

Tibor Kalman, *Wired* Magazine

*The power to create is a discipline.
Imagination is a task that requires dedicated and intentional effort.
Creative genius is not serendipity, chance or raw talent.
Creativity requires discipline.
And that discipline will take on new importance
in this ever-changing business environment.*[258]

Annette Moser-Wellman, President, Firemark, Inc.

*Thinking is the hardest work that there is,
which is the probable reason why so few people engage in it.*[259]

Henry Ford, founder of The Ford Motor Company

*Nothing in this world can take the place of persistence.
Talent will not; nothing is more common than unsuccessful men with talent.
Genius will not; unrewarded genius is almost a proverb.
Education will not; the world is full of educated derelicts.
Persistence and determination alone are omnipotent.
The slogan "Press On" has solved and always will
solve the problems of the human race.*

Calvin Coolidge., 30th President of the United States

*If people knew how hard I worked to get my mastery,
it wouldn't seem so wonderful after all.*[260]

Michelangelo, Renaissance painter and sculptor

*Real creativity has nothing at all to do with casual days.
The absence of discipline and standards doesn't drive creativity. In fact, it's almost the opposite.*

Robert Lutz, CEO of Exide and Former Vice-Chairman and President of Chrysler

*The mastery of integrity comes down to three things: Being authentic with yourself,
being authentic with others, and doing the things you have said you would do.*[261]

Gay Hendricks, *The Corporate Mystic: A Guidebook for Visionaries with Their Feet on the Ground*

*Integrity creates a force field of aliveness, energy, and creativity around you.
An integrity breach clouds the field around you, making creativity impossible.
Lack of integrity leaches energy from you, your colleagues, and the company.*[262]

Gay Hendricks and Kate Ludeman, *The Corporate Mystic*

GENESIS of GENIUS

MASTERING POWER ARC™/ CREATIVE GUIDANCE SYSTEM®

TEAM IDENTITY & MISSION

COLLECTIVE BRAND – Mastering the POWER ARC™:
The Creative Process moves us past separateness - so that we may align toward higher, shared Purpose. We need a way to cross the artificial boundaries in organizations - a bridge to collaboration and information exchange, so that we may tap into the full energy and collective imagination of the Team. Then we begin to see the power of co-creation.

> *I'm struck by how those who built enduring, great companies were driven first and foremost by an inner creative urge. They would have continued to challenge themselves and push forward even if they didn't have to. That is not only why they reached the top, but also why they stayed there so long.*[263]
> — Jim Collins, author of *Built to Last*

After all is said and done, after all the management studies and business books announce how and why some teams and companies excel and others don't, even the gurus circle back to acknowledge that sustainable success is *"driven first and foremost by an inner creative urge."* The essential driver for ongoing excellence in a competitive, turbulent marketspace is unceasing creativity and innovation - not downsizing, rightsizing, or quality initiatives, which, alone, will fail.

"You can't shrink your way to greatness," Tom Peters, *Circle of Innovation* author, observes. **"Think Different,"** Apple Inc., product design leader and innovator, chimes in.

Creativity in business is not just about techniques - it is about creative minds, and an innovation mindset that opens up potentials and frees the mind from limits. A creative perspective is one of abundance, not scarcity. When we focus on problems, or only on what already exists, our scope of potential is immediately limited; any team is confined to working within same limited scope.

When we focus on creation, our possibilities are unlimited; we can create more "pie", rather than merely further subdividing the existing one. Innovative teams and companies do this when they create - not only new products and services - but altogether new categories of products.

> *Clear Vision: Notice that before anything else you selected a target..*
> — Mark Joyner, author of *Simple-ology*

The good news is that the creative energy and genius already exists, inside and outside any team or company. It is *Vision* and *Mission* that direct this elemental and sustaining power.

> *When people are united with their real power -*
> *the power to create what they want to create -*
> *they always choose what is highest in humanity.*
> *They choose good health, exceptional relationships, and love,*
> *and relevant life purpose, and peace and challenges worthy of the human spirit.*
> — Robert Fritz, author of *The Path of Least Resistance*

Here, you will find tools and resources for Teams and Organizations exploring their Mission and Identity (closely associated with "Brand"). In addition, the GUIDE provides a valuable Creative Endeavor Pre-Survey Template teams my use to gain initial input for Vision and Mission (as well as get a jump-start on SWOT Analysis in the next Now Section), and Team/Organization Master ARC Examples, Worksheet and Team Summary Guidesheet.

11 TOOLS FOR EXPLORING MISSION & IDENTITY

We have emphasized the importance of determining *Vision* and *Mission*, as the first, cornerstone step for any team or organization - as they establish the core *Identity* and essential platform which must be in place *before* effective company, product or service goals and strategies, as well as positioning, messaging and communications may be developed.

Even more important than what *Vision* and *Mission are*, however, is what *Vision* and *Mission do* - and, though it is far too often overlooked, it is critical to engage the team or organization - as much as is possible - in creating these central, guiding statements of shared potential and purpose. Since these are the people who will be living and communicating the *Vision*, and implement the strategies to deliver on the *Mission*, they must be involved in helping *create* them. Organizations should not be surprised to find that *Visions*, *Missions*, and *Goals* devised only by a small, elite group of executives, and then dictated to everyone else, who have had no prior involvement or input into the process, almost always fail to generate the commitment and success executives wish to see.

As the GUIDE has demonstrated, the key here, as *with any creative endeavor*, is to involve all participants to the greatest extent possible throughout the process - thus initiating authentic *co-creation* from the start. At the very least, organizations may involve participants by asking for their input from the outset of a creative endeavor, through the use of a pre-project Survey.

TEAM/ORGANIZATIONAL VISION & MISSION ENGAGEMENT

- **GENESIS OF GENIUS Pre-Survey for Creative Endeavors (Strategic Planning, Team Projects, etc.)**
  On the next page, we will provide an excellent starting-point Pre-Survey, a simple but powerful tool that not only engages all participants and communicates to them they are to be active players in this creative endeavor, but also garners authentic input for Vision, Mission, and for other essential stages (Now and How) of the Creative Process we will introduce in the next sections of the GUIDE.

TEAM/ORGANIZATIONAL MISSION CREATION & BRANDING RESOURCES

- **The Mission Primer: Four Steps to an Effective Mission Statement**
  Richard D. O'Hallaron and David Richard O'Hallaron, Mission Incorporated - 2000

- **The Mission Statement Book: 301 Corporate Mission Statements form America's Top Companies**
  Jeffrey Abrahams, Ten Speed Press - 2004

- **Beyond the Mission Statement: Why Cause-Based Communications Lead to True Success**
  Jim Armstrong, Paramount Market Publishing - 2006

- **The Mission-Driven Organization : From Mission Statement to a Thriving Enterprise, Here's Your Blueprint for Building an Inspired, Cohesive, Customer-Oriented Team**
  Bob Wall, Mark Sobol and Robert Solum, Prima Lifestyles - 1999

- **Say It and Live It: The 50 Corporate Mission Statements That Hit the Mark**
  Patricia Jones and Larry Kahaner, Crown Business - 1995

- **The Fieldstone Alliance Guide to Crafting Effective Mission and Vision Statements**
  Emil Angelica, Fielldstone Alliance - 2001

TEAM/ORGANIZATIONAL CORE IDENTITY & BRANDING CLASSICS

- **The Experience Economy: Work Is Theater & Every Business a Stage**
  B. Joseph Pine II and James H. Gilmore, Harvard Business School Press, Updated Edition - 2011

- **Identity is Destiny: Leadership and the Roots of Value Creation**
  Laurence D Ackerman, Berrett-Koehler Publishers - 2000

- **Marketing Aesthetics: The Strategic Management of Brands, Identity and Image**
  Alex Simonson and Bernd H. Schmitt, Free Press - 2009

- **Positioning: The Battle for Your Mind**
  Al Ries and Jack Trout, Mass Paperback - 1993

The SPIRAL symbol signifies **GENESISOFGENIUS.COM RESOURCES** *- tried-and-true, tested resources and tools, which we recommend through the* GENESISOFGENIUS.COM *web site.*

SURVEY # 10 - CREATIVE ENDEAVOR PRE-SURVEY TEMPLATE

CREATIVE ENDEAVOR PRE-SURVEY TEMPLATE

As we begin the 2____ _____, we would like to spark your thinking and stir your
            YEAR   NAME OF CREATIVE ENDEAVOR
creative juices in preparation for this team planning effort. Please briefly answer the following questions, and
_____ (do not write your name on the survey).
INSTRUCTIONS FOR WHEN/HOW TO RETURN SURVEY

1. I would say our organization's most important accomplishment(s) in the past year was/were
   _____.
   because _____

2. I believe the one (1) thing that would make the biggest difference in increasing the value
   our organization brings to our clients/customers would be _____
   _____

3. My highest hope for our organization is _____
   _____
   _____

4. If I could recommend one (1) thing to improve our organization, it would be _____
   _____
   _____

5. The one (1) aspect of our service I think our organization should consider growing or
   cultivating would be: _____
   _____

6. I believe the three (3) most important issues facing our organization in 2____ will be _____
   _____
   _____

7. I think the two (2) most significant challenges our organization faces in the next 12 months are____
   _____
   _____

8. One (1) new service/product I think our organization should consider offering would be_____
   _____
   _____

9. I think the two (2) most significant opportunities our organization faces over the next year are ____
   _____
   _____

10. I believe our client's/customers' overall impression regarding our services and products would be ___
    _____
    _____

KEY FOR USING SURVEY INPUT FOR VISION/MISSION> Qs 1, 3, 5 AND SWOT ANALYSIS> Qs 10 (STRENGTHS), 4 (WEAKNESS), Qs 2, 5, 8, 9 (OPPORTUNITIES), 7 (THREATS)

EXAMPLE # 11 - TEAM ARC TITLE EXAMPLES

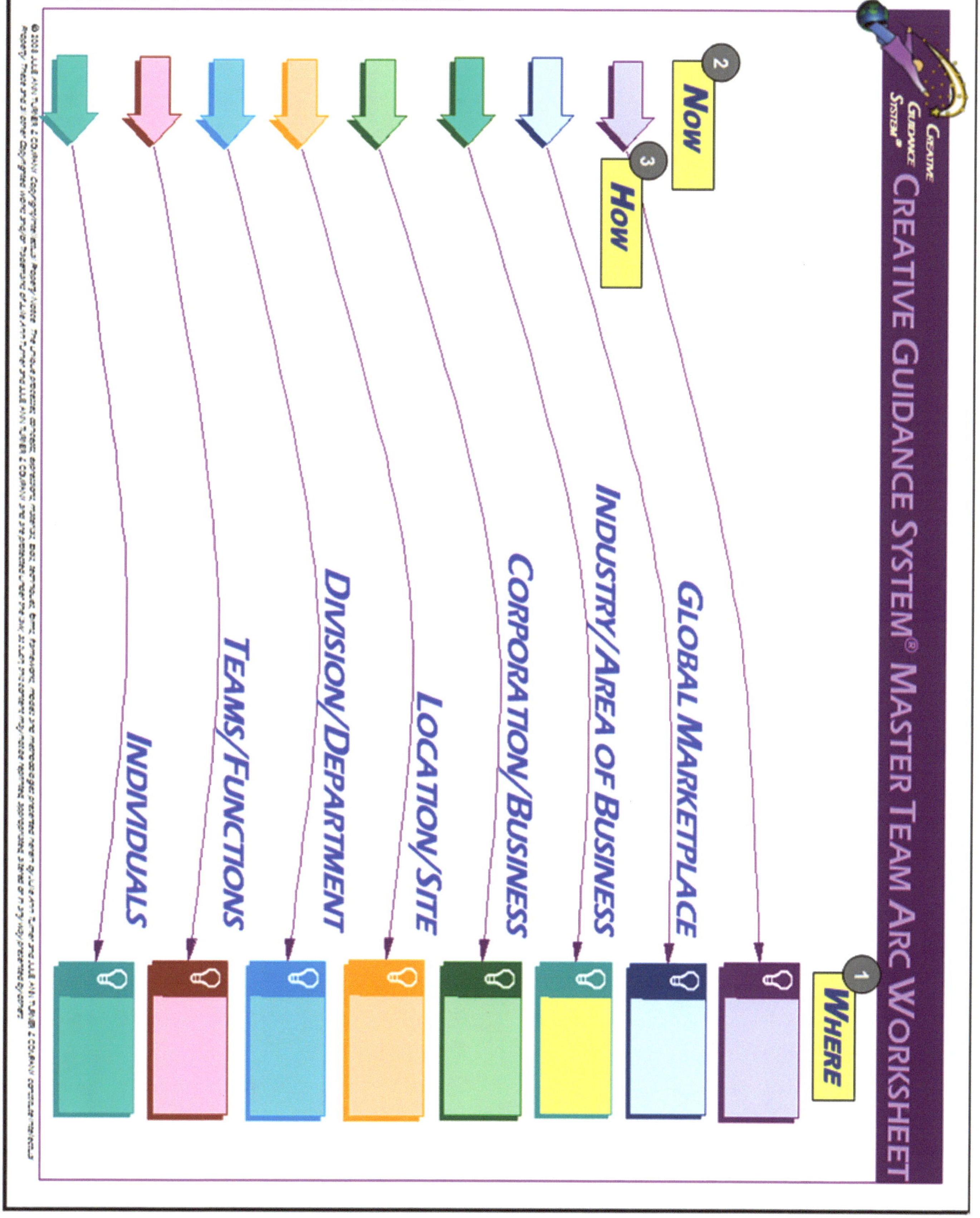

Creative Guidance System® Master Team Arc Worksheet

- INDIVIDUALS
- TEAMS/FUNCTIONS
- DIVISION/DEPARTMENT
- LOCATION/SITE
- CORPORATION/BUSINESS
- INDUSTRY/AREA OF BUSINESS
- GLOBAL MARKETPLACE

1. Where
2. Now
3. How

WORKSHEET # 12 - TEAM ARC WORKSHEET

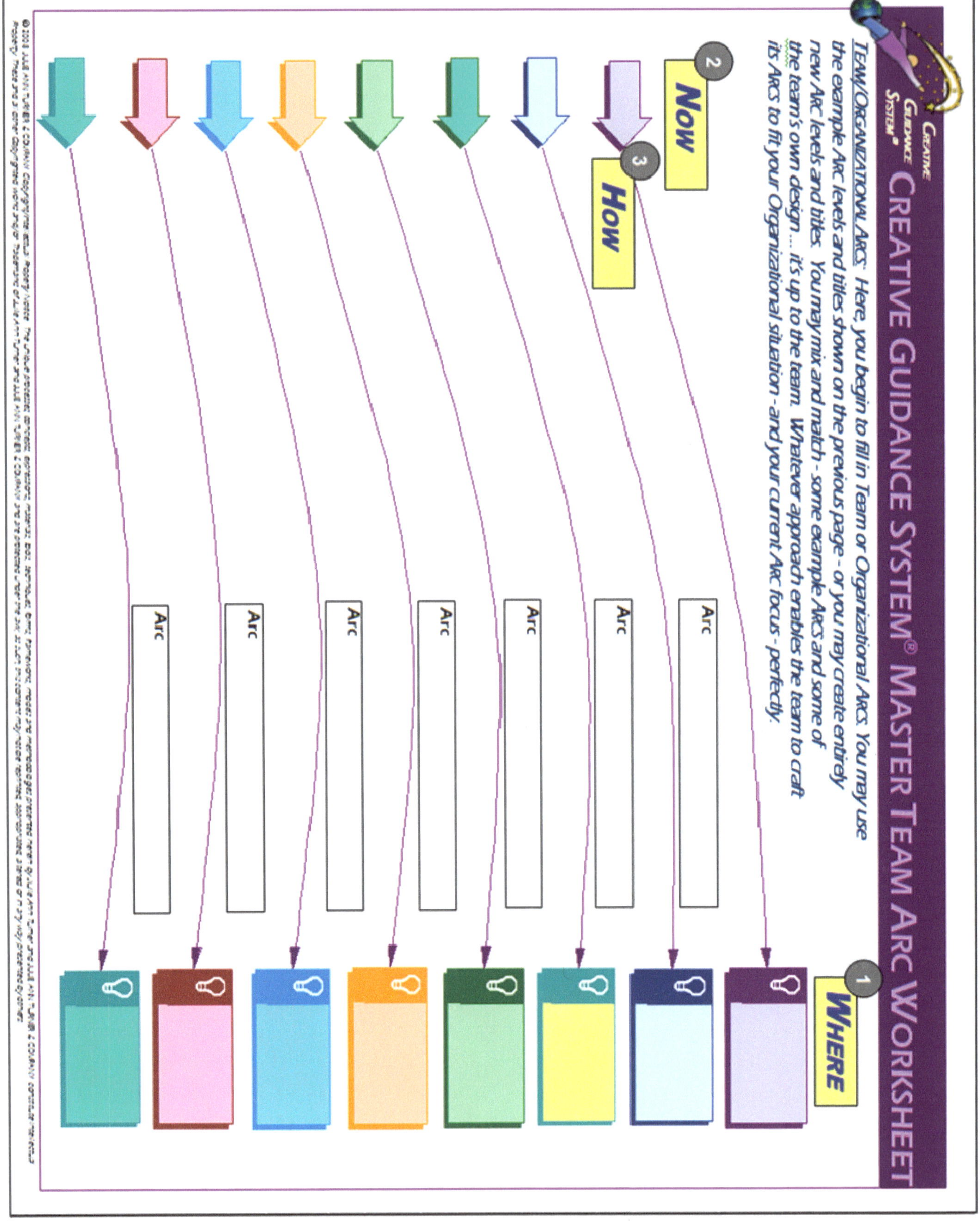

CREATIVE GUIDANCE SYSTEM® MASTER TEAM ARC WORKSHEET

TEAM/ORGANIZATIONAL ARCS: Here, you begin to fill in Team or Organizational ARCS. You may use the example Arc levels and titles shown on the previous page - or you may create entirely new Arc levels and titles. You may mix and match - some example ARCS and some of the team's own design.... it's up to the team. Whatever approach enables the team to craft its Arc to fit your Organizational situation - and your current Arc focus - perfectly.

2 Now

3 How

1 Where

Arc / Arc / Arc / Arc / Arc / Arc / Arc / Arc

To Claim Your Bonus Books, Free Creative Resources, & Innovation Tools visit GENESISOFGENIUSBOOK.COM.

© Julie Ann Turner & Company/CreatorsGuide.com.
All Rights Reserved.

GENESIS of GENIUS

WORKSHEET #13 - MASTER TEAM ARC GUIDESHEET

MASTER TEAM GUIDESHEET. Use this as your portable, always-available MASTER GUIDE SHEET - a simple-but-powerful, One-page summary Team members may carry with them and refer to at any time - which captures the key elements and trajectory of your Master Team Arcs and Visions. All team work from other Worksheets may be consolidated on this sheet, and you may simply jot down "BEST NEXT STEPS" along each Arc as new ideas and opportunities arise to share with the team - using this single sheet as your Team's "real-time" Navigational Guide.

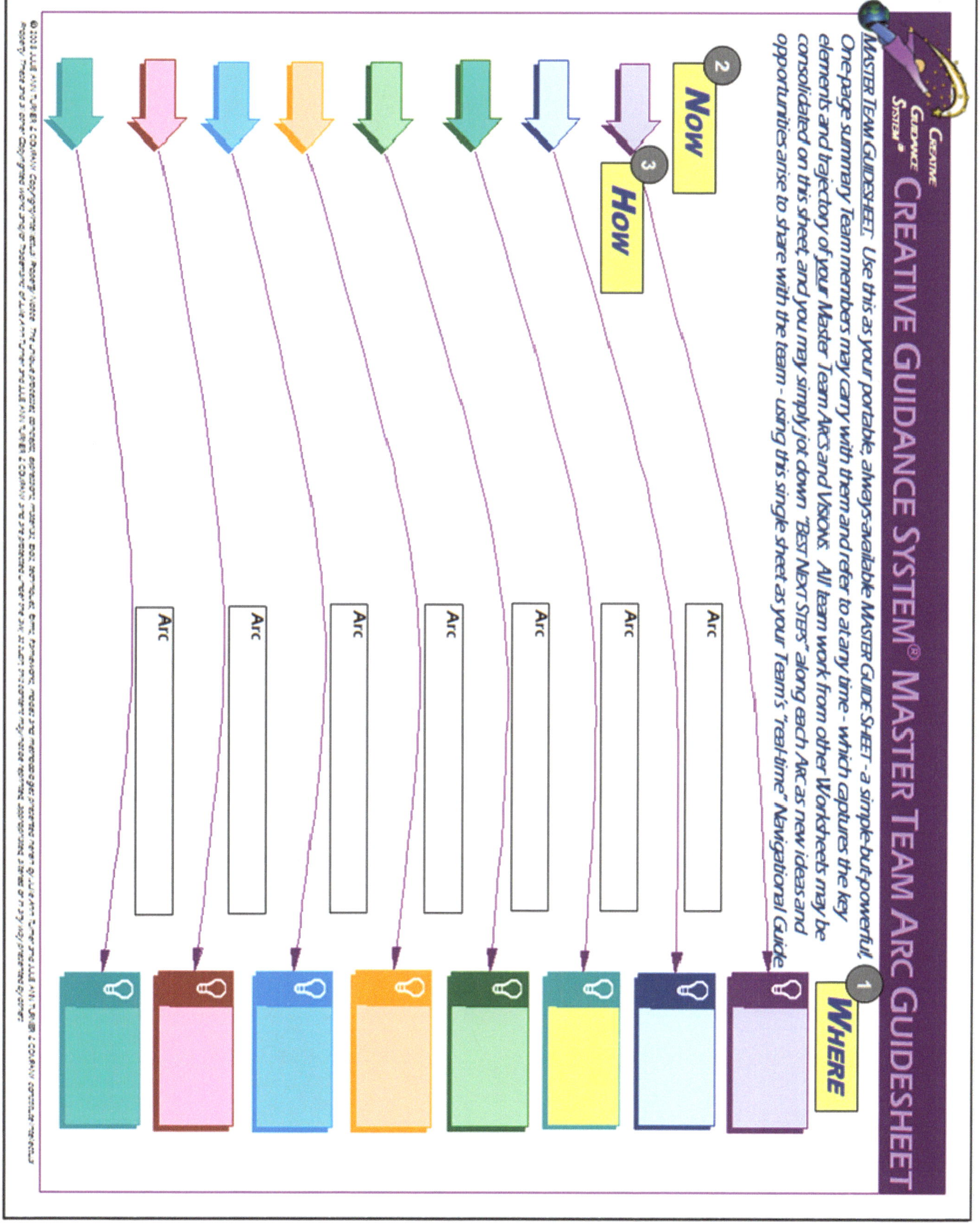

CREATIVE GUIDANCE SYSTEM® MASTER TEAM ARC GUIDESHEET

1 — WHERE
2 — NOW
3 — HOW

(Arc columns labeled "Arc")

CHAPTER NINE
Now

If the world

is in process,

every moment

is a new

and unique one.[264]

Abraham Maslow, psychologist

SNAPSHOT IN TIME

We have discovered the life-altering difference that results when we first imagine WHAT CAN BE, when we first know WHERE we are going – when we first create our Vision and Mission.

This first step in POWER ARC: YOUR CREATIVE GUIDANCE SYSTEM sets a much broader and higher framework within which we may create our lives, work and world, opening to us the full FIELD OF CREATION.

Only *after* we have envisioned WHAT CAN BE, and have a clear image of our *Vision* and *Mission* – our **WHERE**, or most desired destination or experience – are we ready to gain an understanding of WHAT IS or what already exists - to get a picture of our current reality, our "NOW." As we've emphasized, it is this *new order* or *sequence* of thinking – *first* imagining WHAT CAN BE, and *then* considering WHAT IS – that enables us to make the MINDSHIFT from Knowledge to Imagination essential for us to navigate and succeed in the complex, ever-changing space of the 21st Century.

Once we have a compelling *Vision* and *Mission* in place, it is important for us to gain a snapshot of where we are NOW – as this awareness not only frames our journey, but also establishes the crucial "creative tension" that will propel us toward our dreams. When exploring our current reality – our NOW – we use the word "*Scan*" to remind us that the methods we use we in this stage of discovery help us gain a "*snapshot in time*," a description of a *moment* or a *slice* of WHAT IS, captured in the midst of "*a world in process.*" In this stage, we endeavor to gain as full a 360-degree view of WHAT IS as we can, recognizing that we can never have complete information or fully capture current 'reality," as reality itself is ever-changing and elusive. We gain valuable information in this second NOW or *Scan* stage of the Creative Process, which will enable us to view our world from many perspectives,

Again, many of the methods and tools available and useful to us in this stage may be familiar, and that is as it should be; for, as we've said from the outset, our *analytical* thinking and methods are not incorrect, just incomplete. And now that we have placed our exploration in the proper context of the Whole – within the broader framework of the Creative Process - we will find these tools to be much more powerful aids to us in our creative journey.

Charlie Kiefer describes this difference in *The Path of Least Resistance*: "*The unfortunate fact of the matter is that most planning ... is done from the reactive-responsive orientation. Through elaborate methodologies the organization seeks to determine the current state of affairs it faces. It plots its current financial situation, the capacities of its people, and the products it is currently capable of creating ... The organization then takes the almost tragic step of charting a course to optimize performance in light of these current circumstances. In essence, the organization, says, "Given these circumstances, what is the best we can hope to do."*"[265] This, as we've seen, is the primary thinking and planning approach in most organizations. Yet, Kiefer concludes:

> *Imagine instead people in an organization operating from a creative mode. They approach planning, first by determining what they truly want to create, thus in essence becoming true to themselves. And then they analyze current reality (perhaps in exactly the same manner as before). Now, however, it is only to use that analysis as a foundation to build a bridge to what they truly want. Such an organization is on the road to greatness.*[266]

SCAN STATE

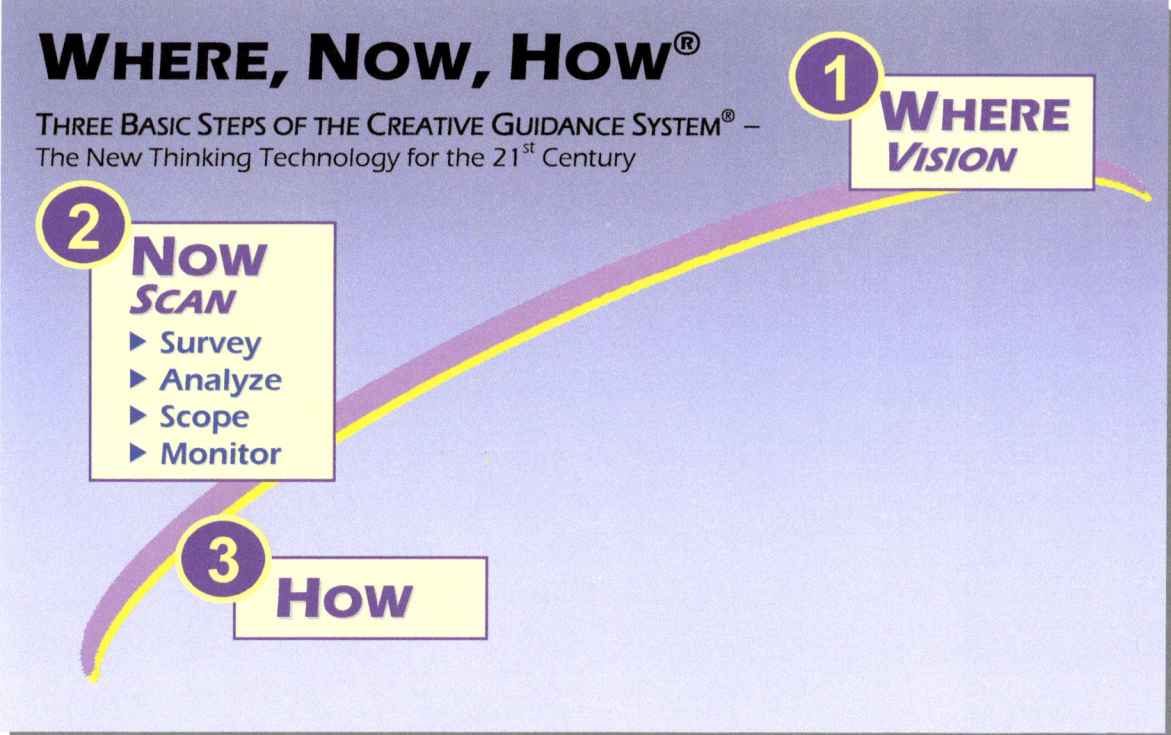

It is in this *creative mode of thought* that we embark on our exploration of Now, the second stage in *POWER ARC: YOUR CREATIVE GUIDANCE SYSTEM*. This new "thinking technology" enables us – and our organizations, which too often have become mired in analysis mode and limited to the realm of WHAT IS – to expand our creative possibilities and shift fully into our creative potential.

In this section, we introduce the four elements in the Now stage, at a level useful both to individuals and organizations:

▶ *Survey* – surveys the current situation, to gain a 360-degree view of *Now*

▶ *Analyze* – analyzes, organizes and evaluates the information gained in the *Survey* step

▶ *Scope* – determines the scope or focus of the creative effort

▶ *Monitor* – monitors the current situation for changes that may affect the process

Remember, the overarching term *Scan* is used to describe this Now stage, to remind us that the four steps above, while initially performed at a specific point in time, are all part of a dynamic and ongoing Creative Process. Therefore, these steps will be repeated as needed throughout the process of creation, to enable us to capture – and adjust in real time to – the changes in our situation and circumstances that inevitably will arise during the creative effort.

Keep in mind that, as we move through each of these *Scan* steps, we will always be keeping our *Vision* and *Mission* in mind, as these provide the essential – and highest – context for our creative journey, context which enables us to make sense of the information we gain, as well as to organize and make choices about, the importance of that information. Keeping our *Vision* always in sight also keeps us from making the all-too-common, but fatal, mistake – that of focusing solely on circumstances or "problems" that lie in the realm of WHAT IS – because we now know WHERE *we are going*, and that destination lies in the realm of WHAT CAN BE.

TWO-FOLD VISION

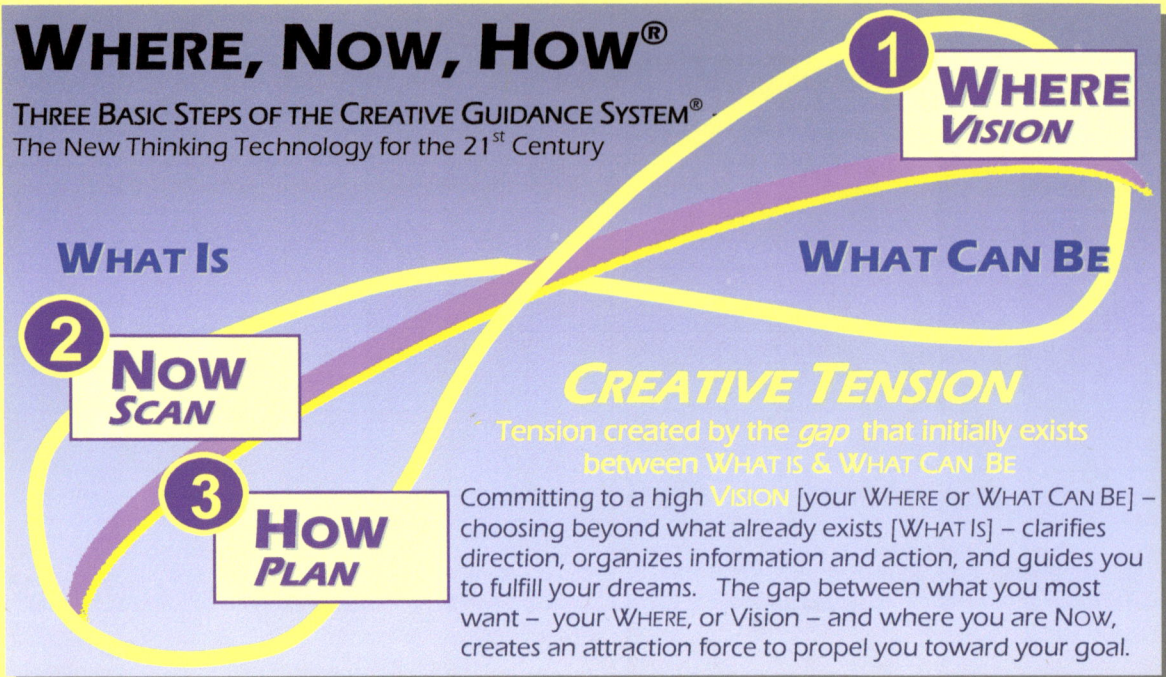

> *If you have built castles in the air, your work need not be lost; that is where they should be. Now put the foundations under them.*
> — Henry David Thoreau, American author and philosopher

Creators have what author Gay Hendricks calls "*two-fold vision*," not only "*a gift for engaging people in big dreams,*" "*but* "*at the same time they can look steadily at right now reality. …they can stand in a future that does not exist and map out the details of how to get there,*" given their "*keen distant vision and equally keen up-close focus.*" Just as important, creators have a systems-view of the Whole, "*the ability to focus on the separateness and the way everything is woven together … a feeling for the wholeness of thing, the people in it and the way it all fits together.*"[267]

Creators constantly hold this dynamic balance between a realization of where they are Now, and a *Vision* of Where they most want to be; this is essential to the art of creation. It is the discrepancy or gap between these two states — between What Is and What Can Be — that establishes "creative tension," the dynamic, positive tension that propels us in the direction of our desired *Vision*. The higher and more compelling our *Vision*, the greater the creative tension to propel us forward. Systems thinker George Land refers to this dynamic force as "future pull."[268] As broadcast journalist Belva Davis says:

> *Don't be afraid of the space between your dreams and reality.*
> *If you can dream it, you can make it so.*[269]

Within this creative field of action, the Field of Creation — framed by What Is and What Can Be — we now have the context to organize the flow of incoming information, to enable us to distinguish our priorities from what is irrelevant, *based on our conscious choices and values*, rather than on random circumstances that enter our immediate space. Our compelling *Vision* acts as an attraction force to focus our energy and actions, to organize information and resources, and to guide us along the path to creating what we most desire. This dynamic, two-fold framework enables us to make sense of the information we gather during the *Scan* stage, and put it to best use in propelling us toward our dreams.

> *You've got to think about big things while you're doing small things,*
> *so that all the small things go in the right direction.*
> — Alvin Toffler, futurist and author of *Future Shock*

SURFING THE SITUATION

In a way, we can think of circumstances like waves, which, as we've noted, are always sweeping into our awareness, often in sets or "clusters" we call "problems."

If we don't see them coming, these waves of circumstance may certainly surprise us, and potentially knock us off our feet (or threaten to wipe us out completely).

That's why we always keep our eyes on our high Vision, and continually Scan the space surrounding us for changes – whether expected or unexpected.

As we've learned, "problems" are simply *sets of circumstances* to which we have given that negative label; these sets of circumstances have no power in themselves, only in the power we give them to affect us or to cause us fear or stress (as we often allow "problems" to do). It is critical to remember that we are travelers in a Field of Information, and *any set of circumstances* is merely a certain *cluster or configuration of information.*

Information cannot hurt us – and we may use it to guide us.

We choose how we view any *situation* or *set of circumstances*. It is entirely possible for us, at one point in time, to view a certain *cluster of circumstances* as a "problem," and later view the *same configuration of circumstances* as an "opportunity." Yet, if we learn to view every set of circumstance merely as *information*, we may separate our *emotions* (such as a stress or fear reaction) from the *information* itself – and recognize *that information is always an invaluable resource that we may use to guide us.*

In fact, now that we have our Vision and Mission in place, we can make much more powerful and accurate assessments about the information we gain in the Scan stage.

We are now better able to make sense of the waves of information we encounter every day, because we are now viewing them in context with what we have *consciously chosen* as most important and valuable to us, framed by the direction we have consciously chosen to go. We now are able to determine, for instance, whether a certain set of circumstances may help move us forward toward our goals, or if that situation is merely a distraction.

We also are able to view *complex clusters of information*, and, through the lens of *Vision* and *Mission*, assess which bits of information might be helpful to us, and which bits are not immediately relevant to us. In this way, our *Vision* and *Mission* enable us to better organize the information that flows in, to identify areas where we need to seek out more information, and to better allocate our resources to focus on and address what is most crucial to us and our goals. *In other words, we are now able to save time, reduce stress, better allocate resources, and be more productive – on the journey to our highest goals.*

In this section of the Guide, we provide simple but powerful tools and methods to enable you to continually monitor the Field of Information unfolding before you, and to "surf the situation" to glean the most important elements to guide you in real time, help you adjust your trajectory as appropriate, and to propel you forward most powerfully.

We also guide you to other resources for further exploration on your own.

GENESIS of GENIUS

SCAN STEP ONE: SURVEY

Now that we have set our trajectory by establishing a compelling *Vision* and *Mission*, we may begin exploring our *current reality* – our *Now*. In this stage of discovery, we endeavor to gain as complete a 360-degree view of WHAT IS as we can. We begin this exploration – whether on an individual level or an organizational level - with the first step in the *Scan* process: *Survey*,

▶ *Scan Step One:* **Survey** *–surveys the current situation, to gain a 360-degree view of* **Now**

In OLDTHINK (which focuses on WHAT IS), as individuals, when asked to describe our current situation, we typically focus on our *circumstances* (often labeled as "*problems*" or "*crises*," as these are generally "*top of mind*" due to their urgency), or even on our "*To-Do Lists*," as these capture the most immediate actions or "tactics" we think will move us forward. The same is true for organizations, departments or teams.

As we've seen, however, *using problems or current circumstances – or even our standard To-Do Lists alone – to navigate by,* often quickly has us bouncing back and forth in *reaction mode* within the limited sphere of WHAT IS, rather than exploring possibilities in *creation mode*, across the unlimited realm of WHAT CAN BE.

In NEWTHINK, or "NAVTHINK," we *Survey* the FIELD OF POTENTIAL, to gain a full view of both WHAT IS and WHAT CAN BE – using methods that give us both an inward-looking and an outward-looking view of the Whole. Fortunately, are several simple but powerful tools – useful for both individuals and for organizations and groups – to help us gain this 360-degree snapshot of our current reality (some tools involve actual surveys and other information-gathering methods with which you already may be familiar; some we share here for your immediate use, and others in the EXPLORESOURCES at the end of this chapter; also, in our advanced online VISIONSPARC resources, we introduce the *P.O.W.E.R. Grid* for gaining this 360-degree view of the Whole).

Constellations of Circumstance – How do you know if the day-to-day events that arrest your attention are a "Crisis" or just a "Circumstance"? The answer? They're all just sets of Circumstances – just constellations of information – that you can only accurately interpret if you know WHERE you are going.

Here, we start with a solid, all-purpose tool for Surveying our environment – called SWOT (Strengths, Weaknesses, Opportunities, Threats) Analysis[270] – which gives us, either as individuals or groups, a fairly quick, multidimensional snapshot our current situation.

For example, on an individual level, you may use *SWOT Analysis* to begin your exploration, by thinking of your personal *Strengths* – your current knowledge, education, skills, unique abilities, physical attributes, interests, and so on – an "internal view" of your attributes or assets as a person. However, in considering *Strengths*, you may also consider "external" assets, such as family and social connections, your work or business network, and your information sources, and even hardware and software you own – as assets that may assist you in reaching your *Vision* and goals.

Similarly, on an organizational or team level, groups may use *SWOT Analysis* to gain an inventory of individual and collective *Strengths* – again, with an "internal view" of the team and organization itself (including institutional knowledge, individual specializations, and so on), and, just as importantly, an "external view" of the team's valuable "*Relational*," *Social*," and "*Creative Capital*"[271] – all of which depend on relationships and collaboration with others.

SWEEPING THE SPACE

Survey

One of the best and fastest ways to gain a 360-degree view of your current reality is to begin with an actual *Survey - a set of key questions you ask —on an individual level*: to yourself and perhaps to your circle of family, friends, and colleagues; *or on an organizational or team level*: to your organization or team members, to collaborators and partners, and to those whom you serve or those who have an interest or an investment in your work (often called "*stakeholders*"). A *Survey* will unearth a wealth of information relevant to *Vision* and *Mission*, as well as to strengths, weaknesses, opportunities and threats (see *SWOT Analysis* below) from diverse perspectives (See *Survey Template #10* with *SWOT Key* in EXPLORESOURCES).

Stakeholders

As noted above, "*stakeholders*" are those who have a "*stake*" in how you, your team or organization meet your commitments and goals, and reach your potential. In an inward-only analysis, we often fail to give stakeholders the attention they deserve; however, considering all stakeholders and their diverse perspectives is essential to gaining a 360-degree view of a personal or organizational "ecosystem." *On an individual level*, stakeholders include you (the individual), family, friends, co-workers, community, and even society as a whole (given your potential life contribution). *On an organizational level*, stakeholders would include your team and staff, related functional groups and divisions/departments, organizational leadership (top executives, board, etc.), customers (current and potential), competitors, influencers (media, analysts, bloggers, etc.), stockholders, community, and society at large.

SWOT Analysis

SWOT Analysis is an ideal starting-point tool to enable us to capture and begin to organize information for our 360-dewgree snapshot of Now. The process involves filling in the four areas or boxes (see below and template in EXPLORESOURCES) – <u>S</u>trengths, <u>W</u>eaknesses, <u>O</u>pportunities, <u>T</u>hreats - applying both an *internal* (inward-looking) and an e*xternal* (outward-looking) view for each one, to gain as complete an inventory as possible for each quadrant (you may even want to conduct a *SWOT Analysis* for your competitors). The Internet is particularly useful for gathering information about external factors, such as threats, opportunities, competitors, and brand perceptions. Answers should be as objective and realistic as possible. As we will see, pivotal issues and success factors will emerge.

Strengths
What are your – or your team's or organization's – advantages, assets and strengths?
- *tangible – personal*, such as physical appearance, health, talents; or *organizational*, such as staff, customers, budget/funding, office space, equipment, software, and information access/resources;
- *intangible* – such as knowledge, skill sets, creativity innovation, networks/collaborative capacities, identity/brand reputation or market perception, etc.)

Weaknesses
What are your – or your team's or organization's – disadvantages, limitations or weaknesses?*
- *tangible – personal*, such as things you do poorly or could improve, physical limitations, or *organizational*, such as staffing, budget/funding, office and information resources; and
- *intangible* – such as knowledge or skill set limitations, lack of motivation or leadership support, negative perception/reputation, etc.)

Opportunities
What are current or emerging opportunities and trends favorable to you – or to your team's or organization's - mission?
- *tangible & intangible* (see above), *local* – such as additional cash flow, etc,, as well as *global* - trends in technology, market, customer or competitor, or global shifts,, etc.

Threats
What are current or emerging threats or obstacles do you – or your team or organization - face?
- *tangible & intangible* (see above), as well as disruptive technologies, market or competitor shifts, staff cuts or conflict, reduced cash flow, tougher job, customer, or market requirements, etc

Also see the advanced VISIONSPARC section, to use the all-new *P.O.W.E.R. Grid* for gaining an dynamic and complete 360-degree view of Now.

GENESIS of GENIUS

CREATION IN CONTEXT

*We have set our trajectory and direction. We have scanned the space before us –
using our Survey tools to gain a 360-degree view of our current reality.
We have reached a critical point in our exploration –
having set the necessary creative framework of WHERE and NOW -
where we have the proper context to allow our analysis of this information
to carry true meaning and true power to guide us forward.*

It is this dynamic balance of tension and harmony within the CREATIVE FIELD that led poets and philosophers over the ages – and writers such as Eckhart Tolle and Deepak Chopra today[272] – to emphasize the power and potential of *the present moment*. Like the ancient sages, S. Marc Cohen compares this moment of possibility with the dynamic tension of an archer's bow:

> *... the [bow's] string being pulled one way by one end of the bow and the other way by the other - enables the bow to perform its function, to be the kind of thing that it is. It seems static, but it is in fact dynamic.*[273]

Now, we have the authentic *context* within which to analyze the rich information
we have gathered – to consider different aspects within the Whole,
to discover patterns and themes emerging within the system.
As Abraham Maslow said, in "*a world ...in process, every moment is a new and unique one.*"[274]
This reveals the essence of the navigational approach –
this *creative guidance system* allows us to dynamically create the future we desire most –
adjusting course and allocating resources *in real time*,
moving consciously and powerfully forward, as co-creators of the future we have imagined.

It is only within this creative framework that we may tap the true power of NOW.
In this creative space, every instant is open to possibility, electric with potential.
Each step moves us forward along the ARC of our Journey, becoming *what we are meant to be*,
as our path spirals ever upward to encompass more abundance, connections and resources.

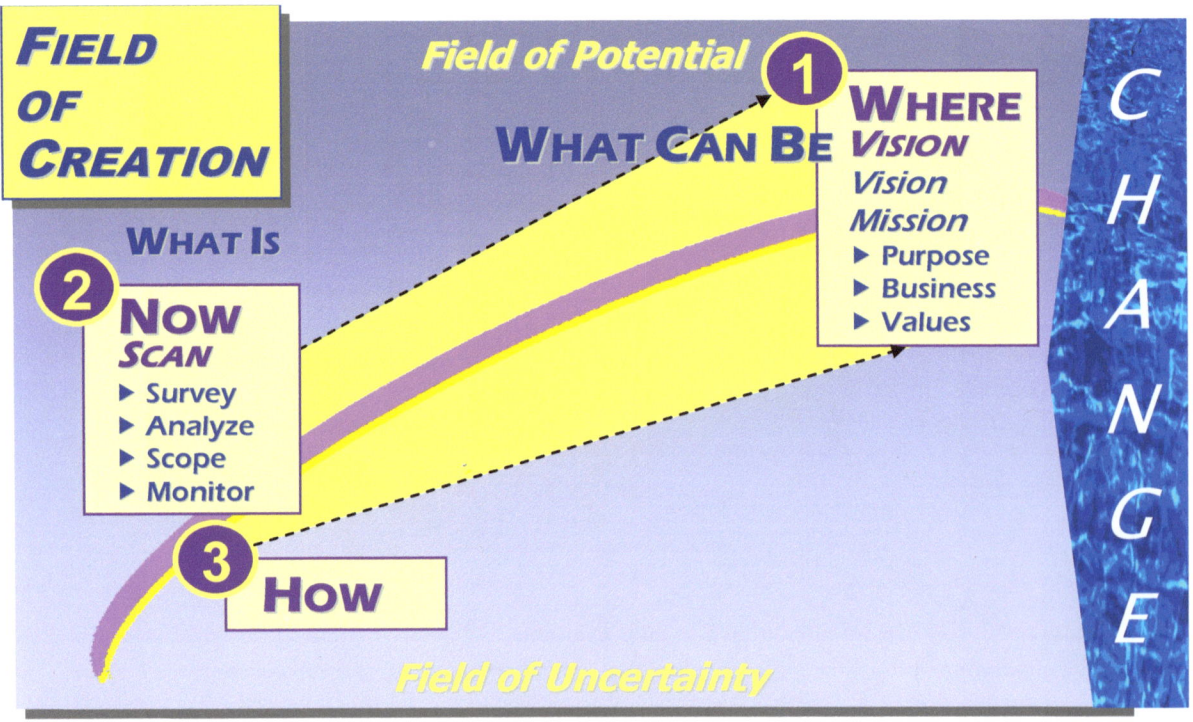

GENESIS of GENIUS

SCAN STEP TWO: ANALYZE

▶ *Analyze* – analyzes, organizes and evaluates the information gained in the **Survey** step

Within the context of our creative framework, the art and magic of the Creative Process – and its self-organizing power – actually begin to emerge and become visible as we sift through the rich information we have gathered in the previous stage of discovery. Drawing from a myriad of viewpoints (inward-looking and outward-looking) – through *Survey* tools such as SWOT and Stakeholder Analysis – we now have before us a collection of diverse contributions (see example SWOT output below).

Yet, it is out of the midst of what initially may look like chaos and disorder that meaningful connections and valuable patterns begin to emerge, almost spontaneously taking form. Across the varied contributions of the many (often gathered from a multitude of locations, as well), we may begin to see recognizable "*clusters*" or related "*constellations*" of information take shape before our eyes. We will pay close attention as these patterns emerge before us, as they bring pivotal issues and success factors into relief against a chaotic background, making it possible for us to identify key points of leverage to propel us along our chosen path.

> • Individual/Personal Example – Personal Exercises/SWOT Analysis (*Career* Arc)
> (Career Vision: Sharing in entrepreneurs' success guided by my business/investing expertise; Mission: To serve entrepreneurs and start-up ventures through my passion for finance)
> *Strengths:* Business–financial acumen; Small business success; strong communication skills
> *Weaknesses:* Hate public speaking; like working independently; competitive nature
> *Opportunities:* Small business a growing market; investor/funding connections; want to serve
> *Threats:* Temptation to "coast" after business success; fear won't live full, authentic life
>
> *Key Pattern/Pivot Point* (arising as "cluster" of potential from analysis above, shown in blue) :
> > Launch one-on-one small business/start-up consulting, with focus on investment/funding

> • Team/Organizational Example – Survey/SWOT Analysis (*Department* Arc)
> (Department Vision: X Corporation is the preferred resource to help small business grow; Mission: To communicate the value of X Corporation, its products and services to key markets)
> *Strengths:* Strong National brand; Experienced team; Executive support; Campaign $ available
> *Weaknesses:* Lack of market focus; Plans/resources not aligned; short-staffed; failure to collaborate
> *Opportunities:* Strong Field support; Small business market potential; New multi-product strategy
> *Threats:* Impending merger; Large business market saturation; Job uncertainty; Losing momentum
>
> *Key Pattern/Pivot Point* (arising as "cluster" of potential from analysis above, shown in blue) :
> > Develop multi-product campaign for small business market, collaborating with Field teams

Framed within the creative Arc of Where and How, analysis becomes more powerful, enabling us to identify high "leverage points" which previously might not have become evident, without an inclusive approach to collect and analyze input from the entire system.

Even in the simplified examples above, we may observe *strategic pivot points* emerging. According to Peter Senge, the inventor Buckminster Fuller compared these "*leverage points*" to a *trim tab* within a boat's rudder– a tiny "rudder within a rudder," which makes it easier to turn a giant ship, through greater leverage of the force of water.[275] As Senge says, "*small, well-focused actions can sometimes produce significant, enduring improvements, if they're in the right place*"; however, we must understand the dynamics of the system to leverage this power.

This analysis will give birth to *Strategic Goals* (or "*Mini-Visions*") in the How stage. But first, these examples also illustrate the next step in the Now stage: *Scope*.

DEATH BY DATA

A lot of analytical stuff will give you incremental improvement, but it won't give you a big leap. You can't time or plan for innovation. It can't come from customer data. It has to come from the heart of somebody with an idea.[276]

Dave Girouard, VP/GM, Google Enterprise

Wow. Did you just read that? The head of Google's software unit for business – the same Google that blows away competition through its powerful analytics and superior algorithms – acknowledges that *analysis* is *not* the path that leads to innovation. Only the human Imagination – *creative* thinking (through the Creative Process), which is *a completely different mode of thinking* from *analytical* thinking – generates innovative leaps.

This point is so crucial for us to grasp – and so contrary to the way we've been taught to think (especially in the business realm) – that it is certainly worthy of a double – or triple – take.

The difference we are highlighting here cannot be overemphasized – as our understanding of it is absolutely pivotal to making the MINDSHIFT that will unlock the creative power that exists within each of us and within our organizations. Yet, this distinction is so subtle, we have seen even the most savvy and experienced traditional strategic planners miss it. Too often, they simply nod dismissively and say, "*Oh, yeah, we all do SWOT analysis, and then create Vision ... how is this different?*"

However, when we explain the difference between WHAT IS (problem-solving) thinking and WHAT CAN BE (potential-driven) thinking), and point out the crucial difference that the *sequence* of the Creative Process makes (*Vision* first, *then* analysis) – it slowly begins to dawns on them : If our starting point is WHAT IS (SWOT or another analysis method), and we use only current or past data as the basis for creating our *Vision*, our *Vision* and goals will be generated from an *already limited* view, and our solutions limited to incremental changes to what already exists (or, at best, extrapolated from has existed in the past, as past data is what much analysis measures; by the time we have the results, the source data is already *past*, not *real-time*, information).[277]

Even in well-intentioned, yet traditional, strategic planning initiatives, it is tempting just to be mesmerized by the results of our analysis, and then to focus on what we can do with whatever capacities we have *now*. If we do, inadvertently, but just as surely, we will be caught once again in the limiting trap of never looking beyond WHAT IS, in to the realm of WHAT CAN BE. In contrast, the CREATIVE GUIDANCE SYSTEM revealed here represents *an entirely different mode and sequence of thought* from that of analysis, a mode that enables us to shift from the limited realm of *Knowledge* to unlimited realm of *Imagination*.

We must therefore take care as we use analytical tools like SWOT Analysis, to consider the results in light of our *Vision* and *Mission*, guarding against the tendency to once again limit our thinking by focusing on the "rear-view" snapshot that analysis so often generates. Again, current data and past trends can reveal valuable insights, but they are always incomplete. And, as much as we may wish it were so, they can't predict –or create – the future.

We've had management by objective and total quality management.
Now it's time for the latest trend in business methodology: management by data. ...
Running a complex enterprise can't be reduced to a spreadsheet, however.
Even the most detailed statistical analysis has limitations, as [Stanford business professor Robert] Sutton acknowledges. For one, conditions may change, rendering the analysis misleading. ...
Jeffrey Pfeffer, Mr. Sutton's colleague ... offers a more insidious pitfall:
Managers can be so focused on perfecting today's business that they lose sight of tomorrow's.[278]

Scott Thurm, business columnist, *The Wall Street Journal*

This truth is critical as we consider the need for creativity – for Imagination – as we realize why our *current knowledge is not enough to navigate and succeed in our constantly changing reality.*

CAUGHT IN THE REAR-VIEW MIRROR

We must constantly be creating - and be conscious that even approaches that worked before will likely no longer be sufficient moving forward, as our realm of reality is always in flux.

Moreover, we must be conscious that our time and other resources may easily become so absorbed in obtaining and analyzing data that we become paralyzed, unable to move forward in the meantime. Certainly, as we've seen, information gained through analysis can provide valuable guidance, highlighting leverage points and emerging opportunities which might not otherwise become evident. Google ably applied results gleaned from its analysis to fine-tune its Internet search algorithm and its formula for aligning ads with relevant online content, to surge past Yahoo, Microsoft and other competitors and seize the search-engine crown.[279] However, the most innovative companies – especially in this networked age – favor a cycle of "*failing fast*" and "*failing forward*," followed by "*continual course correction*" (often described as a "*Ready-Fire-Aim*" approach)[280] – over a "*paralysis by analysis*" approach, every time.

Snapshot thinking alone is insufficient – and often misleading - in a process world.[281]

- *Shifting Cycles* - Even in what appears to be a recurring or cyclical trend, small shifts – by competitors or within the market itself - can disrupt the cycle. For example, as management professor and author Thomas H. Davenport explains, changes in what seemed like predictable mortgage rate cycles misled "even sophisticated lenders and investors," as subprime lending rates dropped: "*For years, default rates followed a predictable pattern based on the borrower's credit score. Last year, that pattern changed slightly and many lenders didn't adjust.*"[282] Cycles shift, competitors adjust, new markets emerge; innovators must be tuned in to navigate changing space.

- *Nothing Fails Like Success* - As we've seen, even experiences and events we consider "successes" can hinder us from remaining flexible and moving on into ever new realms of creative potential; as historian Alfred Toynbee pointed out, "*success*" can easily become "*the nemesis of creativity.*"[283] As *Wall Street Journal* business columnist Scott Thurm notes, Dell captured the lion's share of the PC market through innovations in supply-chain processes. Yet, Dell failed to continue to innovate and sufficiently diversify its business, "making [Dell] vulnerable once Hewlett-Packard matched its expertise." As Thurm says: "*The real trick, then, is to combine these skills, gaining advantage by analyzing today's problems while looking creatively for tomorrow's opportunities.*"[284]

- *Customer Rear-View* – Though it runs counter to the service doctrine of "*the customer is always right*," true innovators - especially those pioneering entirely new markets and industry space - realize customer input can be either a rich source for, or deadly to, innovation. As automaker Henry Ford said:

    If we had asked the public what they wanted, they would have said faster horses.

Leaders have expressed similar warnings for innovators in today's emerging technology markets. George Colony of Forrester Research cautions, "*The customer is a rear-view mirror, Not a guide to the future,*"[285] and technology consultant and former AT&T technologist David Isenberg echoes: "*If you're listening to your customer it's almost preordained that you'll miss the new market.*"[286] Yet, with these cautions in mind, creative organizations are adjusting yet again, by tapping into the creative talent of customer-innovators known as "lead users," who often alter and improve on initial product designs on their own initiative, generating new uses and applications for products beyond what the manufacturers may have envisioned. In addition, as we've noted previously, innovators are wisely plugging into, and creating their own, peer production and crowdsourcing markets to leverage customer creativity. The outcome hopefully will be what designer Dewys Lasdon describes as "*the shock of recognition*": "*… to give the client … not what he wants, but what he never dreamed he wanted; and when he gets it, he recognizes it as something he wanted all the time.*"[287]

True innovators do not try to force their creations to fit what already exists. Consider where technology would be today, if, in the 1950s, engineer Jack Kilby had focused on incrementally tweaking the vacuum tube, rather than inventing the microchip that gave rise to personal computers and the digital age.

GENESIS of GENIUS

SCAN STEP THREE: SCOPE

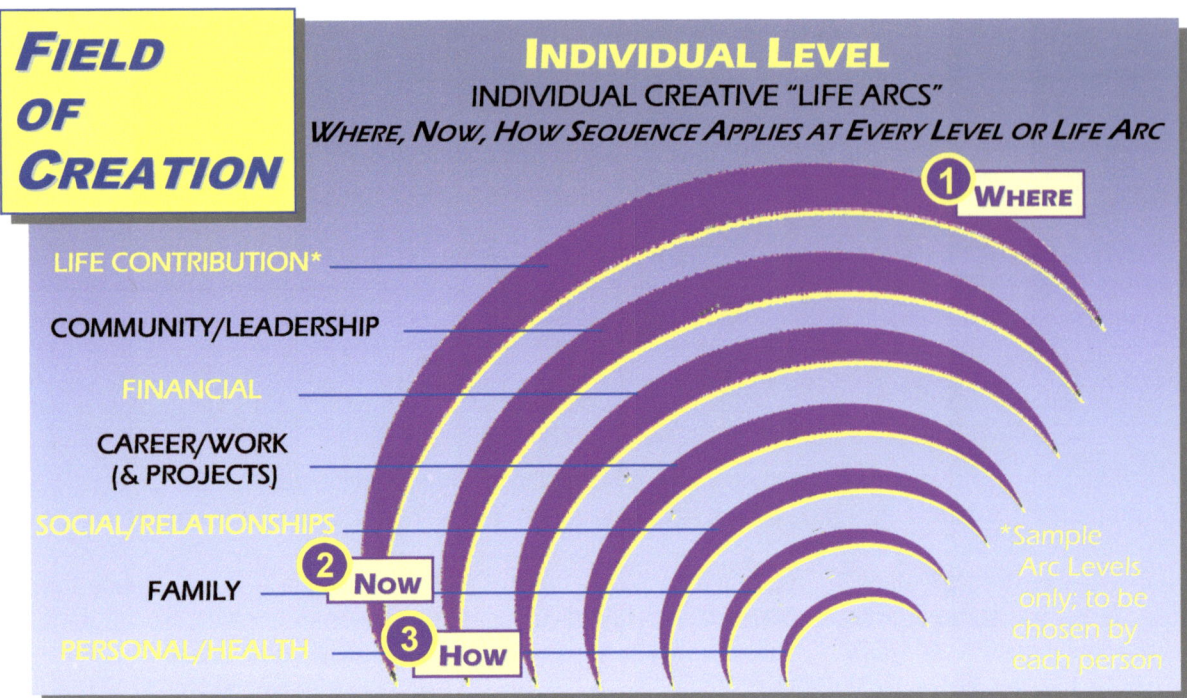

▶ *Scope* – *determines the scope or focus of the creative effort*

One of the most critical steps in any creative endeavor is to determine its Scope – the level and area of focus where an individual or organization will choose to direct its creative energies at a given time.

Perhaps even as you explored *Vision* and *Mission*, and certainly as you have scanned your current reality (through *Survey* and *Analyze* steps), you have discovered ideas and information and uncovered potential goals which may lie on different Arcs – *on different PLANES OF THOUGHT, if you will* – raising the question of which *level* or *Scope* of creation you, personally, or your team, collectively, will choose to focus on at this particular time.

For instance, in using the PERSONAL ARC worksheets, you may already have begun to clarify your high *Vision*, forming some initial ideas around your "*Life Contribution*" ARC (see above). During the process, you also may identified some important elements for your "*Career/Work*" ARC and your "*Community/ Leadership*" ARCS that may relate to this emerging *Life Contribution*.

In this example, we observe the power of using the visual framework of POWER ARC: YOUR CREATIVE GUIDANCE SYSTEM – with its different ARCS – not only to help us imagine our highest goals (as some may never have considered their "Life Contribution," or even their Life Purpose or Vision before), but also to help us identify and focus on different areas of our lives where we may wish to devote more attention.

Here, *POWER ARC: YOUR CREATIVE GUIDANCE SYSTEM* enables us to choose the *Scope* of our creative efforts at any given time.[288] For instance, in the example above, you might choose to focus first on your *Career/Work* ARC – developing goals and strategies (to be discussed in the Now section) for this level as the initial *Scope* of your creative endeavor. At the same time, you still are able to keep the overall framework, and the alignment of the ARCS within it – including potential synergies between your *Career*, *Community*, and *Life Contribution* ARCS - clearly in mind.

DETERMINING SCOPE

As a result, the *Scope* for a given creative endeavor – which a team or organization will ultimately and clearly agree upon, during this step of the *Scan* stage – will naturally result from the unfolding exploration and identification of issues and areas of focus that emerge during the *Survey* and *Analyze* steps. In an Organizational or Team creative endeavor, the question of the *Scope* or focus initially may arise during the WHERE or *Vision* stage, or during early in the HOW or *Scan* stage (particularly as teams begin sorting *Survey* input during SWOT Analysis).

The determination of Scope is actually a natural and necessary part of the discovery process. As the team begins to recognize patterns and organize new information from the Survey step, team members will notice that their emerging goals are associated with different levels or ARCS within POWER ARC: YOUR CREATIVE GUIDANCE SYSTEM.

For example, since the *Survey* step gathers information from across the organizational system, representing input from diverse sources or stakeholders, some of the "clusters" of information that emerge during SWOT Analysis may be most closely related to the "*Industry*" ARC (such as new technologies, industry-wide technical standards, or competitors' product launches), while other patterns may be related to the *Corporation* itself (on the "*Corporate/Business*" ARC), or to a particular *Department* or *Function* (also separate ARCS, as shown in the SYSTEM graphic above).

It is important during the Scope step for the group to identify and clearly agree upon which level or levels the initial creative initiative will focus (subsequent creative efforts may later address additional levels of the situation). We also note here that, although we have introduced the four steps of the HOW or *Scan* stage in a particular sequence which reflects the common flow of these steps, groups often find that the results of their initial analysis lead them to circle back to the *Survey* step to gather more information, perhaps from another stakeholder, for example, or to the *Analyze* step to research an additional area for study, perhaps revealed by their initial SWOT Analysis. As with all steps in the Creative Process, creators often find themselves returning again and again to use tools and techniques as they navigate the changing CREATIVE FIELD before them.

HOW IDEAS DIE

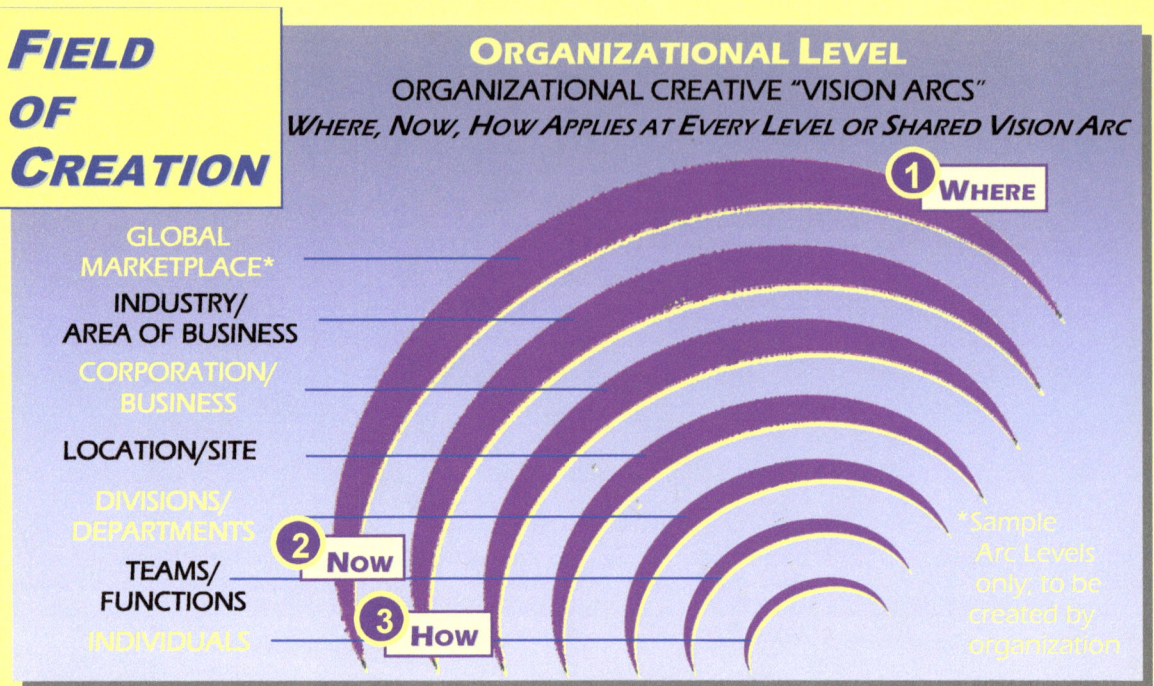

We've all been there - probably more times than we care to remember - sitting through a seemingly endless and unguided meeting, in which each person seems to be holding a conversation with him or herself, each addressing a different aspect of a complex issue:

One person is forcefully arguing for alignment with the Corporation's message and positioning ... another is warning about disruptive technologies arising in the industry ... another about the limitations of the department's budget ... yet another about the lack of cooperation from a separate division in providing urgent data ... and still another about a personnel problem ... all of this, in the same "conversation."

What is occurring — in one simultaneous conversation – is that each participant is addressing a point that lies on *a separate "PLANE OF THOUGHT"* – either on a separate Organizational ARC, as shown above (one person addressing an issue on the "*Corporate*" ARC, yet another on the "*Industry*" ARC), or within *an entirely different stage* of the Creative Process (one person addressing WHERE or *Vision*, while another jumps ahead to HOW).

How often have we witnessed this scenario? One colleague is talking about the potential of a new initiative (WHERE or *Vision* stage), another shoots his or her point by injecting an argument about the current budget (How or scan stage) – and before any new potential or opportunity can be explored fully by the group, the conversation is cut short – many a new idea faces a premature death.

It is no wonder we find ourselves enduring a series of unproductive planning sessions and meetings, wasting tremendous time and energy, and with participants leaving frustrated – blaming the process, meetings themselves, or worse (yet, perhaps more often) - one another – for the lack of progress.

Without a shared framework like the POWER ARC SYSTEM to make this visible, to guide these critical conversations, and to enable the group to agree on the Scope of their creative endeavor, the result is chaos. More than merely frustrating and resource-wasting, however, such unguided conversations often result in the early death of creative thinking. We need a shared SYSTEM for thinking and talking together that generates ideas, rather than killing them.

THE POWER OF PLANES OF THOUGHT

The visual power of POWER ARC is invaluable in enabling teams and organizations to better identify and address different PLANES OF THOUGHT, and to better determine and agree on the Scope of shared creative endeavors.

For example, let's say the group engaged in the conversation on the previous page – the Public Relations/Communications department for the company – recognizes the central *Scope* for their creative endeavor falls along *Division/Department* ARC. With this CREATIVE GUIDANCE SYSTEM framework and tools in hand, the group would begin by clarifying their *Vision* and *Mission* at the *Division/Department* level, then move on to the HOW or *Scan* stage. With the group in agreement on the *Division/Department* as the appropriate *Scope* for their current work, it is clear, for instance, that their *Survey* and *SWOT Analysis* should focus on the *Division/Department* level, as well.

As we could see from the group's initial conversation, the team also has identified a few key questions related to the higher on the *Corporation* ARC – to ensure their efforts align with the "*Corporation's messaging and positioning*," as well as with the *Industry* ARC – to ensure they respond appropriately to any emerging "*disruptive technologies*" they need to address in their communications work. After they complete their work at the *Division/Department* level, the group may decide to move on to the *Team/Function* ARC at a later stage in their creative exploration. Since this CREATIVE GUIDANCE SYSTEM process, and each ARC within it, is "fractal," the group is able to use this *same shared sequence and common tools for each level of creation.*

Realize the power – and productivity – you and your team gain when you are able to guide your thoughts and conversations on the same PLANE OF THOUGHT at the same time?

Rather than chaotic meetings and conversations like the one on the previous page, you and your team will be able to talk and think together in harmony, as the clear WHERE, NOW, HOW sequence and related visual ARCS guide more productive and creative conversations. This not only reduces misunderstanding and miscommunication, but actively facilitates communication and collaboration. By understanding and using the concept of *PLANES OF THOUGHT* and *POWER ARC: YOUR CREATIVE GUIDANCE SYSTEM*, your team will be able to address each question or issue that arises, at the appropriate level, and also clearly see how the different levels or arcs of creation relate to one another (this advantage of the SYSTEM will become even more valuable in the HOW stage, by enabling team members to align their thinking, and to devise synergistic strategies that address issues across more than one ARC at the same time).

In fact, in our creative sessions, participating teams often create a VISION WALL – covering a large section of a wall in the meeting room with paper – on which they draw the *POWER ARC SYSTEM* framework, including the WHERE, NOW, HOW sequence and the group's customized Organizational ARCS. The group then uses this master visual framework as a shared, real-time guide, on which they may physically move to, or post items on, to indicate the appropriate level or stage of thought. They may post ideas and strategies throughout the session, essentially creating a visual "map" of their progress as they go along. Team members are able to guide one another through the WHERE, NOW, HOW sequence – and also are able to suggest when a comment or issue might best be recorded and addressed later related to a more appropriate "plane of thought."

Moreover, the powerful ARC framework enables groups to see more clearly, organize, prioritize and address each level of their creative endeavor, one at a time, in the proper creative sequence.

NAVIGATIONAL THINKING TECHNOLOGY

*It is far better to learn how great companies think,
than to copy what they do.*[289]

Jeffrey Pfeffer, Stanford University Business School, *Leading the Way*

Too often, as individuals and as participants in organizations, we are seduced by the promise of a "silver bullet," lured by the next management fad or self-help "quick fix."

As we've seen, however, while the next benchmark, scorecard, or dashboard may offer us valid information, they will never fill the need for a fundamental shift in human thought, from Knowledge to Imagination.

We are even tempted to approach new thinking in the same old ways, with many attempting to adopt "Innovation" as the latest hot trend – added on as if it were just one more separate "program" for our teams to add to their "skill set."

When we approach innovation in this way, however, we once again miss the crucial truth that creative thinking is a totally different Mindset – one that requires a new navigational thinking technology – new mental programming and a new thought sequence for our brains.

> Creating and maintaining a culture of innovation is important for any business. All companies express interest in innovation — who doesn't want to come up with a new product or process?— but few do much about it. Many companies back away when they see what's actually involved in sustaining innovation. ... I'm a big fan of the Six Sigma philosophy of defect reduction. .... but [defect reduction efforts like] Six Sigma can conflict with innovation because it tries to eliminate different ways of doing things in favor of the "best" way. Innovation thrives on trying new approaches. ...what happens when you only do something once or you actually want to achieve a different outcome? That's the essence of innovation in many cases: Take the same inputs but get a different—and better—outcome. ... I've never believed these two approaches should be in conflict; indeed, they can and should be complimentary. You should measure your innovation processes and look for ways to make them more effective. You should inspect and adapt as you go along. ... You should have an effective investment and development process to nurture the ideas you want to try. ... It's tempting to isolate the innovation efforts from the core of the business ...but this is almost always a mistake ... .[290]

John Parkinson, Technology Consultant, *CIO Insight*

We cannot copy or commoditize our way to innovation. We must change the way we think.

As management expert Tom Peters points out, the long-favored analysis practice of benchmarking, over time, actually results in organizations becoming more and more the same, rather than unique and innovative; if we benchmark, we must allow the input to spark ideas, yet make the ultimate creation our own.[291] As Robert Gandossy and Marc Effron explain, this highlights "*The Myth of Best Practices*":

> Managers everywhere are obsessed with the quick fix. Fads and gimmicks abound.
> The next new thing often promoted by academics or, yes, consultants, promises easy solutions to difficult challenges. And this is understandable. Faced with daunting competitive pressures, global complexity, and a nanosecond world, who wouldn't want to steal from the best?
> But it doesn't work. Cultures are different. Values and beliefs that leaders hold are different. Strategies, customers, history and embedded practices are different. These differences make it difficult, if not impossible, to graft someone else's programs onto your own. ... Best practices, as many people think of them, simply don't exist in the area of leadership. ... believing that the best way to figure out what action to take is to look to your left and your right, and do whatever they're doing - that's not good advice if you're trying to build leaders.[292]

Only by adopting an entirely new navigational thinking technology will we be able to co-create our future.

SCAN STEP FOUR: MONITOR

▶ *Monitor*

Within the context of our creative framework, the art and magic of the Creative Process – and its self-organizing power – actually begin to emerge and become visible.

We see more clearly than ever that our *Scan* stage is an ongoing, dynamic process, a recurring pattern within the overall SPIRAL CREATION process. As with all steps in the Creative Process, we will find ourselves returning again to use tools and techniques as we navigate the changing CREATIVE FIELD before us.

We also see clearly that the power creative *choice* – and the energy that choice releases – may now flow more naturally as we view our Now, always through the lens of our *Vision* and *Mission* (and even these may be further refined, as we gain more information during the *Scan* stage). We are able to maintain the dynamic tension between WHERE and Now, all the while benefiting from the freedom this creative framework allows us.

It is natural, then, that we call our final step in the Now or *Scan* stage "*Monitor*," as it expresses the essence of ongoing exploration of the surrounding and emerging environment of the CREATIVE FIELD .

As the individual or group moves along the ARC towards the "WHERE" destination, noting changes to the current set of circumstances and dynamically adjusting, each participant acts as a "Monitor."

Everyone involved remains observant and constantly scans the field ahead – using the tools and steps of Survey, Analyze, and Scope – in relation to their own contribution, as well as in relation to elements relevant to the needs of the group as a whole – as the creative endeavor progresses.

At the same time, all remain vigilant so that the group does not inadvertently become stalled through focus on any single set of circumstances (a "problem" or "crisis"). In fact, it is critical to success in this dynamic space that individuals and groups not only guard against slipping back into reaction mode, but also proactively *seek out new potentials* and *create change* in the direction of their *Vision* – and are, in fact, always open to discovering an even greater *Vision* as they progress.

For far too long, we have been seduced by *analysis* as our predominant mode of thought, attracted by the mistaken belief that if only we knew an object's – or an organism's or an organization's – parts, we could *control it.* This mode of thought may have seemed a good fit for a mechanical, linear, cause-effect World. Yet, we now realize that we live in a *World in Process*, a world of self-organizing systems, an inseparable Whole within which where there are no parts.[293] Today's science tells us that the cause-effect, mechanical control model is an illusion. All choosing freely, influencing far-reaching effects that emerge spontaneously, organically. Each choice influences others in complex, unpredictable ways.

The point of our analysis is no longer is to control – but to better enable us to create and navigate in an ever-changing World in Process.

The more we can shift into "monitor mode," and push our analysis closer and closer to real-time feedback – the better able we will be to *create our own change* – and actively feed into the direction of change that favors our *Vision*.

THE END OF PREDICTION

In this world, imagination and navigation are far more powerful than knowledge and analysis.

Within a *system*, the "*center*" – the ever-changing outcome the system generates - *emerges organically*, as the result of dynamic, free – but unpredictable - choices within the Whole.[294]

No matter how detailed our analysis may be, these outcomes cannot be controlled or predicted.

We see this power in networks, emerging in every moment through the virtual world of the Internet, where the dynamic choices and creations arise into form and pattern, driven at light speed, into global awareness. This is the mind of the swarm, the hive, the smart mob … the dynamic of the tipping point, of co-creation and peer-production, of "word-of-mouth" branding, social networking, and viral marketing. Each choice influences others in complex, unpredictable ways.

Sometimes, as Duncan Watts, author of *Six Degrees* and expert on self-organizing communities, says "*small events percolate through obscure places by happenstance and random encounters, triggering a multitude of individual decisions, each made in the absence of any grand plan, yet aggregating somehow into a momentous event unanticipated by anyone, including the actors themselves. …*"[295]

Watts sees the increasing power of choice and social networks affecting influence and innovation at all levels. He cites "*rapid changes in the technology of media production, distribution, and consumption are driving a proliferation of choices for consumers – the so-called long tail,*"[296] and acknowledges that some believe this abundance of choice might actually reduce the importance of hit songs, blockbuster movies, bestselling books and other market fads, as advanced search capabilities increasingly enable audiences to find such "niche-oriented" products and services. However, Watts disagrees, arguing that it is "*precisely this proliferation of choice*" that will give ordinary individuals more power to influence others, not less.

… social networking sites such as Facebook, tagging sites such as Flickr, and user-generated content sites such as YouTube are increasingly exposing ordinary individuals to one another's decisions about what they watch, listen to, and buy.

Together, these trends point to a world in which successes will be more dramatic – and also harder to predict – than ever.[297]
   Duncan Watts, "Marketing in an Unpredictable World," *Harvard Business Review*

Though Watts' observations about the power of self-organization apply to marketing and entertainment, his conclusions also apply more broadly to all of us interested in influence and innovation. His recommendation to "*abandon the notion that [we] can either anticipate or determine specific outcomes and instead develop [our] ability to measure and exploit … demand as it arises,*"[298] also applies as we navigate any dynamic system - not allowing analysis to nudge us back into "reaction-mode" thinking – but instead constantly "monitoring" and using feedback to better navigation in real time toward our goals, in the midst of change.

THE SCOUT MOTTO – AND OTHER INNOVATION KEYS

It's no accident that many visionary thought leaders, including *Wired* magazine founder Kevin Kelly and *Wisdom of Crowds* author James Surowiecki, turn to the metaphor of the bee hive as an ideal, organic model of how thriving groups innovate. Both authors emphasize the ingenious "*monitoring*" method bees use to discover ever-newer sources of food: hives depend on a set of "scout" bees, which continually explore the surrounding environment. Upon finding a new nectar source, a scout returns to alert the hive by performing a "waggle dance," where the intensity of the bee's movement communicates the relative potential of the new resource. Thus, by sending scouts in many directions and trusting that one or more will find the best source, Surowiecki notes that the hive arrives at "*the collectively intelligent solution*," and achieves an "*almost perfect distribution to get as much food as possible relative to the time and energy they put into searching*" for new sources.[299]

Likewise, in seeking new sources and potentials for innovation, "*the smart thing is to send out as many scouts as possible*," first," *to uncover the possible alternatives, and then to decide among them.*" As entomologist William Morton Wheeler explains, the bee hive operates as a unified organism: "*like a cell or the person, it behaves as a unitary whole, maintaining its identity in space, resisting dissolution ... neither a thing or a concept, but a continual flux or process.*"[300] Our lesson? Surowiecki concludes: "*One key to this approach is a system that encourages, and funds, speculative ideas even though they have only slim possibilities of success. Even more important, though, is diversity ... in a conceptual and cognitive sense. ... so you end up with meaningful differences among those ideas rather than minor variations on the same concept.*"[301] How does this translate into real-world, "monitoring" terms? Drawing on Watts, as well as Kelly, Surowiecki, and others, we can distill some applicable insights for innovation:

- *Adopt the Scouting Motto* - taking a cue from the hive and other dynamical systems, we would be wise to incorporate a more active, planned deployment of diverse "scouts' – or, better yet, engage everyone in some aspect of scouting as part of the ongoing "Monitor" process – perhaps with each scout assigned to certain "sectors" (markets, trends, etc.),, as well as encouraged and expected to scout outside usual boundaries.

- *Hedge Your Bets* - First, go for quantity in creative ideas (always a key in creative thinking and techniques such as brainstorming). Then, as Watts says, "*increase the number of bets, and decrease their size, acknowledging that hits can't be predicted.*"[302] Invest in more than one creative endeavor, as only the market will tell you which ideas will take off, and thus warrant more investment.

- *Fund for the Future* – Savvy innovation experts always advise setting aside a separate fund for innovation – not only to encourage, but also to reward and communicate that you expect new programs, ideas to emerge as your team co-creates. Few things are more discouraging to creativity than if every new idea is met with "but we have no budget for that." Watts encourages flexible budgets, which may "*quickly be reallocated from unsuccessful bets as ... demand materializes.*" IBM budgets $100 million for innovations in both social and economic realms.[303]

- *Start Small/Fall Forward Fast* – from virtual worlds to physical manufacturing, the direction is toward fast-prototyping and beta-testing; favoring the Ready-Fire-Aim! approach – get the idea, prototype or service out there fast, then adjust as needed, after factoring in feedback (rather than fine-tuning the idea to death before running it by the market). Also, don't require a "blockbuster" initiative before investing in innovative ideas; implement several modest programs, rather than risking all in one high-cost creative initiative, Zappos.com CEO Tony Hsieh says: "*There's still a temptation to come out in a big way and waste a lot of money ... It's better to start small because, until you are actually doing it, you cannot predict the thousand little things that will inevitably happen.*"[304]

- *Engage Social Influence* – As Watts explains: "*Once a product has gained a following... amplify the corresponding social influence signal by directing the attention of a much wider audience toward the individuals or groups who are already enthusiastic about it. This strategy differs subtly but importantly from word-of-mouth or viral marketing strategies that seek to identify so-called influentials in order to solicit their endorsements. Instead, ... in effect, create influentials by selectively modifying social influence patterns as they emerge.*"

- *Track Feedback* - This is where analysis – or "detection, measurement and feedback," as Watts says – pays its greatest dividends in terms of the Creative Process. By using as-close-to-real-time feedback (increasingly possible through the network), we can adjust course toward Vision accordingly, without reverting to reactive mode.

- *Think Process* - In a world in process, we shift from control and prediction to imagination and navigation, not avoiding change, but creating change in the direction of our desired Vision. As Watts says, "*It's a complex dance.*"[305]

BREAKING CREATIVE GROUND

The most critical thing to remember, once an individual or organization has broken new creative ground, is not to try to retrofit their creation to match something that already exists - whether it be an existing product form or an existing job description.

Inventor Jack Kilby had to imagine solutions entirely outside the existing form of the vacuum tubes that powered most of the electronics of his day, in order to design the altogether new form of the *microchip* – an integrated circuit combining miniaturized transistors on a thin slice of silicon. Similarly, Apple computer designers had to move past their mental images of all the existing putty-colored, rectangular-tower-shaped computer box sets that constituted the standard form for PCs, in order to create the multi-colored, rounded-cornered, all-in-one *iMac* that in 1998 rocked the PC industry, and happily shocked computer users with delight. Existing forms – whether *physical* (such as product computer towers) or *mental* (such as existing definitions and descriptions) – literally and figuratively become the "boxes" we want to be able to "think outside of" – but, so often their existing forms are so familiar to us, we hardly notice that these forms may inadvertently limit and shape our efforts to innovate.

Likewise, on a personal level, consider, for a moment, your Career Arc – which you may well be in the process of designing, guided by the step-by-step exercises and worksheets in this section. If you truly are to draw on your unique set of gifts, talents, skill and strengths to design your ideal work, there is no guarantee that the ideal work you discover through the Creative Process will fit neatly into an already existing "job description" – it might, but it might not, nor should you feel you must force it to do so. In fact, once you have expanded your thinking to craft a scope of work that more fully expresses your creative potential, it would be a mistake to think you must stuff it back into an existing box. Instead, realize you are charting new territory, and use the same Creative Process to identify how your "works" may both enable you to contribute to familiar projects and positions, as well as to open a host of brand new opportunities and venues for you.

In fact, the more unique your constellation of gifts, the more likely you will craft unique work – which may well call for an equally new or innovative description or title to communicate, position and promote it. (For example, when the author discovered her unique calling to share the Creative Process, hardly anyone had heard of a "creativity consultant" or "Creative Process consultant"; now, however, this once-new scope of work is slowly becoming more well-known, as well as more "in demand," given ever greater recognition of the need for creative thinking).

In this Age of Imagination, individuals and organizations increasingly will not only adopt the creative mindset, but also will build space and time for creative thinking into their work and lives. They will take an innovation cue from fast-movers like Google, which allows its engineers to spend 20 percent of their work time on "self-directed projects," to encourage and nurture the generation of innovative ideas. Google attributes the creation of such successful new programs as Google News, Gmail, and Adsense for content to employees' use of this built-in innovation time.[306]

The trend to create both physical and mental space for innovative thinking is expanding beyond traditionally "creative" workplaces such as advertising agencies, into the Fortune 500 corporate realm, in the form of playspaces, idea interchanges, brainstorm walls and even meditation rooms.[307] Organizations are also rethinking their basic processes for "*talking and thinking together*," to spark more open, creative, diverse conversations, and are infusing inclusive dialogue techniques to break through traditional but stagnant "meeting modes," to more consciously guide open, innovative thinking , as well as incorporating team celebration and ritual, to continually fuel and nurture a more creative culture.

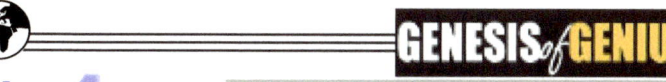

NOW RESOURCES

> **SCAN – MASTERING POWER ARC: CREATIVE GUIDANCE SYSTEM®:**
> We have reached a critical point in our exploration – having set the necessary creative framework of WHERE and NOW - where we now have the proper context to allow our analysis of this information to carry true meaning and true power to guide us forward. Now, we have the authentic context within which to analyze the rich information we have gathered – to consider different aspects within the Whole, to discover patterns and themes emerging within the system. It is only within this creative framework that we may tap the true power of NOW. In this creative space, every instant is open to possibility, electric with potential. Each step moves us forward along the ARC of our Journey, becoming what we are meant to be, as our path spirals ever upward to encompass more abundance, connections and resources.

In a world ...in process, every moment is a new and unique one. [308]
Abraham Maslow, American psychologist

At the close of the previous WHERE chapter, we introduced our *Creative Endeavor Pre-Survey Template* (Survey #10), a powerful information-gathering and engagement tool you may use in creating *Vision* and *Mission*, as well as to gain valuable input for all aspects of the HOW - or *Scan* - stage of the Creative Process, covered in this chapter: Survey, Analyze, Scope and Monitor. As we have noted here, SWOT Analysis may be used by both individuals (along with your LIFE ARC Exercises in Worksheets #1-7) and teams or organizations, and Survey # 10 includes a special key to match specific survey questions to each of the four SWOT Analysis quadrants.

Of course, in this networked age, we almost always have a much broader potential audience than in decades past, and, fortunately, much broader access to research, information, and even production sources, through the Internet. As a result, during the Scan stage of the Creative Process, we should always consider creative ways we might tap into the "global brain" of the Internet during our *Scan* stage, as we *Survey* stakeholders and potential audiences-participants, *Analyze* and *Scope* potential opportunities and assess emerging threats, and especially *Monitor* change much more closely and quickly, if not in real time.

Given our understanding of this *POWER ARC SUCCESS SYSTEM*, however, we now know that all of this information power - this Knowledge - need not move us further into a *reactive* mode of thought, but instead may fuel our Imagination about ways we may harness this emerging information to better create WHAT CAN BE, in the area of our current creative endeavor.

Across the varied contributions of the many Survey sources, we will begin to see recognizable "*clusters*" or related "*constellations*" of information take shape before our eyes. We pay close attention as these patterns emerge before us, as they make clear to us the pivotal issues and success factors that will propel us along our chosen path. Framed within the creative ARC of WHERE and HOW, analysis becomes more powerful, enabling us to identify these high "leverage points," which previously might never have become evident, without our inclusive approach to gain input and participation from the entire system. The patterns that emerge will become *Strategic Goals* (or "*Mini-Visions*") in the HOW stage.

On the next two pages, you will find SWOT Analysis Descriptions (Example #14) and the SWOT Analysis Worksheet (Worksheet # 15), which give you or your team the tools to fill out the four quadrants - <u>S</u>trengths, <u>W</u>eaknesses, <u>O</u>pportunities, and <u>T</u>hreats.

EXAMPLE # 14 - SWOT ANALYSIS DESCRIPTIONS

CREATIVE GUIDANCE SYSTEM® SWOT ANALYSIS DESCRIPTIONS

Strengths
What are your – or your team's or organization's – advantages, assets and strengths?

- *tangible* – personal, such as physical appearance, health, talents; or organizational, such as staff, customers, budget/funding, office space, equipment, software, and information access/resources;

- *intangible* – such as knowledge, skill sets, creativity, innovation, networks/collaborative capacities, identity/brand reputation or market perception, etc.)

Weaknesses
What are your – or your team's or organization's – disadvantages, limitations or weaknesses?

- *tangible* – personal, such as things you do poorly or could improve, physical limitations, or organizational, such as staffing, budget/funding, office and information resources; and

- *intangible* – such as knowledge or skill set limitations, lack of motivation or leadership support, negative perception/reputation, etc.)

* Note: These can then be 'flipped' from negatives to positives, and viewed as opportunities for improvement

Opportunities
What are current or emerging opportunities and trends favorable to you – or to your team's or organization's - mission?

- *tangible & intangible* (see above), *local* – such as additional cash flow, etc., as well as *global* - trends in technology, market, customer or competitor, or global shifts, etc.

Threats
What are current or emerging threats or obstacles do you – or your team or organization - face?

- *tangible & intangible* (see above), as well as disruptive technologies, market or competitor shifts, staff cuts or conflict, reduced cash flow, tougher job, customer, or market requirements, etc

GENESIS of GENIUS

Worksheet # 15 - SWOT Analysis Worksheet

Instructions: Team members fill in the four SWOT Analysis quadrants (either individually or in smaller sub-teams first, then sharing and consolidating input with the full group. Input may come from internal (team knowledge and experience) and external (other stakeholder and research) views (as described in Survey and Analysis sections of this Chapter). To gather input, we recommend the use of Creative Endeavor Pre-Survey Template #10 provided in the Guide, which contains a Key specifying which Survey questions align with each SWOT quadrant.

CREATIVE GUIDANCE SYSTEM® SWOT ANALYSIS WORKSHEET

Strengths	Opportunities

Weaknesses	Threats

To Claim Your Bonus Books, Free Creative Resources, & Innovation Tools visit GENESISOFGENIUSBOOK.COM.

© Julie Ann Turner & Company/CreatorsGuide.com.
All Rights Reserved.

CHAPTER TEN
How

If

you

can

DREAM it,

you

can

DO it.

Walt Disney, creative genius and Imagineer

GENESIS of GENIUS

DOING THE DREAM

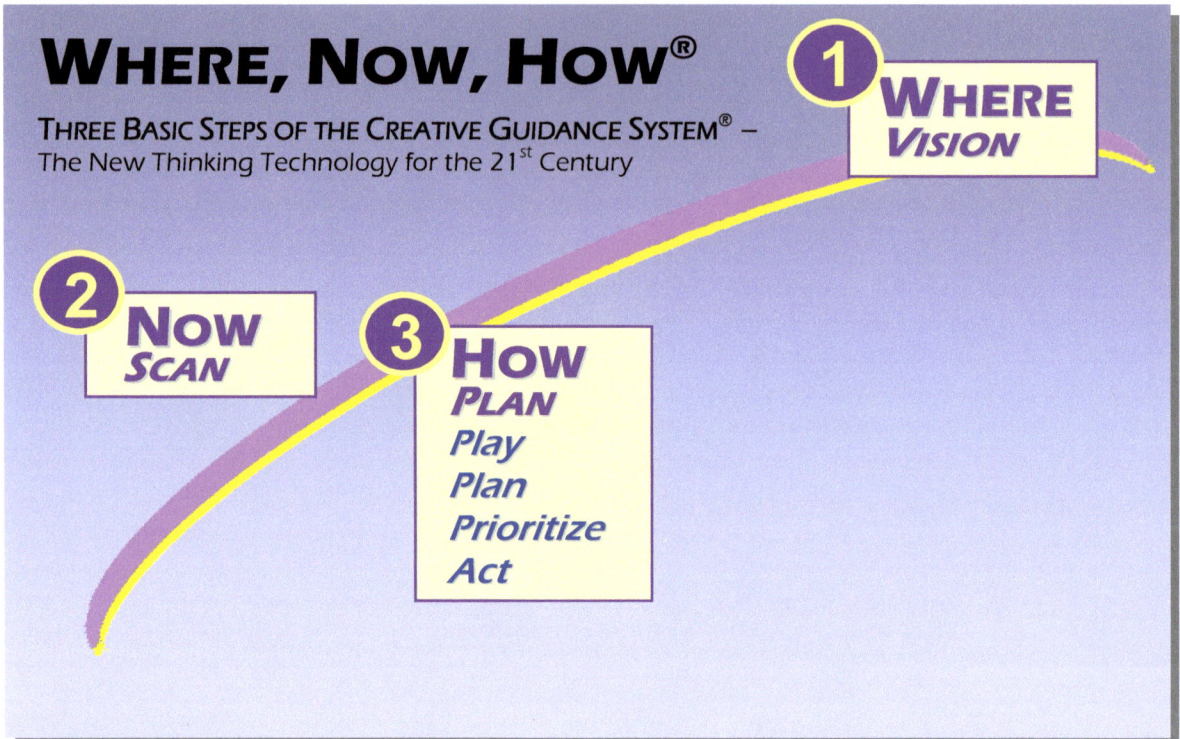

We've dreamed it.
But how many of us know How to turn our dreams into reality?
How to we begin living the life we've dreamed?

As we've learned, Life is always creating.
The Universe is powered by the Creative Process.
If we can learn and consciously apply that master process,
we can live into our potential as creators,
and create the life, work and world we most desire to see.

We've dreamed it. We know WHERE we're going – our *Destination*, our *Vision*, our *Dream* - and we know where we are Now. We've set up a powerful framework based on the Creative Process.

Now it's time to learn How to "live into" the life, work and world we most desire.

In this section, we introduce the four basic elements in the How or *Plan* stage, at a level useful both to individuals and organizations:

▶ *Play* – imaginatively explores multiple possibilities and paths for achieving goals How

▶ *Plan* – generates goals - and organizes ideas and actions to achieve those goals

▶ *Prioritize* – orders potential goals and activities by aligning resources with highest values

▶ *Act* – takes action to implement plans and monitors changes that may affect the process

We introduce the core How steps and tools in this section, and will provide more advanced tools and guidance on planning and navigation in our advanced VisionSPARC training (online only). The section here provides foundational material for both individuals and organizations, with initial examples focusing on the Individual Level. Our advanced VisionSPARC resources focus on Organizational Level examples, with tools and training for the more multidimensional, complex planning involving groups. If you lead an organization or business, see GENESISofGENIUS.COM for details.

SHORTCIRCUIT TO HOW

*In many ways, we are more familiar with planning than with any other aspect of the Creative Process. Just ask us. We know **How** to get things done.*

In our organizations, we often pride ourselves on being *problem-solvers* and *planners*. We know these competitive times call for speed and efficiency, for *do-ers* and *multi-taskers*.[309] Words like *goals, objectives, strategies*, and *tactics* sound familiar and practical. We're good at knowing *what to do*, great at *getting things done*, excellent at *execution*. We can make a *list of things to do* at the drop of a hat. Just ask to see our *calendars* (electronic or paper) or our *To-Do lists*.[310]

*In fact, we're so good **How** thinking, it has become our automatic, default mode.*

And today, it is our near knee-jerk mental jump *past options* to *operation, past envisioning* to *execution* – which virtually ensures that *innovative, creative*, WHAT CAN BE thinking will rarely, if ever, see the light of day. For, as we've seen, one of the quickest ways to shut down creative thinking is to short-circuit the conversation to How, before we know WHERE we're going.

That is why our understanding of full Creative Process and concept of PLANES OF THOUGHT is so critical, as this *sequence of thought* allows us, whether as individuals or as teams and organizations, to *create the space for necessary creative thinking to surface* – so that the imagination involved in envisioning WHAT CAN BE is allowed space to emerge.

In our focus on speed and urgency, on *getting things done*, we often scatter out and rush ahead, before we've even determined if we're headed in the right direction. Recent studies show that this constant demand for speed actually limits breakthrough innovation.[311] And how often are our meetings and conversations cut short in an effort to actually limit new ideas, so we can get on with execution? Yet, as Stephen R. Covey said, it will do us little good to climb the ladder of success if our ladder is on the wrong wall, or to thrash through the vines on a quest through the wrong jungle.[312] We're so busy *doing*, we don't have time to *Plan* – much less *to imagine new possibilities, to envision* WHERE *we're going*, to 'begin with the end in mind," as Covey said.

As Xerox's Chris Turner reminds us: "*Thinking creates the structures that create an organization's behavior. Learn how to rethink, and you start to change.*"[313] It is our thinking technology – our thought sequence – that must change, in order for all the action steps of our How to go in the right direction. If we follow the steps in the Creative Process – presented in this CREATIVE GUIDANCE SYSTEM – then all our experience and efficiency at How, or the *Plan* stage, will translate into vastly greater efficiency, productivity – and yes, speed – in actually achieving our desired results.

In fact, when we think and act together in the sequence presented in this GUIDE, and when all the stages and steps in the Creative Process are followed, we may align our work most effectively for each Life ARC. *Our experience with planning becomes a much greater asset.* Moreover, we not only rediscover creativity and release energy from everyone participating, we also regain the power for the flow of ideas and *strategies* to emerge that can address multiple goals and span more than one PLANE OF THOUGHT at a time. Full energy to achieve our *Vision* may then flow freely, throughout the entire process, enabling us to reach our goals faster, and, drawing on our full potential, reach goals higher than we could ever have before.

Our first question should not focus on "what to do" or HOW *to do it; instead, as we consciously move through the* WHERE, NOW, HOW *sequence, we regain our full creative potential and power.*

PLAN

Unfortunately, most plans are static documents, insufficient for our dynamic World in Process.

"Plan-making" is not the issue. As we've noted, most of know how to create plans. We've had lots of practice. Organizations create plans – often elaborate "Strategic Plans" – massive documents, which, once written, often, sadly, sit on shelves in big binders, gathering dust. Static (or dusty, unused) plans are insufficient for navigating in a real, process world.

On individual level, To-Do Lists often serve as our daily plans. Of course, there is nothing inherently wrong with To-Do Lists, calendars (electronic or paper) and other systems for organizing our next steps – in fact, ultimately, we must have some mechanism through which to move our "best next steps" into our daily line of sight. However, too often, once we've created our plan or To-Do list, we fail to look up again – to reconnect with our purpose, to revisit our trajectory, to reorient our navigational journey.

Planning is a process. Crafting a plan once every 5 years, or even once a year, won't do. We need a dynamic, navigational system to reach the dreams we have envisioned.

A Plan should be a living, navigational document, a dynamic, real-time guide – often rendered in both written and visual form – so that all may participate in its ongoing creation, course adjustment, progress and achievement.

What we present here is a process approach to planning for a process world - what we call "*navigational planning*" (for more on NAVIGATIONAL PLANNING, see p. 366). Our World in Process demands that we have common, *navigational planning* tools – a *shared thinking technology* – to enable us to think, collaborate and act together, navigating change and allocating resources in real-time, and co-creating the results we have set forth in our *Vision*, *Mission* and goals.

Because our highest *Vision* and guiding *Values* (WHERE stage), as well as the insight we've gained from our current 360-degree view of reality (NOW stage), flow through this CREATIVE GUIDANCE SYSTEM, our HOW *Plan* stage will be the culmination of a full cycle of the process. As a result, the ideas, strategies and next steps we generate in this *Plan* stage, based upon this unified work, will carry – and will naturally align with - these guiding *Values* and *Vision*, as well. As we've seen, our Arc framework facilitates this alignment, in a powerful, visual way.

Not only will our new navigational "thinking technology" guide us here, but we may also find ways to tap the power of new web-enabled, collaborative tools – from flexible project software and collaborative meeting tools, to mindmapping and other innovation-enabling software, as well as open tools such as wikis and blogs – not only to gather and exchange real-time information, but to give everyone access to craft, edit, innovate - and continually update - our navigational plans. Some innovative companies are ahead of the curve on this potential, such as Xerox, where the company set up a wiki to enable R&D researchers to collaboratively craft the company's technology roadmap and competitive strategy.[314]

The good news is that, using our navigational planning technology, we don't have to know everything about How to get there in advance (which is a good thing, since, as we've seen, it is impossible to know everything in advance, anyway). As we move through each of these Plan steps, we will always keep our Vision and Mission in mind, as these provide the essential – and highest – trajectory for our creative journey.

FILLING THE GAP

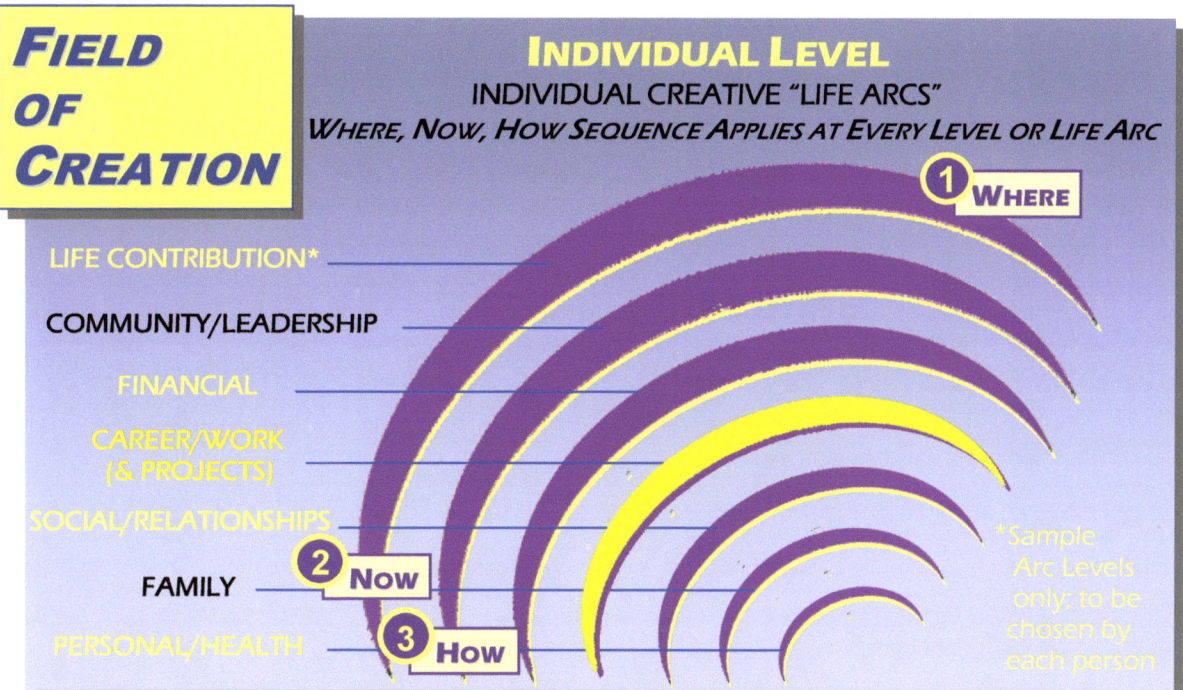

We can think of the How stage as "filling the gap" between our first stage – our WHERE, or Vision or Dream, and our second stage – our NOW, or current reality.

Once we have set up the creative tension established by the discrepancy between our *Now* and our high *Vision – for any level or ARC –* our central focus, necessary resources, and specific steps most important to *How we achieve our dreams* will become evident, emerging spontaneously and almost magically, within the framework we already have created.

To see how the focus for each ARC emerges in this way, we again start with our *WHERE Vision* in mind, and draw on the valuable information snapshot we gained through our *Now Scan* stage (*Scan, Analyze, Scope* and *Monitor*). To illustrate, we focus first on the Individual *Career ARC* (see graphic above), as shown in the example we highlighted previously (p. 345):

> Individual/Personal Example – Personal Exercises/SWOT Analysis (*Career ARC*)
> (*Career* Vision: Sharing in entrepreneurs' success guided by my business/investing expertise;
> Mission: To serve entrepreneurs and start-up ventures through my passion for finance)
> Strengths: Business–financial acumen; Small business success; strong communication skills
> Weaknesses: Lack of public speaking experience; like working independently; competitive nature
> Opportunities: Small business a growing market; investor/funding connections; want to serve
> Threats: Temptation to "coast" after business success; fear won't live full, authentic life
>
> Key Pattern/Pivot Point (arising as "cluster" of potential from analysis above, shown in blue):
> > Launch one-on-one small business/start-up consulting, with focus on investment/funding

Guided by our Vision, and drawing on the information, resources, and possibilities revealed by a Scan of our current state, we may identify valuable patterns emerging - constellations and clusters of information, which will guide us to our most strategic goals for each level or ARC.

MASTER ARCS & MINI-VISIONS

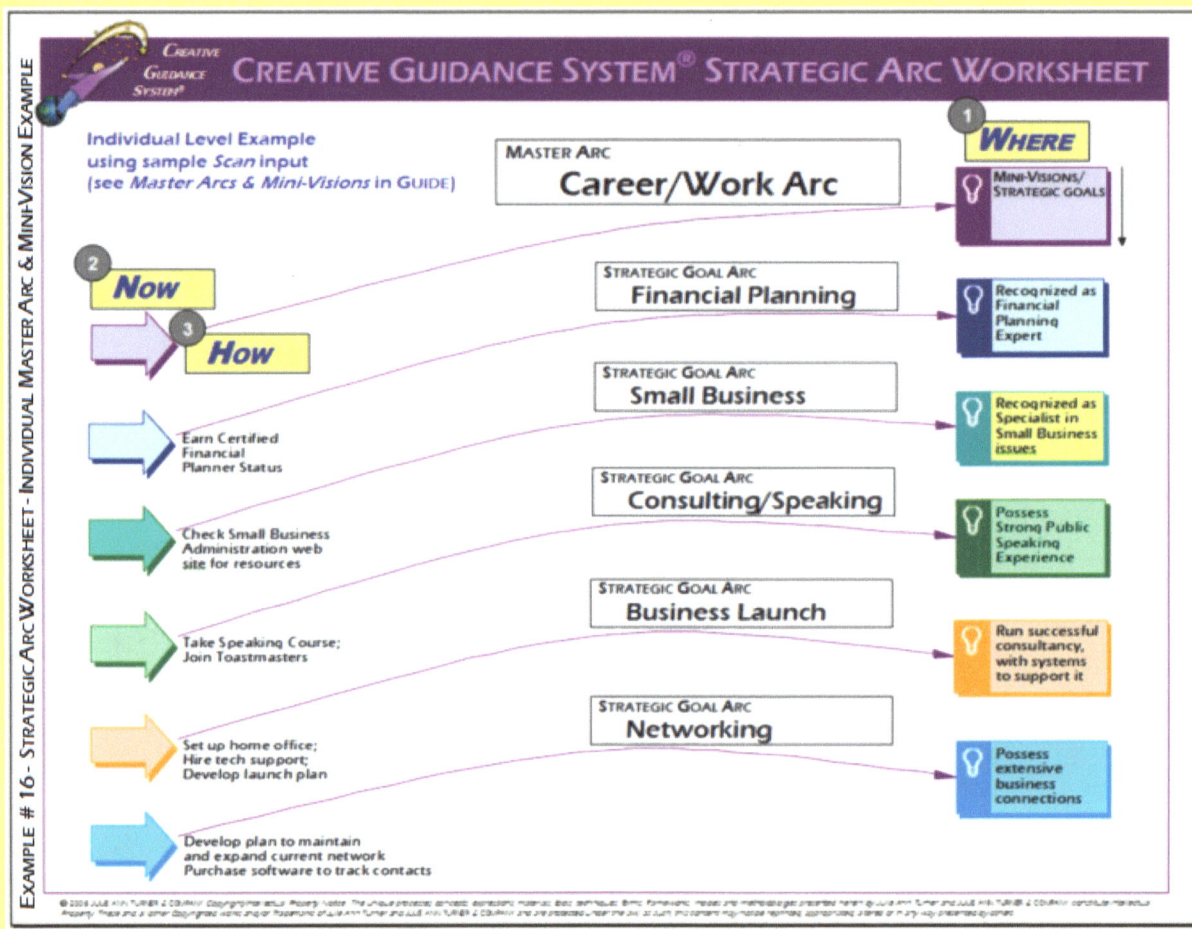

Now, the fractal ARC framework will enable you to simply and clearly focus on the key strategies and next steps for your ARC of immediate focus. Here, drawing on the Individual sample Scan data on the previous page, we show an example focusing on the Career ARC (using Example #16). The power of the fractal ARC framework enables us to simply and clearly "drill down a level" to focus on the Strategic Goals and Next Steps for our ARC of immediate focus.

After identifying patterns and natural "clusters" of related ideas and phrases in your collection of *Scan* information (p. 345), and then major theme areas (some call these "problems" or "issues'); more positively, others call these "critical success factors." In the example above, the individual lists the main strategic focus areas (names or titles for each of the primary themes which emerged during the *Scan* stage, in blue on previous page) which will move him or her toward a specific goal (see instructions and worksheet pp. 376 and 378). Now, we will turn these into *Strategic Goals* or "*Mini-Visions*" – as these form the core of any *Plan*.

Because the same Creative Process works at every level (this is the recurring fractal power of the ARC and the SPIRAL), we create a Vision – which we refer to as a "Mini-Vision" or "Strategic Goal" – for every ARC.

In this way, we are able to ensure we are focused on potential, not problems, at every level.

Now, although you're looking for what you *do* want, you may well first see it in a negative form in your *Scan* input or SWOT Analysis. For example, as we see in our Individual Level example on the previous page, some input initially may be stated in *negative* terms: "*Lack of public speaking experience*" or "*Fear won't live full, authentic life.*" To move toward what we *do* want, we simply "*do a flip*" of the negative statement, to generate a positive one. So, "*Lack of public speaking experience*" (what we *don't* want) simply becomes "*Possess strong public speaking experience*" (a "*Mini-Vision*" of what we *do* want), and so on.

NAVIGATIONAL PLANNING: WHAT WE DO WANT

Notice the power our Creative ARC framework gives us to focus on *what we do want* at each level (shifting us out of the *problem-solving mode* and into the *potential-driven, creative mode* of thinking), and then note how easily we are able to think about and imagine possibilities to achieve our *Strategic Goal* or *Mini-Vision*. For instance, in the example on the previous page, see how naturally ideas for moving us forward along our ARCS begin to flow (we will learn more about how we may generate creative strategies for each ARC in the next section – *Play*).

Our *Strategic Goals* become "*the pivotal planks in our Plan*" – the primary focus areas for each of our Master ARCS, around which we may better organize our efforts and allocate our resources. As we focus on these *Strategic Goals* or *Mini-Visions*, we *know* each decision and step we take will move us toward what we really want, because we have taken the time to determine what our true *Vision, Mission, Values* and *Goals* really are. In addition, because these *Strategic Goals* emerged as the result of the Creative Process, we also know that each of these focus areas represents a key leverage point specific to our lives and work, and, as a result, our efforts in these strategic areas will have the greatest power to propel us forward. (And, if developed within this creative framework, even To-Do Lists can become powerful tools.)

Moreover, we may use the power of this creative, Mini-Vision approach to guide us in every moment – in every situation, project, relationship, conversation or meeting.

At any instant, if we are unsure how to move forward, or we are facing opposition, all we need to do is simply ask "What would success look like in this situation" or "What do we want to have happen now?" Using this navigational system, every decision and interaction will now be initiated at the highest level of thought, infused with creative possibility at every stage, and oriented toward your highest potential, and the greatest potential of the Whole.

Notice also that the relative positions of the ARCS - with the names and order of the ARCS chosen as most important by each individual or group - enable alignment and creative synergy of strategies and resources across ARCS, as well. For example, let's say two of your personal ARCS were "*Quality time with family*" (*Family* ARC) and "*Physical health and fitness*" (*Health* ARC) Because the creative ARC framework enables you to see all your *Strategic Goals* related to one another, you are better able to identify potential ideas that could move you forward on more than on goal at a time – to "kill two birds with one stone," if you will; for instance, with a single strategy – "*Take a walk with my son twice a week*" - you would gain synergy in your time and make progress on both *family time* and *physical health* goals.

By focusing on *what we want to have happen*, we will always be seeking the highest in every situation. We will not be forced into compromise or into choosing some lesser option or "*next best step.*' Instead, we will be able to identify and act on what we call our "*Best Next Step*" - which will always carry us to a higher level of creative possibility and potential.

As we've noted, in this How section, we use examples at the Individual Level, and will focus on the basic, core elements of any *Navigational Plan* – our *Strategic Goals* and "*Best Next Steps*" – saving more detailed Organizational examples and planning elements - such as the distinction among objectives, strategies and tactics - for our advanced VISIONSPARC training (online only).

BEST NEXT STEPS

Infinite choice means infinite possibility.[315]

Mark Joyner, *Simple-ology*

If we create Vision first – at every level - all possibilities remain open to us.

In an unlimited FIELD OF CREATION, our choices determine our trajectory and our path.

Through our conscious, creative choices – we may tap into the infinite possibility and power of the CREATIVE FIELD. Framed within the dynamic tension of each creative ARC, our choices carry much more power, as each choice is aligned with Purpose, with our highest Vision and Values.

We rediscover the truth and freedom of creation: we are not limited by our current abilities, our current resources, or even by what we may currently believe is possible at this moment.
We realize we do not need to match our choices to what we already know exists.
We are free in every instant to make what we call the "BEST NEXT STEP."
We are free to create the future – consciously and intentionally.

To begin, we only need to know our BEST NEXT STEPS.

Once we step into the CREATIVE FIELD, we can navigate the path to attain our dreams.

In this creative, navigational system, each step is a conscious choice we know will move us toward our dreams. The newfound interest in the "law of attraction" is not surprising, in that this principle harmonizes with, and, indeed, is rooted in, the navigational, process-oriented approach encompassed by the Creative Process. We are always creating, as the law of attraction acknowledges, so that we may say in any moment: *"I am in the process of attracting all that I need to do, know or have, to attract my ideal desire,"*[316]

We don't have to know it all right now – we lay down the path as we walk it.

Within the system of the Creative Process, each step opens new and greater possibilities to us. The SPIRAL path takes us ever higher, with each discovery expanding into ever greater potential. Like a mountain climber, who, with each additional arc she walks up the mountainside, can see ever farther – with each step on our creative path, we see farther, and our view of the possibilities expands.

Consider the communication revolution sparked first by the development of writing itself, and then expanded by the development of such creations as paper, the printing press, the telegraph, telecommunications, the Internet, the networked world.

The SPIRAL – and the potential - expands with every ARC.

PLAN STEP ONE: PLAY

We do not stop playing because we grow old. We grow old because we stop playing.
George Bernard Shaw, playwright

▶ *Play* – *imaginatively explores multiple possibilities and paths for achieving goals*

In this GUIDE, we introduce *Play* as essential part of planning.

So often, we underestimate its value, its purpose, and its power, and other planning approaches may rarely, if ever, build play into the process. We believe, however, that infusing the process with play is essential to unleashing an individual's or team's full creative power. Once we have the strategic planks of our plan – our *Strategic Goals* or *Mini-Visions* - in place, we want to approach the creation of our "*Best Next Steps*" and strategies with the same imaginative power and energy as we have to the beginning of the process.

"*Play is how we wire our brains as children, but as adults we tend too much to pave the cowpaths,*" says Lewis Pinault, managing director of Box, a learning lab launched by EDS at the London School of Economics.[317] The old saying holds true, even if we fail to acknowledge it: "*If we always do what we've always done, we'll always get what we've always gotten.*" Albert Einstein, who proclaimed imagination was more important than knowledge, defined insanity as doing the same things over and over, yet expecting a different result.[318] It's no surprise that Einstein, the great thinker, also said that success required equal parts work and play.[319]

Now that we've thought out of the box in developing our "planks in the plan," we want to continue thinking creatively about How we might go about achieving each major *Goal*. After all, we don't want to crawl right back into the box by simply using the "same old ways" we've always used; we want to use our imagination to consider new ways to achieve our *Goals*. Not only that, we want to build imagination and play into our lives and our work. As Gary Schwartz, founder of Intuitive Learning Systems, says: "*Fun is not trivial; it is essential. ... Fun is a psychological state where attitude and judgment are suspended and the mind and body act in harmony to accomplish a goal.*" Schwartz notes that the experience of fun expands awareness, sharpens senses, and involves participants with a sense of positive expectancy. Schwartz adds that play brings us into the present, where we focus only on the object of the "game," and that "*a game changes what you 'should do' into what you 'want to do'*" - a mindset which is perfectly aligned with the Creative Process."[320] What spoils fun and stops the flow of creative thought and energy? Schwartz says, "*any expectation of judgment or the approval or disapproval of others.*" So, as we imagine strategies for reaching our goals, we must create space and allow time for everyone to think freely, to have fun, and to suspend the "voice of judgment" – whether it comes from our own self-consciousness, or from others.

You can't quantify the value of letting people's minds run wild.[321]
Tom Kelley, CEO/IDEO, and author of *The Art of Innovation*

Tom Kelley, CEO of the creative studio IDEO, attributes the company's success to a combination of "boisterous work and play in process," which generates the "incorrigible spirit of play that keeps team members in tune and on edge." From the beginning, *Fast Company* magazine's "manifesto" celebrated this creative spirit, ending with the words: "Make work play."[322] Perhaps it's no surprise that Inc. Magazine also recently proclaimed "fun" as "the new core value" for business.[323] Play also teaches us to navigate - as we learn to make complex adjustments to new situations constantly - and brings out the best of people's abilities.[324]

TOOLS FOR PLAY

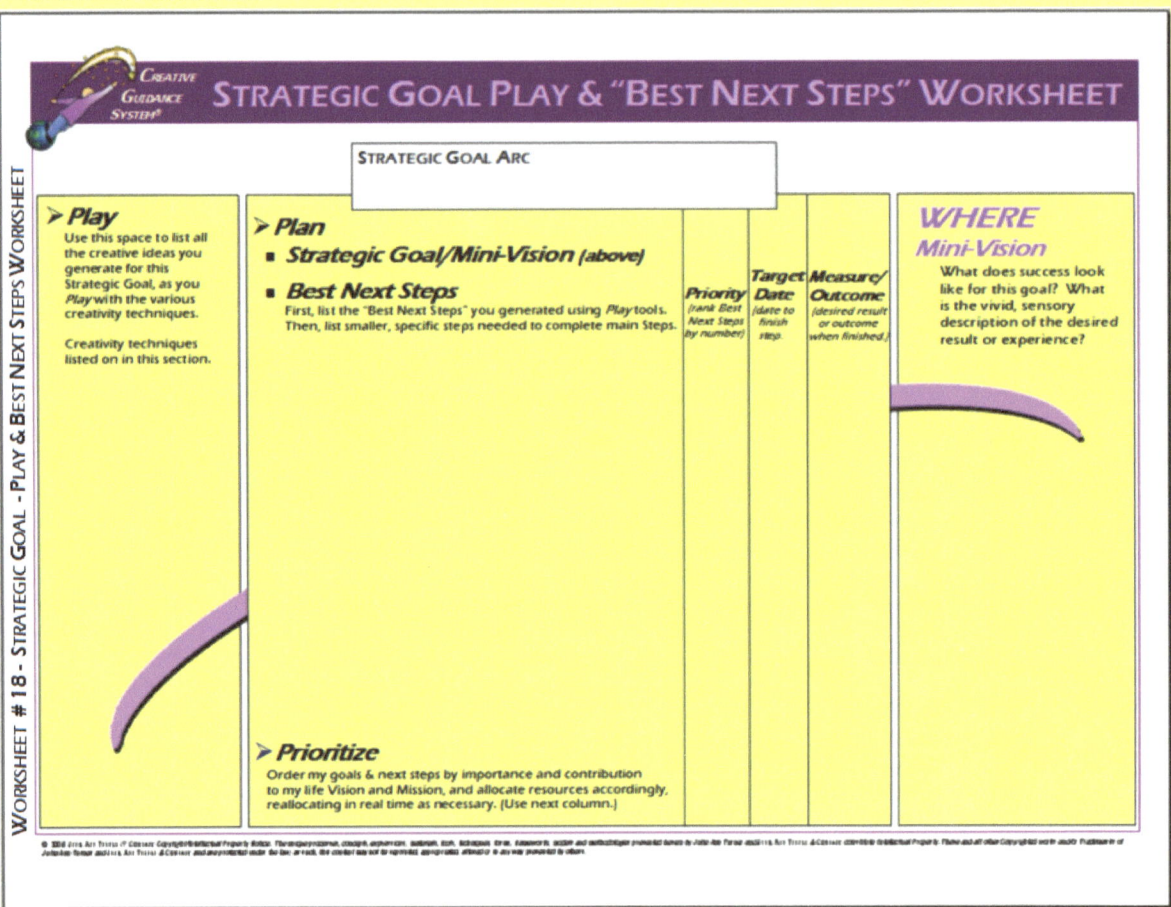

Where is it written that important assignments must be carried out with an air of grim determination? That breakthrough ideas can only emerge in a business-as-usual environment? That work must always feel like, well, work?[325]

Fast Company, "Mind Games"

The good news is, every step of the planning process can not only be creative, but also fun. *Now* is the appropriate stage of the process for you to use the associative creativity tools and techniques we first discussed and introduced on p. 107, as well as additional innovative tools included at the end of this section, to generate fresh ideas for How you might reach each *Strategic Goal* (Worksheets #16-18).

Whether you are seeking to be more innovative as an individual or as a company, adopting the full Creative Process, as well as new creativity tools and techniques, will expand potential, in both life and business.

Moreover, innovative companies across the globe are realizing the importance of creating work spaces that encourage and facilitate play. In fact, IDEO CEO Tom Kelley says *"Creating a great work environment may be as important as hiring the right people. Indeed, in my own experience they're often inseparable."*[326] In addition, companies are now realizing that new technology tools – not only software, but also web-based collaborative tools like wikis and blogs are facilitating idea-sharing and innovation, as well. A key point these companies are recognizing is that, by creating space, opening communication, and encouraging idea exchange – in the workspace and via the Internet - knowledge workers are better able to self-organize and team up dynamically, to meet the needs in a changing market. At *Geek Squad*, in fact, allowing such "play" is not only boosting innovation and idea exchange, but also networking and morale, as workers at headquarters even play online games to stay connected with their colleagues in the company's small satellite office in Anchorage, Alaska.[327] It clearly works to "*make work play.*"

MINDPLAY: REGAINING CREATIVE SPIRIT

Every child is an artist. The problem is how to remain an artist once he grows up.
Pablo Picasso, painter and sculptor

We are all natural creators. Yet somewhere along the way, our naturally creative way of approaching the world gets squeezed out of us ... by an education system that insists only on "correct" answers, rather than creative thinking ... by organizations that measure and reward based only on expected results, rather than on creative efforts that result in mistakes, as well as potential breakthroughs.

Yet, as we've established, our world requires that we shift beyond mere Knowledge to Imagination, and beyond Control to Creation.

As Cisco Systems education lead Charles Fadel and his colleagues at the Partnership for 21st Century Skills note, *"the measure of success in today's economy is not just what you know, but how you use that to imagine new ways to get work done, solve problems, or create new knowledge ... a major part of a person's skill set must be the ability to adapt to new conditions and imagine new solutions."*[328]

Building play back into our lives is a central way we may rediscover our natural creativity.

When you were a child, what did you imagine yourself to be?
What was your favorite role to play, when you imagined what you'd be when you "grew up"?
Remember the freedom and fun of the playground? the colors of Crayons, the smell of Play-Doh, the joy of building new creations with blocks, clay, paste, paper and other simple materials and toys?

In her book *You Don't Have to Go Home Exhausted*, Ann McGee-Cooper encourages us to remember – and to rediscover – the natural creative characteristics of children, who *"seek out things that are fun to do, or else they find a way to have fun at what they are doing ... are curious and usually eager to try anything once ...smile and laugh a lot ... are creative and innovative ... are constantly growing mentally ... will risk often — they aren't afraid to keep trying something they aren't initially good at and aren't afraid to fail ... generally don't worry or feel guilty ... learn enthusiastically ... dream and imagine ... believe in the impossible ... are passionate."*[329] How many of these attributes might we build into our lives? And how might we intentionally incorporate more *play* into our lives?

We may literally add color, toys and art back into our lives. Business leaders at EDS's *Box* center in London literally build structures using Lego toy blocks as part of the learning exercises there.[330] Many high-level leaders incorporate toys in meetings or keep them close at hand at their desks for use during impromptu brainstorm sessions or during their "think time." In fact, building in "think time" is an essential practice and innovation secret of many creative leaders, who realize that our natural creativity needs unstructured, open space and unpressured time in order to emerge and flourish.

In fact, as we have pointed out previously in the GUIDE (p. 114-116), our brains need this unstructured processing time to make new – and often unexpected – connections, which occurs during what British sociologist Graham Wallas called "*incubation*," a key part of the *unconscious* work of the creative process, which the brain carries out below our conscious awareness, if given sufficient time and space to do so. Often, it is when our minds are relaxed or engaged in routine activity that creative breakthroughs come. That is perhaps why Archimedes cried "Eureka!" in the bathtub, and also why Einstein said he always got his best ideas while shaving.[331]

We learn the Creative Process by practicing it - by allowing our minds to play, by expressing our selves and our gifts through art, writing, movement, and more (the courses most often forced out of schools), and by learning the Creative Process step by step, as shared here in GENESIS OF GENIUS.

The thing is to become a master, and in your old age to acquire the courage to do what children did when they knew nothing.
Henry Miller, writer and painter

PLAN STEP TWO: PLAN

▶ *Plan* – *generates goals - and organizes ideas and actions to achieve those goals*

We already have our "planks in the plan" – our *Strategic Goals* or *Mini-Visions* – the key goals we want to navigate toward in our lives, work and world.

Now, all we need to do is choose our top "*Best Next Steps*," of those we generated in the *Play* step. Then, we'll break each main step into smaller steps, by listing the actions it will take to complete each main step. See the example below (as well as worksheet on previous page):

STRATEGIC GOAL: Business Launch

BEST NEXT STEPS

- *Set up home office*

  Action steps:
  - Check Amazon.com for book on home office set-up and equipment
  - Make list of furniture, equipment and supplies I will need
  - Research options for each office component in local stores and online

- *Hire tech support*

  Action steps:
  - Call friends who own small businesses for recommendations
  - Search online for local resources
  - Ask for recommendations at local office technology stores

- *Develop launch plan*

  Action steps:
  - Search online for articles on launching a business
  - Outline launch plan components
  - Use creativity techniques to generate innovative marketing ideas
  - Develop initial launch budget

Notice that the first step, especially when you are starting on a new goal or project, will often be research – just getting more information about what you want to do. In fact, this is an advisable step for most goals, because, during your initial research, you will likely discover new approaches and resources for achieving your goal, and you may also find out that some steps you had listed are not even necessary, thus saving you more time and resources.

You will simply add steps as you go, and you may even break some of these steps down into even smaller, "do-able" pieces.

In this WHERE, NOW, HOW section, we have provided you with a simplified planning process, along with related tools and worksheets, to guide you through the core steps to enable you to move confidently and steadily toward your *Vision* and *Goals*, as well as to navigate through change, by consistently focusing on your *Vision, Strategic Goals* and *Best Next Steps*.

In our advanced VISIONSPARC training, we provide a more detailed planning approach, which includes additional guidance appropriate for teams and organizations or individuals who prefer a more advanced planning approach, including strategic and operational plans, and terms such as objectives, strategies and tactics (a level of detail unnecessary in a basic plan).

PLAN STEP THREE: PRIORITIZE

> ▶ *Prioritize* – *orders potential goals and activities by aligning resources with highest values*
>
> *We each have the same amount of time each day – 24 hours - to accomplish our goals. There is a limited amount that anyone can do in that timeframe, and so we each must make choices about how we spend our time.*
>
> *Our plan, generated by POWER ARC: YOUR CREATIVE GUIDANCE SYSTEM, is oriented around our highest Vision and Values. As a result, our choices – at every level – are always grounded in what is most important and valuable to us.*

Most people can't say that. Since some don't have a plan, and, even those who do, often have not taken the time to determine their *Vision* and *Values*, these individuals are challenged when it comes to choosing where to focus their attention and effort. In a fast-changing world, these people most often wind up simply reacting to whatever circumstances emerge or whatever crisis looks most urgent at the moment. That's why most people find themselves in crisis mode, running from "fire drill" to "fire drill,' as we discussed in the previous section on problem-solving versus creating.

We already have a tremendous advantage, in that we know all our *Goals* are tied directly to our chosen *Vision* and *Values*, and that every action we take to accomplish those *Goals* will move us closer to our dream. Does that mean every step we take will turn out the way we planned? No – because, in many cases, we're still learning the best ways to accomplish our *Goals*. However, even these learning steps – even if they don't turn out exactly as we'd planned – will still be moving us in the right direction, as we may simply orient again toward our *Vision*, and try another way. Moreover, because we are willing to try different approaches – and to be creative at every step – our learning steps will often lead us to new methods and expanded connections that will move us forward faster, which we might never have discovered if not for our creative, navigational mindset.

Because we have taken time to establish a foundation of *Vision* and *Mission*, it will be much easier for us to identify which steps are critical to move us further along our ARC, as well as to avoid being diverted by random circumstances – no matter how urgent they may seem - which have no real relevance to our *Vision* and *Goals*. In addition, we are better equipped to adjust to change and unexpected outcomes, because we have taken a navigational approach to planning. We realize that *planning* is an ongoing *process*, and that we may, at any instant, reorient toward our *Vision* and *Goals* given changing circumstances, adjust our action steps as necessary, and reallocate our resources accordingly, all in real time.

However, because we, like everyone else, do have limited time each day. As part of our navigational approach, we prioritize our *Strategic Goals*, as well as the related action steps to accomplish them, so that we are always focusing our attention and efforts on the most strategic and most high-leverage tasks in any given moment – on the tasks that will best move us forward on our path.

All we have to do is review our Goals and action steps – daily or more often as necessary – and prioritize the most effective order in which we will act on each step, and set target dates to complete each task (see Worksheets 17 and 18). Now, productivity tools - our To-Do lists, calendars (paper or electronic), and software – become truly powerful (see Resources section).

PLAN STEP FOUR: ACT

The possibilities are numerous once we decide to act and not react.
George Bernard Shaw, playwright

▶ *Act* – *takes action to implement plans and monitors changes that may affect the process*

The act of envisioning – in vivid detail - what you most desire carries power.
The very act of imagining and writing down your plan to achieve your Goals carries power.

Every action sets energy into motion – transforming potential into power.
Taking action is a powerful step into the electric field of possibility, into the CREATIVE FIELD.
Now, you have a navigational plan – and a creative guidance system – framed around
your compelling *Vision*, rooted in your highest *Values*, fully aligned with your *Purpose*,
and totally focused on what you most desire.
You are no longer *reacting* to random circumstances,
you are consciously *acting* to realize your dream.

You have created a vivid, experiential *Vision* of the life, work and world you wish to see, and now, you begin to "*live into it, as if it were already true*," as Arnold Schwarzenegger says. Your passion for your dream now fuels your journey, compelling you - at each step - to *act*.

In this CREATIVE GUIDANCE SYSTEM, we have introduced a "plan" as a navigational tool,
as a dynamic, real-time guide – not as a static document that remains on the shelf.
We live in a world in process, so we need flexible, dynamic plans we can adjust
in real time, as we navigate the changing field before us, on the way to our Goals.

As we've learned, it is not enough to *have* a plan – even a navigational one. We must still choose to *act* on it. Our plan is only *potential* until we *act* on it, and we can only act in the present. With each action, we begin transforming potential into reality.

Doing something requires ... doing something! ...
If you want the future to be better than the past, start working on it immediately.[332]
Jeffrey Pfeffer, author of *The Knowing-Doing Gap*

As always, *choice is the mechanism of creation*. We must actually set the plan in motion ... and take the first step into the CREATIVE FIELD. As we've learned, our actions affect the entire system, and our tangible actions communicate our intentions, open new connections to others attracted to our *Vision* and *Mission*, and expand not only our knowledge, but our range of possibilities. Once we act, we start energy moving in a direction; it is no longer just potential.

Because we know all our *Goals* are tied directly to our *Vision* and *Values*, and that every action we take along our ARC will move us closer to our dream, we may move forward with *boldness* – as motivator Anthony Robbins says, we can "*take massive action!*" We have a dynamic plan, with creativity infused at every level – and a master CREATIVE GUIDANCE SYSTEM to guide us at every level, in every moment. The lens of our *Vision* and *Goals* helps us filter incoming information and circumstances. *Vision* and *Mission* serve as the guiding stars of our journey – at any moment, we may "reorient" to our *Purpose*, and reallocate resources in real time.

Whatever you do, or dream you can, begin it.
Boldness has genius, power and magic in it.[333]
Johann Wolfgang Von Goethe, German writer, artist and philosopher

GENESIS of GENIUS

LIFE NAVIGATION SYSTEM

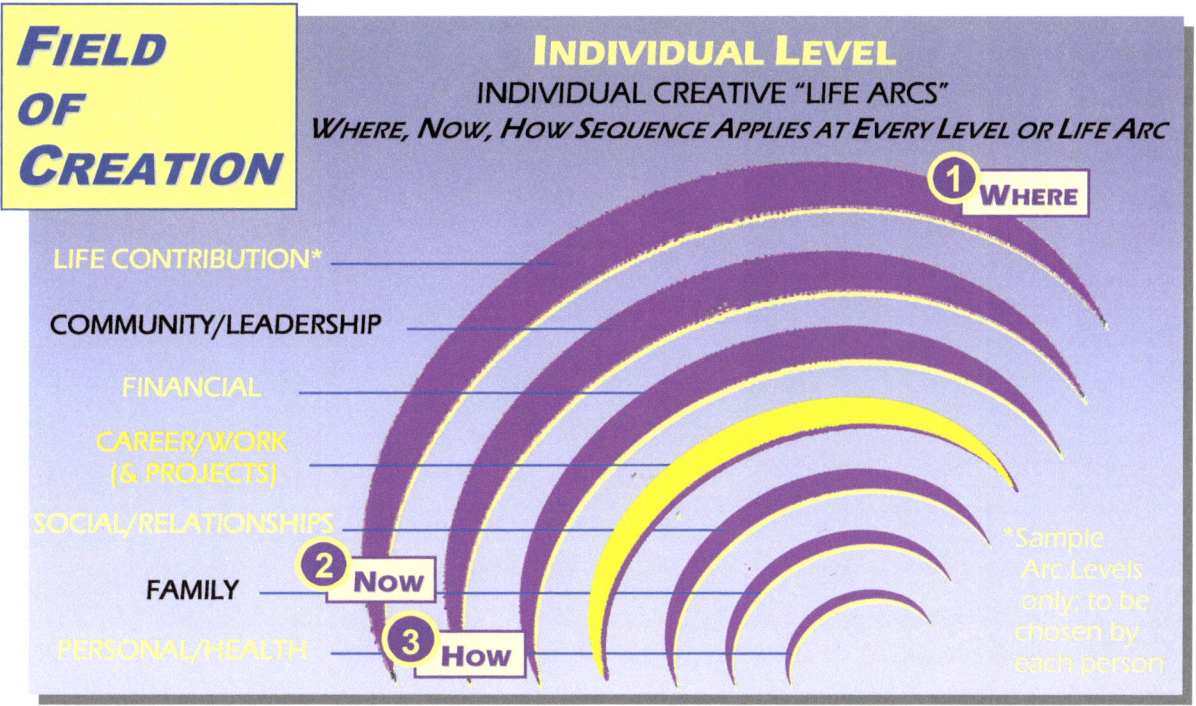

This same powerful Creative Process – WHERE, NOW, HOW – works at every level of creation.

With this simple, recurring three-step process as your own "creative guidance system," you possess the power to navigate and create at every level of your life, work & world.

As you approach completion of one ARC using the process, you simply apply the same sequence and tools to journey to an even higher Goal, or shift to a higher ARC.

We have provided examples in this section of how this ARC to SPIRAL sequence works at the *Career* Level, and, as the graphic above illustrates, *POWER ARC* applies equally well at every level of your life. For example, at the *Project* Level, you may use the three-step process to design the project, by first determining what a successful project will look like, what results it should generate, and what its purpose is – your WHERE Vision. Then you *Scan* the information and resources you have Now, determine other research you may need, and identify the key strategic points or *Goals* of the project (notice that you don't start simply with your current information; you begin by envisioning what the project "can and should be," and then develop it based on that vision). Finally, you *Plan* How to design the project, its components, specific steps, and perhaps even its presentation. Then, you may effectively "shift the ARC" from *design* to *implementation* of the project, starting again at the beginning of the WHERE, NOW, HOW sequence, to determine what successful implementation of the project would look like, and so on.

The same is true of any other level or ARC (those shown above, or those you might create specifically to fit your own life or organization), such as the *Relationship* ARC. Together, you and the person with whom you are in relationship can envision what you both most want out of the relationship (or, what result you both most wish to see if you are facing a specific challenge), and work through the WHERE, NOW, HOW sequence together.

GENESIS of GENIUS

POWER TO POTENTIAL

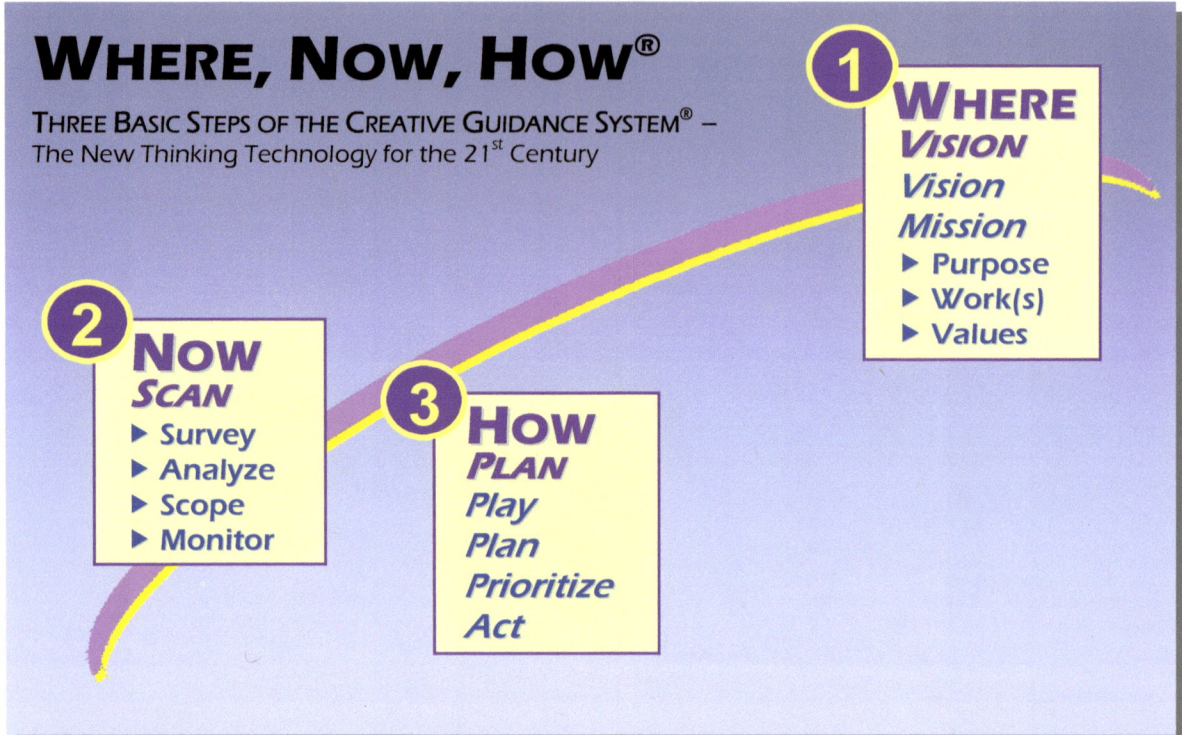

We have arrived full circle, where we first began, but at a much higher plane of thought. We now realize that we already are travelers in an infinite Field of Information – with no artificial buffers to shield us from ever-present speed, complexity and connectedness. We can no longer react fast enough to changing circumstances, and the illusion of control dissolves before us in the light of this new reality. We need an entirely different "mode of thought" – a new "thinking technology" to navigate this Field of Pure Potential. In this new World, the best – and only - way to predict the future is to create it. *We cannot control. But we can create.*

Creative power – *the power to choose something other than what already exists* – exists within each of us. At any moment we choose, we may make the mental leap, beyond current circumstance, to consciously create totally new patterns of thought, new visions, entirely new worlds of possibility. As we do, we step boldly into the Field of Potential.

The only way to traverse this realm is to consciously navigate and create in real time.

POWER ARC: YOUR CREATIVE GUIDANCE SYSTEM is the "new thinking technology" for this Creative Realm. The ARC represents the Creative Process - the translation system by which we may consciously transform energy and information into new forms and desired *Vision.* As we shift our focus from circumstance (external) to creativity (internal), power shifts back to us.

You now possess the knowledge of the core stages and steps of this CREATIVE GUIDANCE SYSTEM, in its core, three-stage form – WHERE, NOW, HOW – a simple but powerful framework you may use to create at every level of your life, work and world. You now possess the mental navigational system and thought sequence, framed around your *Vision* and *Values*, focused on your *Strategic Goals*, and guided by your *Best Next Steps*, to journey to your dreams.

Our advanced VISIONSPARC training (online only) offers more tools for planning, expanding the three-step WHERE, NOW, HOW sequence to five steps, with more depth and guidance on each step (plus a special A.R.C. "Reorienting" section).

GENESIS of GENIUS

MASTERING POWER ARC™/ CREATIVE GUIDANCE SYSTEM®

HOW RESOURCES

NAVIGATIONAL PLANNING – Mastering the CREATIVE GUIDANCE SYSTEM®:

If we follow the steps in the Creative Process – presented in the CREATIVE GUIDANCE SYSTEM – then all our experience and efficiency at *How*, or the *Plan* stage, will translate into vastly greater efficiency, productivity – and yes, speed – in actually achieving our desired results.

It is our *thinking technology* – our thought sequence – that must change, in order for all the action steps of our HOW to go in the right direction. When we think and act together in the sequence presented in this GUIDE, and when all the stages and steps in the Creative Process are followed, we may align our work most effectively for each Strategic ARC.

> *If you employed study, thinking, and planning time daily, you could develop and use the power that can change the course of your destiny.*
> — W. Clement Stone, businessman and philanthropist

Our *Strategic Goals* become *"the pivotal planks in our Plan"* – the primary focus areas for each of our Master ARCS, around which we may better organize our efforts and allocate our resources. As we focus on these *Strategic Goals* or *Mini-Visions*, we *know* each decision and step we take will move us toward what we really want, because we first have taken the time to determine what our true *Vision, Mission, Values* and *Goals* really are.

In addition, because these *Strategic Goals* emerged as the result of the Creative Process, we also know that each of these focus areas represents a key leverage point specific to our lives and work, and, as a result, our efforts in these strategic areas will have the greatest power to propel us forward.

Strategic Goals: Identifying Strategic Goals - The ARCS of Your Navigational Plan

- *Identify Themes* - Drawing on the information from your *Life ARC Exercises* (Worksheets #1-7) and *SWOT Analysis* (Worksheets #14-15), look for patterns in your set of information – for related phrases or bits of information that seem as if they naturally cluster due to their similarities. These "clusters" of information reveal important themes, ideas and issues that span the results of different exercises.

    TIP: One of the best ways to identify themes is to write each phrase of SWOT or POWER input on individual Post-It notes, and then sort the notes and group related phrases, ideas and issues in the same general area on a wall, table, or on flip charts (this method works for both an individual or a team; you may also use this Post-It Notes method with VISION WALL on p. 351, as you did to post *Vision, Mission,* and master ARCS. [334]

- *Complete Clusters* - After the initial sort, you may build on and add to the initial posts generated by the *SWOT Analysis*; however, first be sure to notice (and possibly record or mark original posts in some way) the items and issues which have emerged. The results may surprise you. The major themes that emerge may center around areas you may never have considered as very important before. New areas may emerge that have never been addressed before, but now you see this area listed across several SWOT categories, perhaps more than once. This is the real power of the process, in revealing to us pivotal, but often hidden, issues.

- *Label Strategic ARCS* - Place a "working title" over each set or "cluster" of related ideas and issues that emerges from your *Scan* sorting exercise. These major theme areas (some call these "problems" or "issues"; more positively, others call these "critical success factors") become your Strategic Goals for each ARC. In the Worksheets to follow, you will transform these working titles into Labels and Mini-Visions for each ARC.

First, in the next set of Worksheets, *you will fill in the "planks of your plan" - your Strategic ARCS, Mini-Visions, and Best Next Steps for your current area of creative focus.*
Second, *you will find a wealth of resources for creative Play, as you move Beyond Brainstorming.*
Third, *you will find a host of tools to help you transform your Navigational Plan into daily action.*

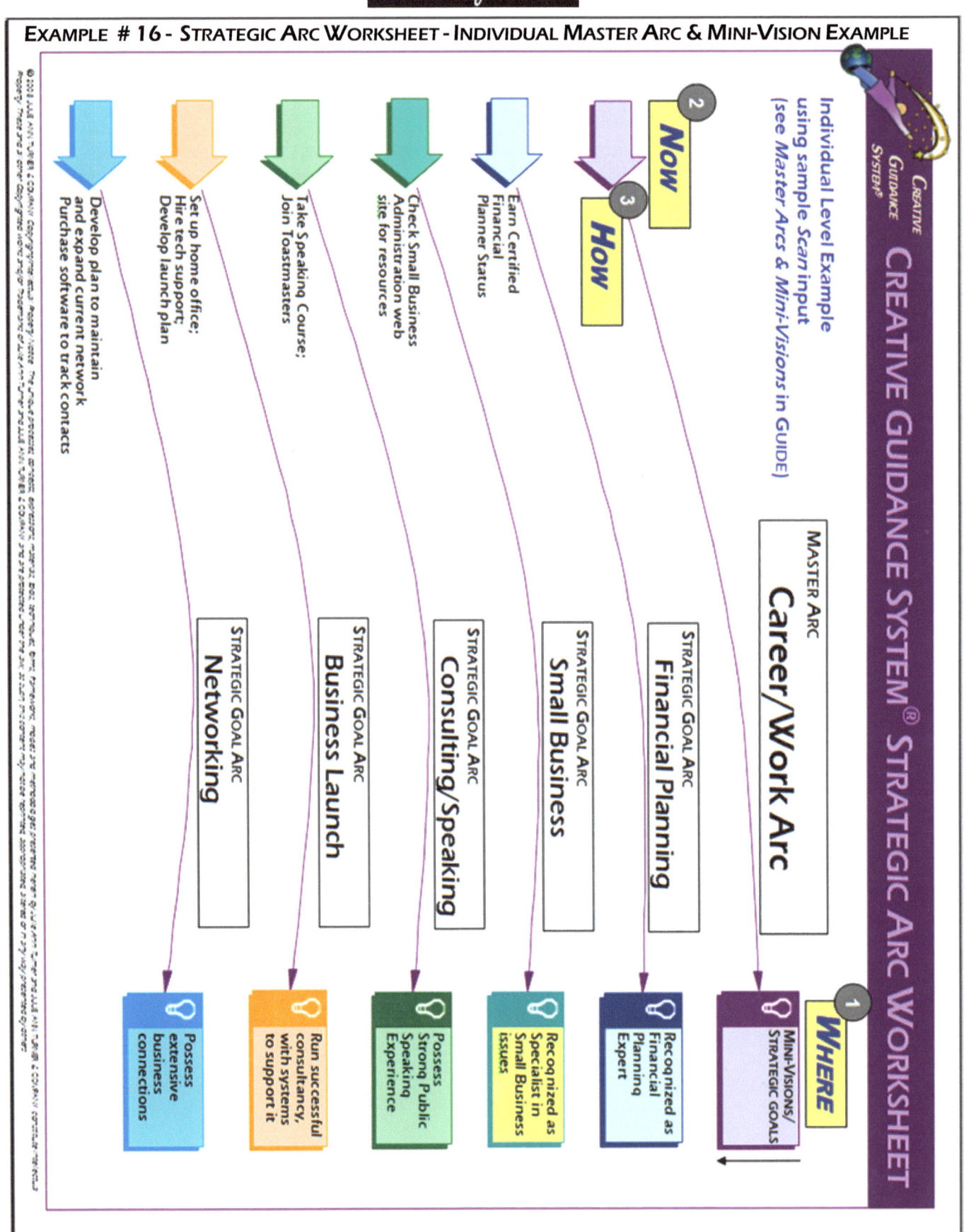

EXAMPLE # 16 - STRATEGIC ARC WORKSHEET - INDIVIDUAL MASTER ARC & MINI-VISION EXAMPLE

WORKSHEET # 17 - STRATEGIC ARC WORKSHEET - INDIVIDUAL OR TEAM/ORGANIZATION

CREATIVE GUIDANCE SYSTEM® STRATEGIC ARC WORKSHEET

Enter the Name of the Primary Arc on which you wish to focus for this plan. Then use "Cluster Analysis" from your Scan (as described in chapter), to identify main issues and/or themes which emerge. Enter the title for each main theme in one of the Strategic Arcs below. Then simply follow the WHERE, NOW, HOW process for each Strategic Arc, creating Mini-Visions and Best Next Steps, prioritizing them, and taking action. Remember, the same Creative Process works at every level!!

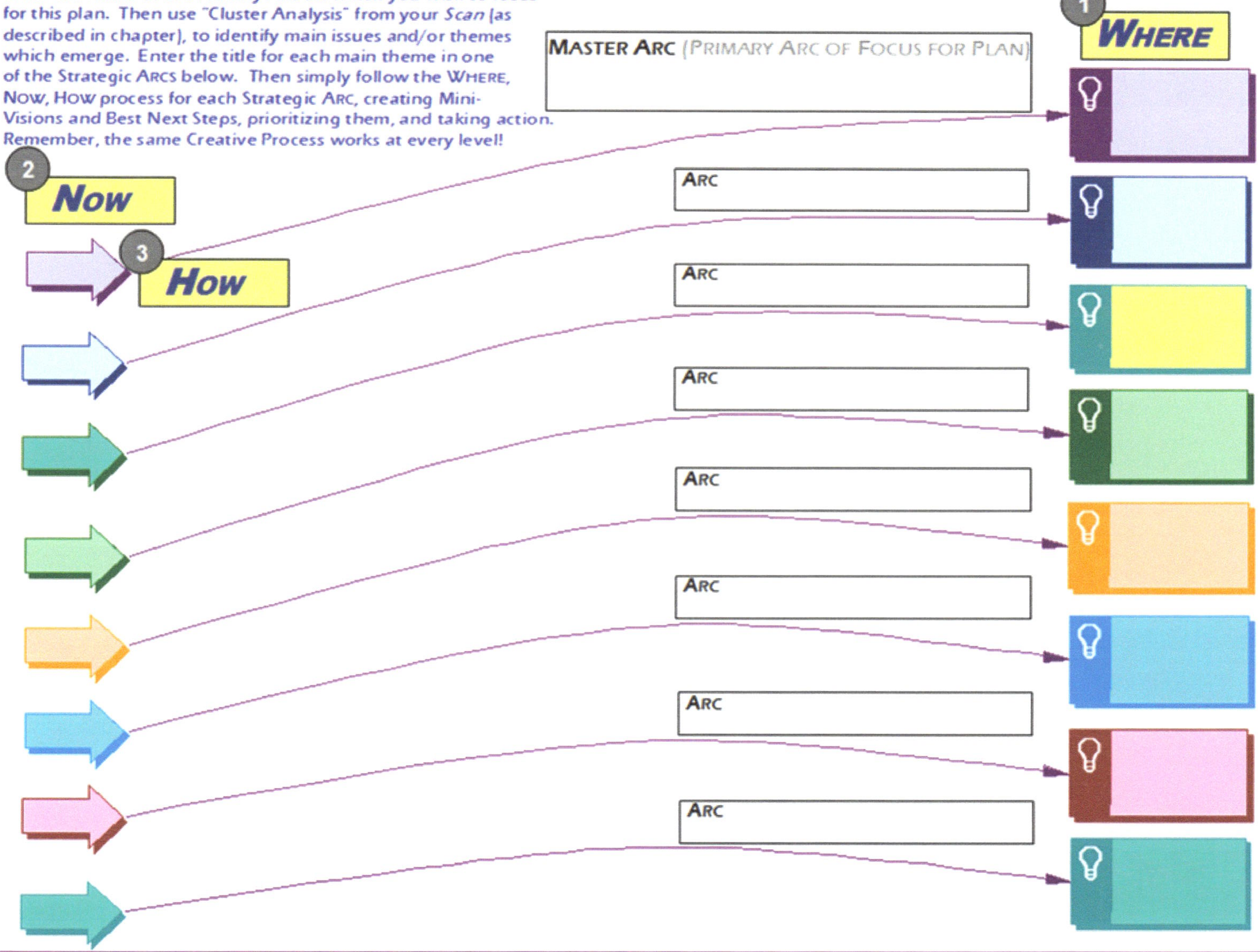

2 — Now
3 — How
1 — Where

MASTER ARC (PRIMARY ARC OF FOCUS FOR PLAN)

ARC | ARC | ARC | ARC | ARC | ARC | ARC | ARC

GENESIS of GENIUS

WORKSHEET # 18 - STRATEGIC GOAL - PLAY & BEST NEXT STEPS WORKSHEET

STRATEGIC GOAL PLAY & "BEST NEXT STEPS" WORKSHEET
Creative Guidance System

STRATEGIC GOAL ARC

▽ Play
Use this space to list all the creative ideas you generate for this Strategic Goal, as you Play with the various creativity techniques. Creativity techniques listed on in this section.

▽ Plan
- **Strategic Goal/Mini-Vision** *(above)*
- **Best Next Steps**
  First, list the "Best Next Steps" you generated using Play tools. Then, list smaller, specific steps needed to complete main Steps.

Priority *(rank Best Next Steps by number)*

Target Date *(date to finish step.)*

Measure/Outcome *(desired result or outcome when finished.)*

▽ Prioritize
Order my goals & next steps by importance and contribution to my life Vision and Mission, and allocate resources accordingly, reallocating in real time as necessary. (Use next column.)

WHERE
Mini-Vision
What does success look like for this goal? What is the vivid, sensory description of the desired result or experience?

To Claim Your Bonus Books, Free Creative Resources, & Innovation Tools visit GENESISOFGENIUSBOOK.COM.

© Julie Ann Turner & Company/CreatorsGuide.com.
All Rights Reserved.

Overview #19 – Where, Now, How Master Summary Snapshot

Creative Guidance System®

WHERE, NOW, HOW® MASTER SUMMARY SNAPSHOT

1 WHERE

My Vision
Where do I most desire to be? What is the vivid, sensory description of the desired experience?

My Mission
———

My Purpose
My unique reason for being. What I seek to contribute to the world through my unique gifts and talents.

My Life Work/Business
What I do. The main method(s) or activities through which I fulfill this purpose.

My Values
What I Care About. The principles or beliefs that guide me as I pursue my purpose.

2 NOW

Scan

▸ **Survey**
Intelligence about my current state of thought and being, gathered through questions, exercises, experiences.

▸ **Analyze**
Deep evaluation of information about my current state and synthesis as input for Vision, Mission & Plan.

▸ **Scope**
Clarity about level and scope of planning focus.

▸ **Monitor**
Ongoing monitoring of current state relative to Vision and Mission.

3 HOW

Plan

▸ **Play**
Use creativity and creative techniques at every level.

▸ **Plan**

■ **Strategic Goals/Mini-Visions**
Describe in short, simple statements the Goal or Mini-Vision I most wish to create for this Arc (a clear statement of tangible results).

■ **Best Next Steps**
List "Best Next Steps" that will move me toward my Mini-Vision.

▸ **Prioritize**
Next, consciously order my Best Next Steps by importance and contribution to my life Vision and Mission, so that the highest potential/pay-off actions are listed first.

▸ **Act**
Take action on the first priority, allocating resources accordingly, navigating and reallocating in real time as necessary. Look for synergistic opportunities, where a single, strategic action may contribute to the achievement of more than one priority at a time. Before moving to each of the other priorities on my list, I will check to be sure that the next action listed is still the best one now available, as I check my progress toward my Vision and Mission at each step.

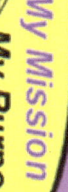

© Julie Ann Turner & Company/CreatorsGuide.com. All Rights Reserved.

PLAY - TIPS & TOOLS TO SPARK IMAGINATION

Play - giving the imagination the time, space and tools for open, creative exploration of our endeavors, thus allowing the energy and inspiration of the Creative Process to flow - is the missing creative catalyst in most of our lives, our work, our plans, and our projects.

For children, we readily acknowledge and support the power of play in developing their imaginations, and in sparking new ideas and potentials in their minds. Yet, as adults, we generally tend to dismiss "play" as "wasted time," even though the same power of play, if nurtured, may generate the ideas, innovations and insights that drive successful work and business. It is time we made space and time for the imagination of adult minds to flourish, for, as we've seen, the future belongs to those who can consciously create it.

Here are some tips, tools and techniques to expand your creative mind, and to give the power of your imagination a place - not only in your dreams - but in your day, your plans, and your life.

- *Plant the Seed Early*

    As we explain on pp. 114-116, the Creative Process has a conscious sequence (our focus here in the GUIDE) and an unconscious sequence (not under our conscious control, but very powerful). The biggest key? Planting the seed early - immerse your mind in diverse ideas and information, and then allow it to operate "behind the scenes." Feed your brain, review your project - then take a walk, sleep on it, go work out. You'll likely be surprised by what emerges - often in an "Aha!" moment, that only needed space to emerge. And the sooner you plant the seed, the more time your brain will have to generate innovative solutions.

- *Rediscover the Joy of Toys*

    If you must, call them "learning aids," "mind tools," or "executive accessories" - but honor your creativity by keeping some strategic toys on hand to free up your right brain and spark your thinking ... yes, at work (a novel idea, encouraging innovative thinking at work). Find some toys that instantly ignite a shift of mind in you - whether they be colorful, squeezable, bendable, tossable, stackable or even sniffable (like Playdoh) - just having them on your desk should make you think "fun!" (And if you're too shy to visit the toy store in person, hop online and cruise the virtual toy aisle at Amazon.com or officeplayground.com.)

- *Go Beyond Brainstorming*

    As we've learned, our brains think through association. Associative thought forms the necessary - but not sufficient – basis for creativity, which shifts our thinking *beyond* existing patterns to create an entirely new concepts or visions than has ever existed before.

    However, it is important to recognize that most "creativity techniques" focus on associative thought, but often fail to provide a mechanism to spark the essential "leap" – the MINDSHIFT – to an entirely new level or plane of thought. For many, the most familiar creativity technique is "brainstorming," a classic which is based on associative thinking.[335] As creativity author Edward de Bono notes, brainstorming typically only uses thoughts or concepts that *already exist in the minds of participants* in order to generate associated ideas, which he says, creates only "variations on a theme," rather than entirely new and innovative ideas.[336] *In fact, almost all creativity techniques are based on associative thinking and matching patterns.*[337] Yet, associative thinking is incremental thinking – it starts from what already exists.

    While useful at some levels, almost all of these "creativity (little "c") techniques" are inherently limiting. Of course, the best way to make the mental leap beyond what already exists is to use the Creative Process, as reflected in this CREATIVE GUIDANCE SYSTEM.

    Here are some additional creative tools to help you move "beyond brainstorming": [See also EXPLORESOURCES *15 Core Creativity Classics* (p. 107), and *Mindmapping* (p. 295)]

EXPLORESOURCES

TECHNIQUES FOR THINKING IN XD

Play helps us move beyond the limits of "problem-solving" (which focuses only on WHAT IS, or what already exists) and beyond basic brainstorming techniques. Edward de Bono and other notable creativity experts emphasize a necessary factor for creative thought – *beyond mere association*: some mechanism to stimulate the "leap" to an alternate "plane of thought" (the term used in this GUIDE), as well as tap into our multidimensional (xD) thinking[338]

Grab-Bag It!

Simply brainstorming can limit creativity to ideas and information already in the minds of those present and, of course, to the ideas sparked by those initial ideas. One way to *stimulate* truly breakthrough ideas — ideas no one may yet have conceived — is to aid your brainstorming with *stimuli* (what de Bono calls "provocations," also called "forced associations"), and use your brain's natural ability to create associations to generate totally new ideas.

Here's how it works: grab some stimuli. *Anything* can be used as stimuli — pictures or words in a magazine (the more far afield from your current endeavor or off-beat the magazine, the better); small desk items or toys (can be pulled from a "grab bag" of interesting, unusual items); images or words from related, or non-related, internet web sites; books in a library or on a bookshelf — the sources for "pocket stimuli" are endless, and easily at hand almost anywhere.

Next, identify an item or piece of stimuli — for instance, a toy airplane. Ask yourself questions about how what you are trying to create is like — or not like — an airplane. Select different attributes of the airplane. How could your project "take flight"? What would make for a "perfect landing" for your new product? This bi-plane has two parallel wings — how could your project build in parallel components, or back-up systems, or redundancy, to enhance performance or reliability? How is your project like a plane? How can you make it take off and then stay in flight?

See how this works? Bounce things off your brain and see what results!

Role-Play It!

Try to look at your creation from many different perspectives. One way is to role play, or take the role of another person. It could be someone from another planet, a child, an elderly person, a famous artist, your fiercest competitor. Useful by yourself, but often more fun with others playing different roles. One of our favorites is the *Martian Buying Committee*, in which several participants play the part of the aliens trying to comprehend a team's idea, product or service, and the rest of the team must come up with creative ways - not just verbal, but visual and kinesthetic (images, gestures, symbols, actions, etc.) to convey the value and essence of the idea, product or service. The exercise itself is very illuminating in stretching creative thinking beyond ordinary limits and generating alternative ways to communicate and persuade.

Experience It!

Get up close and personal. Find a way to get as close as you can to experience the thing you are trying to create (project, product, service, program). Go to a toy store, or actually visit a place related in some way to your project, and find objects that may relate to your creation.

Or, take a cue from Austin advertising agency GSD&M, which actually creates physical spaces within their workplace - Idea City - where the agency's creative minds can become immersed in relevant roles and experiences. The agency contains a *Chili's Bar and Grill* "war room" - complete with booths and decorations from this client's restaurants. Believing that "*your butt's connected to your brain*" - that different forms of information help you put new ideas together - and that "*ideas are serious fun*," GSD&M's workspace contains 30 such client-concept, experiential "war rooms."[339]

Use all your senses — touch, feel, smell — experience it!

EXPLORESOURCES

PUTTING IT ALL INTO ACTION

Remember, we may use the power of POWER ARC: CREATIVE GUIDANCE SYSTEM to guide us in every moment – in every situation, project, relationship, conversation or meeting.

In using this shared "thinking system," we not only rediscover creativity and release energy from everyone participating, we also regain the power for the flow of ideas and strategies to emerge that can address multiple goals and span more than one PLANE OF THOUGHT at a time. Full energy to achieve our Vision may then flow freely, throughout the entire process, enabling us to reach our goals faster, and, drawing on our full potential, reach goals higher than we ever have before.

Instead of problem-centric, our lives and actions will be potential-driven. Moreover, we are better able to integrate all the important aspects of our lives and identify opportunities for alignment and synergy among our Life or Organizational ARCS.

FROM PLAN-TO-ACTION RESOURCES

The all-too-common approach of using problems or current circumstances – or even our standard To-Do Lists alone – to navigate by, often quickly finds us bouncing back and forth in reaction mode within the limited sphere of WHAT IS, rather than exploring possibilities in creation mode, across the unlimited realm of WHAT CAN BE. If we're not sure we're going in the right direction, then focusing only on speed and efficiency will only get us in the wrong place faster.

Instead, however, when our true Vision, Mission, Values and Goals are the result of our conscious use of the Creative Process, we know without a doubt Where we want to direct our focus and our energy. Each of our Strategic Goals - and our Best Next Steps - represent key leverage points specific to our lives and work, and, as a result, our efforts in these strategic areas will have the greatest power to propel us forward. Then, if developed within this Creative Framework, even To-Do Lists can become powerful tools, and efficiency and speed may help us reach our desired goals even faster.

Once your direction and trajectory are set, the following tools and resources may aid your Journey:

- The 4-Hour Workweek: Escape 9-5, Live Anywhere, and Join the New Rich
  Timothy Ferriss, Harmony, Expanded Updated Edition - 2009

- Getting Things Done: The Art of Stress-Free Productivity
  David Allen, Penguin Books - 2002

- Lifehacker: The Guide to Working Smarter, Faster and Better
  Adam Pash and Gina Trapani, Wiley Publishing - 2011

- MindManager
  Mindjet.com (MindManager Mindmapping Software) -
  works to map projects and related tasks, create timeline charts, and synchronize with MS Outlook

- The Now Habit: A Strategic Program for Overcoming Procrastination and Enjoying Guilt-Free Play
  Neil Fiore, Tarcher - 2007

- Search Inside Yourself: The Unexpected Path to Achieving Success, Happiness (and World Peace)
  Chade-Meng Tan, HarperOne - 2012

- Total Workday Control Using Microsoft Outlook: Eight Best Practices of Task and E-Mail Management
  Michael Linenberger, New Academy Publishers - 2013

The SPIRAL symbol signifies tried-and-true, tested resources, which you will find available through the GENESISOFGENIUS.COM web site. Our much-expanded, in-depth version of this initial printed list – is available to you as a registered GUIDE owner, through our site..

Again, consider this set of optional resources as a dynamic launch point for your exploration of creativity. We hope you will be inspired to become a lifetime student of the Creative Process.

WORKSHEET # 20 - CREATIVE GUIDANCE SYSTEM PRACTICE WORKSHEET

CREATIVE PROCESS PRACTICE WORKSHEET

Putting the CREATIVE GUIDANCE SYSTEM to Work

Creative Process Quick Practice Session

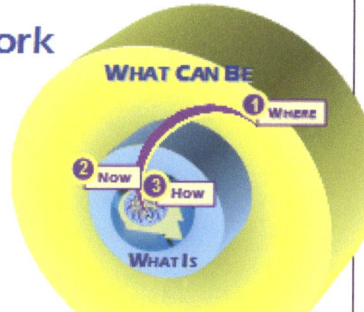

Process Practice #1 - Personal or Project

1. List five (5) things you would like to change or results you would like to create in your life (either personally or for a project on which you are working).

2. Choose one (1) thing to work on - something you would like to create.

3. Write a brief, but vivid description (Vision) of what success in this area or for this project looks like.

4. If you don't have a CREATIVE GUIDANCE SYSTEM® ARC Worksheet handy, simply draw your own ARC on a blank sheet of paper, then number/label the top right - 1. WHERE; bottom right - 2. NOW and 3. HOW.

5. Check your Vision description. Is it compelling? Check for creative tension/future pull between WHERE and NOW. If it's not present, revise your Vision (try closing your eyes and vividly picturing success).

6. Write a brief description of what current reality is in this area. Is there any research or information you need to gather to more fully assess the situation? If so, list this necessary information.

7. List three (3) action steps you might take to start movement toward your goal.

8. Use your creativity for a moment (try some of the creativity techniques we learned). How can you make one of these things fun/enjoyable? More interesting and dynamic?

   - Do a quick "mind dumpster" - write all the ideas you can think of in 3 minutes on a sheet of paper, or one per Post-it Note or note card. In teams, mark the lower right corner of each note with your initials.

   - Note: you may choose this goal to work with your team on creative techniques. If so, be ready to share your Post-Its with your teammates for additional ideas.

   - If you're going this one solo, apply some creativity techniques (e.g., stimuli/associations, grab bag, mindmapping, experiential, etc.).

9. Choose one of your three (3) *Best Next Steps* and then break each action into several smaller tasks. Set a start and target completion date for each one. Remember, *"goals are dreams with deadlines."*

10. Take action on your first priority action. Be ready to adjust. Monitor for opportunities. If you're not having fun or enjoying it, reassess your goals to be sure they align with your Vision and Mission. Adjust as necessary.

11. Keep moving forward. Add more Best Next Steps as they occur to you. Reorient to vision and purpose. Don't worry about seeing the entire path; just take the Best Next Step.

    You're on your way to realizing your dream.

Process practice #2 - Team/Organizational

Use process as above, only a Team or Organizational level. You might choose to create an event, program, campaign, proposal, or something else important to your Vision and Mission.

CHAPTER ELEVEN
CHANGING COURSE

> *Throughout*
>
> *the centuries*
>
> *there were [those]*
>
> *who took first steps,*
>
> *down new roads,*
>
> *armed*
>
> *with nothing*
>
> *but their own vision.*
>
> — Ayn Rand, novelist and philosopher

NAVIGATING THE NEW REALM

You cannot wait for someone else to create change.
You must be part of that change.
Through your own efforts, through your own actions,
through your own creativity and vision, you have to do it.[340]

Congressman John R. Lewis (D) Georgia

Whether we call it the *Field of Information*, the *Creative Field*, or the *Networked World* – we live in a *Participatory Universe*.[341] In this new realm, where real and virtual "worlds" increasingly blend together, one thing is certain: our roles as Creators in this unlimited "*space.*" The shift from Knowledge to Imagination has already taken place ... as visionary Tom Peters reminds us:

Remember: There's no opt-out button.[342]

At every level and in every sphere, the organizing process that generates the emerging world is the Creative Process – as we each choose, consciously or unconsciously, to create something other than what already exists ... and thus shift into the Creative Realm.
Here, we have given you the Master Process and the tools to navigate this uncharted territory.

This New Space is both real and virtual, global and boundaryless. As Walter Truett Anderson tells us: "*Global civilization has no center ... it is a multicentric system ... we are intricately linked in a rich web of economic, political, cultural, and biological systems, networks of networks.*"[343] Similarly, author and tech visionary David Weinstein notes how our networked world and our physical world increasingly cross boundaries and change rules, creating "*a new world we're just beginning to inhabit.*" Here, his words capture the essence, not just of "the web" as the Internet, but "The Web" as the emergence of a new, unbounded civilization.

We're like the earlier European settlers in the United States, living on the edge of the forest. We don't know what's there and we don't know exactly what we need to do to find out: do we pack mountain climbing gear, desert wear, canoes, or all three? Of course, while the settlers may not have known what the geography of the New World was going to be, they at least knew that there was a geography. The Web ... has no geography, no landscape. It has no distance. ... It has few rules of behavior and fewer lines of authority. Common sense doesn't hold there, and uncommon sense hasn't yet emerged ..... .[344]

David Weinberger, *Small Pieces Loosely Joined*

Change is true state of this New Space – everything is perpetually "in process." As we have seen, we can't predict the change, or control it ... but we can, intentionally, *create the change* we wish to see. *Creation is a participatory process. Most significantly, it is a Process of Mind, in which we ourselves are translators, participants, co-creators.* To navigate this new realm of speed and change, we need more than a new plan – we need a fundamental *shift of mind* - from Knowledge to Imagination, from reactive to creative, from limited to unlimited. We need new, shared ways to "choose together" – across boundaries – in real time. In this *Field of Information*, only configuration counts. That means *consciously creating* – new connections and combinations, new categories, and entirely new worlds of possibility.

Now, you have been given the core sequence of that shared, navigational system – this CREATIVE GUIDANCE SYSTEM, *a way of "choosing together," of co-creating in real time – through a common set of principles and tools distilled from the Creative Process. It's time to embark on the Journey.*

CHOOSING IN THE MOMENT

Life is choice. Enjoy your creation.

Jere May, CEO, Technical Focus

*In order to discover, we must embark –
and the first step always seems the most daunting.
Yet, we know it is in this initial step that we break through familiar boundaries,
and free ourselves to move on to undiscovered realms of possibility.*

You already have everything you need to embark.

You don't have to know everything in advance. In fact, as writer Gertrude Stein said:

If you knew it all, it would not be creation, but dictation.[345]

You will, however, have to venture beyond your Comfort Zone.

Choice is the mechanism of creation. On your Creative Journey,
you navigate by your *choices* in each moment, as you move along your ARC toward your *Vision*.

You will encounter obstacles. You cannot travel the heroic Journey without facing them.

Your POWER ARCS and your CREATIVE GUIDANCE SYSTEM help you stay on course, even in the midst of unexpected circumstances, intimidating obstacles, occasional mishaps and unintentional – but inevitable - mistakes. This is how we learn and grow, expand our capacity, and reach our full potential. *All Creators face obstacles and make errors. The great ones embrace them - as invaluable experiences essential for personal growth, and as guides to completing their journey.*

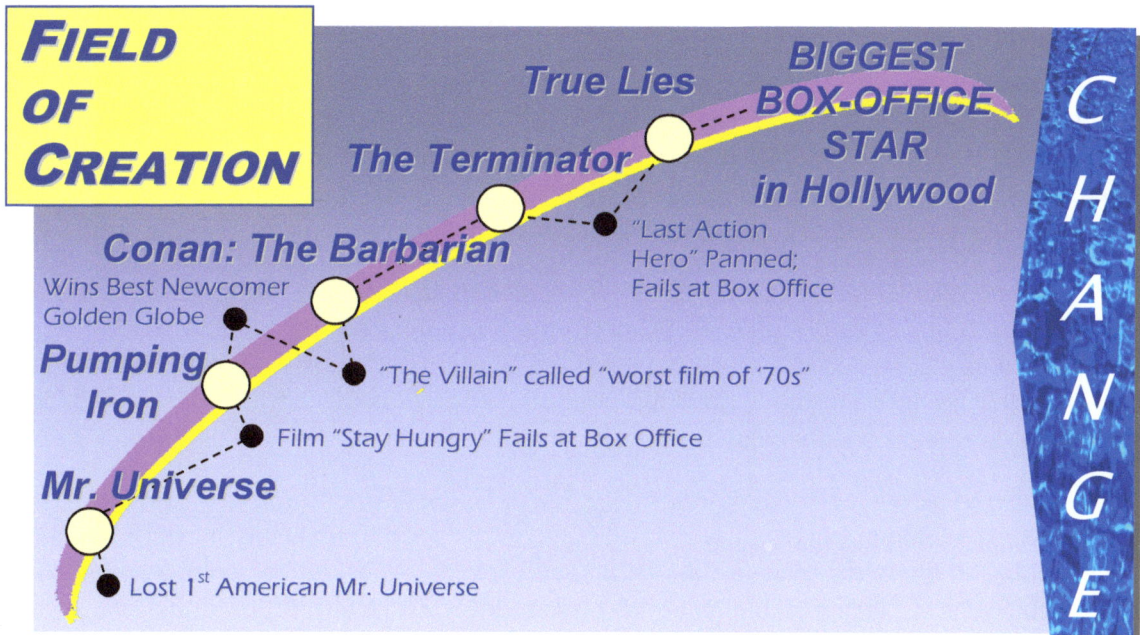

If you get thrown off course, remember – in any instant, you may always choose differently. Reorient toward your Vision, and set forth again.

You are on your Way to living your passion and fulfilling your true potential.

LIGHTSHIFTERS

Take the first step in faith.
You don't have to see the whole staircase, just take the first step.
— Martin Luther King Jr., civil rights leader

You know WHERE you're going.
And you know you are carrying your own light – your inner Vision – within you.
You need not – indeed, cannot - see every step of the path at the outset.
Have the faith to follow as far as you can see now,
and trust that when you arrive there, you'll have more light for the path ahead.

Do not wait: the time will never be "just right."
Start where you stand, and work with whatever tools you may have
at your command, and better tools will be found as you go along. ...
Faith is the art of believing by doing.[346]
— Napoleon Hill, author of *Think and Grow Rich*

Creators are Lightshifters. They trust their current light to carry them forward, and that, as they move further along the ARC of their dream, new options will appear. Along the way, they gain more knowledge and more connections, and far greater possibilities than they could initially have ever imagined open up before them.

A strong passion ... will insure success, for the desire of the end will point out the means.[347]
— William Hazlitt, English writer

The only way to fail is to stop moving forward. Arnold Schwarzenegger overcame a multitude of disappointments, losses, criticisms and even outright movie flops on his journey to become the biggest box-office star in Hollywood. Yet he never lost his focus on his *Vision*, and he steadily steered his way back on track, whenever circumstances did not turn out as he had planned. He successfully navigated his way to his movie-star dream. More than that, Arnold successfully "*shifted the Arc*" – something we'll talk more about later in this section – by consciously envisioning, planning and preparing *in advance* to create *an even higher Arc* – the ARC of his now-successful political career.

This is the essence of Conscious Creation – deliberately using the Creative Process to move ever higher on the SPIRAL of Potential. This potential-driven, creative mindset – what we call the mindset of the CONSTANT VISIONARY (see p. 73) – is essential for individuals who wish to live into their dreams and reach their full potential, as well as for organizations which desire to sustain their success in a competitive, global marketplace.

Creators embrace what Deepak Chopra calls "the wisdom of uncertainty."[348] He points out that it is only in the Field of Uncertainty that all choices are open to us. Only here, in the midst of uncertainty - in the midst of what many might call "chaos" - do we have complete freedom to create, for we may choose among unlimited possibilities. It is within that unlimited, moment of "uncertainty" - in each *instant of choice* – that we possess the greatest creative power.

The ARC of our Journey becomes the organizing force in our lives and our work, as it encompasses our highest *Vision* and *Values*, and leads us to express our greatest passion. We have faith for the Journey because in every instant we choose from within. This is the essence of true intelligence or *"intelligentsia"* – *"to choose from within."*

PREVENTING THE STALL I

There is no security in life, only opportunity.[349]
Mark Twain, writer and humorist

In an ever-changing world, security and control are illusions, because they require that situations stay the same. We cannot force people or situations to stop changing – at least not in the long term. But we can choose – and enable others to choose – to create. Through creative choice, we shift the power flow toward what we want to have happen, instead of fighting against what we don't want to have happen.

The world is in a constant state of flux, yet opportunity lies in the midst of the change and chaos. If we hold tightly to a rigid plan, we close ourselves off from emerging opportunities. But if we know WHERE we're going and have a navigational guidance system, all potentials remain open to us. By viewing every moment through a creative lens, we can learn to use change to our advantage. With this creative guidance system in place, we need no longer be stalled or paralyzed by change.

- *The First Stall – Flying Outside the Comfort Zone* - We all have an internal warning system - which we might call FUD, for <u>F</u>ear, <u>U</u>ncertainty and <u>D</u>oubt – that automatically alerts us when we are crossing into the unknown.

    The zone of the "known" – often called the "Comfort Zone" – encompasses what already exists, what we already know, what we already know how to do, and so on. FUD alerts are automatically triggered by our nervous systems – the old mammalian part of our brains that sends the "fight or flight" survival signal whenever we encounter the unknown. Though this system kept us alive in the caveman era (and our parents tapped into it to warn us of danger when we were children), when just about anything unknown (plants, animals, etc.) might kill us, it works less well for us today, when many new or "unknown' things can just as easily represent opportunity rather than threat.

    Now, even though our advanced brainpower allows us to discern whether new or unknown things might hurt or help us, we still tend to stall at the edge of our individual Comfort Zones. We can, of course, consciously override the FUD system. Indeed, we must choose to do so, because innovation and creation occur beyond the realm of the known. In order to explore new possibilities, we must learn to expect, and be prepared to deal with, the discomfort that arises when we first venture out of our Comfort Zone, realizing that it is only in the open space of new possibilities that we can expand our capacities, create things that never before existed, and discover entirely new worlds.

    Stealth Forms: *Waiting; Procrastination; Forcing solutions to match what already exists; Forcing old solutions on new situations; Getting caught up in busyness, rather than taking new action (mistaking activity for achievement)*

    Navigate! *Start! Keep starting! Take the first step. Then keep taking the* BEST NEXT STEP.

- *The Second Stall – Listening to the Voice of Judgment* - We often think judgment, even self-criticism, can keep us on the right track. We also tend to give power to others' judgments, because we want approval, we want to belong and to "fit in." However, when it comes to creativity, the voice of judgment – whether our own, that of those we know or work with, or that of society – can cut off creative ideas before they even reach your conscious mind, much less reach the light of day. Creativity only emerges as we allow ourselves to suspend judgment. As Michael Ray and Rochelle Myers say in Creativity in Business, "even a slight decrease in judgment can double your creativity."[350]

    Stealth Forms: *Voice of Lack (says 'you don't have or know X, so you can't Y); Perfectionism (expecting it to be perfect the first, and every, time); Only "correct" answers count (often the assessment of education system and many companies, rather than a focus on discovering and creating new things)*

    Navigate! *Don't let what you lack stop you; Start with what you have and know now. Allow for learning.*

PREVENTING THE STALL II

Every adversity, every failure, and every heartache, carries with it the Seed of an equivalent or greater Benefit. ...Failure is nature's plan to prepare you for great responsibilities..[351]
Napoleon Hill, author of *Think and Grow Rich*

- *The Third Stall – Becoming Paralyzed by Chaos* - In a world of complexity and constant change, it is understandable – even inevitable – that we sometimes will feel overwhelmed by incoming information and circumstances, or feel confused or lost in the midst of chaos. First, we, as Creators, have an advantage, in that we realize we no longer have to react to every situation or "crisis" that emerges, and, moreover, we don't have to fear change and chaos. Through our creative lens, we can distinguish which sets of information or circumstances are relevant to our Vision and Purpose, and then, in context of our ARC, we can factor into our Navigational Plan those bits of information or emerging circumstances that can aid us on our journey.

  Second – and this is a very important point – we may realize that it is often only by delving deeper into the Discomfort Zone – into the chaos and uncertainty - that we actually discover the way to dissolve the discomfort altogether. It is a central truth of creation that situations we might label as "problems" or "chaos" often hold the creative keys to resolving them. By being unafraid to step into and explore the chaos, we often discover there realities you (or your group) have not wanted to face, consciously or unconsciously, often those which may have been holding you back for a long time. Yes, doing so will likely feel uncomfortable or even painful at first, however, it is only by traveling through the chaos, that you will get to the heart of the critical issues, and, in being willing to work through the chaos, you may emerge on the other side, free of the hidden weight that has been slowing you down. This process takes courage and commitment, and, again, keeping your eyes on your Vision and Purpose to guide you, as digging through the chaos often is, well, messy. When working through it, things may initially look even messier, before they begin to fall into new order (like cleaning out a closet). You and others may express discomfort and displeasure (in fact, if you do it right, this is inevitable, and an essential, positive step). When you emerge on the other side, however, you will have reclaimed the power you had relinquished to circumstances, negative emotions, past events, or other people, and ultimately be able to move forward, unencumbered, to even higher goals.

  Stealth Forms: Avoiding problems, Overwhelm, Trying to get by with "quick fixes"

  Navigate! *Don't allow circumstances or chaos paralyze you; Keep your eyes on your Vision and follow your ARC through the chaos (the Creative Process is the ARC through Chaos; simply follow the steps)*

- *The Counter Stall – Speeding Up* - Often we think the best response to a chaotic, fast-changing world is simply to speed up, to do or demand even more work and speed. As we've seen, however, this inevitably fails, as we simply can't respond fast enough to every emerging circumstance, and, if we don't know WHERE we are going, speeding up actually works against us. Instead, we recommend …

- *The Master Move – Incubating New Ideas* - Actually slow down – take a break or a walk, sleep on it - to allow time for new information and ideas to percolate, as your subconscious mind continues to rework possibilities and "make sense" of all the information you have fed it.[352] Allow for accident, unfolding opportunities and incorporating what you've learned along the way – you may discover new tools, new connections, or a new frontier (as Christopher Columbus set sail for the Far East, and discovered America). If you can't initially see a way, create a different route, one never tried before. One thing is certain - you can't stand on the shore and expect to discover new worlds. Begin!

- *The Power Stall – Reorienting to Vision and Purpose* – In the midst of a turbulent world, we reclaim our creative power by always directing our attention and action toward our master Vision, by choosing the Creative Way in every instant. Taking action releases potential power. Remember that creations begin with the unseen; they take time to become visible. Orient by your light of your Vision, keep moving forward, following your Navigational Plan, focusing on your dream until it becomes visible.

THRIVING ON AMBIGUITY

In the past, a high tolerance for ambiguity was a quality to be found only in great geniuses like Leonardo [da Vinci]. As change accelerates, we now find that ambiguity multiplies, and illusions of certainty become more difficult to maintain. The ability to thrive with ambiguity must become part of our everyday lives. Poise in the face of paradox is a key not only to effectiveness, but to sanity in a rapidly changing world.[353]
— Michael J. Gelb, *How to Think Like Leonardo da Vinci*

Early on in the massive shift from information to imagination, management guru-turned-innovation evangelist Tom Peters proclaimed that "*a tolerance for ambiguity will be success tool No. 1 for line workers, politicians and corporate chiefs alike.*"[354] Peters realized that certainty and control were management myths, fast fading into memory, and that to succeed in this new World, we "*must be able to not just 'deal with,' but actually thrive on ambiguity.*"[355]

The ability not only to tolerate, but to thrive on, ambiguity, has long been a signature strength of creators. Psychologist Carl Rogers noted this "*openness to experience*" as "*essentially constructive*" to creativity, explaining "*it means a lack of rigidity and permeability of boundaries ... a tolerance for ambiguity where ambiguity exists. It means the ability to receive much conflicting information, without forcing closure upon the situation. ... This complete openness of awareness to what exists at this moment is, I believe, an important condition of constructive creativity.*"[356] Today, a growing chorus is calling for this strength.

To embrace luck, you have to enhance your tolerance for ambiguity. Plan only to a point. The great military strategists from Sun-Tzu to Clausewitz have advised that you can plan only so far into the battle; you have to save lots of room for your adversary's contribution.[357]
— Twyla Tharp, *The Creative Habit: Learn It and Use It for Life*

Our complex, ever-changing world demands that we all learn to navigate through chaos, contradiction, and ambiguity. The secret lies in our creative guidance system. Creators are able to progress steadily toward their dreams, while holding the creative tension between where they are Now – their "current reality" or circumstances – and Where they truly want to be – their desired *Vision* or *Goal*. They walk through chaos and seeming contradiction with boldness and uncommon confidence, because they know each step – and their overarching *Vision* - are grounded in their highest *Values* and directed toward attaining their deepest desires.

When their path leads through chaos, they remain steadfast – not seeking to reduce the tension, by lowering their *Vision* or deciding they've come far enough ... not seeking an easy way out. They realize that, as systems-thinking expert Peter Senge says, "*the easy way out usually leads back in.*"[358] They realize it is the creative tension itself that propels them forward, and attracts to them the resources they most need. They realize that it is in the midst of the chaos, that the greatest breakthroughs emerge – breakthroughs that will not only lead them to their *Goals*, but ultimately will free them from patterns that have been holding them back, so that they may continue to rise to ever higher planes of potential. They *create* change and *embrace* ambiguity.

Effective leaders of innovation (and, in fact, anyone involved in the process) tend to possess a set of qualities and skills that may ... include: Tolerance for ambiguity. The innovation process is inherently ambiguous. It is filled with uncertain outcomes, complex relationships, multiple possibilities, and conflicting ideas.[359]
— James P. Andrew, *Payback: Reaping the Rewards of Innovation*

ON TRUTH & JUDGMENT

The subject of the Voice of Judgment is especially important for Creators, since this is arguably the most powerful force that may keep us from creating, or acting on our creating, or continuing to create through the challenging segments of our ARCs.

As Creators, we learn to keep our own counsel, and to trust that quiet but profound voice of inspiration that springs from within us. In fact, the advice of Hugh McLeod, creator of the cartoon-on-back-of-bizcard, is even more straightforward, in his classic *How to Be Creative*:

> *1. Ignore everybody. The more original your idea is, the less good advice other people will be able to give you. ...You don't know if your idea is any good the moment it's created. Neither does anyone else. The most you can hope for is a strong gut feeling that it is. And trusting your feelings is not as easy as the optimists say it is. There's a reason why feelings scare us. And asking close friends never works quite as well as you hope, either. It's not that they deliberately want to be unhelpful. It's just they don't know your world one millionth as well as you know your world, no matter how hard they try, no matter how hard you try to explain.*[360]

Of course, the ancient philosophers had quite a lot to say about the nature of truth (aletheia) and opinion (doxa),[361] and the master Greek philosopher Plato said that the only things that were true were universal principles – eternal, unchanging principles. The Creative Process is based on such principles. So, as Creators, we would do well to focus on those principles of creation, and on our own internal inspiration and creative guidance system, and give less weight to what others may think or say.

We even need to check what we ourselves thinking, and first, make sure it is valid (grounded in actual evidence and not just hearsay), and second, that it is in line with what really want (our Vision) and what we care most about (Values). It is true that we can be our own worst critics (although, as creators, we often discover there are plenty of others who seem willing to compete for that title). The truth is, we can't believe everything we think. Just because we think it, doesn't mean it is true. And, we can't believe that what others think is necessarily true, either – even if it seems like lots of people think it. From movies to books to television shows, reviewers – even "experts" - have widely divergent views on the same creations. We each must learn to trust our inner voice, and move forward with faith in our creativity.

It is proof of a base and low mind for one to wish to think with the masses or majority, merely because the majority is the majority.
Truth does not change because it is, or is not, believed by a majority of the people.
Giordano Bruno, Italian philosopher

Truth is not determined by majority vote.[362]
Pope Benedict XVI

Popular opinion is the greatest lie in the world.
Thomas Carlyle, Scottish writer

Whenever you find yourself on the side of the majority, it is time to pause and reflect.
Mark Twain, author and humorist

If a million people believe a foolish thing, it is still a foolish thing.
Anatole France, French author

The problems of the world cannot possibly be solved by skeptics or cynics whose horizons are limited by the obvious realities. We need men who can dream of things that never were.
John F. Kennedy, 35th President of the United States

Great spirits have always encountered violent opposition from mediocre minds.
Albert Einstein, theoretical physicist

LOOP OR LEAP

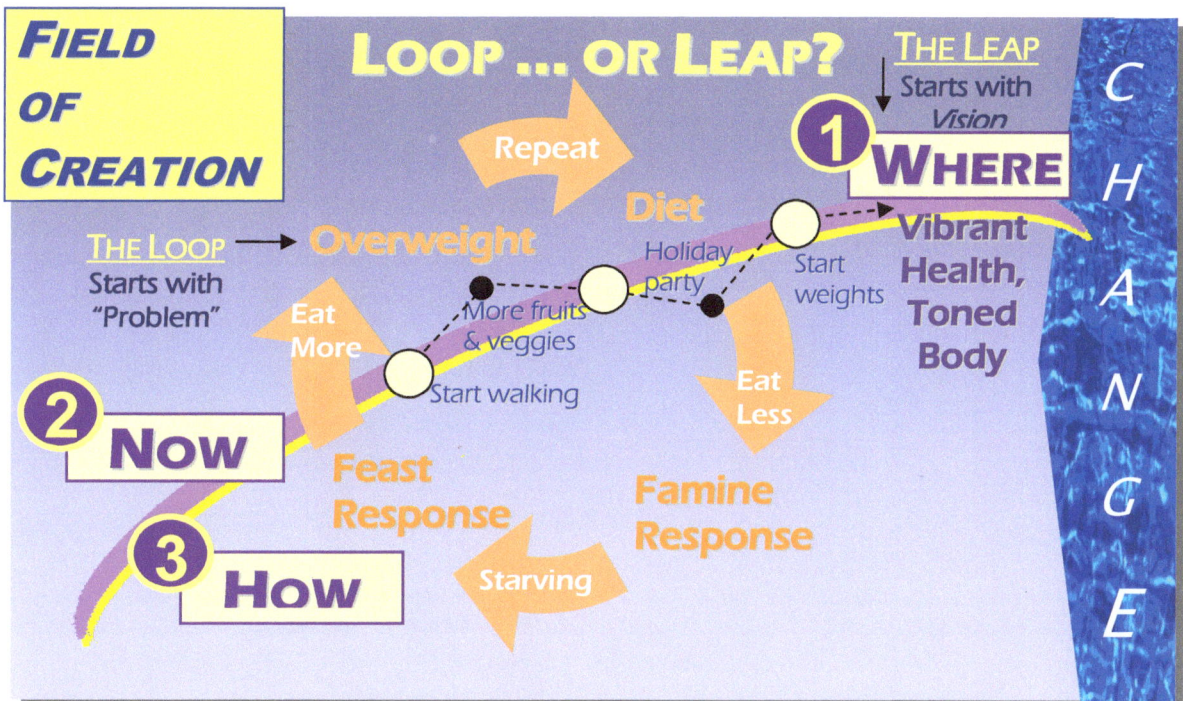

Our thinking leads us to "loop" or "leap." We may always choose a higher Way.

For example, in the "Diet Loop" shown above (orange graphics), as long as we focus on avoiding what we don't want (alternately, we don't want to be overweight, but then we don't want to starve, either), we limit ourselves to a inwardly focused, *closed system* or "loop" of thought, and, in this reactive mode of thought, we are never able to break out of the loop. If we never choose outside the existing system (WHAT IS), we are limited to loops and cycles.

In every instant, however, we may to access choose to leap into the unlimited realm of creative potential - the expansive, ARC-TO-SPIRAL *open system* available to us through the Creative Process (purple arc). In this potential-driven mode of thought, we focus on *what we really want*, our highest *Vision* – here, vibrant health and a toned, fit body. And we realize that, though we still face obstacles (such as tempting holiday parties), we can continue *navigating* through any setbacks (dotted lines), until we reach our *Vision*.

Creative, potential-driven thought is as essential on a larger scale as it is in our daily lives. Consider this exchange between two U.S. presidential candidates, on healthcare:

Mike Huckabee, Former Arkansas Governor: *"… We really have an incredible problem because our [U.S. healthcare] system is upside-down. It focuses on intervention at the catastrophic level of disease rather than focusing on prevention. …We're not going to fix it until we begin to address the fact that this country has put its focus not on wellness, not on prevention, not on health, but on sickness. And that's the single most important and urgent thing that has to be done. …"* Tommy Thompson, Former Gov. Wisconsin (R) and former Secretary of Health: *"We've got a sickness, illness, and disease society. We spend 90 percent of $2 trillion – that's 16 percent of the Gross National Product – on getting people well after they get sick, and less than 10 percent keeping people out of the hospital and nursing homes … lets go to wellness and prevention."*[363]

Our lives – and our world – call us to make a fundamental shift to a creative mode of thought.

OPRAH'S ARC

When she was four years old, Oprah Winfrey recalls standing on the screened-in back porch, watching her grandmother wash clothes in a big iron pot, and thinking:

'My life won't be like this. My life won't be like this, it will be better.'
And it wasn't from a place of arrogance; it was just a place of knowing that things could be different for me somehow. I don't know what made me think that.[364]

Born to unmarried parents, and raised by her grandmother on a farm with no indoor plumbing in Koscuisko, Miss., Oprah (who was named after "Orpah" from the Bible, yet her birth certificate was the only place her name was correctly spelled) began her Creative ARC with a *Vision* far beyond – and much higher than – the view from that back porch in Mississippi.[365] Yet, from the start, Oprah says:

All my life I have always known I was destined for greatness.[366]

It was Oprah's strong belief that enabled her to overcome such humble beginnings and enormous life challenges, and to navigate unceasingly toward her dreams. Hers was certainly a journey of faith, where she believed in her "unseen" but envisioned goals, regardless of the very visible, "seen" circumstances around her, until she rose above them and realized her Vision.[367]

This ability to consistently "*hold the high Vision*" is a core quality of master creators. Dr. Deepak Chopra calls this inner-driven focus on intended goals "*self-referral*," as opposed to "*object-referral*," which focuses on and reacts to current circumstances. Chopra explains: "*Your intent is for the future, but your attention is in the present. ... holding your attention to the intended outcome with such unbending purpose that you absolutely refuse to allow obstacles to consume and dissipate the focused quality of your attention.*"[368] Certainly, it was necessary for Oprah Winfrey to "harness the power of intention' in order to consciously create her life, as she overcame obstacles that have caused many to give up on their dreams.

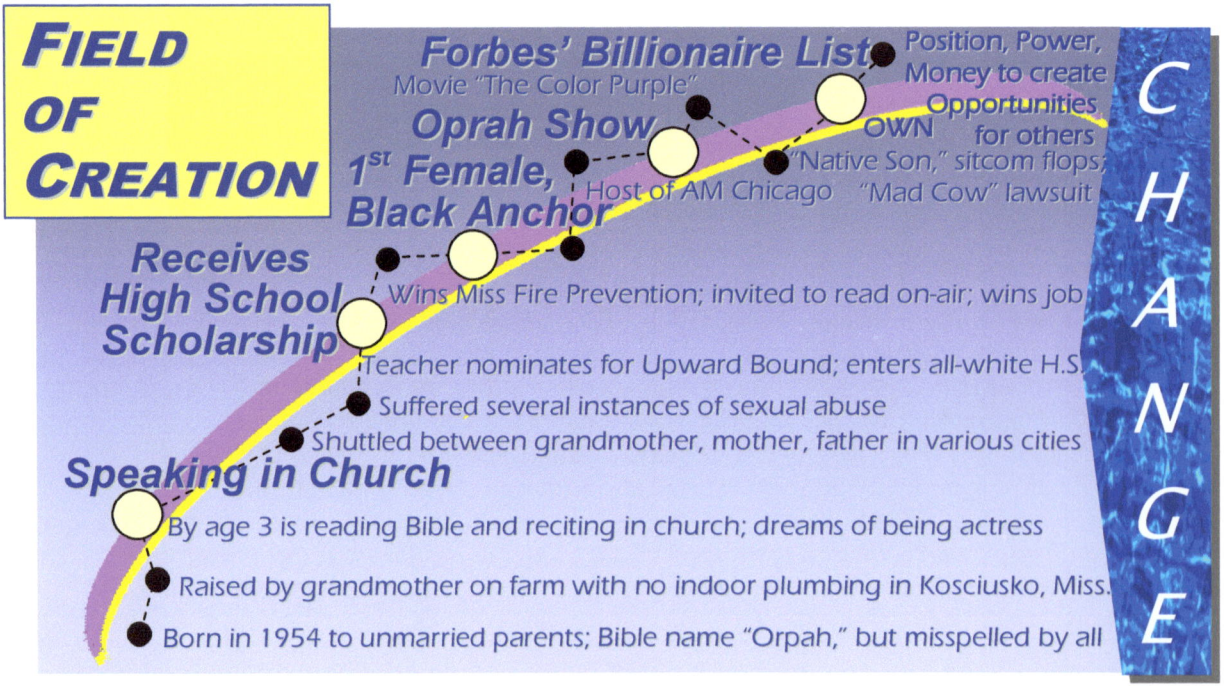

OVERCOMING THE ODDS

The intelligence and talents that would carry Oprah to stardom shone through from an early age. By age three she was reading the Bible and reciting scripture and poetry in church. She recalls: *"And all the sisters sitting in the front row would fan themselves and turn to my grandmother and say, 'Ida Mae, this child is gifted.' And I heard that enough that I started to believe it. … people would say, 'Whew, that child can speak.' And … whatever you do a lot of, you get good at doing it."*[369] Growing up, Oprah spoke at churches across the city of Nashville. And she dreamed of being an actress.

CHILD ORATOR — TALK SHOW HOST-ACTRESS — PRODUCER-PHILANTHROPIST

ARC TO SPIRAL – "SHIFTING THE ARC" TO EVER HIGHER LEVELS

In the background, however, the rest of Oprah's childhood, however, was much less positive. She was shuttled among her grandmother's, her mother's and her father's homes throughout her young life. Her time at her mother's in Milwaukee was the most traumatic, as she suffered several instances of sexual abuse, starting at age 9, and actually lost a child at age 14.[370] She says: *"I became a sexually promiscuous teenager, and got myself into a lot of trouble, and believed that I was responsible for it. It wasn't until I was thirty-six years old, thirty-six, that I connected the fact, 'Oh that's why I was that way.'"*[371] Only years later did Oprah reveal the abuse, in a now-famous segment of her talk show.

Oprah sought refuge in books, and carried her speaking over into school, where her devotionals led her 4th-grade classmates to call her "preacher." *"The kids used to poke fun at me all the time. It didn't bother me because I was so inspired."*

> *I would have been an entirely different person had I not been taught to read when I was an early age. My entire life experience, my ability to believe in myself, and even in my darkest moments of sexual abuse … I knew there was another way. I knew there was a way out. I knew there was another kind of life because I had read about it. I knew there were other places, and there was another way of being. It saved my life, so that's why I now focus my attention on trying to do the same thing for other people. … I don't think you ever stop giving. … I think it's an on-going process. And it's not just about being able to write a check. It's being able to touch somebody's life in such a way that [my 4th grade teacher] Mrs. Duncan touched mine. It's being able to make a child see the light in him or herself. Making someone else see that for themselves.*[372]

In this, Oprah expresses the essence of what being "A CREATOR'S GUIDE" is all about: First, "*We are all Creators*" – we are here to use the Creative Process to discover and express our unique gifts and live into our full potential, and then, "*We are all Creator's Guides*" – we are here to help others do the same. Oprah knows *creation is a process – best next step* by *best next step*.

> *I think that success is a process. And I believe that my first Easter speech, at Kosciusko Baptist Church, at the age of three and a half, was the beginning. And that every other speech, every other book I read, every other time I spoke in public, was a building block.*[373]

NAVIGATING TOWARD DESTINY

My philosophy is that not only are you responsible for your life, but doing the best at this moment puts you in the best place for the next moment.

Oprah's seventh-grade teacher noticed her reading books during the lunch period, and nominated her for the *Upward Bound* program, which led to a scholarship to the all-white Nicolet High School.[374] Oprah was crowned Miss Fire Prevention in Nashville at 17, and was also chosen to attend the White House conference on Youth that same year. Executives at a local radio station were impressed with Oprah during an on-air interview, and they hired her for her first broadcasting job. At 19, as a Tennessee State University sophomore, Oprah was hired by a Nashville TV station as a reporter, and later was hired by a station in Baltimore.[375]

However, it was actually Oprah's failure as a reporter that led to her first talk show.[376]

Instead of firing her, the station gave Oprah a morning talk show, and after her first interview, In 1984, Oprah became the host of A.M. Chicago, which became *The Oprah Winfrey Show*. Oprah was only 32 when the show was syndicated in 1986, and it soon overtook *Donahue* as the nation's top-rated talk show. All through Oprah's early success in radio and television, she also held fast to her childhood *Vision* of becoming an actress. Once again, she used creative principles to envision and "live into" her dream, and to gain a part in *The Color Purple*.

I truly believe that thoughts are the greatest vehicle to change power and success in the world. Everything begins with thoughts. The chair that we are sitting in, the room that we are in, all started because somebody thought it. So I thought of The Color Purple *for myself. I know this is going to sound strange to you. I read the book. I got so many copies of that book. I passed the book around to everybody I knew. If I was on a bus, I'd pass it out to people. And when I heard that there was going to be a movie, I started talking it up for myself. I didn't know Quincy Jones or Steven Spielberg, or how on earth I would get in this movie. I'd never acted in my life. But I felt it so intensely that I had to be a part of that movie. I really do believe that I created it for myself. I wanted it more than anything in the world, and would have done anything to do it. ... I feel that luck is preparation meeting opportunity. ... I sort of began to create my own luck.*[377]

Quincy Jones saw Oprah's show while in Chicago on a business trip, arranged an audition, and hired her to play the part of Sophie, for which she was nominated for an Academy Award. Oprah's career as an actress has met with mixed success, overall. Her second film, *Native Son*, based on Richard Wright's novel, actually flopped at the box office, as did the pilot for a proposed sitcom set to star Oprah as a talk-show host.[378] Yet, Oprah has shepherded several films to movie and television – including *Beloved* and *Before Women Had Wings*, some less well received than others. She continues sharing through her OWN Network and her shows.

[Television] is very important to me because it is a platform for being able to make a difference in people's lives, to influence them to change for the better. I don't want to give that up – until it's time. ... As long as I can be an influence and make a difference, that's what I want to do. But I also want to act because I think that it's very important to create work that, for one, puts the black cultural experience on screen.[379]

Oprah continues creating. In 2007, she opened a school for disadvantaged girls in South Africa: "*I understand what it means to be poor and not have your possibilities revealed to you. So I feel if I can do that for as many young girls as I can reach, I would have served part of my purpose here.*" She calls the experience "*a supreme moment of destiny.*"[380]

GENESIS of GENIUS

AL GORE'S ARC

Few in history have experienced the height of success – and the devastating loss – on the world stage, as has Al Gore, Jr. Having won the popular vote, but lost the U.S. presidency, in the disputed 2000 presidential election – former Vice President Al Gore could have chosen to fade quietly into the background. Instead, he picked himself up, dusted off his slideshow on the threat of global warming, and jump-started an international environmental revolution to save the planet. His story shows that it does not matter how far off course one might find oneself, in any instant, it is still possible to choose a higher way, and navigate again toward your life's high goals.

Born in 1948, the son of U.S. Congressman Albert Arnold Gore, Sr., young Al Gore would spend his school years in Washington, D.C., and his summers back on the family farm in Carthage, Tennessee. In 1952, his father was elected to the U.S. Senate, where he took strong but controversial stands supporting integration, and later, opposing the war in Vietnam. Al Jr. would attend St. Albans preparatory school in D.C., serve as football team captain, play basketball – and, after a school dance, meet his future wife, Tipper (then Mary Elizabeth Aitcheson). He would then head to Harvard, where he was elected freshman class president.[381]

It was at Harvard where Al Jr. would gain his first in-depth education about environmental issues and global warming, directly from oceanographer Roger Revelle, who did much of the pioneering work on the greenhouse effect and global warming – about which Al Gore would write his best-selling 1992 environmental book, *Earth in the Balance*.[382]

> *My parents taught me that the real values in life aren't material but spiritual. They include faith and family, duty and honor, and trying to make the world a better place.*[383]
> Al Gore, Jr., 2000 Presidential Nomination Acceptance Speech

It would seem that Al Jr. would be destined to enter politics, however, he had a broader life *Vision* – to serve and to influence public policy – whether through politics or through writing, which was actually his primary choice. In fact, after serving as an Army journalist in Vietnam – a war both he and his father opposed (a position which cost Al Sr. his Senate seat) – Al Jr. returned home disillusioned by politics, and settled in as a reporter for the Carthage newspaper.

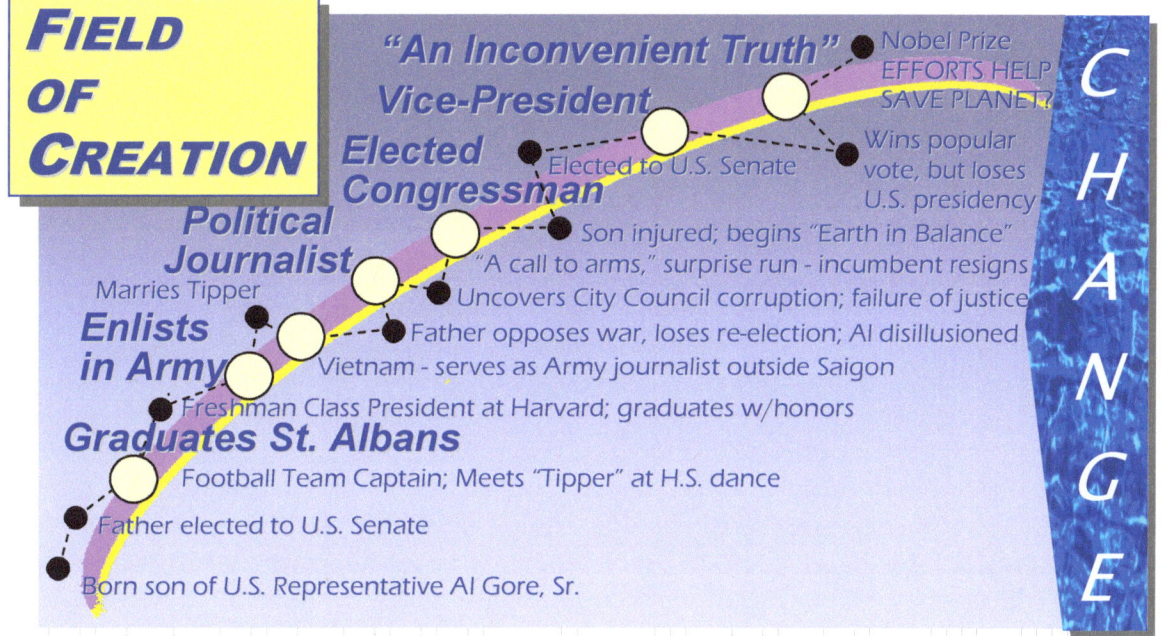

COMMITMENT TO VISION

However, it was Al Gore's coverage of corruption in the local city council, and a failure of justice in a case he had part in investigating for paper, that ultimately led him back to politics.

It was a kind of call to arms. This [political] process held nearly sacred is being defiled, and good people need to jump in and help the forces of good prevail.[384]

In his words, "*I decided that I could not turn away from service at home - any more than I could have turned away from service in Vietnam.*"[385]
And so, for Al Jr., politics reemerged from the background, accelerated significantly by the surprise resignation of veteran U.S. Congressman Joe Evins in 1976. Al Jr. was elected to the U.S. House of Representatives in November of that year. In 1984, he was elected to the Senate, and then made a failed run for president in 1987, after faring well in initial primaries, but ultimately withdrawing.

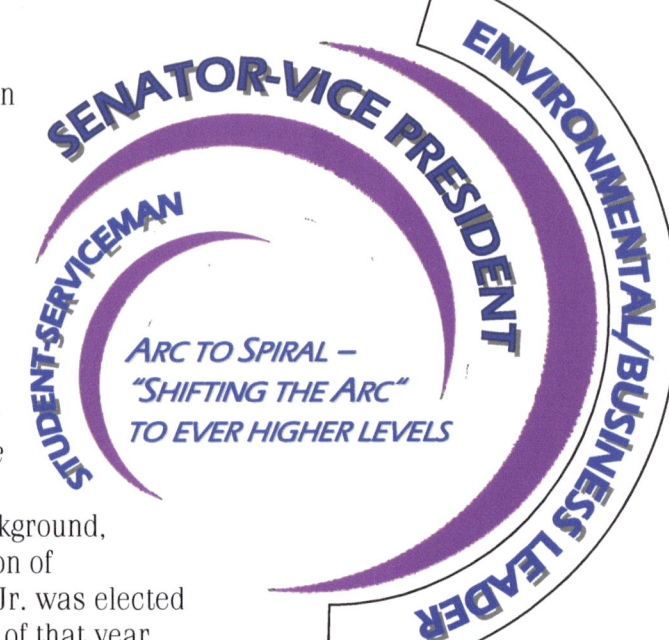

ARC TO SPIRAL – "SHIFTING THE ARC" TO EVER HIGHER LEVELS

STUDENT-SERVICEMAN · SENATOR-VICE PRESIDENT · ENVIRONMENTAL/BUSINESS LEADER

We have to accept responsibility for choosing the destiny of America.

In 1989, Al's son was hit by a car and seriously injured. While his son was recuperating, Al began writing *Earth in the Balance*, which would be published in 1992 – just six months before Bill Clinton would announce Al Gore as his vice-presidential running mate. His two terms as Vice President were not without their own challenges, but Al continued to spearhead national policy to protect the environment, as well as initiatives to spur growth of the Internet (then called "The Information Superhighway"). In 1999, Al Gore, Jr. announced his candidacy for the presidency, and accepted the Democratic nomination in August 2000. In his acceptance speech, he placed the environment front and center on his agenda, and attributed his entry into politics to his commitment to helping preserve the planet.

That's why I ran for Congress. In my first term, a family ... wrote a letter and told how worried they were about toxic waste that had been dumped near their home. ... And ever since, I've been there in the fight against the big polluters. Our children should not have to draw the breath of life in cities awash in pollution. ... On the issue of the environment, I've never given up, I've never backed down, and I never will. And I say it again tonight: we must reverse the silent, rising tide of global warming.[386]

And so, Al Gore Jr., stayed true to his words – and to his high *Vision* – and despite his bitter and controversial 2000 presidential loss, he redoubled his efforts to lead the fight to save the planet from environmental devastation. His book *An Inconvenient Truth* was an instant bestseller, the movie won an Academy Award, and the campaign led to the 2007 global concert *Live Earth*, to raise awareness of environmental solutions. A recent *Fast Company* cover featured Al Gore's remarkable comeback, as well as his continued success in the business realm (on the boards of Google.com and Apple Inc.), the growth of his citizen-journalism-driven cable venture *Current TV* (won an Emmy Award), an investment firm "based on a new definition of sustain-ability," his third bestselling book *An Assault on Reason*. To top it off, in 2007, Al Gore won the Nobel Peace Prize.[387] All because he believed his own, and the country's, ability *to choose to create a better future.*

GENESIS of GENIUS

OBAMA'S ARC

What's hard, what's risky, what's truly audacious, is to hope.[388]
    Barack Obama, as U.S. Senator and 2008 Democratic presidential candidate

Although Barack Obama seemed to break onto the national stage in an instant – most notably with his powerful speech introducing presidential nominee John Kerry at the 2004 Democratic National Convention – his journey to this stage led deep into his heritage, through a rebellious youth, and, ultimately, back to the values of hope and service he learned from his mother.

A decisive moment in my life was the transition from high school to college, because I had gone through a difficult time not knowing my father – and was at times an angry young man – and partly because of the values my mother had instilled in me became reawakened in college. It made me serious about not just what I could do for myself, but what I could do for other people. It's what led me to become a community organizer, it's what led me to go into public service, and, ultimately, it's what led me to this stage [as a U.S. Senator and Presidential candidate].[389]

Barack was born in Honolulu in 1961 to a Kenyan father and an American mother, at a time when mixed marriages not only caused significant controversy, but were still illegal in many states. His father Barack (Baraka means "blessing" or "the blessing of God" in Swahili) had won a scholarship as the first African to attend the University of Hawaii, and graduated at the top of his class the year after Barack was born. However, his father left his wife and son to attend Harvard University when Barack was 2 years old, and never returned to them, after he completed his Ph.D. Barack was told that, after receiving his degree from Harvard, his father had returned to Kenya, where he became an economist and an official in the administration of the newly democratic country. He had also remarried and had five children. As Barack would later write, "*my father remained a myth to me, both more and less than a man*" when he was growing up, and much of his life's search for identity and meaning centered around sorting out the truth about his father. In all, Barack spent only about one month with his father – when Barack was 10, his father visited him briefly – and it would be much later in his life before Barack would learn the full story of his father's accomplishments and failures.[390]

To Claim Your Bonus Books, Free Creative Resources, & Innovation Tools visit GENESISOFGENIUSBOOK.COM.

© JULIE ANN TURNER & COMPANY/CREATORSGUIDE.COM.
All Rights Reserved.

FINDING HIS WAY

As a young boy, Barack struggled to come to terms with both multiracial and multicultural experiences. His mother remarried an Indonesian man, and moved the family to Jakarta in 1967, where Barack attended both Catholic and Muslim schools. Wherever he went, it seemed he did not quite belong; his name and his appearance were different from that of his schoolmates (this led him to use the name "Barry" through most of those years). However, his mother's ideals of "*tolerance, equality, standing up for the disadvantaged*" – inspired by the 1960s and the civil rights movement - shaped Barack.[391] Even then, his 4th grade teacher noticed his leadership and protective nature, and remembered his writings that he one day "*hopes to be president.*"[392]

At 10, Barack ("Barry") returned alone to live with his grandparents in Honolulu, where his grandfather's boss (an alumnus) secured a place for Barry in the elite Punahou School. Barack describes the initial experience as "*a ten-year-old's nightmare,*" as the more privileged students asked to touch his hair and if his father was a cannibal. Fortunately, the novelty wore off quickly, and Barack gained an excellent education, graduating in 1979, and then attending Occidental College in Los Angeles. Here, he entered a rebellious phase, dabbled in drugs, and engaged "*in a fitful interior struggle*" to find his own identity, without a role model to guide him. Barack read his father's letters, read the works of black leaders like Malcolm X and Langston Hughes, and skirted the edge with drugs – "*Junkie. Pothead. That's where I'd been headed: the final, fatal role of the young would-be black man*" – in an effort to "*push questions of who I was out of my mind.*"[393] Yet, ultimately, he came to realize he need not choose between black and white – that his identity was forged far deeper than that, in his *Values*, his *Vision*, and a belief that he could create a life of his own.

> *Only a lack of imagination, a failure of nerve, had made me think that I had to choose between them. ... My identity might begin with the fact of my race, but it didn't, couldn't, end there. At least that's what I would choose to believe.*[394]

In 1981, Barack transferred from Occidental College to Columbia University in New York City, where he would graduate in 1983. After initially failing to find community work with a civil rights organization, he worked briefly for a consulting firm, where he rose quickly. However, the idea of community continued to "tug" at his heart, and, before long he began his search again, and moved to a job as a community organizer in Chicago's South Side.[395]

> *The same images [of the civil rights movement] that my mother had offered me as a child ... such images became a form of prayer for me ... they told me ... that I wasn't alone in my particular struggles, and that communities had never been a given in this country ... because this community I imagined was still in the making, built on the promise that the larger American community, black, white, and brown, could somehow redefine itself – I believed that it might, over time, admit the uniqueness of my own life. That was my idea of organizing. It was a promise of redemption.*[396]

LIVING OUT THE DREAM

Ultimately, Barack would choose to live out his Vision of service – drawing on the ideals, values and hopes he gained from his mother, and reconciling the paradox between fulfilling the expectations – and correcting the errors - of his father.[397]

As an organizer, Barack worked with community organizations, service agencies, and local leaders, to enable those in disadvantaged neighborhoods to find – and seek for themselves – creative solutions to their most pressing challenges. In this process, Barack learned the power of stories, and how asking simple, core questions – "*Tell me what matters most to you*" – and listening to heartfelt answers, was essential: "*That's what leadership was teaching me ... beyond surface issues, people carried within them some central explanation of themselves ... Sacred stories.*"[398] Using many elements of the core Creative Process we share in GENESIS OF GENIUS, Barack's goal became "*allowing the people ... to reclaim a power they had had all along.*"[399]

What is our community, and how might that community be reconciled with our freedom? ... How do we transform mere power into justice, mere sentiment into love. The answers I find in law books don't always satisfy me ... And yet, in the conversation itself, in the joining of voices I find myself ... encouraged, believing that so long as the questions are still being asked, what binds us together might somehow, ultimately, prevail.[400]

After two years as an organizer, Barack took his first trip to Kenya, as he prepared to enter Harvard Law School. With his strong *Vision* and sense of *Purpose*, he excelled – in 1990, becoming Harvard Law Review's "first black president in its 104-year history," as *The New York Times* would report. His star was quickly rising, and, upon graduating, he returned to Chicago, joined a civil rights firm handling discrimination cases, taught constitutional law at University of Chicago Law school, and – urged to write his memoirs due to his Harvard Law Review achievement – began writing his first book, *Dreams from My Father*, which would go onto become a bestseller. During this period, Barack met and married his wife, Michelle Barack, and also began attending Trinity United Church of Christ, where his personal faith deepened. Notably, it was Trinity's pastor whose "*Audacity of Hope*" sermon so impressed Barack on his first visit to the church many years earlier, that Barack adopted the title for his second bestselling book, *The Audacity of Hope*, published in 2006.[401]

In 1996, Barack took his first official step into politics, and was elected to the Illinois state legislature for the South Side Chicago district. Perhaps a bit too encouraged by his initial success, however, Barack in 1999 jumped prematurely into a run for the U.S. Congress to unseat Bobby Rush, a four-term congressman – and Barack received what he himself termed a "drubbing," losing 2-1 in the primary. Though chastened, and almost out of money due to campaign expenses (in fact, his *American Express* card was rejected at Hertz counter when he went to the 2000 Democratic Convention, and, as he had no official credentials, he wound up watching the proceedings on TV), Barack still did not give up on his *Vision*. He navigated his way forward, and, in 2003, he announced his run for the U.S. Senate. After several opponents' campaigns faltered, Barack was gaining ground going into the 2004 Democratic National Convention, where he gave his now-famous keynote speech for John Kerry. Barack won the Senate seat in a landslide, and became only the third black senator since Reconstruction, and the Senate's sole, current African-American member.[402]

Now, he leads on a global stage, as the first African-American President of the United States. As he said in his Kerry keynote, "*in no other country on earth is my story even possible.*"[403]

ERIN BROCKOVICH'S ARC

All my life I'd had a feeling inside that something good was going to happen to me, that I had a calling, a destiny, somewhere I was supposed to go, someone I was meant to be. ... Then, slow and late-blooming for sure, I was transformed from a down-and-out single mom to a $2.5 million bonus baby, with a movie having been made about my accomplishments, and several standing-room-only motivationally themed lecture series ... . [404]

To many, Erin Brockovich projects a larger-than-life image, that of an aggressive, outspoken, sexily dressed dynamo, whose rags-to-riches tale became well-known when actress Julia Roberts portrayed Erin in the blockbuster movie bearing her name.

Yet, Erin's struggles on the way to reaching the fairy-tale ending were also larger than life. Her story *Arc* traces a path that reveals critical life lessons: how an ordinary person can accomplish great things by focusing on strengths and minimizing weaknesses; how easy it can be to get off track, and yet how possible it is to find a way back, no matter how dark immediate circumstances may seem; and how – even after someone apparently has "made it" – it still remains necessary to navigate and adjust in the face of unexpected change.

Born in 1960 to an engineer father and journalist mother, Erin was raised with respect for family, the land, health, honesty, persistence and drive, as well as a solid moral foundation and spiritual values.[405] It was these core *Values* – and her unbending belief in her own destiny – that would eventually guide Erin back when she found herself far off course from her intended life path. From an early age, Erin struggled with learning through traditional methods, and "*had a terrible time getting through school*," as she was hampered by dyslexia, a learning challenge which would remain undiagnosed until she was in high school.[406]

[Dyslexia] caused everyone to misjudge my behavior from the time I was a child, to label me as "different" or "difficult," or as "a slow learner. ...I knew I wasn't dumb, even if everyone else thought I was. Overcoming my dyslexia became the first serious obstacle in my life, the first challenge that led me to discover the power and focus of my inner strength. [407]

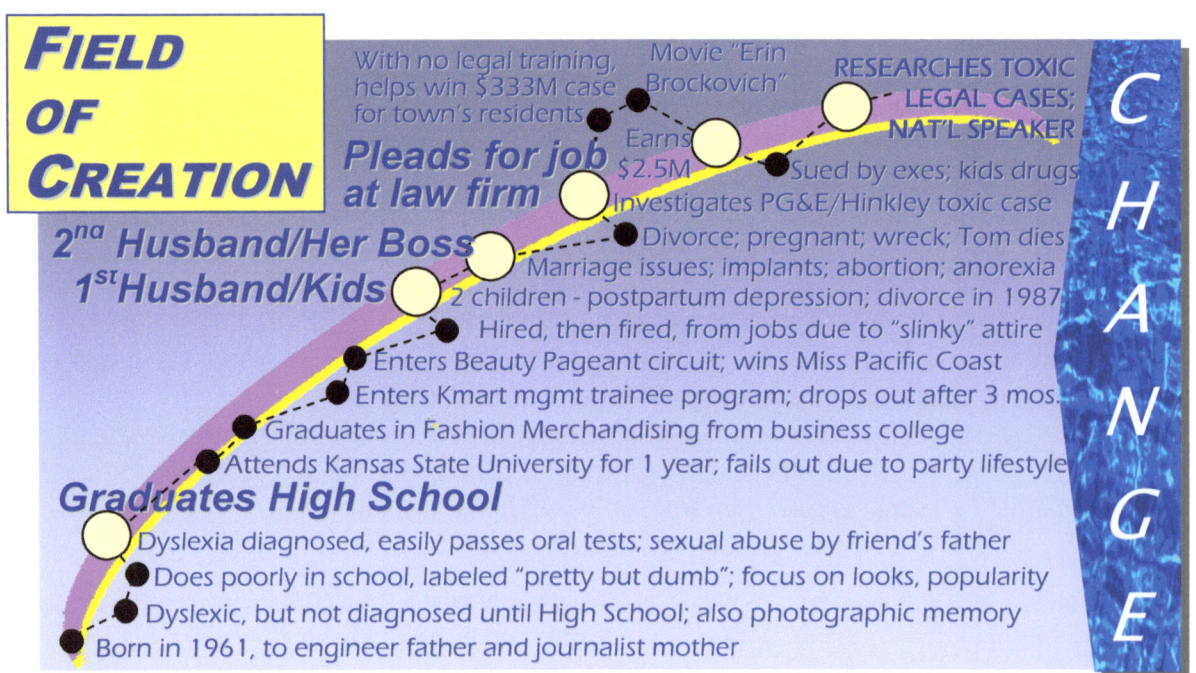

SLOW DOWNWARD SPIRAL

However, as a result of being labeled early on as "pretty but dumb," Erin would, before long, begin to focus on her physical appearance for both approval and attention – a coping method that would contribute to many challenges throughout her life.[408] Fortunately, beauty was not Erin's only strength – her tenacity, her brains, and her photographic memory would eventually shine through and serve her well on her way back toward a higher path.[409]

ARC TO SPIRAL – "SHIFTING THE ARC" TO EVER HIGHER LEVELS

"PRETTY PARTY GIRL" → STRUGGLING SINGLE MOM → FAMOUS LEGAL HEROINE/MOVIE STAR

Thanks to a high school teacher who allowed Erin to take her tests orally (and helped get her dyslexia diagnosed), Erin did graduate high school, and even entered Kansas State University, but barely made it through a year before poor grades and her "pretty" party girl ways intervened. She eventually earned an associate degree in fashion merchandising from a business college, then tried a Kmart management trainee program, but lasted only three months. Still leading with her looks, Erin ventured onto the beauty pageant circuit, even winning the Miss Pacific Coast title, before tiring of the "shallowness" of the pageant scene.[410]

Though she would not realize it at the time, Erin's next steps and her series of choices would initiate a slow downward spiral.

She briefly landed a job with an engineering firm, but was quickly fired because of her low-cut, slinky attire, and Erin began to realize the "*limitations I had imposed on myself by becoming so preoccupied with my physical appearance. ... When it came to looks, I'd always had the power.*" Though her looks might get her in the door, they did not qualify her for a steady job, and Erin learned "*my best personal asset - my just-another-pretty-face-and-figure inclination for having a good time - continued to be my worst professional qualification.*"[411]

Erin met and married her first husband, restaurant manager Shawn Brown, and before long had two children, Matthew and Katie. During this time, as the family moved often from state to state, Erin suffered from pregnancy complications, postpartum depression, panic attacks and weight issues, and before long the marriage itself crumbled, leading to divorce in 1987 and leaving Erin a newly single mother of two. After finding a job as a secretary at a brokerage firm, Erin met and eventually married her boss, Steve Brockovich. Before long, however, that marriage also was failing, with Erin turning to breast implants in an attempt to feel better about herself, as she ended another pregnancy with an abortion, and suffered bouts of anorexia and depression. Just as her second divorce became final, Erin discovered she again was pregnant – and decided to keep the child, despite her circumstances. Then, just four months into the pregnancy, Erin was injured in a serious car wreck, sustaining a herniated spinal cord injury that went undetected. Twice divorced, pregnant with her third child, jobless, and receiving little to no child support, Erin was struggling to hang on.

I was really down on myself, about ready to give it all up, unable or unwilling to face the hard truth that I had no one else to rely on for anything except myself. ... it was time I took control of my life.[412]

COURAGE TO SOAR

The year 1991 would prove to be a pivotal year for Erin Brockovich. Her third child, Elizabeth, was born. Erin moved to Los Angeles, moved in with biker Jorge Halaby, and hired Jim Vititoe to handle her personal injury lawsuit pending from her wreck. Then, her beloved brother Tommy died unexpectedly in a car wreck.

> *There are some things you just have to do. There is no choice, there is no decision, there is no avoidance. ... responsibilities we have to ourselves. I realized that up until that day I had been letting myself down. ... You have to. That was the mindset that had been missing for me. The knowledge, the belief, that I actually had the ability to control my own destiny, as long as I recognized there were some things that had to be done along the way.... I managed to turn the tragedy of Tommy's death into the moment of my own emotional and spiritual rebirth.*[413]

Just at the moment Erin thought that she could go on, she reconnected with the core *Values* her parents had instilled in her, and rediscovered the tenacity – the "*stick-to-itiveness*," as her mother called it – and realized that "*you have to hang in there and keep going no matter what obstacles you run into and no matter how insurmountable they seem.*"[414]

> *Again, it does not matter how far off course one might find oneself, in any instant, it is still possible to choose a higher way, to navigate again toward your life's high goals.*

Though she lost her injury lawsuit, Erin began hounding her lawyer Jim Vititoe and his partner Ed Masry to hire her as a secretary. Ultimately, they gave in, and though Erin's racy attire still offended her co-workers, she had a job, and Jorge was taking care of her kids. Then came the fateful day when Ed dropped a huge box of documents on Erin's desk for a seemingly small case. As she sorted through the files, Erin's tenacity, brains and photographic memory kicked in, and she discovered the telltale blood tests that would reveal the toxic Chromium 6 that Pacific Gas & Electric Company had been allowing to seep into the groundwater in the small town of Hinkley, California, causing residents to suffer ailments from chronic nosebleeds to deadly cancer. Erin had found a cause: "*I saw my own struggles reflected in theirs.*"[415]

Without any formal legal training, Erin Brockovich personally researched and championed the cause of the Hinkley residents, keeping even lawyer Ed Masry committed when he became discouraged. The story of Erin's courage, will and commitment not only led, ultimately, to the largest settlement ever paid in a direct action lawsuit - $333 million from PG&E – but also was translated onto the movie screen in 2000, with Julia Roberts portraying Erin. It is important to note that, even though the victory brought Erin fame, a new career as a legal researcher and motivational speaker, and $2.5 million for her work, she still faced obstacles. Two of her exes tried to blackmail her, claiming she was an unfit mother, and her two oldest children battled drug problems. Still, she was able to navigate on toward her highest *Mission*.

> *I do care a great deal about the environment but my real work and my greatest challenge is trying to overcome deceits that end up jeopardizing public health and safety. ... I am an advocate for awareness, the truth, and a person's right to know. I believe that in the absence of the truth, all of us stand helpless to defend ourselves, our families and our health, which is the greatest gift we have.*[416]

Her message to the world? "*I'm simply Erin Brockovich, and I have tried to make a difference in my life and in all of our lives. ... if I can do something to change our world, then so can you.*"[417]

SHIFTING THE ARC

Arnold Schwarzenegger not only knows how to live into a high Vision, but just as important, he knows how to navigate and change course in real time.

In fact, in 2006 Arnold saved his governorship of the State of California by dramatically adjusting his political course, after an entire set of his conservative, tight-reined budget cuts and anti-union proposals were soundly defeated in 2005, and late in his first term once-high approval ratings were plummeting.
So what did Arnold do? First, he took full responsibility, saying the failed policies were "my mistake." And then he immediately began to listen to the voting public, to reassess his direction, and to dramatically change course. In what *The Wall Street Journal* called an "abrupt about face," Arnold proposed bold strategies to fund education, repair roads, cut car emissions, and raise the minimum wage – embracing a more populist style and policies more traditionally aligned with Democrats than Republicans (which Arnold is). Many began referring to "*The Governator*" as "*Arnold 2.0*."
As a result, his approval ratings rose rapidly, and he easily won re-election in late 2006.[418]

Moreover, in typical Schwarzenegger style, Arnold is still pushing the limits of the possible, extending his leadership to take on development of a universal healthcare system for the entire state, including undocumented immigrants. Many, including senior's groups like AARP, are betting if Arnold can pull this off, "it could break the national logjam" on universal healthcare.[419]

More than just having the essential skills and judgment to navigate and change course along his path, Arnold also has the rare foresight and *Vision* to intentionally "*shift the Arc.*"
We saw this magnitude of creative leap when Arnold shifted from one entire field or industry to another – from bodybuilder to box-office star, and again from entertainment to politics.

Using the Creative Process, Arnold consciously envisions, plans and prepares in advance to move to an even higher Arc – beyond his current path or trajectory.

In his last section, we've seen how other leaders and modern-day heroines have done the same – *shifting their Arcs* to entirely new levels, moving beyond course adjustment and incremental improvements – as necessary as these navigational skills are - leaping from one plane of possibility to another, as they ascend the *Creative Spiral*. Far beyond reacting to circumstances or avoiding change, these Constant Visionaries intentionally *create their own change*.

The ability to *shift the Arc* through the conscious use of the Creative Process is essential, both for individuals who wish to live into their dreams and reach their full potential, as well as for organizations which desire to sustain their success in a competitive, global marketplace.
Do you know what your next Arc will be? Through this Creative Guidance System and the exercises and worksheets in this Guide. you may not only consciously create your *Career*, but your *Life Contribution*. Organizations can not only innovate, but *create entirely new categories*.

GENESIS of GENIUS

DEGREES OF POSSIBILITY

Ideas don't explode; they subvert. They take their time.
And because they change the way we think,
they are less visible than a newly paved national highway or the advent of wall-sized TVs.
After a while, someone notices that we're not thinking about things the way our parents did..[420]
    David Weinberger, co-author of *The Cluetrain Manifesto*

Often, it seems as if some ideas explode onto the scene, suddenly disrupting our awareness.
As we've seen, however, every breakthrough creation was once the merest tiny seed of a
thought, which, after growing slowly and unnoticed in the background, over time may reach
a tipping point, and burst into our consciousness, as if it appeared in its wholeness all at once.

We witness what we often call crazes, fads and even "overnight successes" all the time. Though these may seem ubiquitous for a short time – like the hula-hoop, tie-dyed t-shirts, or Beanie Babies – they are short-lived and soon-forgotten.

Breakthrough ideas, however, hold the power *to shift the* ARC – and even to change the world. These are the ideas that spawn movements and revolution, open our eyes to new realms of possibility and, over time, fundamentally change our WorldView. Those who cling to the status quo, or seek to control, fear them. "*Ideas*," said former communist leader Nikolai Lenin, "*are much more fatal things than guns.*"[421] Some are more global and transformational, like the Space Race or the Internet, and still others are transcendent – ideas like Peace or Freedom, or Rome or America, or like the shift in consciousness from Knowledge to Imagination. Yet they all grow – as well as guide us - behind the scenes.

Sometimes breakthroughs come as new forms in existing categories, or as creations that launch entirely new categories, or as inventions that change how society lives, works and thinks. Many open new worlds by expanding physical movement, communication, or thought itself. From the invention of the wheel, to horse-drawn carts, to boats, to steam engines, to automobiles to airplanes. Or the evolution of stone arrowheads to metal spears to gunpowder and guns to nuclear weapons. Or advances from simple hand tools to the plow to irrigation systems and hydroponics. Or the transformations from stone tablets to paper, from handwriting to the printing press, from the abacus to calculators to mainframes to minicomputers to personal computers. Or the shifts from analog to digital, from telegraph to telephones to digital cell phones, from vinyl records to 8-tracks to cassette tapes to CDs to digital music devices.

Clayton Christensen describes "the Innovator's Dilemma," which occurs when "disruptive innovations" leapfrog existing forms and even "sustaining innovations" (which improve existing products, often incrementally). The creator's of the existing forms are slow to respond or change, due to their investment in the current product or system.[422] They are even less likely to consciously *shift the* ARC *in advance*, to replace their own successful creations, and less able to envision entirely different forms or approaches have never yet existed, as their view of WHAT IS so often blocks their ability to envision WHAT CAN BE.

As we've emphasized, true innovators do not try to force their creations to fit what already exists. They envision forms never imagined before, as Francis Crick and James D. Watson did, in envisioning the structure of DNA. Or, as engineer Jack Kilby did in the 1950s, when, instead of incrementally tweaking the vacuum tube, he invented the new form of the microchip, which gave rise to computers and the digital age. Breakthroughs often lie entirely outside what has gone before, on an entirely new plane of thought. *As Einstein said, we cannot solve problems on the same level in which they were created. Vision itself is inherently disruptive, infused with passion and power. It ignites the* SPIRAL *from which creation comes.*

Before a great vision can become reality, there may be difficulty. Before a person begins
a great endeavor, they may encounter chaos. As a new plant breaks the ground
with great difficulty, foreshadowing the huge tree, so must we sometimes push
against difficulty in bringing forth our dreams. Out of chaos, brilliant stars are born.
    I-Ching, Chinese "Book of Changes"

THE CREATIVE GROUND OF INNOVATION

Like the sun's gravitational pull, innovation also pulls.
It pulls through a compulsion to change, change substantially.[423]
  Tom Peters, *The Circle of Innovation*

Though all too often we try to contain it, control it, minimize it or even ignore it, there ultimately is no avoiding that the Creative Process powers our world. Creativity is the ground of all things, whether tangible or intangible.

Moreover, creativity is more than just a high theory or noble concept – it is the essential force that determines how our lives unfold and how our organizations reach their potential.

As we've discovered, creativity – as well as its cousin, innovation – is a mindset, a different culture, a new way of thinking.

Instead of limited or incremental changes to WHAT IS, creativity and innovation call on us to leap to new realms of WHAT CAN BE. Instead of staying stagnant, or even struggling against the masses in turbulent, competitive space, we strike out for the open space to create entirely new possibilities, new markets, new categories (what W. Chan Kim and Renée Mauborgne call the "*Blue Ocean*," in their business metaphor, and what, on a much more all-encompassing scale, we call the Creative Realm).[424] As the legendary business mind Peter Drucker said, "*Every organization – not just business – needs one core competence – innovation.*"[425]

This requires not merely incremental change, but consciously shifting the ARC – actively envisioning two or three ARCs beyond our current ARC, and beginning to build those higher ARCs far in advance of their full realization in our tangible world. This is the key to overcoming "the Innovator's Dilemma" that so often keeps us, and our organizations, falsely locked into lives and limits (of existing products or services, or even existing success) of far less impact and scope than our full potential holds for us."[426]

As we've noted, however, *innovation* can be framed almost as broadly as creativity itself – as a *mindset* or *ground of thought* – or as narrowly as the "*action and Implementation*" stages of the Creative Process (see pp. 154 327-329, 355-6). In our terms, this means some describe *innovation* as including all three stages of the Creative Process - WHERE, NOW, and HOW – while many others emphasize innovation as focused primarily, or solely, on HOW. As we've seen, although it may be tempting to try to squeeze this creative shift of thought into an old, familiar mold, we cannot shortcut the Creative Process by skipping ahead to HOW, as doing so effectively disconnects any resulting "actions" from the strategic value and power that are framed by, and generated from, the essential first stages of the process. As Drucker said:

Defending yesterday – that is, not innovating – is far more risky than making tomorrow.

For businesses, the *profitability* of ideas is paramount. Yet, it is only within the context of the full Creative Process that innovation gains its power to reshape not only products but categories, and to contribute dramatically to an organization's bottom line (or *Return on Innovation* investment). In *The Seeds of Innovation*, author Elaine Dundon acknowledges this context, in noting that "*without creativity, there is no innovation*," and goes on to define *innovation* as "*the profitable implementation of strategic creativity.*"[427] In this definition, she describes *creativity* as "*the discovery of a new idea*," *strategy* as "*determining whether it is a new and useful idea*, '*implementation* as "*putting this new and useful idea into action*," and *profitability* as "*maximizing added value from the implementation of the new and useful idea.*"

GENESIS of GENIUS

CIRCLES OF INFLUENCE

One of the crucial questions on navigating the ARC is "*Where should we focus our attention?*" We know first and foremost to focus on our *Vision* and *Mission*, filtering information relative to our primary *Goals*, rather than being distracted by any "problem" or particular set of circumstances. We do want to *Scan* the space for information that may help guide or propel us forward (see *Scan* section).

Beyond that, however, how do we know what to pay attention to or expend energy on? Here, we share a useful model that expands on concepts proposed by Stephen R. Covey, called the *Circle of Concern* and the *Circle of Influence*.[428] Simply put, the *Circle of Concern* encompasses those things which *may* affect your path or journey toward your *Goals*, but over which you have no influence or about which you can take no direct action at this moment. These could include anything from a potential stock market downturn to global terrorism to the responses of other people. The *Circle of Influence* encompasses anything that we can act on or influence – and we add, *directly* or *indirectly*. This includes all your *internal* or *Personal Mastery* – how you think, how you feel, how you act, as well as the gifts, talents, experience and skills you may develop. To this inner circle, we have expanded the model to include *Relationships*, through which we may indirectly influence situations and outcomes, and gain information and resources.

It is crucial to understand the value of Relationships as a powerful conduit through which we may expand our influence. As we develop our Personal Mastery – our skills, attitudes, emotions, and especially, our conscious creative thought – and expand our Relationships, our Circle of Influence grows.

Clearly, we want to focus on what we can *Influence*, and not on outside *Concerns* which can only worry us and drain our attention and energy (and which may, ultimately, never actually affect us in the long term). First, we *Scan* any set of circumstances to glean any useful information, and determine if we can take any action or make any contact that would influence the situation. If not, we consciously acknowledge that this currently lies outside our *Circle of Influence*, commit not to allow this situation to distract us, and then actively refocus our attention and energy on our *Vision, Mission* and *Goals* – on *what we can act on or influence.* No matter how turbulent the space ahead may seem, this will keep us on the right path.

With regard to *Relationships*, we make three critical points. First, we *seek the highest* here, as well, That means we expect the best of people (WHAT CAN BE), even if they may not have shown us their best previously. As Abraham Lincoln once remarked, "*I don't like that fellow very much. I must get to know him better.*" Expectations are *powerful*, and research shows that if we expect the best from others, we are more likely to receive it in return (the *Law of Reciprocity*, which Robert Cialdini cites as one of the most powerful triggers of influence).[429] Second, we *set our own limits* with others – we state clearly what we will, and will not, accept in our relationship with them.[430] Finally, we become CREATOR'S GUIDES. As we live into our full creative potential, through the Creative Process, we then help others live into theirs.

> *If you treat an individual as he is, he will remain as he is. But if you treat him as if he were what he ought to be and could be, he will become what he ought to be and could be.*
> Johann Wolfgang Von Goethe, German writer, artist and philosopher

HOLD THE HIGH VISION

I say to you today, my friends, so even though we face the difficulties of today and tomorrow, I still have a dream.
— Martin Luther King, Jr., civil rights leader

Throughout your Creative Journey, hold the high Vision.

How can doing something higher or "harder" actually be easier? Because a high, compelling *Vision* and high expectations – of yourself and of what is possible – increase creative tension, which attracts resources and helps propel you toward your goals and dreams.

When we focus on our own limitations, on competition, on scarcity, we limit our own power. In fact, worrying is actually negative visioning – it saps our energy and reduces our power. Essentially, Albert Einstein said that when we seek to resolve problems on the same level at which we created them, there is no creative tension. As we move to a higher level of thought – from WHAT IS to WHAT CAN BE – we may create compelling new solutions, shared *Visions* which hold power and attraction to shift everyone to a higher level of potential.

Growth and excitement in individuals and companies comes from stretching to achieve things that may not have seemed possible earlier.[431]
— Gay Hendricks and Kate Ludeman, *The Corporate Mystic*

Every thought affects energy flow and carries power. Negative and fearful thoughts reduce our energy and power. Positive, passionate and compelling thoughts increase our energy and power. So, as motivational speaker Tony Robbins says, don't just seek to be good; instead, "*be outstanding.*" Seek the highest in every moment. When we operate at a higher level – on a higher plane – we tap into our full creative power. We direct change.

We hold our highest intention and *Vision* – and our commitment throughout the Creative Process – regardless of the immediate circumstances we may see. We did not depend on circumstances to determine our *Vision* and direction; likewise we do not depend on them for our evidence that *creative change is in process.* We know it is. We set it into motion, and "*as we work the process, the process will work.*" As challenges arise, we will not lower our *Vision*, but instead will adjust our course, and navigate onward toward our high *Vision*. As Stephen Covey says, staying true to our Vision and principles "*will always bear fruit. Always.*"[432]

Life's challenges are not supposed to paralyze you, they're supposed to help you discover who you are.
— Bernice Johnson Reagon, singer and social activist

We are navigating in a realm of infinite potential. The Creative Realm is one of abundance, not scarcity. Rather than further dividing the slices of an existing pie, we create more pie – more capacity, more ideas, more sources, more markets, more categories, more uses of existing resources. Competition is based on scarcity, and engenders conflict. Creation is based on abundance, and engenders collaboration and co-creation.

At each level or plane, we expand capacity. Arnold Schwarzenegger expanded his capacity – and shifted his ARC - to move from Pumping Iron to politics. The Space Race not only opened a new realm of discovery, but spawned a new age of technological creation.

The Spiral widens with every turn, to a higher plane of potential.

ABOUT THE AUTHOR

JULIE ANN TURNER, A CREATOR'S GUIDE is the founder and CEO of JULIE ANN TURNER & COMPANY/CONSCKOUSSHIFT.ME®, a consultancy focused on boosting your team's creativity innovation to breakthrough levels, through exclusive systems and practical tools.

Expert: *Julie Ann excelled as Director of Public Affairs for global telecommunications corporation Nortel, and honed her creativity as Vice President/Senior Executive the international advertising/ public relations agencies Ketchum and Tracy/Locke, Inc. (DDB Needham Worldwide). She holds an M.A. in Communications from the University of Texas at Austin.*

Innovator: *Julie Ann is the creator and founder of the ORBITS OF INFLUENCE® Global Leadership Dialogue, an award-winning social innovation initiative which enables diverse thought leaders to address the key issues and emerging ideas of our communities and world, and founder of the emerging World Sanctuary Project.*

JULIE ANN TURNER
JULIE ANN TURNER & COMPANY/CONSCIOUSSHIFT.ME®

As an author, speaker, executive coach and award-winning social innovator, Julie Ann Turner guides global Thought Leaders and World-Changers to share and profit from their Signature Genius, and live to their highest creative potential.

One of the world's top authorities on the creative process, Julie Ann Turner is the author of the 3-book series **GENESIS OF GENIUS**™ and creator of *POWER ARC*™: *YOUR CREATIVE GUIDANCE SYSTEM*®, through which she shares her expertise and exclusive, innovative model of the master Creative Process. **GENESIS OF GENIUS**™ is based on more than 18 years researching and distilling the master sequence of creation used by all successful thought leaders and visionaries, traced through and distilled from the universal creative archetypes and principles from the most sacred writings of humankind, through philosophy, theology, and science - and on to quantum physics and current systems theory.

She is a thought leader in the global shift to creative consciousness, and is Executive Producer, Creator and Host of the global CONSCIOUSSHIFT Radio Show (250,000+ subscribers worldwide and growing), which features voice and visionaries leading the worldwide co-creative movement, including Seth Godin, Dan Pink, Marianne Williamson, Julia Cameron, Lynne McTaggart, SARK, Fred Alan Wolf, Marilyn Schlitz, Don Miguel Ruiz, and many more.

Julie Ann is the founder and CEO of JULIE ANN TURNER & COMPANY/CONSCIOUSSHIFT.ME *(formerly* CREATORSGUIDE.COM®*), a consultancy and web company specializing in creativity development, innovation and creative counsel, coaching and training; strategic planning; leadership and organizational development; and strategic branding and program development.*

Through Julie Ann's powerful, innovative methods and tools - *drawing on universal creative principles and process and revealed in this* CREATIVE GUIDANCE SYSTEM - you and your organization dramatically enhance individual and team leadership, collaboration, creativity and innovation. Whether you are an individual, seeking to clarify your career/life focus and direction and to more effectively align and integrate your personal, professional and community endeavors ... or a corporation seeking more innovative thinking and team alignment to move your company or department to a new level of effectiveness and teamworking ... our customized programs will propel you to the next level of leadership.

Since 1994, our exclusive systems have guided strategic counsel and planning, team facilitation, marketing strategy, CEO/Executive coaching, and creative counsel and services for corporate executives, entrepreneurs and community leaders, and for more than 40 national and international corporations (including IBM, Nortel, Verizon, IdeaArc, Phillips Petroleum, DDB Needham Worldwide, Ben Hogan Company, Brinker International, and many more). For a complete list and more details, please visit CONSCIOUSSHIFT.ME

ACKNOWLEDGEMENTS

This small space inevitably seems inadequate for me to express fully my gratitude for all who have supported and encouraged me in this life's work. However, though I could never recount all who have contributed in ways small and large to my life and to this work, I do wish to thank a special "slice of the spectrum" among those who have helped light my way.

First and foremost, I wish to thank the Creator, who has given me this life purpose, who leads me on this Journey, who has opened my eyes to the principles, patterns and process that project the glory of All That Is, and who, around each turn in the path of exploration, allows me to experience the inexpressible joy of divine discovery. I honor the miraculous Mind and boundless love of the Creator, who, astonishingly, allows us to participate freely in that Creative Process ... and I honor the Creator's Son, Jesus Christ, who lived that we might love and live more abundantly.

I have undertaken and continue this quest in awe, humility, and deepest gratitude for this gift of purpose, and continue to pray for the wisdom to express adequately the holy truth of the magnificence of the Creator and the Creation ... and to shine a light on the pivotal nature of our role as conscious participants and co-creators of our world, and our role as caretakers of peace and stewards of this fragile planet and its people, which lie in the balance.

I thank my husband, Tim, for supporting and encouraging me all along the way, throughout the creation of this work, and for believing both in me, and in the importance of the work itself. It has taken great patience, faith and love - and I thank him for sharing these gifts with me.

I thank my mother, Anna Sue, whose brilliant mind and creativity have inspired me all of my life, and whose spirit continues to live through me and through this work. I thank my father, Jack, for helping me stay open to all perspectives, and also for nurturing a sense of humor and possibility - as these have enabled me to find my bearings in the midst of the beautiful, but sometimes bewildering, interlacing of chaos and order that is this life. I thank my brother, Steve, my kindred spirit, who believes in me, and means the world to me.

I thank my dearest friend Debora Glennon, without whom I would not have completed this work. Her tireless support and encouragement held me up through the tough times, consistently turned discouragement into determination, and helped me remember the joy and love that always lives behind the words and work.

I thank the special spirits of Pat Porter, Phillip Shinoda, and David Young, whose confidence in my contribution and belief in this creation - not to mention their reading and recommendations - have helped shape and polish this work. I also thank the small but invaluable circle of advance reviewers, whose honest feedback and generous comments enhanced the work - Paul Babin, Marla Crockett, Terry Flowers, Tim Palmer, Rusty Rueff and Pamela Shoemaker. I thank Marisa Murgatroyd for her branding vision, and Marnie Pehrson for her guidance for the book launch.

For his unique and extraordinary Universe and Oz graphics, I thank graphic designer Lee Collison. For faithfully and patiently crafting the Creator's Guide graphics to match my vision, I thank Greg Colunga; for his web wizardry, I thank Anthony Gill (almost every day); and for his remarkable creativity and MoonGames photography showcased on the book covers, I thank Laurent Laveder.

I also thank the entire ORBITS OF INFLUENCE Global Leadership Dialogue community of social innovators and cadre of phenomenal facilitators and volunteers, for their belief in the power of dialogue and visioning to transform potential conflict into creative potential, as this work embodies and expresses the practical application of the principles of the Creative Process presented in this work. Special thanks to Arcilia Carrasco-Acosta, Gerald Borders, Bob Lilly, Jr., Nadine Bell, Seymour Bell, Dirk and Jane Velten, Tasnim Benhalim, Shabnam Modgil, Pat Porter, Mike Ghouse, Najma Chouse, Marlene Gorin, Garry Castro, Raul Treviño, Jay Forte, Elizabeth Frank-Jones, Sharon Bailey, Beverly Wright, Farrukh Hamid, Bill Matthews, Judie Arkow, Phil Ritter, Susan Gore, Suzie Katz, Michael Edwards, Mary Greene, Sylvia Komatsu, Amanda Harris, Farai Chideya, Fernando Torres-Gill, Judy Nadler, Chris Abraham, Hal Hinson, Christine Byers, Chris Koski, Chris Turner, Kathryn Parsons, David Young, Faith Kuczaj, Brenda Raine, Khadijah Jannah, Millicent Boykin, Mohamed Elibiary, Oliver Johnson, Marcia Zidle, Ann Faulkner, Guy Gooding, Bill Tucker, Steve Mittlstet, Andrew Jones, Leigh Ober, Carol Gregston, Yolanda Nolan, Tracy Brown, Marcia Zidle, Cynthia Shinda, Linda Tunnell, Vanessa Baker, Beth Adcock, Froswa Booker-Drew, Dawnetta Miller, Carol Tucker, Hollye Chacon, Leo Cusimano, Chris Phipps, Cynthia Wireman, Kerri Aiken, Robert Manley, Robert Quintana, Cherry Werner, Jay Tzo, Irma Landis, Young Eui Choi, C.A. Engleton, Thomas Tsang, Ken Tarango, Jennifer Wimbish, Claire Gauntlett, Pam Gist, Gretchen Riehl, Dan Rogers, Lew Sayers, Olivia Guerra, Gwen May, Sheryl May, Sonya Spencer, Bill Faulkner, Lennijo Henderson, Kathy Yates, Elsie Burnett, Susan Wehe, Joe Sullivan, Carrie Schweitzer, Dan Rogers, Delores Elder-Jones, Kay Coder, Sue Jones, Deb Yoder, Mwauna Davis, Judy Elimelech, Gretchen Riehl, Suvarna Desai, Ora Howard, Joe Martinez, Joel Riley, and Kathy Yates.

Finally, I thank all the creators whose works have inspired me and provided insight, which include (a necessarily partial list, in no specific order): David Bohm; Margaret Wheatley; Michael Ray; Stephen Covey; Thomas Moore; David Whyte; William Mahony; Fred Alan Wolf; Rudy Rucker; Michael Schneider; Malcolm Gladwell; Tom Friedman; Tom Peters; Daniel Pink; Marianne Williamson; Bernie Siegel; Joseph Jaworski; Peter Senge; Richard Florida; Paul Ray; Sherry Anderson; Juanita Brown; Mihaly Csikzentmihalyi; Kevin Kelly; Seth Godin; David Weinberger; Daniel Yankolovich; Linda Ellinor; Glenna Gerard; Julie Cameron; Harrison Owen; Matila Ghyka; Robert Lawlor; Bruce Rawles; William Isaacs; Steve Chandler; Richard Bolles; Laurence Boldt; Barbara Sher; Alvin Toffler; Teresa Amabile; Robert Fritz; L. Frank Baum; Joseph Campbell; Trinh Xuan Thuan; Gary Zukav; Arnold Schwarzenegger; Oprah Winfrey; Barack Obama; Al Gore, Jr.; Erin Brockovich; Martin Luther King, Jr.; Plato, Aristotle, Heraclitus, Lao Tzu, Pythagoras, Leonardo da Vinci, Alfred North Whitehead, and all of the great philosophers, mystic poets, writers and artists throughout time; for, to paraphrase Tyler Volk, seeing and sharing the "*metapatterns*" ... for "*singing the songs that existed before we knew there were songs to sing.*"[cdxxxiii]

A

Abundance, xxx, xxxi, 31, 77, 117, 131, 144, 154, 157, 209, 225
Adaptation, xxi, 20, 64, 76, 77, 121, 128, 152, 170, 234
Age of Imagination, xvii, 16, 88, 156
    Creative Age, xxxi, 74
    Once & Future, 20, 38
Agricultural Revolution, 222
Al Gore, Jr., 197, 198, 212, 242, 243
Alignment, xxvi, 29, 57, 74, 75, 81, 90, 103, 104, 119, 123, 124, 131, 148, 150, 151, 162, 163, 166, 176, 183, 210, 225, 226, 237
America, ii, 201, 14, 132, 190, 198, 206, 233, 239
American Idol, 80
Analysis, 9, 63, 66, 69, 126, 128, 138, 139, 143, 144, 145, 146, 147, 149, 152, 153, 154, 155, 157, 164, 237
Arc, xviii, 2, 28, 34, 44, 48, 151, 167, 193
Archetype, 2, 17, 38, 48, 223, 235
Aristotle, 103, 108, 212, 221, 235, 237
Arnold Schwarzenegger, 43, 44, 45, 46, 47, 48, 49, 53, 54, 59, 64, 66, 73, 90, 173, 188, 197, 205, 209, 212, 223, 237
Association, 23, 181, 182
Authenticity, xiv, xxv, xxvi, 2, 36, 49, 77, 86, 103, 113, 123, 126, 130, 132, 144, 145, 157, 164, 165, 229
Autopoiesis (Self-Creation), 121

B

Barack Obama, 199, 200, 201, 212, 243
Becoming, xxviii, xxxi, 10, 17, 34, 47, 66, 107, 108, 109, 125, 138, 144, 152, 156, 157, 196, 201, 203, 229
Belief, xiii, xxv, xxix, 18, 31, 34, 69, 90, 106, 107, 127, 153, 194, 200, 202, 204, 211, 212, 224, 227, 228, 229
Best Next Steps, 163, 195, 240
Biology, xxviii, 121, 186, 235
Blogs, 80, 117, 163, 169
Bohm, David, 126, 212
Boldness, 130, 173, 191, 205
Brain, 23, 109, 170, 181, 182, 239
Brainstorming, 73, 155, 181, 182, 224
    Beyond Brainstorming, 73, 181
Branding, xxvi, 105, 154, 210
Business, xxi, xxv, 14, 48, 63, 66, 70, 73, 102, 109, 112, 113, 116, 118, 122, 127, 130, 131, 142, 145, 146, 147, 152, 164, 168, 169, 171, 181, 196, 198, 203, 207, 229, 231, 233, 235, 236, 238, 241

C

Campbell, Joseph, 34, 39, 89, 100, 103, 212, 223, 227, 228
Change, xv, xvi, xvii, xviii, xxi, xxii, xxiii, xxiv, xxvi, 3, 11, 12, 20, 26, 29, 31, 36, 38, 44, 46, 48, 49, 52, 56, 57, 64, 67, 69, 71, 73, 75, 76, 78, 88, 99, 105, 107, 112, 113, 116, 119, 122, 124, 127, 129, 146, 152, 153, 154, 155, 157, 162, 163, 171, 172, 176, 186, 189, 190, 191, 192, 196, 202, 204, 205, 206, 207, 209, 223, 225, 226, 227, 230, 237, 242
Chaos, xv, xxi, 20, 21, 23, 28, 44, 118, 122, 145, 150, 188, 189, 190, 191, 206, 211
Character, 10, 86, 106, 108, 113, 229
Choice, xiv, xvi, xviii, xx, xxix, xxxi, 3, 6, 8, 16, 22, 23, 28, 34, 35, 36, 38, 49, 50, 66, 67, 69, 73, 76, 77, 78, 80, 81, 85, 88, 89, 90, 103, 104, 106, 110, 111, 113, 119, 120, 123, 124, 125, 129, 131, 141, 148, 153, 154, 167, 171, 173, 175, 186, 187, 188, 189, 193, 197, 198, 200, 201, 204, 221, 222, 225, 226, 240
Chopra, Deepak, 108, 144, 188, 194, 230, 237, 241, 242
Circumstances, 9, 26, 36, 38, 45, 62, 65, 66, 67, 68, 70, 71, 72, 73, 74, 76, 77, 78, 80, 81, 86, 88, 89, 90, 103, 112, 138, 139, 140, 141, 142, 153, 172, 173, 175, 183, 187, 188, 190, 191, 194, 202, 203, 205, 208, 209, 237
    Configuration of Information, 12, 20, 65, 74, 141, 186
    Constellations of Circumstance, 36, 65, 66, 67, 74, 76, 141
Civilization, 80, 186
Cluetrain Manifesto, 206, 244
Clusters (see also Strategic Goals), 65, 121, 141, 145, 149, 157, 164, 165, 176
Co-Creation, xv, xvi, xviii, xxvii, xxix, xxxi, 29, 57, 80, 117, 122, 126, 128, 129, 131, 132, 152, 154, 155, 209, 226, 227
    Co-Creators, xxvii, xxviii, 38, 144, 186, 211
Collaboration, 10, 14, 57, 105, 117, 119, 131, 142, 145, 151, 163, 209, 210
Compromise, 123, 124, 166
Conflict, xxi, 124, 152, 209, 212, 233
Consciousness, xvi, xxviii, 4, 5, 11, 36, 38, 79, 80, 88, 107, 130, 168, 206, 227, 234
Consulting, 145, 147, 156, 164, 200, 210, 230
Context, xxv, xxvi, xxix, 23, 72, 73, 138, 139, 140, 141, 144, 145, 153, 157, 190, 207, 237
Control versus Creation, xxi, 9, 26, 38, 68, 69, 80, 120, 121, 123, 128, 153, 155, 175, 181, 186, 189, 191, 203, 204, 206, 207, 225
Copernicus, 5
Covey, Stephen, 112, 113, 209, 212, 223
Creation, xx, xxii, xxvi, xxvii, xxviii, xxix, xxxi, 2, 6, 14, 20, 21, 23, 28, 29, 34, 35, 36, 38, 49, 57, 67, 74, 76, 77, 82, 85, 87, 88, 91, 95, 99, 100, 103, 119, 120, 121, 123, 128, 129, 131, 140, 142, 148, 151, 152, 156, 163, 167, 168, 173, 174, 182, 183, 187, 189, 190, 192, 195, 206, 209, 211, 223, 225, 226, 227, 241
Creative Arc
    Life Arc, 66
Creative Capital, 128
Creative Consciousness, xv
    Conscious Creation, 42, 44
Creative Guidance System®, ii, xii, xvi, xviii, xxi, xxiii, xxvi, 201, 2, 17, 18, 20, 26, 28, 29, 31, 36, 38, 39, 44, 45, 46, 47, 49, 50, 52, 54, 56, 57, 59, 73, 74, 75, 76, 77, 78, 81, 83, 85, 91, 104, 107, 109, 111, 117, 119, 123, 124, 127, 131, 138, 139, 144, 146, 148, 149, 150, 151, 157, 162, 163, 172, 173, 174, 175, 176, 181,

183, 186, 187, 189, 191, 192, 205, 210, 221, 225, 226, 237
Creative Process, xx, xxvi, 35, 102, 108, 118, 139, 170, 225, 226, 227, 232, 235
    Creative Process Manifesto, 240
    MetaProcess, xvii
Creative Spectrum, xiv, xxv, 49, 225
Creative Tension, 81, 138, 140, 144, 153, 164, 167, 191, 209, 225
Creativity, xv, xvi, xvii, xviii, xxii, xxv, xxix, xxx, 3, 11, 14, 19, 20, 23, 48, 49, 63, 67, 69, 70, 72, 73, 74, 76, 80, 86, 89, 100, 103, 105, 109, 110, 119, 120, 122, 125, 126, 127, 130, 131, 146, 147, 155, 156, 162, 169, 170, 171, 173, 175, 181, 182, 183, 186, 189, 191, 192, 207, 210, 211, 224, 227, 231, 239
    Creative Thinking, 63, 64, 65, 68, 69, 77, 88, 95, 138, 139, 146, 150, 152, 155, 156, 162, 166, 170, 182, 193
    Definitions, xiii, 18, 65, 68, 102, 156, 198, 207
Creator, ii, xxvii, xxviii, xxix, xxx, xxxi, 201, 34, 47, 195, 208, 211, 212, 221
Creator's Guide, ii, xxii, xxv, xxix, xxx, 201, 5, 8, 29, 39, 42, 45, 50, 64, 69, 90, 121, 140, 149, 161, 170, 191, 192, 194, 206, 210, 212, 221, 222, 224
CreatorsGuide.com, ii, 201, 221
Crew, 75, 120, 121, 129
    NASA, 120, 121, 232
Csikszentmihalyi, Mihaly, 107
Culture, 2, 80, 102, 105, 126, 127, 128, 152, 156, 207, 229, 233, 236
Culture of Innovation, 128, 152, 233

D

Desire, xiii, xvii, xx, xxii, xxiii, xxxi, 18, 29, 31, 35, 44, 48, 68, 82, 87, 91, 99, 102, 103, 104, 105, 109, 110, 117, 140, 144, 161, 167, 173, 188, 205, 225
Destiny, 38, 76, 79, 176, 196, 198, 202, 204
Dialogue, 126, 129, 156, 212
Digital, 147, 206
Dimensions, xvi, xxv, 20, 57, 77, 80, 81, 89, 110, 117, 225, 226
Discovery, viii, xiv, xxv, 6, 11, 14, 34, 39, 49, 111, 121, 138, 142, 145, 149, 167, 207, 209, 211, 226, 227
    Rediscovery, xxx, 49, 100
Disruptive Technology, 150, 151
    Innovations, 206
Diversity, xxv, 23, 117, 124, 125, 128, 129, 155
Divine, xxvii, xxviii, xxix, xxx, 38, 100, 108, 110, 211
DNA, 206, 230
Dot.com, 128
Dream, viii, xvi, xviii, xx, xxiii, 3, 23, 28, 35, 39, 44, 45, 47, 50, 54, 56, 85, 86, 87, 88, 89, 91, 95, 103, 113, 128, 129, 138, 140, 161, 163, 164, 167, 170, 172, 173, 175, 181, 188, 190, 191, 192, 194, 196, 205, 206, 209, 221, 226, 227, 230

E

Economy, 11, 80, 155, 170, 186, 233, 237
Ecosystem, 143

Education, 90, 106, 142, 170, 189, 197, 200, 205
    Schools, 63, 90, 106, 170, 189, 200, 228
    Testing, xxvi, 48, 106, 128, 155, 203, 204
Education Sphere, 90, 106, 142, 170, 189, 197, 200, 205
Einstein, Albert, xxiv, xxx, 11, 14, 20, 26, 76, 103, 124, 168, 170, 192, 206, 209, 221, 224, 240
Energy, xiii, xvii, xx, xxvii, xxviii, xxix, xxxi, 2, 18, 22, 23, 35, 57, 65, 68, 69, 72, 74, 76, 77, 81, 83, 89, 95, 99, 101, 103, 104, 105, 107, 109, 110, 113, 119, 120, 123, 124, 129, 130, 131, 140, 150, 153, 155, 162, 168, 173, 175, 181, 183, 208, 209, 225, 227, 240
Environmental Sphere, 117, 197, 198
Erin Brockovich, 90, 111, 202, 203, 204, 212, 227, 231, 243
Evolution, 2, 206
Expression, ii, xv, xxii, xxix, 201, 48, 99, 102, 105, 107, 108, 110, 127, 221

F

Facebook, 154
Fear, xiii, 18, 65, 69, 77, 88, 100, 108, 111, 141, 145, 164, 190, 206
Field of Creation, 14, 38, 78, 89, 95, 124, 130, 140, 153, 173, 205, 227, 229
    Creative Field, 14, 29, 89, 144, 149, 153, 167, 173, 186, 225
Florida, Richard, 128, 212, 229
Force, xii, xvi, xxvii, 2, 20, 23, 49, 77, 81, 86, 88, 89, 95, 110, 111, 118, 120, 121, 124, 126, 127, 129, 130, 140, 147, 156, 188, 189, 192, 206, 207, 222, 225, 237
Form, xii, xviii, xxv, xxvii, xxix, 14, 17, 21, 23, 28, 31, 34, 36, 39, 43, 47, 48, 49, 50, 56, 69, 74, 80, 83, 85, 104, 105, 106, 107, 118, 121, 127, 128, 129, 132, 145, 154, 156, 163, 165, 175, 181, 182, 200, 206, 221, 223, 224, 237
Fractal, 21, 28, 57, 151, 165
Friedman, Thomas, 10, 11, 14, 212
Future, viii, xii, xv, xvii, xviii, xx, 6, 9, 12, 14, 25, 26, 28, 29, 31, 35, 39, 52, 56, 64, 67, 80, 81, 86, 89, 90, 107, 113, 116, 120, 125, 126, 127, 129, 140, 144, 146, 147, 152, 167, 173, 175, 181, 194, 197, 198, 223, 230, 238

G

Galileo, xxiv, 5, 6
Gandhi, Mahatma, xxiii, 64, 90
Genesis, xxi
Gifted and Talented, 195
Gladwell, Malcolm, 15, 212
Global Brain, 157
Globalization, 127
Google, 146, 147, 156, 198
Greatness, 17, 59, 64, 125, 128, 131, 138, 194, 235

H

Healthcare, 6, 193, 205, 236
Heraclitus, 212
Hero, xx, 22, 34, 35, 39, 44, 48, 66, 100, 103, 105, 222, 223, 235
Hill, Napoleon, 11, 188, 190, 241
Holographic, 100, 111, 117
Holy Grail, 228
Humor, 211

I

Identity, xxvii, 23, 57, 99, 102, 105, 107, 108, 109, 111, 117, 120, 121, 155, 199, 200, 227, 228, 229
Imagination, xiv, xv, xvii, 6, 9, 10, 12, 49, 50, 73, 74, 76, 89, 90, 95, 112, 118, 122, 123, 126, 127, 131, 154, 155, 162, 168, 181, 191, 200, 224, 241
Information, ii, xxi, 201, 12, 14, 20, 23, 26, 65, 67, 71, 72, 74, 76, 78, 80, 83, 89, 99, 104, 105, 109, 121, 127, 128, 131, 138, 139, 140, 141, 142, 143, 144, 145, 146, 147, 148, 149, 152, 153, 157, 163, 164, 165, 171, 173, 174, 175, 176, 181, 182, 190, 191, 208, 221, 224, 227, 233, 234, 237, 239
Innovate, xviii, xxi, 75, 127, 147, 155, 156, 163, 205, 239
Innovation, xxi, 2, 11, 12, 14, 73, 74, 75, 80, 127, 128, 129, 131, 146, 147, 152, 154, 155, 156, 162, 163, 169, 170, 189, 191, 207, 210, 233, 239, 240
Intelligence, 11, 67, 74, 81, 99, 105, 121, 128, 188, 195
    Intelligentia, 81
    Multiple Intelligences, 234
Internet, 14, 95, 121, 143, 147, 154, 157, 167, 169, 186, 198, 206, 229, 238, 244
Intuition, 238

J

Journey, xiv, xxi, xxiii, xxiv, xxvii, 17, 23, 36, 49, 56, 108, 138, 139, 163
Jung, Carl, xxviii, 102, 108, 221

K

Keller, Helen, 36, 90, 97, 223
Kelly, Kevin, 121, 155, 212, 232, 238
King Jr., Martin Luther, 64, 86, 90, 100, 103, 188, 209, 212, 228
Knowledge vs. Imagination, xviii, 9, 11, 12, 14, 20, 26, 48, 49, 67, 73, 74, 80, 112, 123, 126, 142, 146, 154, 168, 169, 170, 173, 175, 188, 204, 236, 237
Koestler, Arthur, 226
Kuhn, Thomas, 14

L

Lao Tzu, 212
Leaders, xxv, 14, 64, 90, 100, 102, 103, 116, 118, 119, 121, 122, 128, 131, 152, 170, 188, 191, 200, 201, 205, 206, 209, 210, 238
Leadership, xviii, xxv, 2, 36, 38, 76, 90, 102, 103, 116, 120, 121, 122, 125, 128, 129, 143, 152, 200, 201, 205, 210, 227, 236
Legacy, 110
Lens, xvi, 5, 6, 14, 26, 36, 66, 67, 70, 71, 101, 123, 129, 141, 153, 173, 189, 190
Leonardo da Vinci, 191, 212, 241
Light, ii, xxii, xxvii, 20, 23, 26, 65, 76, 77, 80, 99, 100, 101, 107, 111, 112, 117, 138, 146, 154, 162, 175, 188, 189, 190, 195, 211, 226
Logic, 26, 31, 69, 125
    Linear Thinking, 26, 31, 69, 95, 153
Loop or Leap, 193

M

Mahony, William, 212
Malthus, Thomas, 9
Marketspace, 75, 131
Maslow, Abraham, 108, 137, 144, 157, 235, 236, 237, 239
Mental Model, xiv
Meta- (, xvii, 2, 17, 19, 23, 29, 48, 155, 207
Metacosm, xvii
Microsoft, 118, 147, 183, 223, 239
Mind, xiv, 49
Mindset, xvii, xxix, 22, 77, 126, 127, 128, 131, 156, 168, 172, 188, 204, 207
Mindshift, xvi
Mirror, xxii, xxx, 29, 105, 147
Mission, xv, 108, 113, 117, 120, 125, 231, 232
Monitor, 141, 153
Moore, Thomas, 102, 103, 107, 108, 212, 228, 230, 231
Music, 103, 105, 129, 206, 228, 229
MySpace, 105, 229

N

Navigation, xvii, xviii, xxi, xxvi, 6, 26, 29, 38, 46, 47, 52, 56, 69, 75, 78, 80, 88, 107, 112, 121, 123, 124, 126, 129, 138, 142, 146, 147, 149, 153, 154, 155, 161, 167, 168, 171, 173, 174, 175, 183, 186, 187, 191, 194, 197, 202, 204, 205, 209
Navigational Planning, 74, 152, 163
    Strategic Planning, 67
    Strategic Planning, 132
    Strategic Planning, 230
    Strategic Planning, 232
    Strategic Planning, 236
Networked World, 12, 105, 117, 142, 155, 167, 186, 229, 235
New Science, 80
Now, ii, xviii, 201, 28, 43, 45, 48, 49, 54, 56, 57, 64, 67, 71, 72, 80, 81, 83, 85, 88, 89, 131, 132, 138, 139, 140, 142, 143, 144, 145, 146, 148, 151, 153, 157, 161, 162, 163, 164, 165, 168, 169, 171, 172, 173, 174, 175, 183, 186, 189, 191, 201, 207, 221, 229, 233, 234, 237, 238, 242

O

Oprah Winfrey, 194, 195, 196, 212, 242
Orbits of Influence, ii, 201, 212, 221
Order, xiii, xxx, 18, 21, 23, 26, 28, 38, 45, 73, 87, 88, 118, 120, 126, 127, 129, 138, 155, 156, 162, 166, 170, 172, 176, 181, 187, 189, 190, 194, 211, 212, 230, 234, 237

P

Paradigm, 20, 36
Paradox, xxix, 85, 99, 112, 121, 191, 201, 227
Participation, xvii, xxvii, xxviii, 11, 14, 23, 75, 80, 105, 120, 157, 163, 211, 225, 229
Passion, xiii, xxii, 18, 77, 89, 103, 105, 106, 107, 113, 145, 164, 173, 187, 188, 206, 223, 230
Peer Production, 80, 147
Perception, xviii
Peters, Tom, 11, 112, 131, 152, 186, 191, 207, 212, 224, 229, 236, 237, 238, 239, 241, 244
Physics, xxviii, 103, 222, 225, 226, 235
    Physicist, xxiv, xxx, 11, 76, 124, 126, 192, 234
    Quantum, 20, 36, 89, 222, 225, 226
Pink, Daniel, 15, 212
Planes of Thought, xxviii, 124, 126, 129, 151, 175, 181, 182, 206
Plato, xxviii, 103, 192, 212, 221
Possibility, xiii, xiv, xvii, xxviii, 5, 6, 8, 9, 18, 19, 20, 23, 28, 29, 36, 38, 42, 46, 49, 68, 71, 73, 76, 80, 81, 85, 88, 89, 90, 107, 121, 129, 131, 139, 142, 144, 155, 157, 161, 162, 164, 166, 167, 168, 173, 175, 183, 186, 187, 188, 189, 190, 191, 196, 205, 206, 207, 211, 226
Potential
    Potentia, 108, 235
Potential-Driven, 76, 77, 146, 166, 183, 188, 193
Power, ii, viii, xii, xiv, xv, xvi, xvii, xviii, xx, xxi, xxii, xxiii, xxiv, xxvi, xxvii, xxviii, xxix, xxx, xxxi, 2, 3, 8, 9, 11, 12, 16, 17, 22, 23, 26, 28, 29, 31, 34, 35, 36, 38, 39, 44, 47, 48, 49, 50, 56, 57, 64, 65, 67, 68, 74, 77, 78, 80, 81, 83, 86, 87, 88, 89, 90, 95, 99, 100, 102, 103, 104, 105, 106, 107, 108, 110, 121, 123, 124, 126, 127, 129, 130, 131, 141, 144, 145, 146, 148, 151, 153, 154, 157, 162, 163, 165, 166, 167, 168, 173, 174, 175, 176, 181, 183, 188, 189, 190, 194, 196, 201, 202, 203, 206, 207, 209, 212, 221, 222, 225, 230, 244
    Authentic Power, 77
Power of Choice, xvi, xxviii, 3, 77, 154
Power of Us, 148
Principle, xxvi, 38, 196, 210, 225
Problem, xxi, 63, 64, 65, 66, 67, 68, 69, 70, 71, 72, 74, 75, 76, 77, 78, 81, 86, 88, 122, 124, 129, 130, 131, 139, 141, 142, 146, 147, 150, 153, 162, 165, 166, 170, 172, 176, 182, 183, 190, 192, 193, 204, 206, 208, 209, 224, 238
Problem-Centric, 65, 68, 70, 71, 74, 76, 77, 183
Problem-Solving, 63, 64, 65, 68, 70, 71, 146, 166, 172, 182
Progress

The Idea of Progress, xxxi, 64, 85, 128, 150, 151, 153, 163, 166, 191
psychological, xv, xxv, 168, 234, 240
Psychology, xxviii, 239
Purpose, ii, xiv, xx, xxii, xxiii, xxx, xxxi, 17, 28, 29, 31, 35, 49, 50, 56, 57, 65, 69, 101, 103, 107, 109, 111, 113, 117, 124, 125, 128, 130, 131, 132, 142, 163, 168, 174, 194, 196, 211, 228, 234
    Calling, xxxi, 108, 112, 156, 191, 202
Pythagoras, 212

Q

Questions, xx, xxi, xxvii, xxviii, 35, 39, 42, 43, 54, 76, 78, 83, 87, 88, 91, 106, 107, 119, 124, 143, 148, 149, 151, 157, 162, 182, 200, 201, 208, 225, 241

R

Revolution, 4, 11, 167, 197, 206
Rilke, Rainer Maria, xxvii
Rise of the Creative Class, 229, 241
Rome, 206

S

Scan, 150
Schneider, Michael, 212
Scope, xv, xvi, xxi, 3, 68, 71, 74, 85, 89, 131, 139, 148, 156, 207
Self-Organization, 69, 117, 120, 121, 127, 128, 145, 153, 154, 224
Senge, Peter, 71, 81, 102, 105, 116, 120, 125, 145, 191, 212, 225, 229, 231, 232, 233, 237
Senses, 6, 91, 95, 168, 182
Shakespeare, William, 67, 100
Shaw, George Bernard, 7, 8, 64, 67, 82, 88, 103, 168, 173, 221
Speed, xvi, xxi, 3, 11, 12, 14, 20, 26, 29, 38, 54, 71, 76, 80, 121, 127, 154, 162, 175, 176, 183, 186, 190
Spheres of Influence, 123
Spiral, xviii, xxv, 2, 28, 29, 42, 44, 48, 144, 157, 203, 235
Spiritual, xiii, xv, xvi, xxiii, xxv, xxvii, xxviii, xxix, xxxi, 2, 18, 36, 80, 102, 108, 109, 118, 131, 168, 197, 202, 204, 211, 225, 226, 234, 235, 238, 239
St. Philip's School, 106, 230
Stakeholders, 143, 149, 157
Star Trek, xiii, 18
Star Wars
    The Force, xxvii, 81, 99, 145, 198, 222
StarPilot, xiii, 33, 34
Stock Market, 208
Story, xxiii, 2, 34, 39, 42, 43, 44, 47, 48, 54, 59, 90, 100, 105, 106, 117, 125, 197, 199, 201, 202, 204, 230, 232, 243
    Myth, 2, 23, 26, 34, 48, 199
    Story Arc, 42, 44
Strategic Goals (see also Mini-Vision), 164
Strategy, xxi, 2, 145, 155, 163, 166, 207, 210, 236

Subconscious or Unconscious, 36, 50, 170, 181, 190, 222, 234, 235
Success Factors (see also Strategic Goals), 143, 145, 157, 165, 176
Surowiecki, James, 15, 155
Survey, xvi, 70, 157, 236
SWOT, 131, 142, 143, 145, 146, 149, 151, 157, 158, 159, 164, 165, 176, 236
Systems Theory, 12, 20, 25, 26, 29, 67, 69, 77, 80, 107, 119, 120, 121, 128, 140, 153, 155, 163, 182, 186, 189, 191, 206, 210, 222, 223, 229, 232, 235, 239, 240

T

T.S. Eliot, 85, 98, 107, 221, 226
Technology, 5, 11, 14, 20, 26, 38, 75, 80, 88, 121, 147, 149, 152, 154, 163, 169, 171, 237
Terrorism, 208
The Dark Side, 50, 202
The Way, xiii, xv, xxiii, 18, 22, 29, 36, 39, 41, 42, 44, 46, 47, 48, 50, 56, 67, 72, 83, 89, 90, 100, 105, 122, 125, 126, 127, 140, 146, 152, 170, 172, 173, 188, 190, 202, 204, 206, 211, 222, 242
    Dao or Tao, 22, 222
Thinking Technology, 26, 28, 56, 83, 139, 162, 163, 175, 176
Thoreau, Henry David, 8, 103, 110, 140
Thought Leaders, xix, xxv, 155
    Global Thought Leaders, 126
Thuan, Trinh Xuan, 212
Tipping Point, 154, 206
Toffler, Alvin, 11, 140, 212
Tolerance for Ambiguity, 191
Training, 69, 90, 120, 204, 210, 232, 236
Trajectory, 46, 47, 50, 72, 73, 78, 80, 89, 103, 141, 142, 144, 163, 167, 183, 205, 237
Trust, 127, 129, 188, 192, 235
Truth, viii, xxvi, xxvii, xxix, xxxi, 6, 8, 17, 18, 31, 36, 38, 39, 46, 50, 65, 80, 81, 85, 88, 111, 112, 113, 127, 128, 129, 146, 152, 167, 190, 192, 199, 203, 204, 211, 225, 229, 237

U

Universe, ii, xxviii, 23, 68, 81, 88, 89, 107, 110, 221, 222, 226

V

Values, ii, xxvi, 201, 11, 38, 72, 74, 80, 108, 109, 112, 113, 117, 120, 123, 124, 125, 127, 128, 140, 145, 161, 168, 172, 182, 197, 199, 201, 202, 207, 208, 221, 226, 229, 235, 238

Vision, xiii, xiv, xvi, xxii, xxiv, xxx, 14, 18, 43, 49, 53, 81, 86, 104, 106, 108, 109, 116, 117, 120, 122, 124, 125, 140, 174, 185, 186, 198, 206, 212, 225, 235
VisionSPARC, ii, xviii, 201, 29, 49, 142, 161, 166, 171, 175, 221
VisionSPIRAL, ii, xviii, 201, 29, 49, 221
Visual Thinking Technology, 148, 151
Volk, Tyler, 212, 244

W

Washington, Denzel, 106
We are All Creators, ii, xxx, 201, 221
What Can Be, xvii, xxix, 2, 3, 9, 38, 46, 59, 63, 64, 66, 68, 71, 77, 78, 80, 81, 85, 89, 91, 120, 121, 126, 138, 139, 140, 142, 146, 157, 162, 183, 206, 207, 208, 209
What Is, xvii, xxix, 2, 3, 9, 46, 59, 63, 64, 66, 68, 71, 74, 77, 78, 80, 81, 85, 88, 91, 111, 120, 126, 138, 139, 140, 142, 146, 182, 183, 193, 206, 207, 209, 234
Wheatley, Margaret, 69, 99, 107, 109, 117, 119, 212, 224, 227, 230, 231, 232, 233, 234, 238
Where, ii, xviii, xx, 201, 6, 28, 34, 35, 45, 47, 49, 54, 56, 57, 64, 68, 70, 71, 72, 73, 74, 76, 77, 81, 83, 84, 85, 86, 87, 88, 91, 106, 112, 123, 124, 129, 138, 139, 140, 144, 145, 149, 150, 151, 153, 157, 161, 162, 163, 164, 169, 171, 174, 175, 183, 188, 190, 191, 207, 208, 221, 223, 239
Whitehead, Alfred North, 212
Wholeness, xv, xxvii, 100, 109, 140, 206, 234
Whyte, David, 36, 212
Williamson, Marianne, 100, 103, 110, 212, 228
Work or Work(s), xii, xvii, xviii, xxi, xxiv, xxv, xxix, xxxi, 14, 17, 21, 28, 29, 31, 38, 39, 48, 49, 52, 56, 57, 59, 69, 70, 75, 78, 83, 87, 88, 90, 91, 95, 99, 102, 103, 104, 105, 107, 108, 109, 110, 111, 113, 117, 118, 121, 122, 125, 126, 127, 129, 130, 138, 140, 142, 143, 151, 152, 156, 161, 162, 163, 165, 166, 168, 169, 170, 171, 173, 174, 175, 176, 181, 182, 183, 188, 189, 190, 192, 196, 197, 200, 204, 206, 209, 211, 212, 224, 225, 226, 228, 229, 230, 232, 233, 234, 238, 239, 240, 242
    Opus, 102, 228
World in Process, 138, 155, 173, 225
Worldscape, 14
WorldView, xv, 5, 6, 8, 12, 14, 15, 20, 26, 36, 38, 42, 46, 47, 74, 80, 206

Y

YouTube, 154

Z

Zola, Emile, xx

GENESIS of GENIUS

NOTES & REFERENCES

Photo Credits:

Cover Art/Design: Julie Ann Turner
Guideman Art/Design: Julie Ann Turner, Greg Colunga/New Media Gateway
Inside Cover/Design: Julie Ann Turner

Cover photos by permission of photographer Laurent Laveder - www.pixheaven.net - from his MoonGames series.

Certain images and/or photos on this page are the copyrighted property
of HemeraTechnologies Inc./BizArt: 17 (fractal), 18, 44

Certain images and/or photos on this page are the copyrighted property of JupiterImages and are being used with permission under license. These images and/or photos may not be copied or downloaded without permission from JupiterImages"/Clipart.com: xxi, xxvi, xxvii, xxviii, xxiv, xxix, xxx, 17, 22 (Vitruvian Man), 24, 25, 33, 36, 37, 38, 55, 56, 57, 65, 66, 71, 74, 76, 79, 80, 81, 85, 87, 90, 92, 94, 97, 98, 99, 100, 102, 105, 106, 109, 113, 114, 116, 120, 121, 127, 134, 135, 139, 140, 142, 143, 144, 145, 148, 150, 151, 152, 153, 154, 155, 157, 158, 159, 161, 162, 163, 164, 165, 166, 167, 168, 169, 171, 172, 173, 174, 175, 177, 179, 180, 182, 185, 187, 188, 190, 193, 194, 195, 196, 197, 198, 199, 200, 201, 218, 232, 254, 267, 269, 273, 288, 210, 299, 300, 302, 302, 305, 343 (graphics), 345, 363

Certain images and/or photos on this page are the copyrighted property of Lee Collison/Graphic Artist and Julie Ann Turner & Company: xiii, xix, xxii, xxiii, xxv, 11, 12, 42, 70

Certain images and/or photos on this page are the copyrighted property of Microsoft Office Media Elements (under Microsoft license): xii, xiv, xv, xvi, xx, 5, 6, 8, 17, 22 (leaves), 28, 31, 32, 33, 35, 39, 41 (rose), 43, 45, 47, 48, 49, 53, 54, 60, 64, 69, 75, 77, 78, 93, 125 (telescope, earth), 128, 191, 237

Certain images and/or photos on this page are the copyrighted property of Julie Ann Turner & Company:
Cover art, inside cover art, back cover art, xvii, 1, 9, 10, 13, 14, 15, 21, 22 (Vitruvian Man/art), 23, 29, 34 (Chinese Character by commission), 41, 50, 54, 59, 60, 61, 62, 63, 68, 82, 84, 88, 89, 96, 101, 103, 104, 110, 111, 112, 115, 117, 118, 119, 125 (design), 126, 129, 130, 131, 132, 133, 137, 147, 156, 183, 184, 186, 202, 204, 206, 209, 210, 214, 220, 222, 223, 225, 228, 229, 231, 234, 235, 238, 239, 241, 243, 245, 246, 247, 248, 249, 251, 252, 255, 256, 257, 258, 260, 261, 263, 264, 265, 266, 268, 270, 271, 272, 274, 275, 276, 277, 281, 283, 285, 286, 287, 289, 292, 293, 294, 295, 304, 310, 314, 315, 319, 323, 324, 326, 334, 335, 336, 338, 339, 340, 343, 344, 348, 349, 350, 358, 359, 361, 364, 365, 367, 369, 374, 375, 377, 378, 379, 380, 384, 387, 393, 394, 395, 397, 398, 400, 402, 403, 405, 408

Nautilus Photo by R.E. Young, Univ. of Hawaii, Tree of Life Project. Used by Permission.: 20

Golden Spiral created with MathCad Software, Mathsoft Engineering and Education, Inc., Mathcad. Used by Permission: 20

Gogh, Vincent Van (1893-1890). The Starry Night. 1889. Oil on Canvas, 29 x 36 ¼.
Acquired through the Lille P. Bliss Bequest. The Museum of Modern Art, New York, NY, U.S.A. Digital Image © The Museum of Modern Art/Licences by SCALA/Art Resource, NY: 27.

Daisy Photo © Scott Hotton, Smith College. Used by Permission.: 28

Trademarks:

The following are trademarks of their respective companies: Amazon.com, Blogger, Chili's Bar & Grill, Crayon, Digg, eBay, Google, Facebook, Flickr, Inspiration, Kickstarter, Lego, LinkedIn, Mathcad, Mathsoft, Microsoft, Mindjet, Mindmanager, MoveOn.org, Play-doh, Posterous, Post-it Notes, Second Life, StumbleUpon, TagWorld, Technorati, Toobers & Zots, trendwatching.com, Twitter, Volkswagen, Wikipedia, YouTube, Zolo, Zoob.

GENESIS OF GENIUS™, POWER ARC™, CREATIVE GUIDANCE SYSTEM™, CONSCIOUSSHIFT™, WHERE, NOW, HOW™, VISIONSPARC™, VISIONSPIRAL™, CREATOR'S GUIDE®, CREATORSGUIDE.COM™, CREATIVE ARC™, CREATE YOUR LIFE, WORK & WORLD®, CREATIVE RENAISSANCE™, ORBITS OF INFLUENCE®, WHERE GLOBAL THOUGHT LEADERS GATHER® are trademarks of JULIE ANN TURNER & COMPANY/CREATORSGUIDE.COM, as indicated throughout the GUIDE by SMALL CAPS. All Rights Reserved.

Extensive efforts have been made to ensure the information in this book series and course is accurate , and extensive research has been conducted to ensure information and quotes are attributed to their original authors and sources as much as is possible and to the extent source information was available and accessible, as we highly respect the creative expressions and contributions of creators around the world. In addition, multiple editors have made every effort to ensure the book series is error-free. However, though we are all creators, and capable of magnificent contributions - we are also human. So, if you find a typographical or grammatical error, or find anything in this publication which you believe may be in error, please let us know at constructivecomments@creatorsguide.com. Perhaps your creative gift or contribution, in part, is helping find such errors, and we value and appreciate your help, as we endeavor to make GENESIS OF GENIUS an ever-improving, ever-expanding resource for creators worldwide.

---

[1] T.S. Eliot, "Little Gidding" from *Four Quartets* (1942,1943 by T.S. Eliot; renewed 1971 by Esme Valerie Eliot) in *The Norton Anthology of English Literature*, Vol. 2, 4th Edition ed. M.H. Abrams et al. (New York: W.W. Norton & Company, Inc., 1979). 2292.

[2] Shunryu Suzuki, *Zen Mind, Beginner's Mind* (New York: Weatherhill, Inc., 1973), 21.

[3] Ibid, 14.

[4] Business Consultant Fritz Dressler quoted by Thomas Petzinger, Jr. in "The Resurgence of the Small and Other Trends to Watch," *The Wall Street Journal* (New York: Dow Jones & Co., Inc., January 9, 1998).

[5] Albert Einstein, *The Quotable Einstein*, ed. Alice Calaprice (Princeton, N.J: Princeton University Press, 1996), 199.

[6] Rainer Marie Rilke, *Letters to a Young Poet*, trans. M.D. Herter Norton (New York: Norton, 1993), 35.

[7] Plato, *Timaeus*, trans. Benjamin Jowett (Upper Saddle River, Prentice Hall, 1997).

[8] "Vocatus atque non vocatus deus aderit," inscribed over the door of psychologist Carl Jung's Zurich home, cited in *Synchronicity: The Inner Path of Leadership*, Joseph Jaworski (San Francisco: Berrett-Koehler Publishers, Inc., 1998), 191.

[9] Albert Einstein, "My Credo," in *Living Philosophies: A series of Intimate Credos*, ed. Henry G. Leach (New York: Simon and Schuster, 1931), 3.

[10] Aburdene, *Megatrends 2010*, xv-xvi.

[11] Peter H. Thomas, *LifeManual: A Proven Formula to Create the Life You Desire* (Victoria, BC: LifePilot, 2005), 116.

[12] Henry P. Stapp, *Mind, Matter and Quantum Mechanics* (Germany: Springer-Verlag, 1993), 195, In a monumentous statement on the power of our choices, Stapp summarizes: "…even though these choices are not fixed by the quantum laws, nonetheless, each such choice is *intrinsically meaningful*: each quantum choice injects meaning, in the form of enduring structure, into the physical universe."

[13] Of course, these parallel models by necessity simplify the theories and principles of each of these great thinkers' views (which we already have described in more detail) – however, the essential point here is the similarity in areas or levels of *focus* , which in turn have affected, and continue to affect, our world views. As Zukav notes, although Aristotle and Newton differed on their views, their focus was still on the material, physical world.

[14] Zukav, *The Dancing Wu Li Masters*, 21-22. As Zukav notes, although Aristotle and Newton differed on their views, their focus was still on the physical world.

[15] According to researchers at the John F. Kennedy Library and Museum, the quotation "Some men see things as they are and say, 'Why'? I dream of things that never were and say, 'Why not'?" was made famous by Robert Kennedy during his 1968 Presidential campaign, where he often used it as a kind of slogan (although the researchers noted they had not identified the phrase specifically in a written text). As they note, the quotation originated from words spoken by the serpent in George Bernard Shaw's play Back to Methuselah, and was used by President John F. Kennedy in his speech to the Irish Parliament on June 28, 1963: "Speaking as an Irishman

[Shaw] summed up an approach to life: 'Other people,' he said, 'see things and say: why - but I dream things that never were and say: why not.'"
http://www.jfklibrary.org/Historical+Resources/Archives/Reference+Desk/Quotations+of+Robert+F.+Kennedy.htm

[16] Thomas Malthus, An Essay on the Principle of Population, 6th edition, 1826 (http://www.econlib.org/library/Malthus/malPlong.html). Library of Economics and Liberty.

[17] Karl E. Case and Ray C. Fair, Principles of Economics (New York: Prentice-Hall, 2003).

[18] Agricultural Revolution. (2007). In Britannica Concise Encyclopedia. Retrieved March 29, 2007, from Encyclopædia Britannica Online: http://www.britannica.com/ebc/article-9354753
"The Agricultural Revolution: Gradual transformation of the traditional agricultural system that began in Britain in the 18th century. Aspects of this complex transformation, which was not completed until the 19th century, included the reallocation of land ownership to make farms more compact and an increased investment in technical improvements, such as new machinery, better drainage, scientific methods of breeding, and experimentation with new crops and systems of crop rotation. The agricultural revolution was an essential prelude to the Industrial Revolution."

[19] Malthus, Thomas Robert. (2007). In Encyclopædia Britannica. Retrieved March 27, 2007, from Encyclopædia Britannica Online: http://www.britannica.com/eb/article-222944.

[20] Friedman, *The World is Flat*, 443.

[21] Aburdene, *Megatrends 2010*, xv-xvi.

[23] Friedman, *The World is Flat*, 197.

[24] Friedman, *The World is Flat*, 176.

[25] Ibid.

[26] Friedman, *The World is Flat*, 181.

[27] Ibid.

[28] 1998 Timberland print advertisement.

[29] Chang, "The Tao of Star Wars," The Exploration Network (http://www.exn.ca/starwars/taoism.cfm), from interview/article by Gloria Chang, 'The Tao is kind of, well, a force that pervades the universe," says Anne Collins Smith, a philosophy and classical studies professor at Susquehanna University in Selinsgrove, Pennsylvania. "It is the source of the universe, but it also IS the universe.' ... "Tao, often translated as the way or the path, is the ineffable, eternal, creative reality that is the source and end of all things. Te refers to the manifestation of Tao within all things. Thus, to fully possess Te, one must be in perfect harmony with one's original nature. Sound familiar? 'Be one with the force, Luke," advises his teacher Obi-wan Kenobi, as our hero learns the 'ways of the Force.' "

[30] George Lucas, *Star Wars: Episode IV - A New Hope*, 1977.

[31] Lynne McTaggert, *The Field: The Quest for the Secret Power of the Universe*, xiii-xiv, 331. "Human beings and all living things are a coalescence of energy in a field of energy connected to every other thing in the world. This pulsating energy field is the central engine of our being and our consciousness, the alpha and the omega of our existence. There is no 'm'" and 'not-me' duality to our bodies in relation to the universe, but one underlying energy field. This field is responsible for our mind's highest functions, the information source guiding the growth of our bodies. It is our brain, our heart, our memory – indeed, a blueprint of the world for all time. The field is the force, rather than germs or genes, that finally determines whether we are healthy or ill, the force which must be tapped in order to heal. We are attached and engaged, indivisible from our world, and our only fundamental truth is our relationship with it. 'The field,' as Einstein once succinctly put it, 'is the only reality.'"

[32] George Lucas, *Star Wars: Episode IV - A New Hope*, 1977.

[33] The only difference between energy and matter is the configuration of information – whether vibration, wavelength, pattern, sound, sight, gas, chemicals, molecules, and so on.

[34] Quantum physics tells us that we can never really just observe – as part of the system, our actions, our thoughts, and even our observations themselves impact the system. In fact, quantum physics tells us that even the act of observing essentially constitutes a choice that affects the system as a whole. In a way, we are "accidental

creators," in that our choices, whether conscious or unconscious, have the power to" collapse the wave of quantum potential" into particle or material form.

[35] Wheatley, *Leadership and the New Science*, 20. "This world has also challenged our beliefs about objective measurement, for at the subatomic level the observer cannot observe anything without interfering or, more importantly, participating in its creation."

[36] Alan Kay, Apple Computer Fellow: "Don't worry about what anybody else is going to do... The best way to predict the future is to invent it. Really smart people with reasonable funding can do just about anything that doesn't violate too many of Newton's Laws!" — Alan Kay in 1971, inventor of Smalltalk which was the inspiration and technical basis for the MacIntosh and subsequent windowing based systems (NextStep, Microsoft Windows 3.1/95/98/NT, X-Windows, Motif, etc...). Alan Kay, in an email on Sept 17, 1998 to Peter W. Lount According to Alan Kay: "The origin of the quote came from an early meeting in 1971 of PARC, Palo Alto Research Center, folks and the Xerox planners. In a fit of passion I uttered the quote!"

[37] Campbell, *The Hero with a Thousand Faces*, 36, 39.

[38] Joseph Campbell, The Power of Myth with Bill Moyers (New York: Random House, 1991), 151. "Furthermore, we have not even to risk the adventure alone, for the heroes of all time have gone before us. The labyrinth is thoroughly known. We have only to follow the thread of the hero path, and where we had thought to find an abomination, we shall find a god. And where we had thought to slay another, we shall slay ourselves. Where we had thought to travel outward, we will come to the center of our own existence. And where we had thought to be alone, we will be with all the world."

[39] Daniel Boorstin, 1962.

[40] William Jennings Bryan 1860 - 1925.

[41] Zhuangzi, quoted in David L. Hall and Roger T. Ames *Thinking from the Han: Self, Truth, and Transcendence in Chinese and Western Culture* (New York: State University of New York Press, 1998), 181.

[42] Antonio Machado: "Travelers, there is no path. Paths are made by walking."

[43] *Quest: The Spiritual Path to Success*, Vol. 2 (New York: Simon & Schuster Audio, 1996).

[44] Eamonn Kelly, *Powerful Times: Rising to the Challenge of Our Uncertain World* (Upper Saddle River, NJ: Wharton School Publishing, 2006). In his book *Powerful Times: Rising to the Challenge of Our Uncertain World*, author Eamonn Kelly, the CEO and president of Global Business Network, says: "We're not just living through an age of change: we're living through a 'change of age': the most profound inflection point in human history since the Enlightenment."

[45] Helen Keller - "Life is either a daring adventure or nothing. To keep our faces toward change and behave like free spirits in the presence of fate is strength undefeatable."

[46] *Quest: The Spiritual Path to Success*, Vol. 2 (New York: Simon & Schuster Audio, 1996).

[47] Recall that the root of the Greek word *archetypos* is *arche* or *archai* as in "origin" or "something from which the argument proceeds"),

[48] Campbell, *The Power of Myth*, 150.

[49] Steve Chandler, *100 Ways to Motivate Yourself*, (Franklin Lakes, N.J.: Career Press, Inc., 1996) 19-20.

[50] Ibid, 22.

[51] Arnold Schwarzenegger Life Timeline, http://www.schwarzenegger.com/en/life/hislife/timeline/timeline.html.

[52] *Dallas Morning News*, "Looking Presidential: Arnold Schwarzenegger," July 26, 1998; Arnold Talk *Magazine*, November 1999.

[53] Darren Aranofsky and Eric Watson, "Pi" Motion Picture (New York: Harvest Filmworks, July 10, 1998).

[54] Suzuki, *Zen Mind, Beginner's Mind*, 21.

[55] Ibid. p. 14.

[56] Richard Bach, *The Bridge Across Forever: A Lovestory* (New York: Dell Publishing, 1989), 124.

[57] Chandler, *100 Ways to Motivate Yourself*, 19-20.

[58] Lewis Carroll, *The Annotated Alice: The Definitive Edition - Alice's Adventures in Wonderland & Through the Looking-Glass by Lewis Carroll*; ed. Martin Gardner (New York: W.W. Norton & Company, 2000), 65.

[59] Excerpt from 1998 Timberland print advertisement.

[60] Quoted in Tony Robbins, *Awakening the Giant Within: How to Take Immediate Control of Your Mental,*

Emotional, Physical and Financial Destiny! (New York: The Free Press, 1992), 33.

[61] Steve Salerno, "Laughing All the Way," *Worth* Magazine, Sept. 1999.
"For almost 30 years, Southwest's Herb Kelleher has amused himself by revolutionizing air travel. It's no joke to his rivals," *Business 2.0*, Dec. 98.

[62] Alex F. Osborn, *Applied imagination: Principles and procedures of creative problem solving* (New York: Charles Scribner's Sons, 1963). The creativity technique known as "brainstorming" was initially popularized by advertising executive and BBDO co-founder Alex Faickney Osborn in the late 1930s, in his book "Applied Imagination." Osborn also founded the Creative Education Foundation (the "Centre for Applied Imagination") in 1954. Alex Osborn, along with Sidney Parnes, also developed the Osborn-Parnes Creative Problem Solving Process. See http://www.creativeeducationfoundation.org/
James M. Higgins, *101 Creative Problem-Solving Techniques: The Handbook of New Ideas for Business* (New Management Publishing Company, Inc., 1994), 18-19. As Higgins notes, the "Creative Problem-Solving Process (CPS) is comprised of eight basic (and generally sequential) steps: 1) Environmental Analysis, 2) Problem Recognition, 3) Problem Identification, 4) Making Assumptions, 5) Generating Alternatives, 6) Evaluation and Choice, 7) Implementation, and 8) Control. It is significant to note that the first of the four CPS "stages" is "Problem Identification" (followed by "Making Assumptions about the Future," "Generation of Alternatives," and "Choice of Alternatives."
Mark Joyner, *Simple-ology: The Simple Science of Getting What You Want* (New York: John Wiley & Sons, Inc. 2007), 173, 184. On steps to scientific method (Scientific Method – 1. State a problem/question), and Stanford University mathematician G. Polya's 4-Step Problem Solving Method 1. Understand the Problem. First. You have to understand the problem,.." from G. Polya, *How to Solve It* (Princeton University Press, 1957).

[63] Charles Handy, *The Age of Unreason* (Boston, MA: Harvard Business School Press, 1989), xi.

[64] Handy, *The Age of Unreason*, 4-5.

[65] William Shakespeare, *Julius Caesar* 1.2.139-40

[66] Walt Kelly, "We Have Met The Enemy And He Is Us" Pogo strip from Earth Day, 1971. 2005 OGPI (Okefenokee Glee and Perloo, Inc.).

[67] Fritz, *The Path of Least Resistance*, 11.
Tom Peters and other management experts encourage the same idea with the concept of looking for and rewarding "things gone right" (TGR), rather than looking for and punishing "things gone wrong" (TGW). See Peters, *Circle of Innovation*, 463.

[68] W. Edwards Deming spoke of the "85-15 Rule," regarding the relationship between individual performance and the system within which the individual works, and states that if something goes wrong, 85% of what's wrong lies in the system rather than with the individual or thing. See also http://www.deming.rog/deminghtml/wedi.html.

[69] Wheatley and Kellner-Rogers, *A Simpler Way*, 81. "A self-organizing system reveals itself as structure of relationships, patterns of behaviors, habits of belief, methods for accomplishing work. These patterns, structures, and methods are visible. We become entranced by their forms. … Beneath all structures and behaviors lies the real creator – dynamic processes. Processes are not changed by focusing on their effect. Structures and behaviors are artifacts. It does no good to rearrange them."

[70] "The Art of Smart," *Fast Company*, July/August 1999, 85. " … according to some sources, the world has generated more data in the past 30 years than it did in the preceding 5,000 years. . . So, in this Information Age, how do you keep up with all of that, well, information?"

[71] Joyner, *Simple-ology:*, 41, 150-151 on the Magic Number 7.
See also Dijksterhuis, "When to Sleep on It," on limit to conscious mental processing.

[72] Osborn, *Applied imagination*.

[73] De Bono, *Serious Creativity*, x-xi, 38-42.

[74] De Bono, *Serious Creativity*,11-12.

[75] Peters, *Re-Imagine*, 40.

[76] Stuart A. Capper, Peter M. Ginter, Linda E. Swayne, *Public Health Leadership and Management: Cases and Context* (Thousand Oaks, CA: Sage Publications, Inc., 2002), 6.

[77] Albert Einstein - "The mere formulation of a problem is far more essential than its solution, which may be merely a matter of mathematical or experimental skills."

[78] Viktor E. Frankl, *Man's Search for Meaning* (New York: Simon & Schuster, Inc., 1984), 86.

[79] Sandra Anne Taylor, *Quantum Success: The Astounding Science of Wealth and Happiness* (Hay House, Inc., 2006), 5.

[80] Joyner, *Simple-ology*, x,

[81] Danny Hillis, VP R&D, Walt Disney Co. quoted in Thomas Petzinger, Jr., "So long, supply and demand," *The Wall Street Journal*, Jan. 1 2001.

[82] Peter Senge, The Fifth Discipline, 151-154. "Leadership in a learning organization starts with the principle of creative tension. Creative tension comes from seeing clearly where we want to be, our 'vision,' and telling the truth about where we are, our 'current reality.' The gap between the two generates a natural tension."

[83] It seems appropriate, given the recent interest in books and videos focused on "*The Law of Attraction*," to mention that many of the core ideas presented in these materials are in alignment with principles of the Creative Process, and thus, with the CREATIVE GUIDANCE SYSTEM.

This is, of course, as it should be, since, the Creative Process operates through universal principles, including what many call the "Law of Attraction, a concept which may be traced through sacred writings, philosophical themes, and scientific study throughout human history. For example, as Esther Hicks and Jerry Hick, authors of The Law of Attraction (one of the many books with this title or covering this topic), note that these themes can be traced to the "teachings of Abraham," who is considered the father of Judaism, Christianity and Islam. Similarly, the Law of Reciprocity (also called the Golden Rule) – closely related to the Law of Attraction – has deep roots across many religions as well: "Do unto others as you would have them do unto you,' "You reap what you sow," "As a man thinketh, so shall he be," and "It is done unto you as you believe."

As we've noted from the outset, the Creative Process operates through universal principles, which we may use either consciously or unconsciously. We've also established that Creative Process and the CREATIVE GUIDANCE SYSTEM operate at all levels and dimensions of the creative spectrum – from physical to mental to spiritual; the same master Creative Process spans all levels and dimensions.

Also, we've established that we are all already participants in the Creative Field – we can't "not participate" – but we can learn to use the creative process more intentionally, to create the life, work and world we desire.

Many of the concepts that are presented as elements or aspects of "The Law of Attraction" - which is a universal creative principle, closely akin to "creative tension" (in fact, the Law of Attraction may in many cases be another name for the same attraction force, or describe certain aspects of creative tension) - align with creative principles presented here as part of the Creative Process, for example: the concept that we are creating our own lives, that we always have choice in where to focus our thoughts and energy, that what we focus our attention on increases, that our thoughts and feelings may control the flow of energy in our lives, that there is great power in focusing on what we want rather than what we do not want, that there are many dimensions to self – we are physical, mental and spiritual beings.

In many cases, materials on "The Law of Attraction" seem to focus on the mental or spiritual – and we might also say, quantum – aspects or dimensions of creation. To be clear, what we share here is the full Creative Process and its underlying principles (including creative tension and "attraction" forces) and stages, which operate across all dimensions of creation, from spiritual and mental to physical (and thus touch on the role mental and physical action play in creating the results we desire).

The main question may be: Can we achieve what we desire solely with power of mind? As we've noted, principles of quantum physics reveal that we are indeed active participants in a world in process. We're already in the Creative Field. in fact, we can't not be involved. Our thoughts and actions shape reality on all levels. We may either use this creative process consciously, or unconsciously, but we are already, and always, participating. Can this process manifest change on a physical level purely through mental and/or spiritual focus? Quantum physics and growing research (such as Rupert Sheldrake's work in the area of morphic or morphogenic fields) indicate they can. There is certainly an abundance of spiritual, scriptural writings – about miracles occurring in the physical world that were manifested through prayer or mental or spiritual efforts, as well.

For some, these new areas of scientific exploration may provide a challenge in understanding or acceptance. However, because the Creative Process and principles presented here are consistent across all levels of creation, a person may choose to apply these principles at whatever level they wish and feel comfortable accepting.

For example, while some may accept that the Law of Attraction works across "unseen" mental and spiritual levels, it is possible , and totally in alignment with the system presented here, to consider that these principles work powerfully and perfectly well at the physical, tangible level, as well. For example, when an organization co-creates and communicates a clear, higher Vision, it becomes tangible to everyone involved in its creation. The Vision is compelling and holds value – and it attracts the people for whom it holds meaning. Goals and actions organized around this shared Vision may align and guide physical activities to create tangible change or produce physical products, and this process of creation may be propelled by the common mental focus and commitment of the organization. Because the Vision is "visible" and is communicated broadly, new people may be attracted to the effort, and new possibilities and resources may come to light, that previously might not have been discovered or made available. All this creation could be generated, using the same principles of Vision, focus, and so on - without any reference to these principles operating on a purely mental or spiritual level.

Again, the master Creative Process we share here in the GUIDE is based on universal, timeless principles – including, but not limited to, the Law of Attraction - that can be traced throughout history (revealed by science, philosophy and spiritual texts) and operates at all levels and dimensions of creation. The CREATIVE GUIDANCE SYSTEM captures these principles and places them in a simple, but powerful framework, that enables anyone to create the results they want at every level of their lives, work and world.

For more exploration, see:
Michael J. Losier, The Law of Attraction: The Science of Attracting More of What You Want and Less of What You Don't (Victoria B.C.: Michael Losier, 2003).
Esther Hicks and Jerry Hicks, The Law of Attraction: The Basics of the Teachings of Abraham (Hay House, 2006).
Rhonda Byrne, The Secret (Atria Books/Beyond Words, 2006)
[84] Runco, The Creativity Research Handbook.
Koestler, The Act of Creation, 120.
[85] Eliot, Collected Poems, 207.
[86] Sandburg, "Washington Monument by Night," stanza 4, The Complete Poems of Carl Sandburg (Orlando, FL: Harcourt, 1970), 282.
President Ronald Reagan quoted this before a joint session of Congress, April 28, 1981, and added: "As Carl Sandburg said, all we need to begin with is a dream that we can do better than before. All we need to have is faith, and that dream will come true. All we need to do is act, and the time for action is now."—Public Papers of the Presidents of the United States: Ronald Reagan, 1981, 394.
[87] Shakti Gawain, Creative Visualization: Use the Power of Your Imagination to Create What You Want in Your Life (Novato, CA: Nataraj Publishing, 2002), 48.
[88] Gay Hendricks and Kate Ludeman, The Corporate Mystic: A Guidebook for Visionaries with Their Feet on the Ground, (New York: Bantam Books, 1996), 62.
[89] Hendricks and Kate Ludeman, The Corporate Mystic, 48, 56.
[90] McTaggert, The Field: The Quest for the Secret Power of the Universe, xv. "The world of the separate should have been laid waste once and for all by the discovery of quantum physics in the early part of the twentieth century. As the pioneers of quantum physics peered into the very heart of matter, they were astonished at what they saw. The tiniest bits of matter weren't' even matter, as we know it, not even a set something, but sometimes one thing, sometimes something quite different. And even stranger, they were often many possible things at the same time. But most significantly, these subatomic particles had no meaning in isolation, but only in relationship with everything else. At its most elemental, matter couldn't be chopped up into self-contained little units, but was completely indivisible. You could only understand the universe as a dynamic web of interconnection. Things once in contact remained always in contact through all space and all time. Indeed, time and space themselves appeared to be arbitrary constructs, no longer applicable at this level of the world. Time

and space as we know them did not, in fact, exist. All that appeared, as far as the eye could see, was one long landscape of the here and now."

Dossey, Space, Time and Medicine, 115-117. "Subatomic particles are comprehended only through their relationships with all other subatomic particles, and the same can be said for massive bodies – planets, stars, galaxies." (116-7) *Clearly, the world of emotions and feeling are related to the physical word because they generate changes that any scientist can measure. ... The interrelationship of human consciousness and the observed world is also obvious in Bell's theorem. ... What we call physical reality, the external world, is shaped – to some extent – by human thought. Again, the attempts to define reality in terms of no interacting parts – physical matter and human consciousness – fails. The lesson is clear: We cannot separate our own existence from that of the world outside. We are intimately associated not only with the earth we inhabit, but with the farthest reaches of the cosmos."

[91] Campbell, *The Power of Myth*, 285.

[92] Robert K. Greenleaf, *Servant Leadership: A Journey into the Nature of Legitimate Power and Greatness* (Mahwah, NJ: Paulist Press, 1991), 36, 42. On leadership and creativity: "Leaders, therefore, must be more creative than most; and creativity is largely discovery, a push into the uncharted and the unknown." (42) "Leaders must have more of an armor of confidence in facing the unknown - more than those who accept their leadership. This is partly anticipation and preparation, but it is also a very firm belief that in the stress of real life situations one can compose oneself in a way that permits the creative process to operate."

[93] Curt Rosengren, "Spring Board: Richard Tait co-created Cranium as a way to help everyone shine," *Motto Magazine*, May/June 2007, Vol. 3, Issue 2, 61-65, also in *Cranium's "Secret Sauce,"* Created by Richard Tait, Grand Poo Bah, Cranium Inc., http://johnporcaro.blogspot.com/Secret%20Sauce.pdf.

[94] Mark Bernstein, "After Kitty Hawk: How the Wrights Really Learned to Fly," *American Heritage of Invention & Technology*, Summer 2005, Vol. 21, No. 1,12-19.

[95] Erin Brockovich biography, erinbrockovich.com, May 30,2007.

[96] Crayton Harrison and Dianne Solis, "Teens answer the call – and e-mail: Political organizing expected to rely on cell, online networking," *Dallas Morning News*, March 31, 2006.

[97] Joni Eareckson-Tada, a former swimmer and competitive diver who broke her neck in a 1967 diving accident that left her a quadriplegic, learned how to paint by holding a brush in her mouth. See http://www.joniandfriends.org.

[98] McGee-Cooper, *You Don't Have to Go Home From Work Exhausted*, 15. "In a new field of study called psychoneuroimmunology, we are learning that just thinking vividly about an exciting dream or goal, and imaging it as complete with all its benefits, can cause our body to create chemicals and hormones (such as endorphins) that balance our immune system, counter stress, and seem to create new energy."

[99] Joe Dispenza, *Evolve Your Brain: The Science of Changing Your Mind* (Deerfield Beach, FA: Health Communications, Inc., 2007), 267-268. A quick overview of the neurological process that constitutes a stress response proceeds like this: 1. The first response is the most immediate. In it, the autonomic nervous system turns on in response to something real or imagined in our environment. 2. The automatic nervous system passes information along directly through the spinal cord and spinal nerves to the peripheral nerves that are most readily connected directly to the adrenal glands. 3. Once this lightning bolt of information reaches the adrenal glands, they produce adrenaline (also known as epinephrine) that goes immediately into the bloodstream. The first/immediate response takes place in a flash. It produces an adrenal hit that results in a radical altering of our chemical makeup, plus a number of other physiological responses. The body shuts down or limits nonessential functions like digestion, and the blood is diverted from internal organs to the muscles to prepare them for action. We are in a state of heightened awareness and energy. We are ready either to fight or flee."

[100] Quoted in Peter McWilliams, *Life 101: Everything We Wish We Had Learned About Life in School – But Didn't* (Los Angeles, CA: Prelude Press, 1994), 358.

[101] Wheatley and Kellner-Rogers, *A Simpler Way*, 14. "Life organizes around identity. Every living thing acts to develop and preserve itself. Identity is the filter that every organism or system uses to make sense of the world. New information, new relationships, changing environments – all are interpreted through a sense of self. This tendency toward self-creation is so strong that it creates a seeming paradox. An organism will change to maintain its identity."

[102] Quoted in Boldt, *Zen and the Art of Making a Living*, 85.

[103] Campbell, *The Hero with a Thousand Faces*, 39.

[104] Quoted in Boldt, *Zen and the Art of Making a Living*, 93.

[105] Williamson, *A Return to Love*, 190.

[106] Quoted in Boldt, *Zen and the Art of Making a Living*, 96.

[107] Quoted in Boldt, *Zen and the Art of Making a Living*, 50.

[108] Quoted in Boldt, *Zen and the Art of Making a Living*, 89.

[109] From the estate of Dr. Martin Luther King, Jr. http://seattletimes.nwsource.com/mlk/king/words/blueprint.html
Six months before he was assassinated, King spoke to a group of students at Barratt Junior High School in Philadelphia on October 26, 1967.

[110] Michael Ray and Rochelle Myers, *Creativity in Business* (New York: Main Street Books, 1989), 188.

[111] Quoted in Boldt, *Zen and the Art of Making a Living*, 166.

[112] Benjamin Hunnicutt, author (Kellogg's Six-Hour Day Temple Univ. Press, 1996; Saving Work: A Failing Faith), interview in *Fast Company*, Nov. 1999, 194. "*Work has become our new religion, where we worship and give our time. . . . .Until the 20th century, work was secondary to other parts of life. We can see this by looking at the words that mean work in different cultures. The Spanish word for work, 'trabajo, comes from the Latin word for an instrument of torture. The Irish word, 'job,' took on a dual meaning: a temporary assignment, and excrement. Even the Puritans considered work a means to an end, the end being God. But the collapse of traditional cultural structures like family and religion have created a vacuum of belief, which work has grown to fill.... Job-satisfaction studies over the past 20 years indicate that people are looking for identity, purpose and meaning in their work, but very few are finding those things. That's why people are job-hopping, desperately trying to find the work equivalent of the Holy Grail. They aren't finding it because what they're looking for - salvation from a meaningless life and a senseless world - can't be found at work.*"
Andy Law, author of *Creative Company: How St. Luke's became the Ad Agency to End all Ad Agencies*, quoted in *Fast Company*. Nov. 1999, 132. "*Humans are creative, fun and inquiring; yet work for so many is monotonous, complex and dreary. Humans are individual and versatile; yet at work we discover we are all expendable and carefully placed in a well-manicured organogram.*"

[113] "Work: To exert one's mental or physical powers, usually under difficulty and to the point of exhaustion." *The American Heritage Dictionary of the English Language* (New York: Houghton Mifflin Company. 2000).

[114] Warren G. Bennis and Patricia Ward Biederman, *Organizing Genius: The Secrets of Creative Collaboration* (New York: Perseus Books, 1997), 215.

[115] Kahlil Gibran, *The Prophet* (New York: Alfred A. Knopf, 1923), 28.

[116] Senge, *The Fifth Discipline*, 3.

[117] Moore, *Care of the Soul*, 185, 199.

[118] Moore, *On Creativity*.

[119] Quoted in *Zen and the Art of Making a Living*, xiii.

[120] *Creativity: Touching the Divine*, presented by the Catholic Communications Campaign, Video No. 035-4, United States Catholic Conference, produced by Journey Communications, Alexandria, VA, Copyright 1994, United States Catholic Conference, In., Washington, D.C.

[121] Quoted in *Zen and the Art of Making a Living*, 98.

[122] Quoted in *Zen and the Art of Making a Living*, 21.

[123] Paul Cezanne to Louis Aurenche, 10 March 1902.

[124] Quoted in *Zen and the Art of Making a Living*, 199.

[125] Quoted in Michael Michalko, *Cracking Creativity: The Secrets of Creative Genius* (Berkeley, CA: Ten Speed Press, 2001), 85.

[126] Moore, *On Creativity*. "For [Stravinsky], writing music was very much like a person who makes shoes, working at leather and pounding nails and sewing stitches all day long. He said that's what he did ... . He described is one sense of himself as an artist as someone who did the day-to-day craft of making music. He was a maker ... ."

[127] Quoted in *Zen and the Art of Making a Living*, 85.

[128] Greenleaf, *Servant Leadership*, 27-28, 36.

[129] Covey quoted in *Upsidedown Leadership*, 11.
"Leadership Is a Process, Not a Role."

[130] *Quest: Energy, Power & Spirit*, Vol. 3 (New York: Simon & Schuster Audio, 1996).

[131] John Doerr, "Why Zazzle Dazzles John Doerr," *BusinessWeek*, July 21, 2005. "There's this large trend -- I think the next trend in the Web, sort of Web 2.0 -- which is to have users really express, offer, and market their own content, their own persona, their identity. I don't mean identity as in credit cards. I mean like apparel is a way we express our identity, how we dress, the music we listen to."

[132] "The Global Brain: Top 5 Consumer Trends For 2007," trendwatching.com.
See also "*Children Of The Web: How the second-generation Internet is spawning a global youth culture--and what business can do to cash in*," BusinessWeek, July 2, 2007.

[133] The television series "*Ally McBeal*," created by David E. Kelly, ran on the FOX network (1997 to 2002).

[134] Tom Peters, *The Brand You 50: Fifty Ways to Transform Yourself from an "Employee" into a Brand that Shouts Distinction, Commitment, and Passion!*" (New York: Alfred A. Knopf, Inc, 1999).
Daniel H. Pink , *Free Agent Nation: The Future of Working for Yourself* (New York: Warner Books, Inc., 2002).
Florida, *Flight of the Creative Class.*

[135] Melinda Krueger, "Social Networking And Email," (Email Insider: The Inside Line On Email Marketing, Mediapost Publications), May 8, 2007. "To reach Digital Natives, you have to understand the community and respect it. You need to participate, but in an authentic way. A first-class guide to the philosophy can be found on the Word of Mouth Marketing Association's WOM 101 guide. For the nonprofit group mentioned above, it can be as simple as finding young people who are passionate about their cause and active and well-connected in their networks. As Ben McConnell, author of Citizen Marketers, said in a recent talk, there is a fifth "P" of marketing: participation."

[136] Candice M. Kelsey, *Generation MySpace: Helping Your Teen Survive Online Adolescence/How Social Networking is Changing Everything About Friendship, Gossip, Sex, Drugs, and our Kids' Values* (New York: Marlowe & Company, 2007), 40. "Here comes the fun part – creating your own profile. The work inherent in this step is partly why teens are so enamored of MySpace. After all, many see it as a truly creative pursuit, spending hours, days even, 'pimping' or 'tricking' it out to impress friends and other MySpacers."

[137] In Christian belief, the Bible says that others will "know us by our fruits." Matthew 7:18 and 20 "A good tree cannot produce bad fruit, nor can a bad tree produce good fruit. So, then, you will know them by their fruits." Also Luke 6:44 Christians distinguish between being "known" by works (because "works" or expressions may be seen and heard by others), but not "justified" by works, only by faith, a free gift to believers.

[138] Peter Senge, *The Fifth Discipline*, 7. "People with a high level of personal mastery are able to consistently realize the results that matter most deeply to them - in effect, they approach their life as an artist would approach a work of art. They do that by becoming committed to their own lifelong learning."
Tim Sanders, *Love is the Killer App: How to Win Business and Influence Friends* (New York: Crown Business, 2002), 10-11. Tim Sanders, Chief Solutions Officer at Yahoo!:
"… I have found one common truth: Men and women across the country are trying desperately to understand how to maintain their value as professionals in the face of rapidly changing times. Now that the bizworld is moving at velocity once unheard of, many of us can't keep up. … to succeed in tomorrow's workplace, you need a killer application. (What's a killer application? …. basically it's an excellent new idea that either supersedes and existing idea or establishes a new category in its field …). What is that application? Simply put: Love is the killer app. Those of us who use love as a point of differentiation in business will separate ourselves from our competitors … ."

[139] Frankl, *Man's Search for Meaning*, 17, 86-87, 98.

[140] Stephen R. Covey believes that who you are and how you express that essence - which he calls "character" – is more important than anything that you do: "I believe that character (what a person is) is ultimately more important than competence (what a person can do). Obviously both are important, but character is foundational. All else builds on this cornerstone. ... in the long run what we are, our basic character, will take precedence over our skills, our competencies, or even the structures and systems we set up."
"Character First," Interview with Stephen R. Covey, May 1994
"Even the very best structure, system, style, and skills can't compensate completely for deficiencies in character."

[141] Alliance for Nonprofit Management › Frequently Asked Questions › Strategic Planning › FAQ Question on "What's in a Vision Statement?" http://www.allianceonline.org/FAQ

[142] Lawrence Tabak, *If Your Goal Is Success, Don't Consult These Gurus: For years, motivational speakers have celebrated a Yale study on why people succeed. It's powerful! Compelling! Too bad it doesn't exist,* Fast Company, Issue 6, Dec. 1996, 38. "The repertoire of consultants, trainers, and motivational speakers, nothing comes before the power of setting personal goals. And in the annals of personal goal-setting, no story outranks the Yale University Class of 1953. The story, as told by consultants, goes like this: In 1953, researchers surveyed Yale's graduating seniors to determine how many of them had specific, written goals for their future. The answer: 3%. Twenty years later, researchers polled the surviving members of the Class of 1953 -- and found that the 3% with goals had accumulated more personal financial wealth than the other 97% of the class combined! It's a consultant's dream anecdote: a vivid Ivy League success story that documents the cause-and-effect relationship between goals and personal success. It's powerful! It's compelling! also completely untrue -- as the Fast Company Consultant Debunking Unit (CDU) found out."
Fast Company notes that both Zig Ziglar and Tony Robbins cited this story in their books and/or videos. After researching this much-cited study, *Fast Company* research directly with Yale found no record or evidence the study ever existed.

[143] St. Philip's Episcopal School & Community Center Creed, 1600 Pennsylvania Avenue, Dallas, Texas 75215, Headmaster Dr. Terry Flowers, http://www.stphilips1600.org

[144] "An Oasis in South Dallas," *Our Texas*, 1996, 15-18, St. Philip's Episcopal School & Community Center, 1600 Pennsylvania Avenue, Dallas, Texas 75215, Headmaster Dr. Terry Flowers, http://www.stphilips1600.org. Dr. Terry Flowers' study of ten years of St. Philip's graduates found that "alumni achieved 3.6 versus 1.6 average high-school GPAs in comparison to non-alumni,' and found "no high-school dropouts, no one who'd been in prison or in trouble with the law and no teenage pregnancies among a decade of alumni." Dr. Flowers provided the 97 percent graduation rate, and the 88 percent college attendance rate.
David Tarrant, "Community bands together to take back neighborhood, *Dallas Morning News*, June 11, 2007.

[145] *Dallas Morning News* interview, Jan. 8, 2000.

[146] Moore, *On Meaningful Work*.

[147] "If you don't have passion, change," Lauren Hutton, Actress, quoted in *Reader's Digest*, July 1999, 124.

[148] Quoted in Wheatley and Kellner-Rogers, *A Simpler Way*, 58.

[149] Dr. Larry Dossey. Medical City Dallas.

[150] Moore, *On Meaningful Work*.

[151] Csikszentmihalyi, *Creativity*.

[152] Eliot, *Collected Poems*. 178.

[153] Written by Anna Quindlen for 1999 Villanova Graduation Speech (speech was never given for Villanova); Later version reprinted in "A Short Guide to a Happy Life," by Anna Quindlen, (New York: Random House, 2000), 7-9.

[154] Moore, *On Meaningful Work*.

[155] Ibid.

[156] James R. Fisher, Jr., *Personal Excellence Newsletter*, 1998.

[157] Moore, *On Meaningful Work*.

[158] Senge, *The Fifth Discipline*, 144. "Pollster Daniel Yankelovich has been taking the pulse of the American public for forty years. ... Yankelovich as pointed to a 'basic shift in attitude in the workplace' from an 'instrumental' to a 'sacred' view of work. The instrumental view implies that we work in order to ear the income to do what we really want when we are not working. This is the classic consumer orientation toward work - work is an instrument for generating income. Yankelovich uses the word 'sacred' in the sociological not religious sense: 'People or objects are sacred in the sociological sense when, apart from what instrumental use they serve, they are valued for themselves.' "

[159] Deepak Chopra, *The Seven Spiritual Laws of Success* (San Rafael, CA: Amber-Allen Publishing, 1994).

[160] Quoted in Rick Wormeli, *Differentiation: From Planning to Practices* (Stenhouse Publishers, 2007), 9.

[161] Quoted in Troy L. Tate, "The DNA of Successful Leaders: Tapping Your Natural Power To Win Friends and

Influence Others," (San Juan Capistrano, CA: Cumulatius Publishing, 2006), 59.

[162] Quoted in *Zen and the Art of Making a Living*, 182.

[163] Barbara Ann Kipfer. *The Wish List* (New York: Workman Publishing Company, 1997), viii.

[164] Wheatley and Kellner-Rogers, *A Simpler Way*, 88.

[165] Quoted in *The Corporate Mystic*, xvii.

[166] Diana Kunde, "The Driving Force Behind Fast Company," Dallas Morning News, June 28, 1999, interview Diana Kunde with Alan Webber, editor and co-founder, *Fast Company*.

[167] Wheatley and Kellner-Rogers, *A Simpler Way*, 57.

[168] Henry David Thoreau, *Walden* (Stilwell, KS: Digireads Publishing, 2005), 461.

[169] *Quest: Energy, Power & Spirit.*

[170] Ibid.

[171] Ibid.

[172] Ibid.

[173] *Creativity: Touching the Divine,*

[174] *Quest: Energy, Power & Spirit.*

[175] Moore, *On Creativity.*

[176] Erin Brockovich, *Take it from Me: Life's a Struggle, But You Can Win* (New York: McGraw-Hill, 2002), 100-101.

[177] Marcus Aurelius, *Meditations*, trans. Maxwell Staniforth (London: Penguin Books,1974), 95-97.

[178] "Character First," Interview with Stephen R. Covey, May 1994.

[179] Quote from *FranklinCovey Mission Statement Builder* http://www.franklincovey.com/fc/library_and_resources/mission_statement_builder

[180] Suzanne Falter Barns, author, *How Much Joy Can you Stand* (New York: Ballantine, 2000).

[181] Senge, *The Fifth Discipline*, 9.

[182] Lorraine Monroe, "The Monroe Doctrine," *Fast Company*, Sept. 1999, 230.

[183] Paul Cook, CEO, Raychem Corporation, quoted in *Positive Leadership* (Lawrence Ragan Communications, Inc., 1998), 8.

[184] Innovation '98 Conference. a worldwide broadcast on creativity, innovation, and business strategy.

[185] Debra Dunn, General Manager, Hewlett-Packard, "They Hear it Through the Grapevine," *Fast Company*, April:May 1998, 160.

[186] Noel M. Tichy, *The Leadership Engine: How Winning Companies Build Leaders at Every Level* (New York: Collins, 2002), 219.

[187] Bloom, *The Global Brain*, 223.

[188] C.G. Lynch, "Five Things Wikipedia's Founder Has Learned About Online Collaboration," CIO Insider, 2007.
World of Warcraft - often abbreviated as "WoW" - is a multiplayer online game, produced in 2004 by Blizzard Entertainment, as part of the "Warcraft" game series. http://www.blizzard.com/

[189] Quoted in Wheatley and Kellner-Rogers, *A Simpler Way*, 58.

[190] Quoted in Wheatley and Kellner-Rogers, *A Simpler Way*, 13.

[191] Quoted in Wheatley and Kellner-Rogers, *A Simpler Way*, 58.

[192] "Harry Bacas, "Tapping your creativity - Creativity in business," *Nation's Business*, March 1987.

[193] Fred Moody, *The New York Times Magazine*, August 25, 1991.

[194] Andy Warhol, quoted in *Positive Leadership* (Lawrence Ragan Communications, Inc, 1998), 13.

[195] Michael Ray and Rochelle Myers, *Creativity in Business* (New York: Broadway Books, 1986), 3.

[196] John Bogle Founder of Vanguard Group Inc. and pioneer of the index mutual fund, interview with Cheryl Hall, *Dallas Morning News*, June 27, 2007.

[197] *The Corporate Mystic*, xvii-xviii.

[198] Quoted in *Zen and the Art of Making a Living*, 143.
[199] Wheatley and Kellner-Rogers, *A Simpler Way*, 90-99.
[200] Steve Case quoted in Julia Angwin and Martin Peers, "The Re-Emergence of Steve Case: With a Focus on the Far Future, AOL Chairman Prepares to Take More Active Role," *The Wall Street Journal*, Jan. 17, 2002.
[201] Stephen R. Covey, *The Seven Habits of Highly Effective People: Powerful Lessons in Personal Change* (New York: The Free Press, 1989), 101.
[202] Covey, *The Seven Habits of Highly Effective People*, 99, 101.
[203] Covey, *The Seven Habits of Highly Effective People*, 102.
[204] James Barrowman, "Pin the Deputy's Badge on Me," Goddard Space Flight Center.
http://appel.nasa.gov/ask/issues/03/03s_pin_barrowman.php
Charlie Stegemoeller, "Chaos Is the Fraternal Twin of Creativity," Johnson Space Center
Wendy Dolci, "The Enterprise Project," Ames Research Center
http://appel.nasa.gov/ask/issues/15/15s_enterprise.php
Maj. Norman H. Patnode, "Grins & Giggles: The Launch Pad to High Performance
http://appel.nasa.gov/ask/issues/12/12s_stories_grinsandgiggles.php#top
[205] Lisa Reed, "Crew dynamics are vital to a mission's success," Training team lead at NASA's Johnson Space Center in Houston, NASAexplores: April 26, 2001
http://nasaexplores.nasa.gov/show2_articlea.php?id=01-041
[206] Owen Gadeken, "Activation Energy," Defense Systems Management College.
[207] Senge, *The Fifth Discipline*, 293.
[208] Chip Heath and Dan Heath, *Made to Stick: Why Some Ideas Survive While Others Die* (New York: Random House, 2007), 25-27.
[209] Barrowman, "Pin the Deputy's Badge on Me."
[210] Wheatley and Kellner-Rogers, *A Simpler Way*, 58.
[211] Bohm, Wholeness and the Implicate Order, 114.
[212] Marshall and Zohar, *Who's Afraid of Schrödinger's Cat*, 59.
Wheatley, *Leadership and the New Science*, 20, 80-81.
Wheatley and Kellner-Rogers, *A Simpler Way*, 49.
[213] Gord Hotchkiss, "Creating Conversations, One Column At A Time," MediaPost's Search Insider, July 12, 2007.
[214] Grossman, "Time's Person of the Year: You."
[215] Wheatley and Kellner-Rogers, *A Simpler Way*, 34.
[216] Kevin Kelly, *New Rules for the New Economy* (New York: Viking Press 1998); also, a direct quote from Upside Magazine, Dec. 1998, 144.
[217] Barrowman, "Pin the Deputy's Badge on Me."
[218] Thomas Petzinger, Jr., "The Front Lines," *The Wall Street Journal*, Jan. 2, 1997.
[219] Stegemoeller, "Chaos Is the Fraternal Twin of Creativity,"
[220] Jeffrey B. Swartz, President/CEO Timberland Co. in "The Art of Smart," *Fast Company*, July:August 1999, 98.
[221] Eric Hippeau, Chairman and CEO, Ziff-Davis Inc. in "The Art of Smart," 102.
[222] Richard Pascale, Fellow at Oxford University, "Grassroots Leadership," *Fast Company*, April:May 1998.
[223] Wheatley and Kellner-Rogers, *A Simpler Way*, 58.
[224] Chris Turner, Xerox Business Services "Learning Person" and Author, "The Art of Smart," 96.
[225] Quoted in *Zen and the Art of Making a Living*, 492.
[226] Quoted in Clint Sidle, Ron Napier, Patrick Sanaghan, *High Impact Tools and Activates for Strategic Planning: Creative Techniques for Facilitating Your Organization's Planning Process* (New York: McGraw-Hill Professional, 1997), Apple Vision on 206. Author's note: We also mention here that, too often, groups and organizations may become so caught up in disagreements over what is a Vision or a Mission statement, that the creative process becomes paralyzed. We advise that organizations understand that Vision and Mission may always be considered "working versions" – "works in process" – and simply have a starting-point statement is sufficient to enable the group to launch its journey and begin navigating toward these shared high goals; the statement(s) may always

be refined later.

[227] Ray and Myers, *Creativity in Business*, 182.

[228] Senge, *The Fifth Discipline*, 345.

[229] Whole Foods Market (http://www.wholefoodsmarket.com/company/sustainablefuture.html)

[230] Daniel H. Burnham, architect (1846-1912).

[231] Senge, *The Fifth Discipline*, 343.

[232] Jeffrey K. Liker, *The Toyota Way: 14 Management Principles from the World's Greatest Manufacturer* (New York: McGraw-Hill, 2003), 72.

[233] Theodore Zeldin, Oxford historian and author, *Fast Company* Magazine, Dec. 2000.

[234] Deborah L. Flick, *From Debate to Dialogue: Using the Understanding Process to Transform Our Conversations* (Orchid Publications, 1988), 2.

[235] Bohm, *On Dialogue*.

[236] Peter F. Drucker, *Management Challenges for the 21st Century* (New York: HarperCollins, 1999), 119.

[237] Trevor Davis, PricewaterhouseCoopers, UK PricewaterhouseCoopers Innovation Study June 1999 (interview by Robert B. Tucker *Thinksmart*).

[238] Joyce Wycoff and Ruth Hattori, *Innovation Training* (Alexandria, VA: ASTD Press, 2004), ix.

[239] Bob Evans, InformationWeek Editor-in-Chief, www.marketingcomputers.com Magazine, June 1999, 51.

[240] Ibid.

[241] Wheatley and Kellner-Rogers, *A Simpler Way*, 34-35, 38.

[242] Scott Thurm, "Now, It's Business By Data, but Numbers Still Can't Tell Future," *The Wall Street Journal* ("In the Lead" Column), July 23, 2007.
"3M's Innovation Crisis: How Six Sigma Almost Smothered Its Idea Culture," *BusinessWeek*, June 11, 2007 Cover Story
"Six Sigma: So Yesterday? In an innovation economy, it's no longer a cure-all," *BusinessWeek*, June 11, 2007,
Thomas H. Davenport and Laurence Prusak, with H. James Wilson "Reengineering Revisited," *Computerworld*, June 23, 2003
Art Kleiner, "The Battle for the Soul of Corporate America: Hammerism battles Demingism for how the corporation (or society) should be governed in the information age," *Wired* Magazine, Issue 3.08, August 1995
Author's note: As Kleiner explains, corporate "Re-engineering," popularized in the 1990s by Michael Hammer and James Champy in their best-selling business book "Re-engineering the Corporation," primarily involved outside management consultants mapping processes and recommending changes (notably major workforce layoffs and job elimination). However, the failure rate for these initially popular and extremely expensive "re-engineering projects" was acknowledged by the original authors themselves to be "50 to 70 percent," with re-engineering's lack of consideration for "human behavior" cited as the major cause of these the high failure rate. At the national conference "Innovation '98," business restructuring author Gary Hamel acknowledged the shift of thinking: "Reenergizing is more important than restructuring. People are hungry for meaning, for a chance to create." Gary Hamel, business restructuring author, Innovation '98.
See also:
Edward M. Gurowitz, "Why Reengineering Fails," (Center for Management Design, Inc. Generative Leadership Group, 1994).http://www.gurowitz.com/articles/Reengineering.pdf.
John E. Jones, "Re-Engineering: Why it So Often Fails," (Reid Moomaugh & Associates, 1996). "It has been estimated that about two-thirds of re-engineering projects either fail completely or fall significantly short of their hoped-for outcomes. http://www.improve.org/reengfl.html
Later in the 1990s and early in the first decade of the millennium, the hot management trend was "lean management" and "Six Sigma" quality improvement initiatives. Often, these quality initiatives have been viewed by some companies as "innovation" efforts; however, as John Parkinson notes in CIO Insight:
"Creating and maintaining a culture of innovation is important for any business. All companies express interest in innovation — who doesn't want to come up with a new product or process?—but few do much about it. Many companies back away when they see what's actually involved in sustaining innovation. Then there are businesses that really want to make innovation work, but face an internal roadblock: A long-running, moderately successful Six Sigma quality effort led by fanatics. ... Six Sigma can conflict with innovation because it tries to eliminate different ways of doing things in favor of the "best" way. Innovation thrives on trying new approaches.

John Parkinson, "The Conflict Between Six Sigma and Innovation," *CIO Insight*, July 23, 2007.

[243] Thurm, "Now, It's Business By Data, but Numbers Still Can't Tell Future,"

[244] Wheatley and Kellner-Rogers, *A Simpler Way*, 80.

[245] The psychologist Carl G. Jung contributed, as a central part of his theory, the concept of "psychological types," upon which many current personality styles assessments – most notably the popular Myers-Briggs or MBTI (Myers-Briggs Type Indicator) assessment (developed by Katharine Cook Briggs and her daughter Isabel Briggs, based on Jung's work), used widely within organizations today. Similar typologies and assessments of individual personality styles, learning styles (many derived from Howard Gardner's work on multiple intelligences) and "strengths" (such as the Gallup Organizations' "*StrengthsFinder*," introduced in the 2001 book "Now, Discover Your Strengths," by Marcus Buckingham and Donald Clifton, Free Press), are also popular today, both within organizations and teams, as well as with those seeking to discover talents and potential work for which they may be well-suited.

Jung said his work on psychological types was "one of the greatest experiences in my life to discover how enormously different people's psyches are," (*Collected Works of C.G. Jung*, Vol. 10, Read, Fordham and Adler, Princeton University Press, 137). However, Jung immediately acknowledged that his work – which identified eight main psychological "types" - was never intended to be used to categorize people, a misapplication which Jung said would be "pointless." ("It is not the purpose of a psychological typology to classify human beings into categories – this in itself would be pretty pointless." - from "Psychological Types," C.G. Jung, 146, in *The Essential Jung*, MJF Books: New York, 1983 Princeton University Press) and acknowledged that even within the same "category," no two individual's personality patterns would be exactly alike.

As Calvin S. Hall and Vernon J. Nordby note in A *Primer of Jungian Psychology* (1973, A Mentor Book/Published by the Penguin Group, New York): "It should be noted that Jung's [psychological] typology has been severely criticized by psychologists who insist that people do not fit neatly into eight, or eighty, classes. Each individual, they argue, is unique and not a member of a specific class. These criticisms indicate a misunderstanding of Jung's position. He would not argue about the uniqueness of the individual's psyche, which to him was self-evident. What his typology does is to offer a system for characterizing the significant ways in which people differ from one another."

Most importantly, when Jung talked about the goal of achieving selfhood, he was advancing the idea that opposites ought to be transcended. In other words, one extreme (whose equivalent MBTI type might be INFJ, Introverted, Intuitive, Feeling, Judging) would not be considered "a full self," in the same way that he opposing ESTP (Extroverted, Sensing, Thinking, Perceiving MBTI type) would need to be more fully developed in order for that person to be what Jung called unified, "individuated," or whole - that is, to be "a whole self."

As Anthony Schorr says in *The Essential Jung*, MJF Books: New York, 1983 Princeton University Press, 18): "*Jung considered that habitual attitudes were nearly always carried too far, so that the thinker neglected his feelings, while the intuitive paid too little attention to the facts given by sensation. Introverts were caught up in their inner worlds; while extraverts lost themselves in the press of events. … There was, therefore, within every individual, a striving toward unity in which divisions would be replaced by consistency, opposites equally balanced, consciousness in reciprocal relation with the unconscious. Jung affirmed that personality was manifested by "definiteness, wholeness and ripeness."*"

As Jung says of introversion and extraversion (*he Essential Jung* (MJF Books: New York, 1983 Princeton University Press, 162-163): "*The two types therefore seem created for a symbiosis. The one takes care of reflection and the other sees to the initiative and practical action. When the two types marry the may effect an ideal union. …. No man is simply introverted or simply extraverted, but has both attitudes potentially in him – although he has developed only one of them as a function of adaptation. We shall immediately conjecture that with the introvert extraversion lies dormant and undeveloped somewhere in the background.*" Further, Jung calls this "union of opposites the 'transcendent function" … [a] rounding our of the personality into a whole" (226).

Jung uses the term "individuation" to "denote the process by which a person becomes a psychological "individual," that is, a separate, indivisible unity or "whole" (a process which Jung also views as essentially a spiritual journey p. 19). In addition, it is significant that Jung himself relates this term "whole" with the same idea of physicist Louis DeBroglie, in the sense of something 'discontinuous." (T*he Essential Jung*, MJF Books: New York, 1983 Princeton University Press, 212).

The caution is that some may view their "type" as a given, in the sense of "that's just they way I am – deal with it," rather than viewing their "type" (and those of others) as information about "What Is" for them, as well as a guide for personal development and growth (fully developing – or "maturing," to use Jung's term – in all aspects, to reach full potential).

Some see the popularizing of these typologies and assessments, especially when used as an end in themselves, rather than as a starting point for exploration and development, as particularly ironic, given the fact that Jung's vision was to enable people to illuminate, and to transcend, any limitations on their full potential. If misused in this way, such typologies may be seen to diminish people, making them feel smaller or reducing them to a mere fraction of their full human potential. And, as Arthur C. Martinez, former Chairman of the Board, President and Chief Executive Officer of Sears, Roebuck and Co., says (also quoted on this page): "*You can't shrink your way to greatness.*"

The larger point that may especially missed in a focus primarily on these individual analyses is the significance of the more dynamic nature of behavior generated by and value created within systems (by people interacting in relationship with one another, whether in small groups or large organizations) – an overarching dynamic the importance of which is increasingly emphasized by findings of neuroscience, biology, network theory, physics and a host of other scientific disciplines. These overarching – higher-level and co-creative – effects are, of course, of particular interest to us here in the GUIDE, and particularly relevant as we seek to understand how a shared creative process may enable both individuals, and groups of every size, to integrate but move beyond differences, to achieve higher, common shared visions, missions and goals.

Ultimately, as Schorr explains (T*he Essential Jung*, MJF Books: New York, 1983 Princeton University Press, 229): " The goal toward which the individuation process is tending is 'Wholeness' or 'Integration': a condition in which all the elements of the psyche, both conscious and unconscious, are welded together. … Individuation, in Jung's view, is a spiritual journey; and the person embarking upon it, although he might not subscribe to any recognized creed, was nonetheless pursuing a religious quest. … he is guided by an integrating factor which is not of his own making. This integrating factor … is named the Self; an archetype which not only signifies union between the opposite within the psyche, but 'is a God-image, or at least cannot be distinguished from one.' "

This brings us back, yet again on a higher turn of the spiral, to the essence of hero's journey – and of Aristotle's *potentia* and Abraham Maslow's *self-actualization* – to discover individual and collective Wholeness.

[246] "Managing Those Creative Types." *Gallup Management Journal*,.
Louis Uchitelle, *The Disposable American: Layoffs and Their Consequences* (New York: Vintage, 2007), 193-194. In an interview with author Louis Uchitelle, Thomas Knochan of MIT Sloan School of Management, explains: "*Academics engaged in this research understand social capital as trust, communication, and value generated by people working together. But since no one is able to quantify in dollars the loss of these intangibles, the decision is to go with the visible savings from layoffs. You see this in staffing decisions all the time. You can easily calculate the direct dollar savings from fewer people on payroll.*"

In addition, Uchitelle relates that Judy Hoffer Gittell, an assistant professor of management at Brandeis University's Heller School for Social Policy and Management, who wrote *The Southwest Airlines Way: Using the Power of Relationships to Achieve High Performance*, argues that "*Southwest's singular success in the airline industry is mainly a result of social capital, and she detailed the various ways in which Southwest achieves social capital, including an outsize effort to train people not just in the skills required for their jobs, but in the skill of working togethe*r." Gittell also noted that Southwest "eschews layoff."

[247] Watts, *Six Degrees*, 150.

[248] Watts, *Six Degrees*, 25-26.
Vertosick, *The Genius Within*, 16.
Sheldrake, *The Presence of the Past*, xvii-xviii.

[249] Uchitelle, *The Disposable American*, 194. Uchitelle concludes that "*Layoffs undermine … corporate effectiveness, subtracting from the corporate edge that the layoffs are intended to enhance. … Cutting staff may appear to be sensible, particularly when sales revenue is not keeping up with the costs of production. Getting rid of excess labor brings the two back into balance quickly, and that gets the attention of investors and shareholders. … The irony is in the unreported damage to social capital that layoffs inflict and the costs that are added because of this damage.*" Moreover, in an interview with Uchitelle, Dr. Kim Cameron, an organizational psychologist at the University of Michigan's business school, says: "*The evidence suggests that quality, productivity , and customer service often decline over time, and financial performance – while frequently improving in the short run after downsizing due to promised savings and lower costs – erodes often in the long run.*" Uchitelle notes that many studies support Cameron in this view, as does Frederick F. Reichheld, who argues in his book *Less is More* that "*companies with the highest customer satisfaction are least likely to*

engage in layoffs. So are companies that invest in worker training, avoiding layoffs, and the price of their stocks do better than average."

In addition, the costs for reduction in or elimination of the social capital lost in layoffs – not only the relationships and efficient networks of these individuals, but also the vast subject knowledge and institutional knowledge of these workers, is rarely, if ever, quantified, and virtually never factored into the overall cost to an organization for massive layoffs (not to mention the vast costs to these employees themselves, as Uchitelle's book *The Disposable American* presents through detailed research).

For example, in a July 2007 Research Brief entitled "Retiring Boomers Important in Hand-off to Younger Employees" in July 2007, The Center for Media Research (MediaPost Communications: New York, http://www.centerformediaresearch.com/) noted that: "A recent survey of 28,000 employers in 25 countries, by Manpower, revealed that only 21 percent have implemented retention strategies to keep their senior employees participating in the workforce.

A related May 2007 article – "Companies May Lose Older Workers with Shortsighted Policies" - from Birkman International, Inc., (http://www.birkman.com) which cites the same Manpower study, warns that: "The baby boomers are a significant percentage of the current workforce and are nearly ready for retirement. Experts expect tremendous gaps in competencies and know-how as a result of this demographic wave. Several industries, including electric utilities, oil and gas production, healthcare and the public sector, are already feeling the effects of baby boomer retirements. 'This could be catastrophic, considering that those best able to train replacements will be those that are leaving," said Sharon Birkman-Fink, President and CEO of Birkman International."

[250] Peters, *The Circle of Innovation*, 499.

[251] Ellinor and Gerard, *Dialogue*. xxv.

[252] Martha Heller, "The Top 10 Drivers for Innovation: Council members offer up their own ways of fostering an innovative culture," *CIO* Magazine, April 15, 2004.

[253] Ellinor and Gerard, *Dialogue*. xxv.

[254] Quoted in John-Roger and Peter McWilliams, *Do It: Let's Get Off Our Butts – A Guide to Living Your Dreams* (Los Angeles, CA: Prelude Press, 1991), 286.

[255] Quoted in *Zen and the Art of Making a Living*, 181.

[256] Basil King, quoted in *Converge* Magazine, Aug.- Sept. 2002, 24.

[257] Tibor Kalman quoted in *Wired* Magazine, Jan. 2000, 86.

[258] Annette Moser-Wellman, President, Firemark, Inc., "Prioritizing the Creative Workout" *BrandWeek*, May18, 1998, 28.

[259] Quoted in *Zen and the Art of Making a Living*, p. 199.

[260] Quoted in *Zen and the Art of Making a Living*, p. 181.

[261] *The Corporate Mystic*, 33. Authors' Note: Chapter 1, "Integrity," is one of the best resources and summaries on the topic of integrity to be found in leadership literature.

[262] *The Corporate Mystic*, 29.

[263] Jim Collins, author of *Built to Last*, "Fear Not," *Inc.* Magazine, May 1998, 39.

[264] Abraham Maslow, *Motivation and Personality*, 202.

[265] Charlie Kiefer quoted in Fritz, *The Path of Least Resistance*, 132.

[266] Ibid.

[267] *The Corporate Mystic*, 17.

[268] George Land and Beth Jarman, *Breakpoint and Beyond: Mastering the Future Today* (New York: HarperBusiness, 1993), 12.

[269] Quote attributed to Broadcast Journalist Belva Davis by The History Makers, http://www.thehistorymakers.com.

[270] Henry Mintzberg, The Rise and Fall of Strategic Planning: Reconceiving Roles for Planning, Plans, Planners (New York: The Free Press, 1994). 36. "One single set of concepts underlies virtually all the proposals to formalize the process of strategy formation. Sometimes called the SWOT model (for strengths and weaknesses, opportunities and threats), and most popularly known in the writings of the Harvard business policy people

(especially Kenneth Andrews, in his own books and a textbook with his various colleagues, the basic ideas can be traced back at least to Philip Selznick's influential little book, *Leadership in Administration* (1957)

[271] See also Florida, *The Rise of the Creative Class.*

[272] Eckhart Tolle, *The Power of Now: A Guide to Spiritual Enlightenment* (Novato, CA: New World Library, 1999). See also Chopra, *The Seven Spiritual Laws of Success.*

[273] Marc Cohen, *Readings In Ancient Greek Philosophy: From Thales To Aristotle.*
Ancient astronomers erred in their initial view of the relative movement of the Earth and the other stars and planets – concluding that the Earth was the center of the Universe – because, given their "inward-looking," partial view of our planet made it appear that the Sun, moon and stars moved around the Earth (rather than the other way around). This error arose because the ancients lacked the broader context and higher view of the solar system, within which the actual movements of the stars and planets relative to one another could be accurately assessed. Discoveries such as the unexpected, elliptical movements of the planets – whose seemingly strange shifts in space long puzzled ancient astronomers - could not be discerned without a wider view of the whole system. In the same way, we must have a broader context within which to view the influx of information, emerging events and movements within our space, in order to make sense of this information, to organize, order, prioritize it appropriately, relative to our chosen trajectory – and then use that now-ordered information (now configured as knowledge) to guide us along the path to our goals.

[274] Maslow, *Motivation and Personality*, 202.

[275] Senge, *The Fifth Discipline*, 64-65.

[276] Thurm, "*Now, It's Business By Data, but Numbers Still Can't Tell Future.*"

[277] Information technology initiatives continue to make enormous strides in enabling more efficient communications and information-sharing across organizations, and the growing popularity of data "dashboards," designed to gather and analyze critical information and render it into meaningful form as close to real time as is possible. However, the truth remains that the instant data is captured, it represents a snapshot of one point or segment of time, and even long-running trends can change in an instant, due to a myriad of factors - and unexpected, even globally dispersed, events - which may lie far beyond the reach of our current "nets" of analysis.

[278] Thurm, "*Now, It's Business By Data, but Numbers Still Can't Tell Future.*"

[279] Ibid.

[280] John Cook, *The Book of Positive Quotations* (New York: Gramercy Books, 1993), 511.
Tom Peters, *The Project 50 (Reinventing Work): Ways to Transform Every 'Task' into a Project that Matters,* (New York: Alfred A. Knopf, 1999), 150-151. Ready. Fire! Aim. attributes to Ross Perot (and others such as Harry Quadracci, founder, Quad/Graphics and Wayne Calloway, former PepsiCo chairman p. 150

[281] Thurm, "*Now, It's Business By Data, but Numbers Still Can't Tell Future.*"

[282] Ibid.

[283] D.C. Somervell, *A Study of History, Volume 1* (Oxford: Oxford University Press, 1946), in "Arnold J. Toynbee," 358, 663.

[284] Thurm, "*Now, It's Business By Data, but Numbers Still Can't Tell Future.*"
Olivier Blanchard, "Avoid the Spiral of Doom," *The Brand Builder Blog.*

[285] Peters, *Circle of Innovation*, 326.

[286] Steve G. Steinberg, "Stupid Is Smart," *Wired* Magazine, Issue 6.08, Aug. 1998.

[287] Peters, *Circle of Innovation*, 441.

[288] Because the "*Analyze*" step often focuses the participants in the process, whether an individual or group, on the details of the operations or circumstances, the Creative Guidance System further includes the "*Scope*" step to look at the entire set of circumstances, context or environment related to the planning situation; the activities of the individual or group and the resources and skills available to the individual or group as an entire package. In addition, the *Vision* is evaluated against the *Scope* to make sure that there is alignment between the various aspects of the enterprise, the external environment, including the marketplace, industry and general economic and market forces and trends, and the plan being created.

[289] Jeff Pfeffer, Stanford University Business School, from Robert Gandossy and Marc Effron, *Leading the Way: Three Truths from the Top Companies for Leaders* (Hoboken, NJ: John Wiley & Sons, 2004), 10.

[290] Parkinson, "The Conflict Between Six Sigma and Innovation.

[291] Peters, *Circle of Innovation*, 318. "It's my problem with benchmarking. Benchmark against "the best." But that evades the biggest issue: Those who really make a difference create a … whole new way .. of doing business … in their part of the market. Invent whole new markets. Best of the Best? That wasn't Netscape's approach to the Internet. They wanted to 'be the only ones who do what we do.' "

[292] Gandossy and Effron, *Leading the Way*, "The Myth of Best Practices," 10. "Managers everywhere are obsessed with the quick fix. Fads and gimmicks abound. The next new thing often promoted by academics or, yes, consultants, promises easy solutions to difficult challenges. And this is understandable. Faced with daunting competitive pressures, global complexity, and a nanosecond world, who wouldn't want to steal from the best? But it doesn't work. Cultures are different. Values and beliefs that leaders hold are different. Strategies, customers, history and embedded practices are different. These differences make it difficult, if not impossible, to graft someone else's programs onto your own. It is far better to learn how great companies think - as Jeff Pfeffer, Stanford University Business School Professor says - than to copy what they do."
Jeffrey Pfeffer and Robert I. Sutton, *The Knowledge-Doing Gap: How Smart Companies Turn Knowledge into Action* (Cambridge: Harvard Business School, 1999).

[293] Wheatley and Kellner-Rogers, *A Simpler Way*, 72.

[294] Watts, *Six Degrees*, 52-54.

[295] Ibid.
Johnson, *Emergence*, 13.
Solé and Goodwin, *Signs of Life*, 18.

[296] Duncan J. Watts and Steve Hasker, "Marketing in an Unpredictable World," *Harvard Business Review*, Sept. 2006.
Chris Anderson, "*The Long Tail: Forget squeezing millions from a few megahits at the top of the charts. The future of entertainment is in the millions of niche markets at the shallow end of the bitstream*," *Wired* Magazine, Issue 12.10 - October 2004.

[297] Watts and Hasker, "Marketing in an Unpredictable World."

[298] Ibid.

[299] Surowiecki, *The Wisdom of Crowds*, 26-31.

[300] Kelly, Out of Control, 7.

[301] Surowiecki, *The Wisdom of Crowds*, 26-31.

[302] Watts and Hasker, "Marketing in an Unpredictable World."

[303] Don Tapscott and Anthony D. Williams, "The Wiki Workplace," The *BusinessWeek* Wikinomics Series, March 26, 2007.

[304] Zappos.com CEO Tony Hsieh, "Interview - How Zappos.com Grew So Big So Fast - 10 Strategies Behind Their Success," Marketing Sherpa, *Email Sherpa*, Aug 7, 2007.

[305] Watts, *Six Degrees*, 52-54.

[306] Thurm, "*Now, It's Business By Data, but Numbers Still Can't Tell Future.*"

[307] Creative Environments
John Kao, *Jamming: The Art and Discipline of Business Creativity*, xvii, 65-66, on creative environments at Kodak, GE, Story Street Studios, Canon, The Body Shop, and more.
Gina Imperato, "Greetings from Idea City: Southwest Airlines, Wal-Mart, and the PGA Tour stop here first for their ad campaigns. Inside the new headquarters of GSDM, home of the scarcest resource in business: great ideas," *Fast Company*, Issue 11, Oct. 1997, 149, on GSD&M.
Aburdene, *Megatrends 2010*, 13-14, on meditation in businesses.
Corinne McLaughlin, *Spirituality And Ethics In Business*, The Center for Visionary Leadership. 2004, http://www.visionarylead.org/articles/spbus.htm/
In addition to prayer and study groups, other spiritual practices at companies include meditation; centering exercises such as deep breathing to reduce stress; visioning exercises; building shared values; active, deep listening; making action and intention congruent; and using intuition and inner guidance in decision-making. According to a study at Harvard Business School published in The Harvard Business Review, business owners credit 80% of their success to acting on their intuition.

Apple Computer's offices in California have a meditation room and employees are actually given a half hour a day on company time to meditate or pray, as they find it improves productivity and creativity. A former manager who is now a Buddhist monk leads regular meditations there. Aetna International Chairman Michael A. Stephen praises the benefits of meditation and talks with Aetna employees about using spirituality in their careers. Avaya, a global communications firm that is a spin-off of Lucent/AT&T, has a room set aside for prayer and meditation that is especially appreciated by Muslims, as they must pray five times a day.

Medtronic, which sells medical equipment, pioneered a meditation center at headquarters 20 years ago, and it remains open to all employees today. Prentice-Hall publishing company created a meditation room at their headquarters which they call the "Quiet Room, where employees can sit quietly and take a mental retreat when they feel too much stress on the job. Sounds True in Colorado, which produces audio and video tapes, has a meditation room, meditation classes and begins meetings with a moment of silence. Employees can take Personal Days to attend retreats or pursue other spiritual interests. Greystone Bakery in upstate New York has a period silence before meetings begin so people can get in touch with their inner state and focus on the issues to be discussed.

Stan Richards *The Peaceable Kingdom: Building a Company Without Factionalism, Fiefdoms, Fear and Other Staples of Modern Business* (New York: John Wiley & Sons, Inc., 2001).

Tom Kelley, *The Art of Innovation: Lessons in Creativity from IDEO, America's Leading Design Firm* (New York: Currency, 2001.

Matt Weinstein, *Managing to Have Fun: How Fun at Work Can Motivate Your Employees, Inspire Your Coworkers, and Boost Your Bottom Line* (New York: Fireside, 1996).

Andy Law, *Creative Company: How St. Luke's Became "the Ad Agency to End All Ad Agencies* (New York: John Wiley & Sons, Inc., 1998).

Leslie Yerkes, *Fun Works: Creating Places Where People Love to Work* (San Francisco: Berrett-Koehler Publishers, 2001.

Michael Schrage, "The Proto Project: To learn how to innovate, learn how to prototype. Here's how Microsoft and Boeing make their projects go Wow!" *Fast Company*, Issue 24, April 1999, 138.

John Kao, Innovation Nation: How America Is Losing Its Innovation Edge, Why It Matters, and What We Can Do to Get It Back (New York: The Free Press, 2007).

[308] Maslow, *Motivation and Personality*, 202.

[309] Mounting research indicates that multitasking – an ability listed as a core requirement for most job positions, and long a badge of efficiency and productivity for workers – actually may *decrease productivity, hinder learning*, and even *cause safety concerns.* In addition, studies show continuous multitasking negatively impacts innovation in virtual teams.
See references below.

Carol Mithers, "Multi-tasking adversely affects brain's learning, UCLA psychologists report," *UCLA Magazine*, July 2007 http://www.eurekalert.org/pub_releases/2006-07/uoc--maa072506.php
"Multi-tasking affects the brain's learning systems, and as a result, we do not learn as well when we are distracted, UCLA psychologists report this week in the online edition of Proceedings of the National Academy of Sciences. 'Multi-tasking adversely affects how you learn,' said Russell Poldrack, UCLA associate professor of psychology and co-author of the study. 'Even if you learn while multi-tasking, that learning is less flexible and more specialized, so you cannot retrieve the information as easily. Our study shows that to the degree you can learn while multi-tasking, you will use different brain systems."

Sandra Blakeslee, "Car Calls May Leave Brain Short-Handed," *The New York Times*, July 31, 2001
"Scientists have bad news for people who think they can deftly drive a car while gabbing on a cell phone. The first study using magnetic resonance images of brain activity to compare what happens in people's heads when they do one complex task, as opposed to two tasks at a time, reveals a disquieting fact: the brain appears to have a finite amount of space for tasks requiring attention."

Porter Anderson, CNN, "Study: Multitasking is counterproductive (Your boss may not like this one), " CNN Career, Dec. 6, 2001. "Multitasking is a managerial buzz-concept these days, a post-layoff corporate assumption that the few can be made to do the work of many. But newly released results of scientific studies in multitasking indicate that carrying on several duties at once may, in fact, reduce productivity, not increase it. "In some cases, you could be wasting your employer's time," says researcher Joshua Rubinstein, Ph.D., formerly of the University of Michigan and now with the Federal Aviation Administration (FAA) working on security issues. "And in certain cases" of multitasking, Rubinstein says, "you could be risking employers a dangerous outcome."

Jim Loehr and Tony Schwartz, The Power of Full Engagement: Managing Energy, Not Time, Is the Key to High

Performance and Personal Renewal (New York: The Free Press, 2003), 3-4. "We walk around with day planners and to-do lists, Palm Pilots and Blackberries, instant pagers and pop-up reminders on our computers - all designed to help us manage our time better. We take pride in our ability to multitask, and we wear our willingness to put in long hours as a badge of honor. The term 24/7 describes a world in which work never ends. We use worlds like obsessed, crazed and overwhelmed not to describe insanity, but instead to characterize our everyday lives. Feeling forever starved for time, we assume that we have no choice but to cram as much as possible into every day. But managing time efficiently is no guarantee we will bring sufficient energy to whatever it is we are doing. ... Energy, not time, is the fundamental currency of high performance."
Karen Sobel Lojeski, Richard Reilly, Peter Dominick, "Multitasking and Innovation in Virtual Teams," Paper in System Sciences, 2007. 40th Annual Hawaii International Conference. "The limits of human multitasking capabilities in intense conditions are well understood. However, little is known about how increasing and continuous multitasking impacts innovation in virtual teams. During this investigation, we developed a construct called virtual distance to understand how both perceived and physical distance impacts innovation on virtual teams and applied it to 223 individuals and mangers at seventeen organizations. We then explored virtual distance as a moderator of the relationship between multitasking and innovation. Our results showed that virtual distance has a significant and negative relationship to innovation. We farther found that virtual distance significantly moderated the relationship between multitasking and innovation. When virtual distance is low, there is a positive relationship and when virtual distance is high, there is a significant curvilinear relationship. The results have implications for the selection of virtual team members and virtual project management activities when critical project outcomes include innovation."

[310] Even on individual level, To-Do Lists serve as our daily plans. Of course, there is nothing inherently wrong with To-Do Lists, calendars (electronic or paper) and other systems for organizing our next steps – in fact, ultimately, we must have some mechanism through which to move our "best next steps" into our daily line of sight.

[311] Robert Tucker, "Is Speed Killing Creativity?" *Innovation Network*, on Conference Board Report by Marilyn Zuckerman Michaels, *Speed: Linking Innovation, Process, and Time to Market*, May 2000.

[312] Covey, *The Seven Habits of Highly Effective People*. 98. "It's incredibly easy to get caught up in the activity trap, in the busy-ness of life, to work harder and harder at climbing the ladder of success only to discover it's leaning against the wrong wall. It is possible to be very, very busy without being very effective. People often find themselves achieving victories that are empty, successes that have come at the expense of things they suddenly realize were more important to them. ... How different our lives are when we really know what is deeply important to us, and, keeping that picture in mind, we manage ourselves each day to be and do what really matters most. If the ladder is not leaning against the right wall, every step we take just gets us to the wrong place faster. We may be very busy, we may be very efficient, but we will also be truly effective only when we begin with the end in mind."

[313] "The Art of Smart," *Fast Company*.

[314] Tapscott and Williams, "The Wiki Workplace."

[315] Joyner, *Simple-ology*, 229.

[316] Losier, *The Law of Attraction*, 52.

[317] "Toying with Creativity," Scientific American Mind, *Scientific American*, 2004, 8.

[318] Albert Einstein quoted in *Simple-ology*, 6.

[319] Albert Einstein quoted in *Business 2.0*, Oct. 1999, 252.

[320] Gary Schwartz, "The Power of Play and the Need for Playing," *Paradigm* Magazine, The Illinois Institute for Addiction Recovery, Vol. 9, No. 2, Spring 2004. "Fun produces a unification of mind and body and creates full involvement. Fun is not trivial; it is essential. ...Fun is not an escape from reality. It is a doorway into reality. Fun is a psychological state where attitude and judgment are suspended and the mind and body act in harmony to accomplish a goal. ... What spoils fun? Judgment and opinion block flow and stop the fun. In fact, any activity that takes attention away from full involvement with the self-chosen task at hand spoils the fun."

[321] Kelley, *The Art of Innovation*, 6, 63, 134.

[322] "Manifesto: A letter from the founding editors," *Fast Company*, Handbook of the Business Revolution, Issue 1, October 1995, 8.

[323] "Fun. Frivolous, we know - unless you want to attract and keep good employees and customers," *Inc.* Magazine, Aug. 2007.

[324] Neva L. Boyd, from the essay, "A Theory of Play," 1971, Play and Games Theory in Group Work: A collection of Papers (Chicago: Office of Publications, University of Illinois).

[325] Cheryl Dahle, "Mind Games," *Fast Company*, Issue 31, Dec. 1999, 169.

[326] Kelley, The Art of Innovation, 134.

[327] Tapscott and Williams, "The Wiki Workplace.

[328] Charles Fadel, Margaret Honey, & Shelley Pasnik, "Assessment in the Age of Innovation," *Education Week*, Vol. 26, Issue 38, May 23, 2007, 34,40.

[329] McGee-Cooper, *You Don't Have to Go Home From Work Exhausted!*

[330] "Toying with Creativity," *Scientific American*, 8.

[331] Koestler, *The Act of Creation*, 209.

[332] Alan M. Webber, "Why Can't We Get Anything Done? Stanford B-school professor Jeffrey Pfeffer has a question: If we're so smart, why can't we get anything done? Here are 16 rules to help you make things happen in your organization." *Fast Company*, Issue 35, May 2000, 168.

[333] Quoted in *Do It: Let's Get Off Our Butts*, 286.

[334] Post-it Notes is a trademark of the 3M Corporation.

[335] Osborn, *Applied imagination*.

[336] De Bono, *Serious Creativity*, x-xi, 38-42.

[337] De Bono, *Serious Creativity*, 11-12.

[338] De Bono, *Serious Creativity*, 36.

[339] "Greetings from Idea City," *Fast Company*, 140.

[340] The Honorable John R. Lewis (D) Georgia, 2007 University of Vermont Commencement Address, May 20, 2007.

[341] Dossey, *Space, Time & Medicine*, 50.
Zukav, *The Dancing Wu Li Masters*, 28.

[342] Peters, *Re-Imagine*, 55.

[343] Anderson, *All Connected Now*, 251-255.

[344] David Weinberger, *Small Pieces Loosely Joined: A Unified Theory of the Web*, Online edition, http://www.smallpieces.com.

[345] Gertrude Stein - If you knew it all, it would not be creation, but dictation.

[346] Napoleon Hill, Napoleon Hill's Keys to Success: The 17 Principles of Personal Achievement (New York; Penguin, 1994), 218.

[347] Quoted in *Zen and the Art of Making a Living*, 279.

[348] Chopra, *The Seven Spiritual Laws of Success*, 86-89.

[349] Quoted in *Zen and the Art of Making a Living*, 453.

[350] Ray and Myers, *Creativity in Business*, 42-51.

[351] *Think and Grow Rich, Napoleon Hill.*

[352] Joyner, *Simple-ology*, 41, 150-151.

[353] Michael J. Gelb, *How to Think Like Leonardo da Vinci: Seven Steps to Genius Every Day* (New York: Dell Publishing, 1998), 150.

[354] Tom Peters," A Very Big Deal Indeed," Column, Sept. 03, 1993. http://www.tompeters.com/col_entries.php?note=0054201.

[355] Peters, *Circle of Innovation*, 245.

[356] Florida, The Rise of the Creative Class, 168.

[357] Tharp, *The Creative Habit*, 123.

[358] Senge, *The Fifth Discipline*, 60-61.

[359] James P. Andrew and Harold L. Sirkin, *Payback: Reaping the Rewards of Innovation* (Cambridge, MA: Harvard Business School Press, 2007), 195.

[360] Hugh McLeod, *How to Be Creative*, www.gapingvoid.com, http://www.gapingvoid.com/Moveable_Type/archives/000932.html
"1. Ignore everybody. The more original your idea is, the less good advice other people will be able to give you. When I first started with the cartoon-onback-of-bizcard format, people thought I was nuts. Why wasn't I trying to do something more easy for markets to digest, i.e., cutie-pie greeting cards or whatever? You don't know if your idea is any good the moment it's created. Neither does anyone else. The most you can hope for is a strong gut feeling that it is. And trusting your feelings is not as easy as the optimists say it is. There's a reason why feelings scare us. And asking close friends never works quite as well as you hope, either. It's not that they deliberately want to be unhelpful. It's just they don't know your world one millionth as well as you know your world, no matter how hard they try, no matter how hard you try to explain. Plus, a big idea will change you. Your friends may love you, but they don't want you to change. If you change, then their dynamic with you also changes. They like things the way they are, that's how they love you—the way you are, not the way you may become."

[361] Geldard, *Remembering Heraclitus*, 127.

[362] Quoted in *Pope Benedict XVI: His Life and Mission* (New York: Jeffrey P. Archer, 2005), 163.

[363] *This Week with George Stephanopoulos*, "The Iowa Debates/Republican," moderators George Stephanopoulos and David Yepsen, ABC News (Washington, D.C.: Council on Foreign Relations Essential Documents, Republican Debate Transcript, Aug. 5, 2007), http://www.cfr.org/publication/13981/republican_debate_transcript_iowa.html?breadcrumb=%2Fpublication%2Fby_type%2Fessential_document.

[364] *Acheivement.org*, "Interview: Oprah Winfrey" (Chicago: February 21, 1991), http://www.achievement.org.

[365] Deborah Tannen, "Oprah Winfrey, The *Time* 100: The Most Important People of the Century," *Time* Magazine, Magazine (New York: Time, Inc, June 8, 1998).

[366] Honie Stevens, "From Rags to Riches: Oprah Winfrey," (Folkstone, Kent: *Saga* Magazine, May 2002).

[367] Hebrews 11:1, "Now faith is the substance of things hoped for, the evidence of things not seen." (Holy Bible, King James Version).

[368] Deepak Chopra, *The Seven Spiritual Laws of Success: A Practical Guide to the Fulfillment of Your Dreams*, (San Rafael, CA: Amber-Allen Publishing and New World Library, 1994), 75-77.

[369] *Acheivement.org*, "Interview: Oprah Winfrey."

[370] Tannen, "Oprah Winfrey, The *Time* 100: The Most Important People of the Century," *Time* Magazine; George Mair, *Oprah Winfrey: The Real Story*, (Seacaucus, N.J.: Carol Publishing Group, 1998), 20.

[371] *Acheivement.org*, "Interview: Oprah Winfrey."

[372] Ibid.

[373] Ibid.

[374] Ibid.; *Oprah Winfrey: The Real Story*, 16.

[375] Stevens, "From Rags to Riches: Oprah Winfrey"

[376] *Acheivement.org*, "Interview: Oprah Winfrey."

[377] Ibid.

[378] Richard Zoglin, "Oprah Winfrey, Abused Child and Young Beauty Queen, Was Awful As an Anchorwoman, But Now Runs TV's Highest-Rated Daytime Talk Show with Curiosity, Humor and Empathy," *Time* Magazine (New York: Time, Inc, Aug. 08, 1988).

[379] *Acheivement.org*, "Interview: Oprah Winfrey."

[380] Richard Zoglin, "10 Questions For Oprah Winfrey," *Time* Magazine (New York: Time, Inc, Dec. 15, 2003).

[381] KERA Unlimited," The Choice 2000: Gore Chronology," Frontline, Oct. 2000, http://www.pbs.org/wgbh/pages/frontline/shows/choice2000/gore/cron.html.

[382] Melinda Henneberger, "Al Gore's Journey: A Character Test at Harvard - On Campus Torn by 60's, Agonizing Over the Path," *The New York Times* (New York: The New York Times Company, June 21, 2000).

[383] CNN Transcripts, Democratic National Convention, "Al Gore Accepts His Party's Presidential Nomination,"

(Atlanta: CNN/Turner Broadcasting System, Inc., August 17, 2000), http://transcripts.cnn.com/TRANSCRIPTS/0008/17/se.04.html.

[384] Melinda Henneberger, "Al Gore's Journey: Headlong Into Politics - Birth of a Candidate: Al Gore Goes Into the Family Business," *The New York Times* (New York: The New York Times Company, August 11, 2000).

[385] CNN Transcripts, "Al Gore Accepts His Party's Presidential Nomination."

[386] Ibid.

[387] Walter Gibbs And Sarah Lyall, "Gore Shares Peace Prize for Climate Change Work," *The New York Times* (New York: The New York Times Company, October 13, 2007).

[388] Steve Dougherty, *Hopes and Dreams: The Story of Barack Obama*, (New York: Black Dog & Leventhal Publishers, Inc., 2007), 19.

[389] *This Week with George Stephanopoulos*, "The Iowa Debates/Democratic," moderators George Stephanopoulos and David Yepsen, ABC News (Washington, D.C.: Council on Foreign Relations Essential Documents, Republican Debate Transcript, Aug. 19, 2007), http://www.cfr.org/publication/by_type/essential_document.html.

[390] Barack Obama, *Dreams from My Father: A Story of Race and Inheritance* (New York: Three Rivers Press,1995, 2004), 12; Dougherty, *Hopes and Dreams*, 127, 43, 46.

[391] Barack Obama, *The Audacity of Hope: Thoughts on Reclaiming the American Dream*, (New York: Crown Publishing Group, 2006), 29.

[392] Kirsten Scharnberg and Kim Barker, "The not-so-simple story of Barack Obama's youth: Shaped by different worlds, an outsider found ways to fit in," *Chicago Tribune*, March 25, 2007.

[393] Obama, *Dreams from My Father*, 93; Dougherty, *Hopes and Dreams*, 42, 48. 52-54.

[394] Obama, *Dreams from My Father*, 111, 227.

[395] Dougherty, *Hopes and Dreams*, 53, 61, 66.

[396] Obama, *Dreams from My Father*, 135-135.

[397] Ibid., 200, 220, 226-227.

[398] Ibid., 188-190.

[399] Ibid., 242.

[400] Ibid., 438.

[401] Dougherty, *Hopes and Dreams*, 37, 67, 77, 80.

[402] Dougherty, *Hopes and Dreams*, 24, 27-28, 85.

[403] Ibid., 102.

[404] Brockovich. *Take it from Me*, 170.

[405] Ibid., 29-30.

[406] Ibid., 177, 31-32.

[407] Ibid., 26.

[408] Ibid., 31.

[409] Ibid., 43.

[410] *The Biography Channel*, "The Real Erin Brockovich," LA Justice/People, April 3, 2000, 96-98 http://www.thebiographychannel.co.uk/biography_story/1564:1812/3/Erin_Brookovich.htm
Austin Bunn, "Erin Brockovich: The Brand," *The New York Times Magazine*, April 28, 2002; Brockovich, *Take it from Me*, 52-55.

[411] Brockovich, *Take it from Me*, 38-39.

[412] Ibid., 12-13.

[413] Ibid., 72.

[414] Ibid., 95, 100, 97.

[415] Ibid., 77.

[416] Erin Brockovich, "Erin Brockovich Philosophy," http//: www.brockovich.com.

[417] Brockovich, *Take it from Me*, 164.

[418] Christopher Cooper and Jim Carlton, "He's Baaack – Facing Re-Election, Schwarzenegger Switches Course:

Huge Spending Plans Revive His Fortunes in California While Irking Republicans," *The Wall Street Journal* (New York: Dow Jones & Co., Inc., June 3-4, 2006).

[419] Anna Wilde Mathews and Rhonda L. Rundle, "Crunch Time – Schwarzenegger Fights to Save Health Plan: Governor Would Levy Fees to Cover All in State; Rival Democratic Bill," *The Wall Street Journal* (New York: Dow Jones & Co., Inc., July 17, 2007).

[420] Keith H. Hammonds, "Internet 101: According to "The Cluetrain Manifesto" coauthor David Weinberger, the Web has been underhyped. That's right, underhyped. In his new book, "Small Pieces Loosely Joined," Weinberger offers a unified theory of the Web -- and rules for tapping into its real power," *Fast Company* Magazine (New York: Mansueto Ventures, Inc., March 2002),132.

[421] *Understanding Mass Media*, Jeffrey Shrank, (Skokie, IL: National Textbook Company, 1981), 127.

[422] Clayton M. Christensen, *The Innovator's Dilemma: When New Technologies Cause Great Firms to Fail*, (New York: HarperCollins Publishers, 2000).

[423] Peters, *The Circle of Innovation*.

[424] W. Chan Kim and Renée Mauborgne, *Blue Ocean Strategy: How to Create Uncontested Market Space and Make Competition Irrelevant*, (Boston: Harvard Business School Publishing Corporation, 2005).

[425] Peter F. Drucker, *Management Challenges for the 21st Century* (New York: HarperCollins, 1999), 119.

[426] Christensen, *The Innovator's Dilemma*.

[427] Dundon, *The Seeds of Innovation*, 6, 16.

[428] S Covey, *The Seven Habits of Highly Effective People: Powerful Lessons in Personal Change* (New York, Fireside/Simon & Schuster Inc., 1989), 81.

[429] Robert B, Cialdini, Ph.D., *Influence: The Psychology of Persuasion* (New York, William Morrow and Company, 1984, 1993), 17.

[430] Maria Arapakis, *Softpower!: How to Speak Up, Set Limits, and Say No Without Losing Your Lover, Your Job, or Your Friends*, Warner Books, 1990).

[431] *The Corporate Mystic*, 63.

[432] Covey, *Quest: Discovering Your Human Potential*; Covey, *The Seven Habits of Highly Effective People*, 22.

[cdxxxiii] *World Scripture*, 212.

[cdxxxiii] Volk, *Metapatterns: Across Space, Time and Mind*, 210, 242-244.

www.ingramcontent.com/pod-product-compliance
Lightning Source LLC
Chambersburg PA
CBHW041829300426
44111CB00002B/28